THE APATHY
OF EMPIRE

THE APATHY OF EMPIRE

Cambodia in American Geopolitics

James A. Tyner

UNIVERSITY OF MINNESOTA PRESS
MINNEAPOLIS • LONDON

Copyright 2024 by the Regents of the University of Minnesota

All rights reserved. No part of this publication may be reproduced, stored in a retrieval system, or transmitted, in any form or by any means, electronic, mechanical, photocopying, recording, or otherwise, without the prior written permission of the publisher.

Published by the University of Minnesota Press
111 Third Avenue South, Suite 290
Minneapolis, MN 55401–2520
http://www.upress.umn.edu

ISBN 978-1-5179-1508-7 (hc)
ISBN 978-1-5179-1509-4 (pb)

A Cataloging-in-Publication record for this book is available from the Library of Congress.

Printed on acid-free paper

The University of Minnesota is an equal-opportunity educator and employer.

To
MICHAEL DEAR

In framing a government which is to be administered by men over men, the great difficulty lies in this: you must first enable the government to control the governed; and in the next place oblige it to control itself.

—JAMES MADISON, *The Federalist Papers*

Contents

Introduction / 1

1 Into the Breach / 25

2 Bracketing War / 57

3 Bordering War / 103

4 Aterritorial Wars / 135

5 A Widening War / 163

6 The Perfidy of Geopolitics / 203

Epilogue / 241

Acknowledgments / 261

Notes / 263

Index / 337

INTRODUCTION

At the door of geography may be laid the blame for many of the
age-long struggles which run persistently through history.
—Nicholas J. Spykman, "Geography and Foreign Policy, I"

On Thursday, April 30, 1970, Richard Nixon, president of the United States,
informed the American public of his decision to send U.S. and South Vietnamese armed forces into neutral Cambodia. "We take this action," Nixon
explained, "not for the purpose of expanding the war into Cambodia but
for the purpose of ending the war in Vietnam and winning the just peace
we all desire." Standing before a map of Southeast Asia, Nixon pointed first
to South Vietnam then to North Vietnam. He explained that North Vietnam
already occupied parts of neighboring Laos and now threatened eastern
Cambodia. If successful, Nixon warned, North Vietnam's military advances
would completely outflank South Vietnam's western border and thus place
U.S. and South Vietnamese forces "in an untenable military position." In
response, Nixon said that the deployment of allied combat troops into
Cambodia marked not an invasion but an "incursion."[1] Evocative of a brief
or small-scale operation, Nixon's word choice downplayed ongoing military operations even as it elevated the geopolitical importance of the action.
The defense of Cambodia was important enough to deploy American military forces but, then again, not necessarily important enough to warrant a
full-scale invasion.

Much has been made of Nixon's decision to initiate military operations
into Cambodia. Within weeks of the so-called incursion, several scholars
held a symposium on "The United States Military Action in Cambodia,
1970, in the Light of International and Constitutional Law."[2] Since that
opening forum, a veritable cottage industry has emerged to consider the

2 / Introduction

legality of Nixon's use of military force and the lessons it holds for contemporary foreign policy.[3] Military scholars and historians, likewise, continue to document and debate both the operation and the subsequent Cambodian Civil War.[4] Decidedly less attention, however, has been paid to the importance of Cambodia to America's grand strategy and national security interests during the Cold War. Most often, Cambodia is portrayed as a sideshow to America's war in Vietnam.[5] Alternatively, it is seen as a pawn in the tripolar geopolitical chess match waged between the United States, the Soviet Union, and the People's Republic of China.[6] However, to render Cambodia as peripheral to America's war in Vietnam is to sidestep the fundamental problem Cambodia posed to U.S. officials on the question of national security: How to differentiate some areas as central and others peripheral? To that end, a straightforward question frames my project: Was Cambodia central or peripheral to U.S. national security interests during the Cold War?

The resolution of this question is far from simple and requires a critical reading of America's unfolding grand strategy from the Second World War forward. My project, therefore, is an exercise in critical geopolitics in general and a study of practical geopolitics in particular. Geopolitics, Simon Dalby explains, is about the practice of statecraft and addresses "both matters of importance and their geographical arrangements, which in turn situate and constrain states in their rivalries and struggles for power."[7] Building on this notion, John Agnew and Stuart Corbridge define geopolitics as "the division of global space by institutions (states, firms, social movements, international organizations, armed forces, terrorist groups, etc.) into discrete territories and spheres of political-economic influence through which the international political economy is regulated materially and represented intellectually as a natural order of 'developed' and 'underdeveloped,' 'friendly,' and 'threatening' areas."[8] *Practical geopolitics* constitutes that domain of policymaking and geopolitical reasoning whereby officials articulate national interests and rationalize concrete diplomatic overtures and military operations.[9] Geopolitical practice, therefore, is always contingent and always contextual, subject to an ever-changing constellation of political, economic, and military conditions across a range of spatial scales.

The practical determination of Cambodia's status to U.S. policymakers, I argue, provides a particularly important case study in that it underscores the spatial uncertainties inherent in America's national security concerns and

Introduction / 3

overarching grand strategy during the Cold War. In the following chapters I chart, from Franklin Roosevelt to Nixon, the vicissitudes of U.S. foreign policy as policymakers vacillated on Cambodia's geopolitical importance to the war in Vietnam. As the centrality of Vietnam waxed and waned throughout the Cold War, Cambodia's geopolitical status remained shaded by its neighbor. Cambodia, in essence, occupied the penumbra of America's war in Vietnam. *The Apathy of Empire* is an effort to provide clarity to this geopolitical problem.

National Security, Grand Strategies, and Geopolitics

In common usage, *national security* is frequently equated with *national defense*, and to a degree this equivalence is accurate. National security is concerned fundamentally with those military or diplomatic practices necessary to protect one's nation from physical harm, such as from foreign invasion or domestic insurgency. However, for policymakers national security is more capacious, in that it implies protection, through a variety of means, of vital economic and political interests, the loss of which could threaten the fundamental values and interests of a state.[10] In other words, national security indicates the securement of a way of life, often framed in abstract terms like "freedom," "liberty," and "independence." That said, national security concerns—or interests—are not self-evident and, in practice, both civilian and military officials routinely define and redefine what constitutes a nation's interests.[11]

National security is manifest geographically. This is understood as the physical defense of one's homeland, that is, protecting the territory and people of a state against attack in order to ensure survival with fundamental values and institutions intact.[12] However, national security is also conditioned by the uneven geographies of economic and political interests that exist across multiple spatial scales. Take, for example, so-called natural resources, such as oil, coal, or timber. As Philippe Le Billion details, resources "vary in their spatial location, relative abundance, physical characteristics, technologies of extraction and transformation, use, social and environmental impacts, and economic value."[13] As such, governments frequently invest heavily in the military protection of critical infrastructure and trade routes of key resources.[14] However, the territorial control of resources is not, as Matt Huber explains, simply about imposing politics on natural stuff; rather, the

4 / Introduction

processes of territorially delimiting control and access to resources actively constitute the state.[15] To that end, the presence or absence of key resources greatly mediates whether a region or state is considered central or peripheral to any given state's national security interests.

National security is spatial, also, in the sense that vital interests cross both domestic and foreign policy. On the one hand, national security must be understood in the context of foreign policy, defined as the policies of a state that encompass all official relations with other state and nonstate foreign political entities. On the other hand, establishing and defending national security priorities is often circumscribed by political and economic linkages between both foreign and domestic policies. In other words, the domestic economic impact of certain national security policies links domestic interests and policies to the international security landscape. Similarly, domestic interests are important in establishing national security priorities and interests. Examples of national security concerns that operate at the nexus of domestic and foreign policies include economic sanctions and embargoes, trade policies, and border security.[16]

In order to achieve and secure national security interests, states have at their disposal a number of instruments, including diplomatic, military, and economic components. Taken together, these represent the basis of a state's *grand strategy*.[17] Conceptually, grand strategy expands on the notion of *strategy*, that is, a plan for applying resources to achieve certain defined objectives.[18] However, grand strategy is considerably more broad in scope and encompasses, in the words of Basil Liddell Hart, the sense of "policy in execution."[19] Thus, for any particular policy objective sought, the key grand strategic decision is choosing the right instrument, or the right combination of instruments, appropriate under particular political, economic, and military conditions.[20] Notably, a key distinction between foreign and domestic policy and national security policy is, to a degree, the likelihood of the use of the military as the primary instrument for implementing national security policy.[21]

Grand strategy is not reducible to military strategy, but the two are closely related. When policymakers determine that military force will be used to serve the ends of policy, the strategy must be put into practice and is achieved at both operational and tactical scales of action. Tactics are concerned with the details of battle, that is, the total range of possible ways military forces, from just a few soldiers to entire fleets and armies, can be deployed in combat.[22] Spatially, tactics are focused at the scale at which singular battles and engagements are planned and fought. Operations are concerned with the scale at which military campaigns are planned and conducted. It is through the operational level that tactical actions serve the requirements of the overall military strategy.[23] In other words, at the operational scale, schemes of warfare are planned to attain goals set by the overall military strategy through a suitable combination of tactics.[24] Thus, the overall grand strategy circumscribes military strategy by setting national security goals and establishing political restraints on the conduct of war, including limitations at both operational and tactical scales.

In practice, grand strategy retains an important spatially normative function. Peter Feaver, for example, argues that grand strategy "refers to the collection of plans and policies that comprise the state's deliberate effort to harness political, military, diplomatic, and economic tools together to advance that state's national interest. Grand strategy is the art of reconciling ends and means. It involves purposive action—what leaders think and want."[25] Hal Brands echoes these remarks, affirming that a grand strategy constitutes a "conceptual framework that helps nations determine *where* they want to go and how they ought to get there."[26] Accordingly, as a prescriptive "policy in execution," grand strategies project forward a *desired* spatial order or *nomos*.[27] As defined by the German legal theorist Carl Schmitt, nomos signifies a "unity of space and law, of order and orientation."[28] That is, when "understood in its original spatial sense . . . nomos is the immediate form in which the political and social order of a people becomes spatially visible."[29] On this point, the concept of spatial order is both the process and the project of grand strategies, in that grand strategy "entails order extended in time, space, and milieus . . . [and] attempts to impose coherence and predictability on an inherently disorderly environment composed of thinking, reacting, competing, and conflicting entities." Simply put, as Peter Layton suggests, grand strategy tries to construct the future and, in doing so, deliberately remakes geography to conform with national security interests.[30]

This is not to say that grand strategies emerge fully formed, born of "statesmen, generals, and diplomats huddled around a tabletop map of the world, calculating how best to defend vital 'national interests' from a hostile

6 / Introduction

international environment."[31] Such a caricature belies the contested nature of national security planning. [32] Instead, grand strategies are the product of an assemblage of actors operating within myriad political, economic, and military institutions. In addition, the articulation of grand strategy does not necessarily translate into reality. The drafting of planning reports or the issuance of national security strategy documents may provide the framework of a desired spatial order but does not guarantee the desired end will come to fruition. On that note, it is perhaps best to think of grand strategies as "organizing principles" or even "grand principles" that circumscribe the pursuit of national security interests.[33]

In summation, national security policy is primarily concerned with formulating and implementing national strategy involving the threat or use of force to create a favorable geopolitical environment for national security interests.[34] Integral to national security policy is the formulation of grand strategy, an organizing principle that sets the limits of diplomacy and military strategy. Moreover, as a policy of execution, grand strategy seeks to enact a particular spatial order, or nomos, to secure those conditions necessary to achieve one's national security interests. All grand strategies, therefore, are informed by certain "geopolitical codes," that is, assumptions about vital interests in the world, potential threats to these interests, and feasible responses.[35] Throughout the Cold War, for example, U.S. national security interests and subsequent grand strategy was framed around a spatially infused language of "blocs," "containment," and "dominos."[36] Here, the practice or enactment of grand strategy necessarily situated some states or regions at the *center* of national security concerns while simultaneously situating others toward the periphery of geopolitical importance.

Having thus sketched the conceptual terrain, in the following section I detail how national security concerns have, since the Second World War, served as the fulcrum of American practical geopolitical reasoning thereby delineating the American postwar spatial order.

The Genesis of American National Security Doctrine

In the United States, the seeds of national security as geopolitical discourse were sown during the Second World War.[37] However, as a guiding doctrine, national security did not fully germinate until the Cold War, nourished especially in the soils of Vietnam. Steadily, anticommunism was grafted onto the national security discourse and soon overshadowed competing frames of geopolitical interpretation. As Emily Rosenberg writes, the meanings of "national security" for US policymakers emerged only within the context of the Cold War.[38] Accordingly, national security as geopolitical discourse can only be understood as the product of American proxy wars.

Prior to the 1930s, there prevailed in the United States a general feeling of spatial immunity from foreign threats, an era C. Vann Woodward describes as a period of "free security."[39] Free security, Woodward explains, was based on nature's gift of three vast bodies of water—the Atlantic Ocean to the east, the Pacific Ocean to the West, and the Arctic Ocean and polar ice cap to the north. This *organic defense* was "provided free in the sense that it was enjoyed as a bounty of nature in place of the elaborate and costly chains of fortifications and even more expensive armies and navies that took a heavy toll on the treasuries of less fortunate countries and placed severe tax burdens on the backs of their people."[40] Accordingly, as Preston explains, Americans rarely felt vulnerable and an ideology of expansionism—evident initially in the displacement and dispossession of Native Americans—was propelled by a sense of providential opportunity and Manifest Destiny. Indeed, no "foreign" wars have been fought on American soil since the War of 1812. As Preston concludes, "In American foreign relations, it was an age of offense, not defense."[41]

U.S. imperialism abroad was inherently offensive, captured best by the phrase "gunboat diplomacy." Behind the façade of "open" trade, the United States acquired, by force or by fiat, a string of territories throughout the Caribbean and the Pacific. Expansionism, Preston writes, was propelled by the national *interest*—what is desired for expanding power and influence—rather than by national *security*—what is required for basic protection.[42] To that end, U.S. policymakers framed their mission as the fulfillment of "Manifest Destiny." Coined by John O'Sullivan in 1845, the phrase signified America's position in the world as being guided by Providence to overspread the North American continent "for the free development of our yearly multiplying millions."[43] In time, the concept of manifest destiny became almost inviolable, a dictum that seemingly justified—indeed, sanctioned—the right to continental and, later, overseas expansionism.[44] President Theodore Roosevelt evoked this sentiment at the dawn of the twentieth century, proclaiming that "we are now . . . face to face with great world problems;

8 / Introduction

that we cannot help playing the part of a great world power; that all we can decide is whether we will play it well or ill."[45]

This is not to suggest that a defensive component was entirely lacking in America's overseas imperialism. The historian and naval officer Alfred Thayer Mahan, for example, advocated for a powerful navy and a vast maritime network of coaling stations and bases to safeguard both key strategic chokepoints and the markets America acquired.[46] Defensive measures were to protect overseas territories; there was little concern that the territorial integrity of the continental United States was in jeopardy. Notably, though, Mahan was one of the few individuals to question the prevailing wisdom of free security.[47] Together with Rear Admiral Stephen Luce, Mahan challenged the long-held assumption that America's protection owed most to its size and isolation rather than to U.S. naval strength. This proposition was given added impetus by Benjamin Tracy, secretary of the navy (1889–93), who argued that the "defense of the United States absolutely requires the creation of a fighting force." Tracy expounded that "we must have a fleet of battleships that will beat off the enemy's fleet on its approach, for it is not to be tolerated that the United States, with its population, its revenue, and its trade, is to submit to attack upon the threshold of its harbors." Moreover, such a naval force was to include both offensive and defensive capabilities. As Tracy concluded, "We must be able to divert an enemy's force from our coast by threatening his own, for a war, though defensive in principle, may be conducted most effectively by being offensive in its operation."[48] Despite these admonitions, however, most policymakers remained firm in their conviction that the best defense for America's territorial integrity was selective and limited engagement in foreign affairs.

America's belated participation in the First World War is testimony to this belief. As Preston writes, the reason the United States did not join the war in 1914 was simple: there was no compelling reason to do so. In fact, the United States benefitted from its neutrality. According to Michael Neiberg, the war, and trade with Britain and France specifically, pulled the United States out of an economic recession and created a positive trade balance with Europe. In fact, Americans were able in 1914–15 to force the Allies into trade terms that increasingly benefitted U.S. banking, agriculture, and industry.[49] As the war progressed, however, more voices rose in alarm. Speaking before Congress in 1915, for example, Senator Henry Cabot Lodge warned that America's "national defense is not only imperfect and unbalanced but that it has grave and in some instances fatal deficiencies." He continued: "Unarmed, unready, undefended, we offer a standing invitation to aggression and attack. . . . The ocean barrier which defended us in 1776 and 1812 no longer exists."[50]

Conventional accounts hold that during the interwar years, between 1919 and 1941, the United States turned inward, deliberately and explicitly avoiding any foreign entanglements that might imperil America's own security. And yet, even a cursory glance at American military interventions belies this myth. During the 1920s, for example, the United States deployed military forces to China, Costa Rica, Guatemala, Honduras, Nicaragua, Panama, Russia, and Turkey.[51] In addition, American economic and cultural interests expanded across all continents, embodied by entrepreneurs such as Henry Ford and missionaries proselytizing in Africa and Asia.[52] Conspicuously, U.S. policymakers frequently justified these ventures as wholly defensive, that is, conducted to protect vital U.S. interests abroad. This is notably clear from the remarks of Cordell Hull, U.S. secretary of state. Speaking before the National Press Club on March 17, 1938, Hull explained that "the primary objectives of our foreign policy are the maintenance of our country and the promotion of the economic, the social, and the moral welfare of our people." He clarified that "from time immemorial it has been the practice of civilized nations to afford protection, by appropriate means and under the rule of reason, to *their* nationals and *their* rights and interests abroad." To that end, Hull acknowledged that "methods and means of affording protection abroad vary according to the places in which and the circumstances under which protection is called for." However, it remained "a policy of affording appropriate protection—under the rule of reason, in such form as may be best suited to the particular circumstances, and in accordance with the principles we advocate—is imperatively needed to serve *our* national interests."[53] In other words, it was both reasonable and necessary to promote and support military intervention abroad in defense of vital U.S. interests. That acquiring these "vital interests" abroad could be considered imperialist was left unspoken.[54]

It was not until the late 1930s, as the specter of another global war loomed on the horizon, that sustained and substantial attention was devoted to the concept of national security. This is not to say that the phrase "security" was

10 / Introduction

unheard of prior to this time. Rather, as Rosenberg documents, its usage was restricted largely to social or economic security and was directed at the level of the individual.[55] This is seen most clearly in the Depression-era New Deal programs of Franklin D. Roosevelt, namely the Social Security Act of 1935. However, the prospect of war heralded a new school of American geopolitics, exemplified by the writings of Edward Mead Earle, Nicholas Spykman, Margaret and Harold Sprout, Albert Weinberg, Jean Gottmann, and Alfred Vagts.[56] More and more, as Dexter Fergie explains, national security framed a novel way of imagining the world, one in which a permanently prepared United States would confront seemingly omnipresent threats.[57]

From the outset, national security was ambiguous in its constitution. In this regard, we recognize that national security—as a discourse—is exceptionally pliable and subject to (re)interpretation according to specific geopolitical conjunctions. In fact, it is precisely this opacity that gives value to the phrase. In the U.S. context, for example, national security discourses held (and continue to hold) a number of elements in common. During the late 1930s, Albert Weinberg, a political scientist at Johns Hopkins University, provided a working definition: "National security is the condition in which external attack, direct or indirect, by armed force or other means, upon the nation's territorial domain, rights, or vital interests is not likely to be made or, if made, to succeed."[58] Weinberg's definition is important insofar as it established notions of fixed geographies as central to the understanding of national security. Nicholas Spykman best articulated this mindset, postulating that geography "is the most fundamentally conditioning factor in the formulation of national policy because it is the most permanent." "Ministers come and ministers go," Spykman reasoned, "even dictators die, but mountain ranges stand unperturbed."[59] Even so, Spykman tempered his hyperbole, suggesting instead that "the geographic characteristics of states are *relatively* unchanging and unchangeable." More pressing, Spykman underscored that geography so conceived was a "conditioning rather than . . . a determining factor." For Spykman, the phrase "conditioning" was chosen carefully, in that he did not mean to imply that "geographic characteristics play a deterministic, causal role in foreign policy."[60]

Those policymakers who followed in Spykman's wake often were less circumspect in their understanding of geopolitical relations. In part, this

Introduction / 11

restricted view of geography was adopted in response to the contours of the Second World War and a reinterpretation of America's place in the world. America's once-secure position was no longer secure, as Nazi Germany and Imperial Japan steadily laid claim and waste to country and colony throughout Europe and Asia. As John Thompson remarks, "Reliance on geographical location and America's own military capacity to protect the physical integrity of the North American homeland gave way to an assumption that the safety of the United States from external attack depended upon the balance of power beyond the western hemisphere."[61] Crucial to this geopolitical axiom was the control of the Eurasian landmass.

The geopolitical centrality of Eurasia to global dominance was a longstanding position among both civilian and military strategists. Since 1904 the British geographer Halford Mackinder postulated that Eurasia was the "geographic pivot" on which world politics turned. In the United States, the work of Mahan and Lewis Einstein further emphasized the importance of Eurasia with regard to America's national interests. However, the general consensus within Washington in the 1930s was to adopt a position of isolationism or, more properly, one of noninterventionism. Indeed, the much-ballyhooed narrative of American isolationism is largely a myth, one that reinforces the illusion of America as a reluctant superpower. U.S. policymakers were, on the whole, never adverse to flexing America's geopolitical muscle; indeed, from the mid-nineteenth century onward, the United States had gradually accumulated a string of territorial possessions throughout the Pacific and the Caribbean. From the Aleutians through Midway, Guam, Samoa, the Hawaiian Islands, and the Philippines to Puerto Rico and the U.S. Virgin Islands, America's maritime empire spanned the western hemisphere. The United States was "isolated" only to the extent it was buffered by its overseas possessions; and it was "reluctant" to project its power only to the degree its military capabilities were not overstretched.

As the German war machine ran rampant across Poland and France in 1939–40, U.S. President Franklin D. Roosevelt, in his geopolitical rhetoric, broadened the coordinates of America's "home defense."[62] On the evening of December 29, 1940, for example, Roosevelt delivered a momentous message to the American public. He began: "This is not a fireside chat on war. It is a talk on national security, because the nub of the whole purpose of your President is to keep you now, and your children later, and your

12 / Introduction

grandchildren much later, out of a last-ditch war for the preservation of American independence and all of the things that American independence means to you and to me and to ours." Noting the growing military strength of Germany, Italy, and Japan, Roosevelt cautioned that the United States faced a "new threat" that required "courage and realism." The president explained that Britain alone was left standing to confront this threat and that if the British failed, then "the Axis powers [would] control the continents of Europe, Asia, Africa, Australia, and the high seas." Effectively, the United States would "be living at the point of a gun," a "new and terrible era in which the whole world . . . would be run by threats of brute force." As such, Roosevelt told his listeners that it was necessary to plan "our own defense with the utmost urgency" not for the purpose of war but instead to serve as "the great arsenal of democracy." Roosevelt envisioned a massive national effort to "increase the production of munitions" and the manufacture of "guns, planes, [and] ships."[63] The modern doctrine of national security was born. Until Roosevelt, no American statesman had presented security as having two equal parts—physical and normative, territorial and ideological.[64] From this point forward, this geopolitical dualism mediated the unfolding of the American spatial order.

Toward an American Spatial Order

The Second World War strengthened the bridge between geography and politics. Writing in 1943, Alfred Vagts surmised that "geography has been a more useful handmaid of military leaders" and that it was "through geography that military men have very often approached politics and foreign affairs."[65] Indeed, Vagts concluded that geopolitics, effectively, was "plainly geography gone imperialistic, geography being made to provide arguments and reasons . . . for one's own expansion."[66] On this note, Roosevelt's arsenal of democracy would prove crucial in determining the outcome of the Second World War; it would provide also the foundation for America's postwar planning and the establishment of an American nomos. As Fergie explains, the hardening geopolitical discourse of national security "marked the re-thinking and re-making of U.S. power abroad and at home."[67] Effectively, policymakers in Washington evinced a changed attitude toward global geopolitics. When the war ended, the United States was in a uniquely favorable position. The country controlled just over half of the world's gross national product, most of its food surpluses, and nearly all of its financial reserves. In addition, the war had generated a new industrial revolution that made the United States world leader in most key technologies. And on the military ledger, America's fighting forces were unsurpassed. That the United States held a monopoly on the atomic bomb was, quite literally, overkill.[68] Given these material conditions, many U.S. policymakers sought to construct a global economy centered on American national interests.[69] They were also prepared, if need be, to kill for this spatial order.

America's postwar spatial order did not materialize fully formed. Nor were its coordinates predetermined. That is to say, there was nothing inevitable or teleological about America's geopolitical dominion that coalesced in the post–Second World War era. Rather, the solidification of America's spatial order was built upon an edifice of national security policies and programs forwarded by decision makers within the U.S. government. As such, we should be mindful that the nascent form that America's spatial order ultimately assumed was the culmination of choices often marked by contradictions and uncertainties; that is, America's spatial order, albeit an aspiration that frequently crossed political parties, was the product of internecine power struggles that played out in the halls of government and on the fields of battle.

The U.S. accession to global hegemony, Dalby explains, required a reconceptualization of the U.S. role on the world stage. This, in turn, required a political reorientation away from prewar isolationist tendencies in favor of global intervention.[70] Standing in the way, however, stood the Soviet Union. Although briefly allied with the United States during the Second World War, the Soviet Union was almost always the supreme enemy for many U.S. policymakers. And when the war ended in 1945, it was the Soviet Union that continued to pose the greatest threat to the American nomos.[71] For U.S. policymakers it was necessary therefore to deter and to contain perceived Soviet expansionism throughout Europe and beyond. Consequently, set against the specter of possible Soviet global domination, during the early years of the Cold War, no imperiled state was deemed peripheral. The loss of freedom anywhere in the globe, U.S. policymakers cautioned, would have a ripple effect that would endanger America's allies globally. In the words of U.S. President Harry Truman, to do nothing would "endanger the people of the world" and, in turn, "endanger the welfare" of the United States.[72]

14 / Introduction

In blunt terms, for Truman, the United States was "no longer adequately protected by geography."[73]

Containment was not a policy prescribed all at once but was instead a concept developed over time and adjusted as political, economic, and military conditions warranted.[74] In turn, U.S. officials balanced diplomatic and military options at and between multiple scales. In the months immediately following the end of the Second World War, for example, the Joint Chiefs of Staff (JCS) affirmed that "the basic purpose for maintaining United States armed forces is to provide for our security and to uphold and advance our national policies, foreign and domestic. The essentials of our military policy are determined by our national policies." To that end, the national policies explicitly mentioned included "maintenance of the territorial integrity and security of the United States, its territories, possessions, leased areas and trust territories" and "advancing the political, economic and social well-being of the United States." Tellingly, the report clarified that the "maintenance of the United States in the best possible relative position with respect to potential enemy powers" must be prepared, whenever necessary, "to take military action abroad to maintain the security and integrity of the United States."[75]

The unfolding of America's embryonic spatial order was not without disagreement. In the late 1940s, many U.S. intelligence analysts calculated that the Soviet Union did *not* pose a military threat. For these dissenters, according to Melvyn Leffler, there was nearly universal agreement that the Soviets, while eager to expand their influence, desired to avoid any military engagement with the United States.[76] In September 1947, for example, a Central Intelligence Agency (CIA) report determined that "the U.S.S.R. is unlikely to resort to open military aggression in present circumstances."[77] Certainly, there was concern that Soviet control over much of Eastern Europe, and its raw materials would abet Russia's economic recovery, enhance its war-making capacity, and deny important foodstuffs, oil, and minerals to Western Europe.[78] However, the CIA report conceded that Russia's "policy is to avoid war, to build up its war potential, and to extend its influence and control by political, economic, and psychological methods." From the vantage point of some analysts working within the CIA, "The greatest danger to the security of the United States is the possibility of economic collapse in Western Europe and the consequent accession to power of Communist elements."[79]

George F. Kennan, a career foreign service officer and director of the policy planning staff in the U.S. Department of State, concurred with the CIA assessment.[80] As detailed in a planning report issued on November 6, 1947, Kennan surmised that "the danger of war is vastly exaggerated in many quarters." The Soviet Union, Kennan deduced, "neither wants nor expects war with us in the foreseeable future." In addition, he concluded, "Political advance of the communists in Western Europe has been at least temporarily halted." However, Kennan conceded that the world situation was "still dominated by the effort undertaken by the Russians in the post-hostilities period to extend their virtual domination over all, or as much as possible, of the Eurasian land mass." Effectively, Moscow's objective was to "neutralize our own ability to oppose it by weakening in every way our national potential and by undermining confidence everywhere in our motives and our fitness for leadership." In other words, both American prestige and credibility were at stake, two crucial elements in the projection of the American nomos. For Kennan, "Our best answer to this is to strengthen in every way local forces of resistance, and to persuade others to bear a greater part of the burden of opposing communism." Ultimately, Kennan concluded, "our policy must be directed toward restoring a balance of power in Europe and Asia."[81]

American military expansion was therefore necessary to maintain a geopolitical balance among the world's great powers and, in the process, promote American national security interests. In part, U.S. officials sought to construct a hegemonic spatial order through the establishment of international institutions, such as the United Nations (UN). However, these efforts constituted less an abrogation of U.S. sovereignty than a means to exert greater influence on the global stage. The UN, for example, was, as Bruce Cronin writes, "largely the product of American thinking, American initiative and American influence." And to that end, U.S. leaders "viewed the institution both as the custodian for maintaining a favorable post-war political order and as an important tool for exercising US leadership."[82]

As detailed by the U.S. State Department, "The United Nations is built upon the power relations existing among the United States, Great Britain, Russia, China, and France, and the other members of the war-time coalition. . . . If the balance of this relationship in military potential were to be impaired or upset, the fabric of the United Nations would be weakened or

16 / Introduction

at least would require reexamination. We do not wish this balance to be upset. Therefore, we should retain our military power in greater strength than that which would be needed merely to fulfill our strictly military obligations under the Charter."[83] Effectively, this meant that the United States assumed the right to support international coalitions only to the extent that these served American interests; otherwise, the United States was prepared to achieve its geopolitical ends through unilateral force. Thus, as detailed by the JCS, it was necessary always for the United States to "possess the means for retaliatory or punitive attack against other powers who may threaten the United States or the international peace structure in general." And while the JCS claimed disingenuously that such a military arsenal was not "for purposes of asserting world domination," they did acknowledge that American military power be preeminent and uncontested "to make it unwise for any major aggressor nation to initiate a major war against the opposition of the United States."[84] On this point, U.S. officials began to think seriously about the country's postwar national security, including designs for an elaborate, overseas base system.[85]

U.S. military and civilian planners envisioned an extensive system of overseas bases that would constitute America's *strategic frontier*, beyond which the United States would be able to use force to counter any threats or to frustrate any overt acts of aggression. The extra-territoriality of U.S. military bases could allow also the United States to preserve the formal fiction of nation-state sovereignty, in short, to maintain a physical presence without strictly "occupying" any given state.[86] Within the garrisoned state, however, as well as the entirety of the strategic frontier, U.S. military predominance—that is, defense of the American homeland—was to remain inviolate.[87] This is a point expressed most clearly by the JCS, who counseled the State Department that "in the future neither geography nor allies will render a nation immune from sudden and paralyzing attack should an aggressor arise to plague the peace of the world." Accordingly, the JCS advised that "determination of United States foreign policy should continually give consideration to our immediate capabilities for supporting our policy by arms if the occasion should demand. . . . In the final analysis the greatest single military factor in the security of the world is the absolute military security of the United States."[88]

Introduction / 17

Unlike the slapdash territorial expansion that typified nineteenth-century American geopolitics, America's commitment to the construction of a "strategic frontier" marked the inception of a new geopolitical order, a nomos predicated on American exceptionalism buttressed by military and economic dominance. This position was articulated clearly in a report issued by Truman's NSC in September 1949: "The position of the United States in world affairs is based upon the premise that our security and welfare are inextricably related to the general security and welfare, and upon an acceptance of the responsibility for leadership in world affairs which is called for by the premise." To that end, the United States sought "by unilateral action and through collective effort with other like minded peoples, to establish world conditions under which we can preserve and continue to develop our way of life." This required, in turn, a commitment to "adopt and effectively maintain programs which will both safeguard its security and welfare against the threats posed by the USSR, and lead to the establishment of the world conditions which we seek."[89]

Ironically, for both military and civilian planners, the "road to security was paved with feelings of insecurity."[90] Indeed, as Thompson explains, America's national security discourse has since the end of the Second World War been predicated on a geopolitical paradox. On the one hand, "The dramatic extension of America's overseas involvement and commitments . . . has reflected a growth of power rather than a decline of security," and yet, on the other hand, "the full and effective deployment of that power has required from the American people disciplines and sacrifices that they are prepared to sustain only if they are persuaded that the nation's safety is directly at stake."[91] In other words, America's Cold War stratagem was always fundamentally contradictory, so much so that it is perhaps best to describe U.S. geopolitics as one of national (in)security.

America's growing sense of vulnerability was given added impetus when, in August 1949, the United States lost its monopoly on the atomic bomb. Initially, and publicly, many U.S. officials downplayed the significance of the Soviets' emerging nuclear program. On September 23, for example, Truman announced that the United States had evidence that "an atomic explosion" occurred in the Soviet Union and that "this probability [had] always been taken into account" by his cabinet. He concluded that the test underscored

18 / Introduction

the need for the "truly effective enforceable international control of atomic energy." On the same day, Dean Acheson, the U.S. secretary of state, also released a statement affirming that the "event" signaled "no change in our policy."[92]

Behind the walls of the White House a different mood prevailed.

On September 30, 1950, Truman approved a report prepared by his National Security Council on "United States Objectives and Programs for National Security," otherwise known as NSC-68. The report advocated, in part, a dramatic increase in defense spending, particularly in the form of covert operations directed against the Soviet Union and its satellites.[93] In so doing, the report effectively set the parameters for U.S. national security over the coming years. The Soviet Union, as assumed in NSC-68, was "developing the military capacity to support its design for world domination." To achieve this objective, Soviet efforts were directed "toward the domination of the Eurasian land mass."[94]

NSC-68 was normative in orientation. As the distillation of practical geopolitical reasoning, the report advocated "a much more rapid and concerted build-up of the actual strength of both the United States and the other nations of the free world." Thus, NSC-68 called for a substantial increase in defense expenditures and military readiness on a global scale in order to bring about America's strategic frontier. The tone was also highly aggressive. To confront the Soviet challenge, it was "not an adequate objective to seek to check the Kremlin design, for the absence of order among nations is becoming less and less tolerable." Instead, the security of American core values and vital interests "demands that we make the attempt, and accept the risks inherent in it, to bring about order and justice by means consistent with the principles of freedom and democracy." That said, not all peoples of the world would be afforded the opportunity to exercise *their* freedom and democracy. Falling short of advocating war, the report acknowledged that it was "necessary to have the military power to deter, if possible, Soviet expansion, and to defeat, if necessary, aggressive Soviet or Soviet-directed actions of a limited or total character."[95]

Left unspecified were the geographic particulars of America's new spatial order. In broad terms, the core of the U.S.-imposed strategic frontier was self-evident: a ring of defensive positions throughout the Pacific and the Atlantic. Strategically, these forward bases would serve as a check on Soviet expansion. However, American resources were finite and, inevitably, hard decisions would have to be made. For Kennan, the objective was global equilibrium, that is, to balance the scales of geopolitical importance. In practical terms, this meant that U.S. foreign policy efforts center on Eurasia. According to Kennan, the Soviet Union was "taking advantage of the power vacuums left by the collapse of Germany and Japan" following the conclusion of the Second World War; as such, U.S. policy "must be directed toward restoring a balance of power in Europe and Asia."[96] This was in fact the premise codified in NSC-68, as U.S. analysts reaffirmed that "Soviet efforts" were "directed toward the domination of the Eurasian land mass."[97]

Beyond Eurasia, however, the specific contours of America's strategic frontier remained very much in doubt. John Ferguson, deputy director of the Policy Planning Staff, conceded that "to achieve any of our objectives, certain areas are clearly of more importance than others, and where the importance is of a critical nature to us we shall have to so conduct ourselves and so determine our policy that we assure the commitment of this strength to our purposes."[98] In bald terms, as Schelling writes, "many territories are just not worth a war."[99] As detailed in the coming chapters, the unfolding American nomos would always be marked by a fluid political geography, with strategic importance in constant circulation depending on broader geopolitical currents, both domestic and foreign. Spaces were coded as central or peripheral to American national security concerns, with the allocation of financial and military resources distributed according to a hierarchy of perceived geopolitical importance.

The spatial coding of the American nomos was always a contested process, for it was not always clear which regions or countries constituted the core or the periphery. Certainly, the so-called Great Powers of France, England, Germany, and the Soviet Union were central. Beyond these, however, a complex assemblage of historical, cultural, political, economic, and geostrategic elements mediated the relative centrality or marginality of any given area. France, for example, was central, but what of its southwestern neighbor, Spain?

The challenge, for U.S. strategists, was to determine where—and if—to draw a line in the sand. Indeed, as detailed in a paper prepared by the Department of State in cooperation with the Joint Chiefs of Staff, it was determined that "the United States cannot accept the concept of any 'stop-line'

20 / Introduction

on the ground as a *casus belli*, inasmuch as decision on such matters must depend not upon geography alone but upon the general situation which may exist locally and globally at the time of the aggression, the nature of the attack, and the apparent firmness of purpose of the attacker." Markedly, the report cautioned also against any public pronouncement that might imply the existence of a "stop-line." Any "public definition," the report explained, "would be a grave mistake for, on the one hand, it would invite aggression up to the line and, on the other, would probably increase our overt commitments to go to war in given situations."[100]

During the early years of the Cold War, one region stood out as being especially problematic: French Indochina. Composed of present-day Cambodia, Laos, and Vietnam, French authorities divided the region into five separate political entities: Tonkin (in northern Vietnam), Annam (central Vietnam), Cochinchina (southern Vietnam), Cambodia, and Laos.[101] From a purely defensive calculus, Indochina posed no risk to the security of the United States. However, following the Second World War, local revolutions in the region would profoundly affect America's geopolitical relations with France. In fact, U.S. policymakers understood Indochina primarily through the lens of European geopolitics, thus affecting strategic planning.

Charting the coordinates for America's proposed strategic frontier in Indochina and elsewhere would, in time, inform and impact America's diplomatic overtures and military interventions. As Stephen Kinzer details, "The United States repeatedly used its military power, and that of its clandestine services, to overthrow governments that refused to protect American interests."[102] U.S. operatives during the Cold War, for example, routinely and repeatedly supported, promoted, or facilitated the overthrow of several governments or opposition leaders, including those of Mohammed Mossadegh in Iran (1953), Jacobo Árbenz in Guatemala (1954), Patrice Lumumba in the Democratic Republic of the Congo (1961), Nelson Mandela in South Africa (1962), Ngo Dinh Diem in South Vietnam (1963), Joao Goulart in Brazil (1964), Sukarno in Indonesia (1965), Georgios Papandreou in Greece (1967), and Salvador Allende in Chile (1973). Far from exhaustive, this list does not include the myriad failed or aborted coups concocted by the CIA, including numerous attempts to overthrow Fidel Castro in Cuba and Norodom Sihanouk in Cambodia.

Most of the leaders deposed by U.S. and allied officials were democratically elected; few were ardent communists. Their tragic sin was invariably to challenge the corporate interests of the United States and its allies.[103] Indeed, as Walter LaFeber explains, although the need to spread American-style democracy throughout the world supposedly shaped U.S. foreign policy, this aspiration was accompanied by more rhetoric than reality. In actuality, U.S. policymakers demonstrated a willingness to work with dictators, terrorists, drug lords, and military juntas to the extent that these authoritarian regimes remained sufficiently anticommunist on the one hand and pro–U.S. business on the other.[104]

During the early years of the Cold War, however, it was not yet clear how—or if—Indochina would assume a central or peripheral place within the American nomos. As indicated, control over the Eurasian land mass remained central; beyond this certainty, significant disagreement among various policymakers remained. Indeed, in the early 1950s, many high-ranking officers in the U.S. military counseled *against* involvement in Indochina based on their conception of America's grand strategy. Given America's growing number of overseas commitments, officers such as J. Lawton Collins, Hoyt Vandenberg, and Matthew Ridgway did not believe they had the resources to get involved in areas of peripheral significance such as Indochina.[105]

State Department official Kennan captured some of the uncertainty clouding America's haphazard geopolitical practice. Early in his tenure as director of the Policy Planning Staff, Kennan was asked by Dean Acheson, then undersecretary of state, to "trace the lines of development of our foreign policy as they emerged from our actions in the past, and to project them into the future, so that we could see where we were going." Reluctant at first, Kennan subsequently provided in February 1948 "a general view of the main problems" of U.S. foreign policy, effectively a geopolitical calculus of the unfolding American nomos. Sweeping in their geographic scope, Kennan's concerns were outlined for most of the world's regions, including an evaluation of U.S. national security interests in the "Far East."[106] Kennan began with the bold claim that "we are greatly over-extended in our whole thinking about what we can accomplish, and should try to accomplish, in [the Far East]." For Kennan, it was imperative to "recognize our own limitations as a moral and ideological force among the Asiatic peoples."

22 / Introduction

In other words, and symptomatic of a latent racism within the evolving American spatial order, Kennan remained unconvinced that America's *core values* were applicable to future diplomatic relations in Asia. Kennan reasoned that "we must observe great restraint in our attitude toward the Far Eastern Areas. The peoples of Asia and of the Pacific area are going to go ahead, whatever we do, with the development of their political forms and mutual interrelationships in their own way. This process cannot be a liberal or peaceful one." Here, Kennan alludes to the ongoing anticolonial movements that were sweeping across Asia, including those underway in Indochina. Simply put, for Kennan the "Far East" was a backward region, an element that contributed to its instability. "All of the Asiatic peoples," Kennan cautioned, "are faced with the necessity for evolving new forms of life to conform to the impact of modern technology. This process of adaptation will also be long and violent." As such, Kennan determined, it was "not only possible, but probable, that in the course of this process many peoples will fall, for varying periods, under the influence of Moscow, whose ideology has a greater lure for such peoples, and probably greater reality, than anything we could oppose to it."[107]

Portentously, Kennan outlined the coordinates U.S. policymakers would follow in Indochina for the next quarter-century. "We would be better off," Kennan concluded, "to dispense now with a number of concepts which have underlined our thinking with regard to the Far East. We should dispense with the aspiration to 'be liked' or to be regarded as the repository of a high-minded international altruism. We should stop putting ourselves in the position, of being our brothers' keeper and refrain from offering moral and ideological advice. We should cease to talk about vague and—for the Far East—unreal objectives such as human rights, the raising of the living standards, and democratization." Instead, for Kennan, the proper course of action was "to be primarily military and economic." And to that end, Kennan advised that U.S. policymakers "should make a careful study to see what parts of the Pacific and Far Eastern world are absolutely vital to our security, and we should concentrate our policy on seeing to it that those areas remain in hands which we can control or rely on."[108] Notably, in 1948 neither Indochina in general nor Cambodia specifically assumed even a cursory mention in Kennan's appraisal of global geopolitics. Within a matter of years, however, all that would change: so much so that in 1969–70 Nixon authorized the secret—and illegal—bombing and invasion of Cambodia.

Critical geopolitics is about making arguments about geopolitical conjunctures and about trying to understand those conjunctures. *The Apathy of Empire* constitutes one such argument: namely to document the geopolitics of America's military intervention in Cambodia as part of the broader war in Indochina and to critically interrogate how a seemingly peripheral state, Cambodia, came to be central to the American nomos.

[1]

INTO THE BREACH

> Communist aggression in Indochina represents one of the most serious present threats to the free world.
>
> —JOHN FOSTER DULLES, speech before the U.S. Congress

The surprise Japanese attacks on Pearl Harbor in 1941 demonstrated to many scholars and policymakers in the United States that enemies could reach across the oceans to strike at America's heart; advances in air power and missile technologies throughout the late 1940s and into the 1950s only raised the alarm of even more devastating attacks in the future.[1] Writing in the aftermath of the atomic bombings of Hiroshima and Nagasaki, for example, Harold and Margaret Sprout warned that "most Americans simply cannot imagine themselves huddling in underground shelters, fighting incendiary fires, picking in the charred ruins of their burned-out homes." As such, rather than holding a misguided belief that "it can't happen here," the Sprouts counseled that the security of the United States required greater resolve; indeed, they warned that "ordinary" Americans "have yet to grasp the changing character of war, and the bearing of that upon our own future."[2] This mindset would become a recurrent theme within America's national security discourse: it was better to fight the enemy abroad than wait until they appeared on America's doorstep. To do so, however, required a particular geographic literacy to determine where the most grievous threats lurked. In this opening chapter I document America's early involvement in Indochina; in subsequent chapters, I provide a critical reading of America's geographic assessment of Cambodia's centrality to U.S. national security interests.

The Genesis of the American Nomos

The Second World War is properly seen as a turning point in the emergent spatial order of the United States. Relatively untouched by war, and

26 / Into the Breach

in possession of an enormous industrial potential that had produced war materiel not only for its own military but also for those of its allies, the United States was in a unique position.[3] And many officials within the FDR administration were prepared to capitalize on America's ascendancy on the world stage. Indeed, as Ivo Daalder and James Lindsay explain, the foreign policy questions America faced at the end of the war had little to do with what the United States *could* do abroad; the immediate questions dealt with what the United States *should* do abroad.[4] Michael Adas captures this sentiment:

> The economic and military power the United States was able to project on a global scale in a war that was so devastating to its industrial rivals served to bolster Americans' long-held belief in their nation's exceptionalism. But it also intensified the paradox that had muddled exceptionalist thinking from the time of the earliest European settlement in North America. Although Americans deemed their nation's historical development both unprecedented and unique, they also saw American institutions, ideas, and modes of organizations as models for all societies. The experiences of the Second World War heightened the moral and millenarian dimensions of this teleology.[5]

Even as fighting raged across Europe and the Pacific at the war's zenith, elite elements within the U.S. government and private sector outlined postwar settlement plans that would ostensibly guarantee peace, economic growth, and stability into the indefinite future. These plans included the promotion of free markets and of private property—as opposed to nationalized businesses or colonies outside the reach of U.S. investors. Effectively, the objective was to construct an unfettered spatial order for trade and economic development, enforced by the "benevolence" of U.S. hegemony. Indeed, reminiscent of earlier expansionist practices—notably military interventions in the Caribbean, Central America, and the Pacific islands—U.S. officials claimed to act with universal interests in mind, unlike the self-centered profiteering of European colonialism. To that end, many policymakers in the United States viewed their role in quasi-religious terms— a divine right to lead the world's downtrodden to financial salvation. In practice, however, officials confronted myriad obstacles, not least of which was the appropriate response to the geopolitical contradictions wrought by resurgent nationalisms and anticolonial movements intensified by the Second World War. Mark Lawrence ably summarizes the geopolitical complexities faced by U.S. policymakers: for Lawrence it was a question of "how to balance their desire to win the favor of anticolonial nationalists in Asia and Africa against their determination to form partnerships with Western European governments that wished to preserve their strong influence, if not outright control, in those same places."[6] On this point, U.S. officials recognized, or rather *sensed*, the dawn of a new spatial order: the old colonial regimes were crumbling as new nationalist governments were forming, and the United States was prepared to step into the breach.

During the Second World War, Roosevelt made clear his opposition to the restoration of European colonialism, notably in Asia.[7] Shortly before his death, for example, Roosevelt expressed concern "about the brown people in the East." FDR acknowledged that there were "1,100,000,000 brown people" who were resentful of being "ruled by a handful of whites." America's goal, Roosevelt explained, was "to help them achieve independence."[8] Roosevelt was far from altruistic in his sentiments. European colonialism effectively cut off large swaths of territory from U.S. influence and, because of that, the establishment of pro-Western states was favored. However, the belief among Roosevelt and many of his advisors was that the formerly colonized peoples, and especially those in Indochina, were not ready for self-government. According to Secretary of State Cordell Hull, "Emergence of these regions as self-governing countries would appear desirable as soon as they are capable of self-rule, either as independent nations or in close voluntary associations with western powers, for example as dominions."[9]

From a practical standpoint, Roosevelt supported the creation of trusteeships for former European colonies. Roosevelt, however, never developed a coherent plan for his notion of trusteeships and, indeed, was frequently and deliberately vague when discussing his intentions.[10] When, in March 1943, Roosevelt explained to Anthony Eden, then serving as British ambassador to the United States, the idea of an international trusteeship for Indochina and other territories, including Korea, Manchuria, and Formosa, he was less than forthright.[11] In part, Roosevelt was sensitive to the volatility of the idea of trusteeships, especially with his British allies, and was understandably reluctant to articulate any policy that would jeopardize the wartime coalition.[12] Of equal importance, the president's plans for a postwar

28 / Into the Breach

world were not widely supported among U.S. policymakers. Indeed, dissension was notably present among senior military officials, who determined that American security interests in the postwar environment required that the United States control formerly Japanese-held islands in the Pacific, but only under conditions that would not allow any international agency or foreign government to interfere.[13] On that point, members of America's military institutions worried that their endgame to establish a global archipelago of military bases was jeopardized by Roosevelt's antipathy toward colonialism and his proposed idea of trusteeships.

Markedly, although Roosevelt opposed the return of European colonialism in general, much of his ire was directed toward France. In the summer of 1940 France was defeated militarily by Nazi Germany. Subsequent agreements brought about an armistice that promised French sovereignty despite being occupied by German troops. A new government was proclaimed, named after the site of its administrative center in Vichy, France. As part of the armistice, the Vichy government would continue to control the French Empire, including its colonies in Indochina. There, colonial officials wanted to retain the vestiges of French sovereignty and, ultimately, hold fast to its possessions until the war was concluded. Consequently, French officials were compelled to enter into a collaborative relationship with the Japanese government.[14] In August 1940, the governor-general of Indochina signed a general accord with Japan; this allowed French officials to remain in effective control of Indochina in return for placing all military facilities and economic resources at Japan's disposal. As Gary Hess explains, the sudden collapse of the French government in the face of German aggression in 1940 convinced Roosevelt that France had become a decadent nation that no longer deserved the status of a major power.[15] Roosevelt was equally convinced that after the war France would not be a stabilizing force in Asia and should not be allowed to retake possession of Indochina.[16] Indeed, by January 1943 Roosevelt was adamant that many of France's "colonial possessions . . . would not be returned" after the war, and he expressly harbored "grave doubts as to whether Indo-China should be" returned.[17] For Roosevelt, the geographic calculus was clear: "After 100 years of French rule in Indochina, the inhabitants were worse off than they had been before."[18] Such a condition, if left unchecked, could only weaken America's objectives in Asia.

Roosevelt's preoccupation with Indochina, however, ran deeper than his antipathy toward the French government. Indeed, the president and many of his senior advisors recognized the potential economic and strategic importance of Indochina for the postwar world—a fact that mitigated against the return of French colonial rule. On September 8, 1944, for example, Hull noted that Southeast Asia, but specifically the territories comprising Indochina, "are sources of products essential to both our wartime and peacetime economy." He continued: "They are potentially important markets for American exports. They lie athwart the southwestern approaches to the Pacific Ocean and have important bearing on our security and the security of the Philippines. Their economic and political stability will be an important factor in the maintenance of peace in Asia."[19] The resumption of French colonialism was anathema to an envisioned world order based on open access and free markets.

America's military involvement in Indochina began during these years. In the waning months of the Second World War, operating in northern Vietnam, covert agents of the U.S. Office of Strategic Services—the predecessor to the Central Intelligence Agency—formed an alliance with a young nationalist, Ho Chi Minh, and his Viet Minh (Viet Nam Doc Lap Dong Minh Hoi, or League for the Independence of Vietnam) guerrilla army. Since 1941 the Viet Minh had been fighting Japanese troops occupying the former French colony and, as Marilyn Young explains, these Vietnamese nationalists became, in a formal sense, allies of the United States, Great Britain, and the Soviet Union in a joint struggle against the Axis powers and collaborationist regimes such as Vichy France.[20]

Under the Roosevelt administration, the U.S. State Department was deeply divided on the proper course of action in Indochina specifically but Southeast Asia more generally. At risk of oversimplification, two "camps" struggled over U.S. policy in Southeast Asia. On one side stood members of the U.S. State Department's European division. By and large, these analysts were indifferent, if not outright hostile, to the demands of Asian nationalists such as Ho Chi Minh. For these officials, Europe already held center stage and, as such, counseled that the United States should not jeopardize relations with its European allies by interfering in colonial affairs marginal to U.S. interests.[21] On the other side stood analysts working within the Office of Far Eastern Affairs. As a whole, these individuals were sensitive

30 / Into the Breach

to nationalist aspirations in Asia and advised that the continuation of European sovereignty could be tolerated in Asia only *if* combined with explicit pledges of eventual independence for the former colonies. This was the course taken by the United States in the Philippines. A possession of the United States since 1898, the Philippines was granted independence in 1946. However, through the imposition of unfair trade and security treaties, the United States effectively controlled the economic and political fortunes of the Philippines, all to the benefit of U.S. corporate interests.[22] U.S. officials, in turn, believed that the Philippines could become a model for European powers to emulate—but only on one condition. Strategically, U.S. officials sought to impose an "open door" framework that would allow unfettered American access to markets and resources throughout Southeast Asia.[23] A European presence was tolerable only to the extent that such influence did not restrict U.S. military or business activities.

With Roosevelt's death, the pendulum within the U.S. State Department —and by extension, the overall U.S. policy toward Indochina—swung to the Europeanist side. In May, President Harry Truman conveyed to French representatives that "the American people and the American government realize that the French nation has emerged with renewed strength and vigor from the catastrophe which it suffered and that it has demonstrated its determination and its ability to resume its rightful and eminent place among the nations which will share the largest measure of responsibility in maintaining the future peace of Europe and the world." Truman proclaimed, "A strong France represents a gain to the world."[24] Effectively, the "Europeanists" within the U.S. government argued that the United States could not impose its views on unwilling allies and should not, in any event, risk cooperation with France or the United Kingdom for the abstract principle of anticolonialism.[25]

Just three weeks after Roosevelt's death, French Foreign Minister George Bidault received assurances from the U.S. Acting Secretary of State Edward Stettinius that the United States was *not* in opposition to the restoration of French sovereignty over the French Empire, including Indochina.[26] In turn, French officials over the ensuing months began to reframe—at least rhetorically—their ambitions in Indochina. According to Jean Chauvel, secretary general of the French Ministry for Foreign Affairs, the French position was to formulate a policy that would have "certain advantages for the

Into the Breach / 31

US and Britain" and that therefore would "insure American and British interest in the future of Indochina." That is, French officials hoped to "operate Indochina in a general way" that was not only a "lucrative business" for France but also one that was "advantageous to the other occidental powers."[27]

In the end, the trusteeship plan, Roosevelt's most conspicuous postwar goal for an area that had been an integral part of a European empire, remained unrealized. And yet, the kernel of Roosevelt's plan, of autonomous governments beholden to "friendly" foreign powers, was firmly planted in Cold War soil. Indeed, this was the attitude of key British officials. In March 1944, for example, Eden professed that the goal for colonial territories should be economic, social, and political advancement and an autonomous status rather than independence. Indicative of the prevailing racism that permeated the question of colonialism, Eden surmised that the colonized peoples were incapable of self-government and were thus "subject" to "both economic and military dangers."[28]

In August 1945, the atomic bombing of Hiroshima and Nagasaki by the United States brought an abrupt end to the Japanese Empire. This is significant, as Evelyn Colbert explains, because none of the colonial powers— France, the Netherlands, or the United Kingdom—were prepared to move immediately and in strength into the Japanese-occupied colonies. The result was that Asian nationalists, notably the Viet Minh, were afforded a brief but significant hiatus to consolidate their positions. On September 2, 1945, the day Japan formally surrendered, Ho Chi Minh declared the formation of an independent Democratic Republic of Vietnam (DRV). He opened his speech with quotations lifted from the American Declaration of Independence and France's Declaration of the Rights of Man and the Citizen. He spoke of equality and unalienable rights and harshly criticized the brutality and undemocratic character of colonialism. Above all, he asserted the right of the Vietnamese people to be free—a right to which the "entire Vietnamese people are determined to mobilize all their physical and mental strength, to sacrifice their lives and property in order to safeguard their freedom and independence."[29] Ho Chi Minh's proclamation, however, went unheeded by the international community, and French forces moved to reclaim their former colonial possessions. As Young writes, "By October 1945, it was clear that the only people ready to recognize the freedom and independence of Vietnam were the Vietnamese themselves."[30]

32 / Into the Breach

As the prospect for war grew ever more likely, both French officials and Viet Minh nationalists turned to the United States for help. On the one hand, French diplomats appealed to the United States for ships to transport additional troops to Indochina and for arms and ammunition to equip them. On the other hand, Ho Chi Minh voiced his hope that the long-standing relationship between the Viet Minh and the OSS would translate into American support. With this in mind, on September 21, he sent the first of several personal appeals to Truman.[31]

U.S. policy in Indochina was at the first of many crossroads that American presidents would face throughout the Cold War. As Lawrence explains, "The competing demands of colonizer and colonized in Vietnam posed the dilemma more urgently than anywhere else, and the solutions that Americans offered helped to set patterns that would play out globally throughout the Cold War."[32] In fall of 1945, the choice favored by the Truman administration was essentially to do nothing. Not wanting to assume responsibility for a situation that threatened to spiral out of control, the Truman administration ignored Ho's appeals but also limited their support of the French. Notably, the United States did not participate in the protracted and eventually abortive negotiations between the Viet Minh and France throughout the early months of 1946.[33] Practically and pragmatically, in the interest of improving relations with France, the Truman administration, by doing nothing, gave the French a free hand in Indochina.[34]

French officials faced their own dilemma. Their primary objective was to reestablish control over Indochina. More precisely, as Young summarizes, "France defined its well-being in terms of repossessing its lost colony, not only as a balm to wounded national vanity, but because of a reasonable fear that an independent Vietnam would threaten French interests in the economically far more significant colonies of Algeria, Morocco, and Tunisia."[35] Officials were concerned also with diverting scarce resources from domestic reconstruction. From their vantage point, the ideal solution was to resolve the problem diplomatically rather than militarily. Appropriately, French diplomats forwarded a proposal that would grant limited autonomy to the Vietnamese while still maintaining effective control. In broad outline, the agreement would recognize the DRV as an "independent" and "free" state within the French community; Vietnam would have its own parliament, army, and finances; it would also be part of an Indochinese federation that would include Cambodia and Laos. A referendum would be scheduled throughout the three "components" of Vietnam—Tonkin, Annam, and Cochinchina—to determine the final political status of Vietnam.[36] The Preliminary Convention, as the compromise solution was known, was anything but a compromise from Ho Chi Minh's viewpoint. Indeed, despite the trappings of independence, the convention placed both Vietnam's ultimate sovereignty and unification at risk. French authority was persevered and the specter of a referendum left in doubt whether Vietnam would become a single country or (potentially) three separate republics.[37]

By November 1946, armed conflict erupted between French forces and the Viet Minh, and fighting soon spread throughout Vietnam. In the beginning, French officials were optimistic. On the domestic front, early on, the war was immensely popular and garnered support across the political spectrum. Conservatives, liberals, socialists: all were in like agreement that Indochina, in some form or another, should remain within the French colonial empire.[38] That French armed forces appeared to have the upper hand only added to the sense of purpose and optimism. As the war progressed, most major cities and towns came under French control and the Viet Minh appeared vulnerable.

Wars are fickle, though. Despite early success on the battlefield, French officials voiced concern over the long-term prognosis. Still recovering from the devastation wrought by the Second World War, France was in no position to fight a protracted and costly guerrilla war against the Viet Minh. To do so would jeopardize the economic and political security of France.[39] This was precisely the strategy adopted by the Viet Minh General Vo Nguyen Giap.[40] Sacrificing the urban areas in the short-term, the Viet Minh prepared for long-term victory. Despite France's initial military superiority, the Vietnamese had something more important: time.

Outside of France, world reaction to the deepening of hostilities was tempered. None of the Great Powers—the Soviet Union, the United Kingdom, or the United States—did much to prevent the outbreak of war and, once war arrived, did little to resolve the conflict. The Soviet Union, not unlike the United States, remained focused on events in Europe and, as such, prioritized diplomatic relations with France over the Vietnamese. British officials, concerned also with maintaining dominion over their own colonial possessions, hoped for a political solution but otherwise supported in

34 / Into the Breach

principle the sovereignty of France in Indochina. Officials in the United States, on the whole, remained divided on the war.[41] Certainly, a broad consensus existed in Washington that colonialism was unacceptable to the emergent spatial order; that said, the precise course of action for a postcolonial world remained unclear.[42] Within weeks, many U.S. officials stationed in Asia expressed grave doubts regarding America's role in the conflict. On January 7, 1947 Paul Josselyn, the U.S. consul general in Singapore, forwarded a letter from Abbot Low Moffat, head of the State Department's Southeast Asia Division, advising that Truman's "hands-off policy" was based on European considerations and signified the appearance of U.S. approval of the French military conquest of Vietnam. Prompt U.S. action was necessary to bring the war to a swift conclusion in order both to save lives and to protect America's position in Southeast Asia. Even if the French were militarily successful, hatred among the Vietnamese would, in the end, threaten all Western interests in the region. At this critical juncture, Moffat explained to the Truman administration the "deep need for US moral leadership"[43]

Other voices attempted to provide clarity. George Marshall, U.S. secretary of state, explained in a February 1947 memo to the U.S. embassy in Paris, "We have only [the] very friendliest feelings toward France and we are anxious in every way we can to support France in her fight to regain her economic, political and military strength and to restore herself as in fact one of [the] major powers of [the] world." No doubt referencing the previous administration's attitude toward France and the resumption of colonial authority, Marshall clarified that "in spite of any misunderstanding which might have arisen . . . in regard to our position concerning Indochina they must appreciate that we have fully recognized France's sovereign position in that area and we do not wish to have it appear that we are in any way endeavoring [to] undermine that position, and [the] French should know it is our desire to be helpful and we stand ready to assist [in] any appropriate way we can to find [a] solution for [the] Indochinese problem." However, Marshall called attention to the nagging problem of supporting the restoration of colonial rule. "We cannot shut our eyes," Marshall stated, "to the fact that there are two sides [to] this problem and that our reports indicate both a lack [of] French understanding of [the] other side." On this point, Marshall warned against the folly of forwarding a "dangerously outmoded colonial outlook" in Indochina. Instead, Marshall intimated the need for the French government to establish a new relationship with the peoples of Indochina in order to challenge Ho Chi Minh. That said, Marshall made clear "we do not lose sight [of the] fact that Ho Chi Minh has direct Communist connections and it should be obvious that we are not interested in seeing colonial empire administrations supplanted by philosophy and political organizations emanating from and controlled by [the] Kremlin." For Marshall, the Indochina problem was no longer "of a local character," that is, a struggle between France and the Viet Minh. Of the proper course of action to pursue, though, Marshall tersely concluded, "Frankly we have no solution [to the] problem to suggest."[44]

In fact, a solution was forming. On March 12, 1947, U.S. President Harry Truman spoke before a joint session of Congress.[45] The impetus for Truman's speech was not the war in Indochina but instead the communist threat brewing both in Greece and Turkey. The implications, though, were plain to see. The British government had recently announced that it would no longer provide military and economic assistance to the Greek government in its struggle against the Greek Communist Party; British assistance to Turkey would also be withheld. In Washington, U.S. officials believed that the Soviet Union supported the Greek communist war effort and thus worried that if the communists prevailed, the Soviets would gain the upper hand in southern Europe. In reality, the Soviet involvement in the Greek civil war was minimal and was not a threat to Turkey at the time. However, by 1947 the discourse surrounding the "Soviet threat" had already come to play a crucial role in the conduct of American foreign policy.[46] Now, the gauntlet had dropped, and the United States was on a course that would markedly define subsequent decisions regarding Indochina.[47] In short order, a peripheral anticolonial conflict would assume a central role in America's spatial ordering of the Cold War and its global crusade against communism.

In what became known as the "Truman Doctrine," the president established that the United States would provide political, military, and economic assistance to all democratic states under threat from external or internal authoritarian forces. "One of the primary objectives of the foreign policy of the United States," Truman affirmed, "is the creation of conditions in which we and other nations will be able to work out a way of life free from coercion." Indeed, it was this purpose that prompted the United States to

36 / Into the Breach

enter the previous war against Germany and Japan. As such, Truman warned, "We shall not realize our objectives . . . unless we are willing to help free peoples to maintain their free institutions and their national integrity against aggressive movements that seek to impose upon them totalitarian regimes."[48] Truman, remarkably, downplayed the threat of communism. For Truman, it was totalitarian rule—regardless of ideology—that posed the gravest threat; in other words, when Truman spoke of the incompatibility of "two ways of life," he was referring to totalitarianism and democracy, not communism and capitalism.[49] The president continued: "Totalitarian regimes imposed on free peoples, by direct or indirect aggression, undermine the foundations of international peace and hence the security of the United States." In the aftermath of the war, however, Truman explained that the "peoples of a number of countries of the world have recently had totalitarian regimes forced upon them against their will." It was therefore incumbent upon the United States "to support free peoples who are resisting attempted subjugation by armed minorities or by outside pressures." Truman, in addition, laid bare his geopolitical reasoning. "It is necessary only to glance at a map," Truman counseled, "to realize that the survival and integrity of both Greece and Turkey" was at stake, for, according to the president, should either of these states fall to totalitarian rule, the regional and global effects would be "immediate and serious." Indeed, as understood by Truman, "Confusion and disorder might well spread throughout the entire Middle East." Were the United States to allow this to happen, the consequences would "have a profound effect upon those countries in Europe whose peoples are struggling against great difficulties to maintain their freedom and independence."[50]

Despite Truman's pledge of global assistance, America's wherewithal to project power and protect its vital interests from the Soviet bloc was still limited. As Brands explains, "Expansive rhetoric aside, the United States clearly lacked the resources to support 'free peoples' everywhere."[51] This was a point underscored by Truman in September 1947. "The fundamental basis of the policy of the United States," Truman declared, "is the desire for permanent world peace." However, the president cautioned that "our resources are not unlimited. We must apply them where they can serve the most effectively to bring production, freedom, and confidence back to the world."[52] It was this geopolitical reasoning that informed Secretary of State Marshall's

Into the Breach / 37

proposal to extend massive economic assistance to the devasted states of Europe. Materialized in the Marshall Plan, the secretary of state explained that the policy of the United States was not directed "against any country or doctrine but against hunger, poverty, desperation, and chaos. Its purpose should be the revival of a working economy in the world so as to permit the existence of political and social conditions in which free institutions can exist." Left unsaid in Marshall's pronouncement was that U.S. policy promoted the free-market economy as the best plan for economic recovery and the best defense against Soviet communism in Western Europe.[53] Essentially, the overwhelmingly economic focus of these early Cold War programs reflected the widespread belief that political systems were largely shaped by economic conditions and that communism flourished in economically depressed regions.[54] Indeed, as Andrew Bacevich explains, American national security interests were based on the removal of barriers that might inhibit the movement of goods, capital, ideas, and people; the ultimate objective was the creation of an open and integrated international order based on the principles of democratic capitalism, with the United States as the ultimate guarantor of order and the enforcer of norms.[55]

For most military and civilian intelligence officials, Eurasia—and specifically Western Europe—remained central in their geopolitical calculations. Such reasoning, however, did not translate into a marginal consideration of peripheral regions, including Indochina. Although Asia was considered secondary in importance—with Japan as the only major industrial center of note—the region was strategically important for other reasons.[56] The task at hand, George Kennan explained, was to "make a careful study to see what parts of the Pacific and Far Eastern world are absolutely vital to our security, and we should concentrate our policy on seeing to it that those areas remain in hands which we can control or rely on."[57] As detailed earlier, this thinking informed the promotion of a "strategic frontier" or "defensive perimeter" that would encircle the western flank of the Pacific Ocean and, in doing so, contain the Soviet threat.[58] Spatially, the concept "was based on the idea that it was possible to draw a clear line between vital and peripheral interests," something that no official wanted to do.[59] Nevertheless, as detailed by Acheson, the proposed perimeter, stretching from the Aleutians through Japan to the Philippines, would act "as a protective shield to all of the Americas and all free lands of the Pacific Ocean" and, from this

38 / Into the Breach

position, the United States would be able to "dominate with air power every Asiatic port from Vladivostok to Singapore and prevent any hostile movement into the Pacific." Simply put, Acheson explained, "With naval and air supremacy and modern ground elements to defend bases, any major attack from continental Asia toward us or our friends of the Pacific would come to failure." In this manner, Acheson believed, it was possible—indeed, vital—to contain the Soviet threat without the fiscal or military burden of long-term commitments to peripheral states. "If we hold this line," he warned ominously, "we may have peace—lose it and war is inevitable."[60]

As war lumbered on in Indochina, the Soviet threat to America's interests was formally codified in a 1948 National Security Council report entitled "The Position of the United States with Respect to Soviet-Directed World Communism." Designated as NSC-7, the report warned that "the ultimate objective of Soviet-directed world communism is the domination of the world." And confronting this threat was the United States, which was "the only source of power capable of mobilizing successful opposition to the communist goal of world conquest." Since the end of the Second World War, the report warned, "the USSR has engaged the United States in a struggle for power, or 'cold war', in which our national security is at stake and from which we cannot withdraw short of national suicide." On that point, NSC-7 underscored the need for a more aggressive foreign policy, a position robust enough to stand up to the Soviet threat. "In view of the nature of Soviet-directed world communism," the report concluded, "a defensive policy cannot be considered an effectual means of checking the momentum of communist expansion and inducing the Kremlin to relinquish its aggressive designs"; rather, the United States required a "world-wide counter-offensive against Soviet-directed world communism," a policy that would involve both "strengthening the military potential of the United States" and "mobilizing and strengthening the potential of the non-Soviet world."[61]

French officials were very attuned to the hysteria and paranoia bubbling up in the United States. The conflict against the Viet Minh had reached a stalemate, and the war had become a drain on the government's coffers. France could continue fighting, the government concluded, only if it obtained additional and substantial financial and military resources from abroad. And while wary of U.S. expansionism, French officials determined that the United States was the logical if not the only choice.[62] All that was required was to recast their *colonial war* against the Viet Minh as a *global war* against communism. To this end, in an effort to downplay their colonial objectives, French officials adopted a two-pronged strategy. On the one hand, Ho Chi Minh was increasingly portrayed as a puppet of the Soviet Union. On the other hand, French authorities forwarded a proposal to establish a "free" Vietnam in opposition to the DRV. This latter strategy, the so-called Bao Dai solution, would provide the appearance of Vietnamese independence while retaining French dominion over the territories; moreover, the United States would provide the necessary financial and military resources to make it all possible.[63]

In September 1947 France announced its intention to unify Tonkin, Annam, and Cochinchina within a single state. This "new" Vietnam would be independent, albeit a member of the French Union. As figurehead for their state-building artifice, French officials turned to Bao Dai, the former emperor who had abdicated to make way for Ho Chi Minh in August 1945. Heralded by the French as the embodiment of Vietnamese nationalism, Bao Dai was the only leader French officials felt could effectively rally the Vietnamese populace away from Ho Chi Minh. Consequently, following a series of negotiations, the Ha Long Bay Accords were signed in June 1948 and the establishment of an "independent" Vietnam formalized. As Fredrik Logevall concludes, "It was disingenuous in the extreme, an ex post factor justification for a war initiated and fought on other grounds."[64]

Despite Truman's proclamation that the United States was prepared to "support free peoples who are resisting attempted subjugation by armed minorities or by outside pressures," many U.S. officials in 1947 continued to remain wary of supporting France's effort. Aware of possible economic and military overreach, several U.S. policymakers counseled to bracket America's overseas ventures. Clark M. Clifford, serving as special counsel to Truman, reasoned that "one of the most fundamental objectives of American foreign policy is that no aggressive military power shall establish itself on the shores of Western Europe."[65] Any diplomatic or military action, therefore, had to be evaluated on that geographic axiom. Asia, though, posed a geopolitical dilemma. What if events in Asia impinged on Europe, either directly or indirectly? How would these relations mediate US policymaking? Solutions to these problems were not immediately apparent. Kennan, for example, held that "while we would endeavor to influence events on the mainland of Asia in ways favorable to our security, we would not regard any mainland areas as vital to us."[66] Here, Kennan simply compounds the problem: Asia is important, just not vitally important.

In late 1947 the CIA provided its assessment. Based on current U.S. national security interests, the "Far East [was] of only third priority from the point of view of containing the U.S.S.R. and eventually redressing the balance of power."[67] For now, the situation in Indochina—although concerning—was still seen as peripheral to America's spatial order. Consequently, Marshall's reasoning appeared to hold sway: The war in Indochina was a colonial war; and although Ho Chi Minh was portrayed as an ardent communist, the fact remained that it was largely the Vietnamese who were resisting subjugation by outside pressures, namely France.[68] Indochina was central inasmuch as France was central to U.S. objectives in Europe. Beyond that, there were plenty of other territories around the world to occupy the attention of Washington.

Still, a consensus to support the Bao Dai Solution was growing among many U.S. officials.[69] In September 1948, the State Department drafted a policy statement that clarified U.S. policy toward Indochina. The long-term objectives of the United States were (1) "to eliminate so far as possible Communist influence in Indochina and to see installed a self-governing nationalist state which will be friendly to the US"; (2) "to foster the association of the peoples of Indochina with the western powers . . . to the end that those peoples will prefer freely to cooperate with the western powers culturally, economically and politically"; (3) "to raise the standard of living so that the peoples of Indochina will be less receptive to totalitarian influences and will have an incentive to work productively and thus contribute to a better balanced world economy"; and (4) "to prevent undue Chinese penetration and subsequent influence in Indochina so that the peoples of Indochina will not be hampered in their natural developments by the pressure of an alien people and alien interests."[70] Hypocrisy notwithstanding, the document is informative in that it lays bare fundamental objectives that would remain central to U.S. foreign policy in Southeast Asia for the next quarter-century. Effectively, the goal was to install and support a pro-Western, noncommunist state as a viable alternative to Ho Chi Minh's Democratic Republic of Vietnam and become a productive member of the emergent capitalist world order.

This latter aim, of a free and independent state of Vietnam participating in the U.S.-controlled global economy, cannot be overemphasized. Beyond the powerful rhetoric of anticommunism, U.S. policy toward Southeast Asia was profoundly affected by larger economic goals. Indeed, a planning paper prepared by the State Department in March 1949 expressed clearly that the objective was to "seek vigorously to develop the interdependence between [Southeast Asia], as a supplier of raw materials, and Japan, western Europe and India, as suppliers of finished goods, with due recognition . . . of the legitimate aspirations of [Southeast Asian] countries for some diversification of their economies."[71] In other words, Southeast Asia—but especially Indochina—was important not for its direct contribution to the economy of the United States but for the resources necessary for economic growth for those pro-Western states allied with the United States.[72] Could this form the basis of U.S. national security policy?

No strategy can be effective, John Gaddis writes, if it fails to match means with ends.[73] The Truman Doctrine implied an open-ended commitment to resist Soviet expansionism. However, with limited financial means and military forces, it was impossible for the United States to encompass the entirety of the free world under its protective umbrella. This "blunt reality," Gaddis explains, "forced the making of distinctions between vital and peripheral interests." Required was a geopolitical strategy based on "the calculated relationship of resources to objectives."[74] As Kennan specified in a Policy Planning Staff report, "there is some misconception in the mind of the American people as to the objectives of the Truman Doctrine and of our aid to foreign countries." Concretely, Kennan countered the belief that the "Truman Doctrine is a blank check to give economic and military aid to any area in the world where the communists show signs of being successful." Consequently, in response both to American public opinion and to other foreign governments, Kennan stressed that it "must be made clear that the extension of American aid is essentially a question of political economy in the literal sense of that term and that such aid will be considered only in cases where the prospective results bear a satisfactory relationship to the expenditure of American resources and effort."[75] Western Europe was clearly a centerpiece of U.S. strategic interests; so too was Japan.

In the immediate aftermath of the Second World War, U.S. policy was to create a weak and compliant Japanese state that could never again threaten

42 / Into the Breach

the international order. However, with the prospect of a communist "takeover" in China looking more likely with each passing day, many U.S. officials looked to Japan as a viable bulwark.[76] To this end, key figures in the State, War, and Navy Departments, as well as influential private citizens, mobilized to reverse existing punitive economic controls and to promote the fastest possible economic recovery of Japan.[77] This shift in emphasis is articulated in a 1948 CIA report on the "Strategic Importance of Japan." In stark terms, the report explained that whoever controlled Japan—either the United States or the USSR—controlled the "Far East." On this point, the report warned, "Extension of Soviet control or domination over North China, Manchuria, and the whole of Korea would result in an incalculable loss of US prestige throughout the Far East" and that "such a condition might greatly facilitate further Soviet extension into Japan itself, which in turn would expedite Communist expansion in Asia against diminishing resistance." More precisely, CIA officials cautioned that "from a purely ideological viewpoint the [Japanese] masses are not attracted to the banner of Communism because of their innate conservatism and their traditional fear of the USSR," there remained the possibility that communism could make inroads in Japan. "Communism's advantages in Japan," the CIA premised, "lie largely in the economic field." In fact, according to intelligence officials, "until the Japanese people are shown tangible evidence of economic recovery they will remain susceptible to Communist anti-government and anti-Occupation propaganda."[78] Under the right conditions, though, CIA officials reasoned, Japan could "develop into a free, independent nation capable of exerting a stabilizing influence in Asia"; otherwise, the "probability that Japan would eventually succumb to Communist domination would become almost a certainty."[79]

To make this possible, though, Japan required substantial resources and access to markets—the very conditions that impelled the Japanese government to wage war in the 1930s.[80] U.S. officials in Japan who were running the postwar occupation and their superiors in the Pentagon and the State Department believed that Japan could not be rehabilitated unless Japan had access to the markets and raw materials in Southeast Asia.[81] As explained by U.S. Army Assistant Secretary Tracy Voorhees, Japan's economic recovery depended on keeping communism out of Southeast Asia, promoting economic recovery there, and in further developing Southeast Asia as the principal trading area for Japan.[82] Consequently, to facilitate Japan's rapid economic recovery, U.S. policymakers adopted a "southern strategy" that would simultaneously contain a potential communist China and open a new economic zone in Southeast Asia for Japan.[83] Indochina was increasingly seen by many U.S. officials as the keystone of this geoeconomic objective and thus the source of ongoing frustration in their dealings with the French. In contrast to the defensive perimeter concept, however, this shift indicated the possibility of committing U.S. resources to the mainland of Asia.

Echoing the long-standing tension between recognition of French sovereignty over Indochina and the appearance of supporting the restoration of colonial rule or the creation of a puppet government, the State Department underscored the communist threat posed by the Soviet Union. A 1948 policy statement on Indochina prepared by the State Department conceded that the United States is prepared "to support the French in every way possible in the establishment of a truly nationalist government in Indochina which, by giving satisfaction to the aspirations of the peoples of Indochina, will serve as a rallying point for the nationalists and will weaken the Communist elements." As such, "Some solution must be found which will strike a balance between the aspirations of the peoples of Indochina and the interests of the French."[84] In the end, the policy statement perfectly represented the paradoxical nature of U.S. foreign policy: the commitment to support France for the sake of stability in Europe threatened to undermine relations with the nationalist ambitions of former colonies throughout Asia and Africa. However, the refusal to support France opened the door for world domination by the Soviet Union and its communist minions. The Bao Dai Solution, while not mentioned in the document, appeared as the most promising path forward.[85]

Throughout 1948 and early 1949 U.S. officials remained frustrated with the recalcitrant French government. Concerned that false promises of real independence would backfire, Washington struggled to find a suitable approach to wrestle concrete concessions from the French. As expressed by the State Department, "We are naturally hesitant to press the French too strongly or to become deeply involved so long as we are not in a position to suggest a solution or until we are prepared to accept the onus of intervention."[86] Compounding the issue were domestic concerns surfacing in the United States. "A staunch and undifferentiated anti-Communism," Logevall

44 / Into the Breach

writes, "became the required posture of all aspiring politicians, whether Republican or Democrat."[87] Thus, while the Truman administration early on enjoyed bipartisan support for many of its major policy initiatives, Cold War paranoia soon constrained policy decisions regarding U.S. intervention in Indochina. Indeed, as Brands explains, in this charged atmosphere, distinctions between vital and nonvital interests were all the more difficult to make, and a setback anywhere—no matter how peripheral the location— could easily be politically damaging to the administration.[88]

Anticommunist fervor in the United States demanded that Vietnam not be lost. However, unless the United States was prepared to assume the burden in full, the Truman administration had few viable options. Events in early 1949 offered a faint glimmer of hope. On March 8, 1949, Bao Dai and French president Vincent Auriol concluded the Élysée Accords. These agreements reconfirmed Vietnam's autonomy and her status as an Associated State within the French Union; Laos and Cambodia would receive the same status in July and November, respectively. In addition, the new State of Vietnam was promised its own army for internal security reasons, but with the proviso that the army would be equipped and directed by France. Notably, also, Vietnam's foreign and defense relations would remain under French control. In short, Paris retained ultimate sovereignty backed with vague assurances that genuine independence would be forthcoming.[89]

Although the plan fell far short of genuine independence, several key U.S. officials threw their weight behind the Accords. In March 1949, Jefferson Caffery, U.S. ambassador to France, explained that Bao Dai represented the "only foreseeable opportunity for [an] anti-Communist nationalist solution in Indochina" and, given the "declared policy" of the United States to prevent the "spread of communism in [Southeast Asia] and of supporting truly nationalist movements in that area," the country should seriously consider the full support of the proposed arrangements. Caffery conceded that if Bao Dai failed after receiving U.S. support it could be construed as a blow against America's position in Asia; the only alternative would be to negotiate with Ho Chi Minh—something the ambassador assumed was not possible.[90] Later that year, David Bruce, Caffery's successor in Paris, concurred, noting that "there seemed to be a choice of only two horses to back in Indochina—Ho Chi Minh and Bao Dai. There was no third man or third force. Ho Chi Minh, whatever he might think in his secret heart, was identified with Stalinist communism. We could not consistently back him even if we were prepared to make the major break with France which this would entail. The alternative was Bao Dai with his imperfections."[91] Bruce also realized that the current structure of the proposed Bao Dai state was far from satisfactory; however, he remained convinced that the "agreements [could] afford as much room for satisfying Vietnamese aspirations [of] self-rule and international status as [the] Vietnamese themselves are now able to cope with." In the end, Bruce believed that French officials could be "constantly and successfully pressed for liberal interpretation and implementation."[92]

Caffery was correct in his assumption that negotiations with Ho Chi Minh were out of the question. As Secretary of State Acheson explained, "All Stalinists in colonial areas are nationalists," thus making the question of whether Ho Chi Minh was a nationalist or communist irrelevant. To Acheson, the Vietnamese leader was an "outright Commie" whose objective was to subordinate the state to "Commie purposes" through the "ruthless extermination" of all opposition groups.[93] Here, Young explains, was "a formula that at one blow met the needs of America's anti-colonial ideology and the reality of its postwar position as hegemon of world capitalism. By definition, Communists could not be genuine nationalists; by definition, America supported genuine nationalism. Therefore, those people the United States supported were nationalists, the rest were Communist stooges."[94] Such a hardline position would have severe repercussions when U.S. policymakers confronted states that pledged adherence to neutrality. As Acheson explained in a telegram dispatched to diplomatic and consular offices throughout South and Southeast Asia, it was the position of the United States that "Asian nations cannot remain neutral toward communism as neutrality amounts to supine acceptance [of] commie domination and is regarded as weakness by [the] enemy."[95]

Certainly not all U.S. officials were in agreement with Acheson. Kennan's position deviated considerably from that of Acheson. Indeed, as Gaddis writes, Kennan objected vigorously to the notion that the United States had to resist communism wherever it appeared.[96] Kennan, for example, counseled that "further areas of Asia may fall into communist hands," primarily because most peoples of the region were "dangerously vulnerable to communist penetration" by virtue of "political immaturity," a general "state of flux and instability," and "stubborn misconceptions about western nations,

46 / Into the Breach

including ourselves, arising out of past experiences with colonialism and imperialism." And Kennan conceded that if portions of Asia fell to the Soviets, it "would be a serious blow to the stability of [the region] and to [the] immediate prospects of [the] people immediately concerned." Furthermore, Kennan acknowledged, it "would constitute [a] definite deterioration of [the] world situation." Still, Kennan concluded that "it would not necessarily be fatal or irreparable . . . and no cause either for despair or lack of self-confidence on our part." U.S. efforts should concentrate on "those areas—often modest in extent—where our help really can serve [a] useful and constructive purpose."[97] In other words, Kennan believed strongly that direct military intervention to prevent communist takeovers in areas peripheral to America's national security interests would only propel the United States into a series of civil wars from which it would be difficult to extricate itself.[98] Kennan underscored that the Russians hadn't attacked any state militarily since the Second World War and that "their successes, such as they have been, have been primarily in the minds of men." Indeed, "Military occupation or direct military action [was] not always [a] foolproof remedy."[99] As Kennan detailed elsewhere, "Success in the conduct of foreign policy . . . rests ultimately . . . with the power and will to discriminate, wisely, prudently and in ways that cannot be labelled as offensive, in the application of our national power. Anything that tends to strap us up, to inhibit such discrimination, leads to inflexibility, loss of buoyancy and eventual impotence in foreign affairs."[100] By this point, however, Kennan and his pragmatic approach to national security were being swept aside by Cold War panic and paranoia.

As Kennan's more prudent approach to diplomatic methods steadily fell into disfavor, America's increasingly militant anticommunist ideology provided an operational order and orientation to the unfolding struggle in Indochina. This is not to suggest that the path forward was unobstructed. Despite his anticommunist fear-mongering, even Acheson realized that the Bao Dai Solution was imperfect and risky. Alluding to the imminent downfall of Chiang Kai-shek's nationalist forces in the ongoing Chinese Civil War, Acheson acknowledged that no amount of U.S. military or economic aid could save the Bao Dai government—even if the state's sovereignty was recognized by other powers, and it had plenty of opportunities to achieve its national aims—unless it could rally support against the communists.

This could only happen if the new government extended representation to its people and demonstrated real leadership.[101] In other words, any effort at state building entailed considerably more effort than simply signing an agreement, a belief affirmed by Acheson himself. Acheson foreshadowed the fundamental dilemma that would confront later civilian and military officials: America's objective in South Vietnam was never simply a matter of state building but rather a confluence of state building, nation building, and government building. Here, the secretary of state confessed his fear that the French government was unlikely to make further concessions and that U.S. efforts to force the issue would likely miscarry. Acheson hoped, though, that France would carry out its obligations detailed in the Accords and that the Vietnamese nationalists, in turn, would appreciate the true character of the approaching Chinese menace. That said, Acheson also worried that the French government was "offering too little too late" and, should the attempt falter, the United States should not rush into the breach and jeopardize its remaining prestige in Asia.[102]

With Mao Zedong's communist victory in China in October 1949, coming on the heels of the Soviet Union's first successful test of an atomic weapon, most opposition to America's deepening involvement in Indochina dissipated. The outcome of the Chinese Civil War, Hess details, profoundly affected the thinking of U.S. policymakers, notably in the affirmation of Southeast Asia as the likely next battleground in the struggle against international communism. Plans were drawn up to utilize economic and military assistance extensively in the region as a means to assure the survival of pro-Western governments in Indonesia, Thailand, Burma, the Philippines and, especially, Indochina.[103] As Bruce warned, "the Indochina problem" was one in which "the Western World had high stakes" in that it "involved nothing less than the extension of Soviet control to Southeast Asia."[104]

With the hardening of Cold War ideologies in the United States, most officials in Washington failed to recognize that their objectives remained at cross-purposes with their counterparts in Paris. Since the earliest formulations of the Bao Dai Solution, U.S. policymakers saw the building of an independent state as the most viable solution to the geographic containment of communism. French policymakers, conversely, conceived of the effort as a means for maintaining French control in Vietnam: a method to preserve a colonial state in a new world order increasingly opposed to old-fashioned

48 / Into the Breach

colonialism.[105] This geopolitical disconnect would place severe constraints on U.S. policy throughout the 1950s.

The Territorial Trap

As part of the Bao Dai Solution, French officials created and recognized the Associated State of Vietnam on January 29, 1950. The following day, the Soviet Union—after five years of geopolitical intransigence—formally recognized the Democratic Republic of Vietnam (DRV) with Ho Chi Minh as its president and prime minister. For U.S. officials, Soviet recognition seemed to provide evidence of nefarious Soviet influence and confirmed suspicions that Ho Chi Minh was nothing more than a minion of the Soviet Union. That recognition of the DRV by the Soviet Union had not materialized earlier, or that it was clearly in response to French machinations in southern Vietnam, mattered little. From the moment the Truman administration announced its recognition of the French-backed Associated State of Vietnam, Washington was committed to a project of state-building and—although it wasn't appreciated at the time—the additional projects of nation building and government building. On this point, the Truman administration mistakenly drew parallels with postwar reconstruction in Europe. That is, the success of the Marshall Plan in restoring Western Europe encouraged U.S. advisors to apply the same formula in various degrees around the world to any state threatened by communism, including the embryonic pro-Western Vietnamese state.[106] However, there was one fundamental flaw in this calculus: in Indochina, it wasn't about rebuilding a war-ravaged state as in Europe; rather, it was about the building and bordering of an entirely new state out of the remnants of a former colony. Anticommunist paranoia cast a shadow over the path of U.S. foreign policy and American officials became ensnared in a *territorial trap* of their own making.

The practice of geopolitics has long privileged the sovereign, territorial state as the "singular actor of modern world politics."[107] Indeed, as John Agnew explains, "Territory has been the singular spatial modality for much of what goes for international relations and political theories."[108] Within Western political philosophy, territory was (and largely remains) conceived as a fixed, unmovable, unchanging entity, whose finite limits determined the beginnings and ends of sovereignty, control, and statehood; accordingly, these were the common elements through which territory was understood and, as such, constituted a trap inasmuch as they limited thinking about alternative ways in which the understanding and analysis of territory could be constructed.[109] In reality, of course, there are myriad ways that "space" can be organized; politics is not necessarily or inevitably confined to state-based, territorial containers.[110] National security as geopolitical discourse, however, circumscribed diplomatic and military options to the carving out of a territorial state where none had previously existed. Consequently, U.S. policymakers interpreted their actions in Indochina as mutually constituting both sovereignty and territory in southern Vietnam. To that end, U.S. foreign policy was increasingly reductionist in its worldview, thereby limiting both diplomatic and military options. Reduced to its most basic formulation, the U.S. objective was simple: to create a sovereign, territorial state in South Vietnam where none had previously existed. And to that end, U.S. policymakers were not merely *defending* an imperiled state; they were actively manufacturing a state that would, ultimately, serve as a loyal ally in the greater spatial struggle of world dominion.[111]

With the formation of the Associated State of Vietnam, defense of the Indochinese peninsula figured prominently in America's geopolitical struggle against the Soviet Union and, by extension, its presumed apparatchik, communist China. On January 31, 1950, Truman directed Secretary of State Acheson and Secretary of Defense Louis Johnson "to undertake a reexamination of our objectives in peace and war and of the effect of these objectives on our strategic plans, in the light of the probable fission bomb capability and possible thermonuclear bomb capability of the Soviet Union."[112] The outcome of this directive was a joint State-Defense study delivered to the National Security Council on April 7. Known as National Security Council 68 or, more simply, NSC-68, the document would in time shape the contours of the Cold War.[113] In alarmist terms, the report delineated the current geopolitical configuration as understood by the Truman administration: "The issues that face us are momentous, involving the fulfillment or destruction not only of this Republic but of civilization itself." Specifically, the framers of NSC-68 warned that the Soviet Union was "animated by a new fanatic faith, antithetical to our own, and seeks to impose its absolute authority over the rest of the world." This fanatical faith, of course, was communism. Coupled with "the development of increasingly terrifying weapons of mass destruction," the report cautioned, "any substantial

50 / Into the Breach

further extension of the area under the domination of the Kremlin" the world as a whole faced "the ever-present possibility of annihilation." The United States, accordingly, was confronted with "new and fateful decisions" to "assure the integrity and vitality of our own society." The report explained, the "United States, as the principal center of power in the non-Soviet world and the bulwark of opposition to Soviet expansion, is the principal enemy whose integrity and vitality must be subverted or destroyed by one means or another if the Kremlin is to achieve its fundamental design." Exemplary of the reluctant superpower myth, NSC-68 affirmed in no uncertain terms that continual U.S. territorial expansion, in the form of overseas military bases, was not something the United States sought out but instead was necessary and justified to prevent a global conflagration. Indeed, the report continues, "Unwillingly our free society finds itself mortally challenged by the Soviet system" for "no other value system is so wholly irreconcilable with ours, so implacable in its purpose to destroy ours, so capable of turning to its own uses the most dangerous and divisive trends in our own society, no other so skillfully and powerfully evokes the elements of irrationality in human nature everywhere, and no other has the support of a great and growing center of military power."[114]

In more concrete terms, NSC-68 concluded that "the Communist success in China, taken with the political-economic situation in the rest of South and South-East Asia, provides a springboard for a further incursion in this troubled area."[115] This would be a recurrent theme. A National Intelligence Estimate produced later that year reaffirmed that "an intensification of Communist efforts to secure Indochina is to be expected." This assessment, in particular, determined that the "Chinese Communists are already furnishing the Viet Minh with materiel, training, and technical assistance. If this assistance proves inadequate to enable the Viet Minh to accomplish its objectives, it is estimated that it will be supplemented, as necessary, by the introduction of Chinese Communist forces into the conflict."[116]

In May 1950 Acheson, Marshall's successor as secretary of state, announced U.S. plans to provide $15 million in military aid to support the French war effort in Indochina.[117] At this point, the war was no longer (in theory) to restore French sovereignty over Indochina; the objective was to establish and defend the sovereignty and territorial integrity of the Associated State of Vietnam against communist insurgents—the Viet Minh—

and their Chinese and Soviet handlers. In support of this financial commitment, the Military Assistance Advisory Group (MAAG), Indochina was formally established.[118] The working relationship between French and U.S. officials was fraught from the beginning, however. A major point of contention was the belief among many U.S. officials that all forms of U.S. aid provided to the war effort be distributed directly to the allied Vietnamese forces, discreetly through MAAG. This would bolster the idea of an independent, noncommunist, nationalist alternative to the Viet Minh and remove the stigma of neocolonialism. French authorities rejected these requests; to do otherwise would have jeopardized the restoration of their colonial empire. As such, the French government threatened to withdraw from Indochina— a scenario Paris knew the Americans would not allow to happen.[119]

The outbreak of war in June 1950 on the Korean peninsula cast a dark shadow over America's Indochina policy. Similar to Vietnam, Korea was politically and territorially divided after the Second World War. Notably, as Steven Lee explains, Korea was not a formal participant in the war, and yet it was the only nonbelligerent to undergo a military occupation. Following Japan's defeat, the Allied powers determined that Korea would be partitioned, temporarily at the 38th parallel, until national elections could be held to determine its political fate. However, U.S. occupation policies in "South Korea" were from the outset designed to contain Soviet influence on the North and to secure an American sphere of influence. With the failure to come to an agreement with the Soviets on an acceptable policy for the unification of the two Koreas, in 1947 the United States took the Korean issue to the United Nations. Consequently, under UN auspices, elections were held in the South in 1948, which brought Syngman Rhee and his conservative Korean Democratic Party to power.[120]

Parallel to U.S. policy in Indochina, Washington's strategy toward Korea was linked to its regional and global strategies designed to rebuild Japan as an economic engine, powerful enough to withstand the feared expansionism of the Soviet Union.[121] Hence, the United States injected substantial sums of material and financial aid into Rhee's Republic of Korea. In turn, the Soviet Union supported the newly formed Democratic Republic of Korea—better known as North Korea—and its communist government led by Kim Il Sung. Neither Kim nor Rhee was satisfied with the geopolitical partition of the peninsula into two states; as such, both claimed jurisdiction over the entirety

52 / Into the Breach

of Korea. Kim however struck first, launching a military invasion of the South that caught officials both in Seoul and in Washington off guard. For U.S. officials, however, the political context of the war was readily understood. Indeed, the North Korean attack was interpreted as a Soviet-inspired move toward the larger goal of world domination; by getting its satellites to drive back Western spheres of influence, Moscow could remain relatively detached from the responsibilities of conflict while its global objectives were being accomplished.[122] On June 27 Truman declared that "the attack upon Korea makes it plain beyond all doubt that Communism has passed beyond the use of subversion to conquer independent nations and will now use armed invasion and war."[123] Equally important, the Korean conflict for U.S. officials became a struggle for credibility, to prove that it was possible to promote liberal democracy abroad to withstand the challenge of international communism.[124] It mattered little that South Korea, as an "independent nation" was an artifice of Cold War calculations. For Washington, South Korea was a "free" sovereign state whose territorial integrity was threatened by foreign aggression.

It is important to recognize that both South Korea and Vietnam figured centrally in American security concerns predominantly because of Asia's geographic proximity to the Soviet Union. As detailed in a 1951 National Security Council (NSC-48/5) report, U.S. "objectives, policies and courses of Action in Asia should be designed to contribute toward the global objective of strengthening the free world vis-à-vis the Soviet orbit, and should be determined with due regard to the relation of the United States capabilities and commitments throughout the world." That said, the report continued, "in view of the communist resort to armed force in Asia, United States action in that area must be based on the recognition that the most immediate overt threats to United States security are currently presented in that area." In other words, the United States was purportedly *reacting* to military actions in Asia—Korea and Indochina—that were initiated by Soviet expansionism. According to NSC-48/5, "Current Soviet tactics appear to concentrate on bringing the mainland of Eastern Asia and eventually Japan and the other principal off-shore islands in the Western Pacific under Soviet control, primarily through Soviet exploitation of the resources of communist China." If Moscow achieved its objectives on the mainland of eastern Asia, this "would substantially enhance the global position of the USSR at the expense of the United States, by securing the eastern flank of the USSR and permitting the USSR to concentrate its offensive power in other areas, particularly in Europe." It was imperative, therefore, to "forestall communist aggression" both on the Korean peninsula and throughout Southeast Asia.[125]

During the early weeks of the Korean War, the poorly equipped and outnumbered U.S. and South Korean troops were pushed south and faced imminent defeat. However, a successful counterattack following a surprise amphibious landing at Inchon in September seemed to turn the tide. U.S. forces under the command of General Douglas MacArthur pressed their advantage and, in October, invaded North Korea, advancing rapidly toward the Yalu River along the DRK-China border. In turn, China intervened, sending approximately three hundred thousand troops into the conflict, pushing the American forces south of the demarcation line. From that point forward, the war ground to a stalemate that would last until an armistice was signed on July 27, 1953.

To a certain extent, as John Prados writes, the onset of the Korean War made the U.S. course of action in Vietnam irreversible.[126] Having committed itself to the defense of pro-Western governments seemingly threatened by Soviet aggression, U.S. officials in 1950 severely circumscribed the diplomatic options available for subsequent decision makers. Moreover, the conduct of the war in Korea conditioned future military strategies regarding possible armed intervention in Indochina. On the one hand, both U.S. military and civilian analysts cautioned that conventional warfare, not counterinsurgencies, posed the greatest and gravest threat to the security and survivability of South Vietnam. On the other hand, the specter of possible Chinese (or Soviet) military intervention always remained in the realm of possibility. Both of these apparent lessons would in turn mediate subsequent U.S. strategic thinking.

Against this backdrop, U.S. officials struggled to match rhetoric with reality. Indeed, within months of the Truman administration's decision to recognize the Bao Dai government, tensions emerged over the political, economic, and social construction of the new, pro-American Vietnamese state. Absent a viable government, there was little chance South Vietnam could withstand a military onslaught comparable to North Korea's invasion of its southern neighbor. In other words, U.S. officials perceived that the demarcation of

54 / Into the Breach

South Vietnam as a state was futile unless it was accompanied by both nation building and government building. And to that end, U.S. officials confronted two interconnected problems. On the one hand, Bao Dai failed to measure up to U.S. expectations as a competent leader to garner support among his citizens, and on the other hand, French authorities refused to make any substantial progress toward the building of an effective South Vietnamese government.[127] U.S. officials had reached another crossroads.

In January 1950 Kennan professed his belief that war "on a grand scale" could not achieve positive aims for a democracy. His comments were directed primarily to the development and possible use of atomic weapons, but his remarks extended more broadly into the promotion of military means to political ends. Indeed, regarding the prospect of war against the Soviet Union or any other totalitarian state, he suggested, "it would be useful . . . if we were to recognize that the real purposes of the democratic society cannot be achieved by large-scale violence and destruction." He explained, "For such positive purposes as we wish to pursue, we must look to other things than war: above all, to bearing, to example, to persuasion, and to the judicious exploitation of our strength as a deterrent to world conflict." For Kennan, the United States could not "have a clear and sound national policy unless it is based on a correct appreciation by our people of the role and possibilities of the various weapons of war, and of warfare itself, as instruments of national policy."[128]

With the adoption of NSC-68, Kennan's conception of national security was all but eclipsed. Whereas Kennan sought to block Soviet expansion by a variety of political, economic, psychological, and military measures, NSC-68 concentrated almost exclusively on military options.[129] That said, there remained a sense, both within civilian and military circles, that the United States not squander its resources unwisely. On that point, officials appeared to retain elements of Kennan's concept of asymmetrical response, with its concern for the conservation of limited resources and its implied distinction between vital and peripheral interests.[130] Writing in the months following the onset of war in Korea, the Joint Chiefs warned that "the Korean incident has created a situation under which there must be an urgent and frank re-appraisal of the global position of the United States military potential." Noting that "the geopolitical security of the United States requires diplomatic, psychological and military coordination of the highest order," it was necessary that no further diplomatic effort or moral commitment be made pending a comprehensive review of US security interests. The Joint secretaries thus emphasized "the impossibility of the United States undertaking alone the protection of the free world from Soviet aggression." "Our view," they concluded, was "that we must not attempt to build up United States military power to defend all these areas where they Soviets in one guise or another might attack." To do otherwise "would badly dissipate our strength."[131] Some locations, in short, would remain peripheral to American national security interests. Although the United States was committed to the containment (and possible rollback) of communism—as in Korea—many U.S. advisors were disinclined to risk all-out war, limited or otherwise, against the Soviet Union or China. This required a more nuanced approach to bracket future conflicts, especially in Indochina.

[2]

BRACKETING WAR

> It is recognized that the consequences of a general war would
> be appalling.
>
> —U.S. State Department Report

Any strategy, grand or otherwise, implies both an objective and the means to attain it.[1] There exist myriad instruments by which a policy objective may be achieved, and these can be usefully categorized under four main instruments: diplomatic, intelligence assets, military, and economic.[2] In practice, of course, these overlap and interact, and not necessarily in a coherent or comprehensive manner. For my present purposes, a key consideration of these instruments is the conjunction of military strategy and geopolitics.[3] Notably, the threat or use of armed force cannot always lead directly to policy objectives; that said, military operations can alter the power relations through which policies can be pursued.[4] This is significant, in that the advocacy of military action becomes just another means to an end, with the immediate consequences of strategic violence dismissed in light of political objectives. Accordingly, a crucial component of any grand strategy is a corresponding military strategy, understood here as the application of military resources to help achieve grand strategic objectives.[5] In turn, once it has been determined that military force will be used to serve the ends of policy, the strategy must be put into practice; this, in turn, is achieved through actions planned and performed at the *tactical* and *operational* levels. Here, the former is concerned with the details of combat, for example the deployment of forces, engagement with the enemy, and interactions among the various units. However, it is through the operational level that tactical actions serve the requirements of the overall military strategy, for the operational level provides an analytical framework within which tactical actions can be

58 / Bracketing War

integrated to serve the overall military strategy. As such, there is an important *geographic* dimension to the operational context of tactics, one that includes logistics and lines of communication, the position and movement of enemy forces, key locations such as cities, bridges, and other terrain features.[6]

In this chapter I pick up the chronicle of America's intervention in Indochina under the presidential administration of Dwight D. Eisenhower. Specifically, I detail how U.S. military and civilian officials and advisors understood the objectives in South Vietnam as a crucial component to the broader strategy to establish an American spatial order. In doing so, however, I underscore the recurrent tensions in Washington's effort to secure a defensive perimeter in Asia and the challenges of distinguishing between vital and nonvital interests.

A Geopolitical Paradox

With the forwarding of NSC 7, Truman's National Security Council (NSC) advocated for a more muscular U.S. foreign policy. This was followed with a report on America's capabilities of "providing military assistance" to the "nations of the non-Soviet world." The NSC premised that the "success of certain free nations in resisting aggression by the forces of Soviet directed world communism is of critical importance to the security of the United States." In fact, according to Truman's security council, "Such military assistance from the United States would not only strengthen the moral and material resistance of the free nations, but would also support their political and military orientation toward the United States, augment our own military potential by improvement of our armaments industries, and through progress in standardization of equipment and training increase the effectiveness of military collaboration between the United States and its allies in the event of war." That said, the NSC recognized that the United States could not adequately fund or supply *all* governments in the so-called non-Soviet world; indeed, the report makes clear that support would be provided only "with selected non-communist nations." This qualification was entirely pragmatic, in that military assistance to foreign governments in the periphery should never "jeopardize the fulfillment of the minimum material requirements of the United States armed forces." Regardless, the provision of armaments was far from altruistic, for aid-receiving governments were expected "to provide strategic raw materials to the United States in return for military assistance."[7]

Conventional wisdom within the U.S. intelligence community continued to hold that Europe remained the pivot of Cold War security threats. However, as detailed in the previous chapter, there existed also the paradoxical presumption that Southeast Asia was central to America's European-based national security interests. In August 1948, for example, Charles Reed of the U.S. State Department noted that "there is every indication that Moscow is turning more and more attention to the Far East, particularly to Southeast Asia." For Reed, this development did not necessarily translate into the need for immediate and decisive action; in fact, Reed suggested that "it may well not be in the interest of the US" to get involved in national movements in Southeast Asia.[8] Reed's memorandum, however, did signal a growing concern that Southeast Asia was *in some way* central to America's national security interests. This sentiment would intensify in the coming years.

Indeed, within four years, U.S. officials more strongly connected the fate of Southeast Asia to America's position in the world. In 1952, Paul Nitze, then director of the Policy Planning Staff, held firm that the "loss of Southeast Asia would present an unacceptable threat to [the] position of [the] U.S., both in [the] Far East and world-wide."[9] And to that end, Southeast Asia's vitality to U.S. interests was registered twofold. On the one hand, policymakers still portrayed Southeast Asia as being important because of the raw materials the region offered both for the United States and its allies, notably Japan. On the other hand, these resources were thought to be coveted by the Soviet Union precisely to deny these to the United States and its allies. This is expressed in a November 1951 National Intelligence Estimate that concluded, "From an economic point of view, control of Southeast Asia would be of considerable strategic importance to the Communists by increasing their capabilities for weakening the West through denying food to India and Japan and denying strategic raw materials to Japan and the industrial countries of the West."[10] Among the resources identified, rice, rubber, and tin stood out. Southeast Asia was considered important also because of its geostrategic location. Situated between East and South Asia, the region was important for control of vital land and sea routes, thus impacting military and economic concerns. In 1952 the Joint Chiefs of Staff affirmed

60 / Bracketing War

that "Communist domination of Southeast Asia would almost completely deny the Pacific littoral of Asia to the West."[11]

Within Southeast Asia, Indochina—but specifically Vietnam—came to be seen as the lynchpin of the region. Indeed, Vietnam was the principal domino, and its loss would supposedly set off a chain reaction, leading to the downfall of neighboring states. "The loss to the Communists of the Tonkin Delta in Indochina," the JCS warned, would facilitate the "continued Communist expansion in Southeast Asia" and "would probably lead to the collapse of Burma and Thailand, and to a dangerous weakening of internal security in Malaya, Indonesia and the Philippines." For the JCS, the threat of falling dominoes was far from abstract, in that each threatened state held its own particular geopolitical importance. "The mainland communications between China and Southeast Asia," the JCS noted, "are channeled through the Tonkin Delta, the retention of which in friendly hands would render aggression by Chinese Communist ground forces against Southern Indochina, Thailand and Malaya very difficult." Burma, likewise, held geostrategic importance because it was "the land route from China for an invasion of the Indian sub-continent and is the back door entrance for a conquest of Thailand." Thailand, also, was "of strategic importance because it lies astride the communication routes to the South" and "would provide useful base facilities in enemy hands for an invasion of Malaya and for operations against Allied sea communications in the Gulf of Thailand and the South China Sea." Spreading outward, "the loss of Southeast Asia . . . would have strong repercussions in India, Pakistan and Ceylon." Ultimately, from the vantage point of the JCS, the "reestablishment of Western influence in the region" following the loss of Southeast Asia "would be a difficult, if not insurmountable, problem."[12]

Despite the warnings forwarded by the JCS, both civilian and military officials continued to question the *degree* of geopolitical importance the region held for America's national security. Behind the façade of geopolitical certainty, most policymakers were attuned to the opacity of national security interests. It simply was not possible to definitively separate the world into central or peripheral status. During a joint meeting of State Department officials and the JCS, General Hoyt Vandenberg counseled, "It seems to us that there must be a decision regarding the political importance of the fall of Indochina, or for that matter of all Southeast Asia, to the eventual position of the United States in the world." He clarified that "if the loss of these areas is really as important to the United States as it appears to be to the JCS, then the U.S. must decide whether it intends to live, or indeed can live, in a world that has gone by." Simply put, the general explained, "The JCS has to know whether the U.S. must hold in this area or go down. With that decision in hand the JCS would have the necessary directive to figure out the cost and requirements of the necessary military action." "If [the region] is not as important as we believe," Vandenberg concluded, "then we should know that and should know, furthermore, where the line is on which we have to hold." For the JCS, vague statements to contain communism and to provide security in Southeast Asia—or any region—were impractical. Both logistics and economics limited the military's capabilities and capacities to adequately defend the entire world. If, for example, a decision was made to defend Indochina, Vandenberg explained, "all the requirements for this area will have to be obtained by shifts from other areas." On this point, however, the State Department was unable—or unwilling—to specify with any degree of certainty or clarity where to draw the line in defense of U.S. national security. Nitze, for example, held that "no one can give you a statement that anything is so important that any cost whatever is worthwhile."[13]

The exchange between State Department officials and members of the JCS captures well the slapdash decision-making that often underscored America's commitment to Indochina. As Hal Brands explains, "When it comes to foreign policy, there is never enough of anything to go around. Money, troops, intelligence assets, time, and other finite resources are always insufficient to neutralize every threat and exploit every opportunity."[14] The same holds for military strategies, operations, and tactics. Was Indochina of sufficient importance—now or in the near future—to reallocate precious resources? When Vandenberg pressed his counterparts if the State Department was prepared to let go Indochina, Nitze quipped, "We do not let something go simply because it is not absolutely important." In short, all in attendance agreed that Indochina—and by extension, Southeast Asia— was important; left unclear was whether the region was *absolutely* important. This question would plague subsequent administrations, so much so that ultimately Indochina symbolized both the resolution and the uncertainty of U.S. foreign policy.

62 / Bracketing War

The degree of *military* intervention in Southeast Asia was further complicated by broader geopolitical relations, notably the support of America's two principal allies, France and the United Kingdom. In late 1951, for example, the State Department acknowledged that "while we recognize the importance of Southeast Asia and are concerned that the countries in the area do not fall into the Communist camp, we cannot at this time accept the commitment of U.S. ground forces to the defense of the area."[15] Nitze, likewise, affirmed that it was "an overriding objective of U.S. policy to avoid U.S. engagement with China alone, without allies."[16] On this point, however, it was clear to many policymakers that neither France nor the United Kingdom were prepared to commit, militarily, to the defense of Southeast Asia. The United Kingdom, for its part, had vested interests in the region, notably Hong Kong, Malaya, and Singapore. That said, most U.S. advisors believed that British support would primarily be political. And France, of course, was actively fighting in Indochina, but its commitment was wavering. By 1952, it was plain to see that France was actively seeking a way out of this morass. As explained by H. Freeman Matthews, deputy undersecretary of state, "If it comes to a showdown between French interests in Western Europe and French interests in Southeast Asia, I feel sure that the French will decide for Western Europe and pull out of Indochina."[17] That showdown was not far off.

Eisenhower's Commitment

The Franco–Viet Minh War was in its seventh year when Dwight D. Eisenhower assumed the U.S. presidency in January 1953. By this point, the United States was shouldering 40 percent of the cost of war, with little to show for its investment. The incoming administration bemoaned the defensive-minded military strategy adopted by France; indeed, Eisenhower bristled that French military leaders had for years squandered their numerical superiority against an ill-equipped enemy. Equally important, U.S. officials feared that as long as the French government was effectively fighting for the restoration of colonial rule in disguised form, the war was unwinnable. Under such conditions, the Vietnamese populace faced only two choices: continued subjugation under French rule or compliance with Ho Chi Minh and the communists. Bao Dai had proven unable to generate any appreciable support, and the Associated State of Vietnam continued to drift rudderless into dangerous shoals.[18] Still, Eisenhower perceived the war in Indochina as part of the greater Cold War geopolitical conflict and was steadfast in his determination to prevent a communist takeover of the country. As the president would later explain, "It was important that we not show a weakness at this critical time and that we not let the Russians think that we might not resist in the event that the Communists attempted to step up their present tactics in Indochina and elsewhere."[19]

In response to Eisenhower's demands to strengthen the war effort, French general Henri Navarre proposed a major military offensive consisting of a set-piece battle to disrupt North Vietnamese supply routes through Laos, an additional ten battalions of French troops, and a substantial increase in South Vietnamese troops. And in return for its apparent newfound commitment to military victory, France was rewarded with an additional $385 million in funds, with another $400 million promised for 1954.[20] For Eisenhower, the trade-off was pragmatic. America's foreign policy was simply "gambling thousands to save billions." To do otherwise would be to allow the communists to continue "chipping away [at] any part of the free world," an outcome that was intolerable for Eisenhower. "Where in the hell can you let the Communists chip away any more?," the president asked. "We just can't stand it."[21]

On paper, the so-called Navarre Plan was tailored to U.S. specifications; indeed, in key ways the French military operation was concocted more for U.S. geopolitical considerations.[22] By this point, the protracted war was increasingly unpopular in France, with a sizeable proportion of French citizens in support of a negotiated settlement. A decisive victory on the battlefield would, in theory, force the Viet Minh to cede ground politically and accept a political settlement favorable to Paris. In fact, French officials agreed in early 1954 to place Indochina on the agenda of a previously scheduled East-West conference in Geneva.[23] In light of these geopolitical developments, the fear of many U.S. officials were being realized, that is, the prospect of an end to the Franco–Viet Minh War and the loss of part if not all of Vietnam to communism. As such, the Navarre Plan assumed even greater importance, for whichever side prevailed in the coming battle would likely hold the upper hand in any future negotiations.

Navarre planned initially to combine his scattered forces and to initiate a major offensive in the Red River delta; the intent was to draw the Viet Minh

64 / Bracketing War

into a large-scale conventional battle whereby superior French firepower would win the day. Navarre, though, was personally skeptical of the plan and acknowledged that the French government adopted it to gain additional U.S. aid. The Eisenhower administration, likewise, was doubtful of the plan's success but, having few options, was compelled to support the strategy.[24] Regardless, Navarre was forced to abandon much of the plan even before he had a chance to fully implement it. In late 1953, the Viet Minh commander, Vo Nguyen Giap, launched an invasion in central and southern Laos, intensified guerrilla activity in the delta, and prepared for a major strike into northern Laos. Navarre was forced to disperse his troops to meet the multiple threats.[25]

By early 1954, both the French and Viet Minh had committed sizeable forces in the vicinity of Dien Bien Phu, a village located in the extreme northwest of Vietnam. Navarre established a position at the intersection of several major roads near the Laotian border in an effort to disrupt an anticipated invasion and, once again, to draw the Viet Minh into a set-piece battle. In a broad valley surrounded by forested hills, just under eleven thousand elite French forces defended a garrison supported by artillery and aircraft. Navarre recognized the geographic flaw of his strategy, notably that his forces were susceptible to enemy fire from the hilltops. However, he consoled himself that the Viet Minh would be unable to move their artillery through the jungle and set up positions overlooking the garrison. And in the event that that should happen, the French could call upon their superior airpower.

On March 1954 Giap's forces laid siege to Dien Bien Phu, exploiting the flaw that Navarre dismissed. Far from a motley assortment of untrained and ill-equipped peasants, Giap had under his command 49,000 combat soldiers and upwards of 15,000 logistical support personnel. Most important, though, Giap had a tactical terrain advantage. Occupying the high ground—an accomplishment thought impossible by French military officials—Giap had an excellent observational point over the French positions and was able to direct his artillery with pinpoint precision. In addition, the dense foliage permitted Giap to hide his artillery and antiaircraft guns from French counteroffensives and to shift his infantry around the French perimeter without detection.[26] With these advantages, in the initial phase of the battle, the Viet Minh captured most of the outlying strongpoints of the encircled camp and conducted repeated assaults against the main garrison. Soon, the airfield at Dien Bien Phu—the garrison's only lifeline—was cut off. Problems were compounded by poor weather, which frequently made any airdrop of supplies impossible.

As the military situation deteriorated, French officials, notably Armed Forces Chief of Staff Paul Ely, pleaded for U.S. military assistance. Diehard hawks and anticommunists, such as Vice President Richard Nixon and Admiral Arthur Radford, pushed strongly for U.S. military intervention. Others who remained unconvinced of the strategic importance of Indochina, such as Army Chief of Staff Mathew Ridgway, argued against any form of military action. For his part, Eisenhower hedged his bets. During a meeting with his National Security Council on April 6, the president stated unequivocally that "there was no possibility whatever of U.S. unilateral intervention in Indochina." Eisenhower, however, did not rule out military intervention but was adamant that the United States would not respond without allied support. Part of Eisenhower's reasoning was informed by domestic considerations. Secretary of State John Foster Dulles clarified that it would be impossible to get U.S. Congressional authorization for American unilateral action in Indochina unless three conditions were met. First, U.S. military intervention had to be part of an international coalition that included the other free states of Indochina and the British Commonwealth territories. Eisenhower underscored that the United States would not "become the colonial power which succeeded France." He recognized that without any clear and definite invitation from neighboring Asian states, U.S. intervention would be construed as colonial in intent. Second, the French must agree to accelerate their independence program for the Associated States so that there could be no question of U.S. support of French colonialism. Here, again, U.S. officials realized that their objectives in Indochina were contradictory to those of France. Third, the French must agree not to pull their forces out of the war if American troops were deployed.[27]

For Dulles, the decision to intervene militarily and, if so, to what degree, was not yet necessary, although French forces were clearly on the ropes. In the interim, all efforts were to be directed toward the organization of a regional grouping for the defense of Indochina. The so-called united action plan had long been under consideration with the secretary of state, who was in frequent communication with both French and British representatives, as well as other foreign dignitaries. Four days earlier, for example, Dulles

66 / Bracketing War

explained to Roger Makins, British ambassador to the United States, that "the situation in Indochina had reached a serious stage" and that "there was a threat of a French collapse or of a French desire to reach a settlement on terms which would result in the loss of Indochina and the rest of Southeast Asia to the Communists." According to Dulles, Soviet Russia and communist China posed a "grave threat to the whole free community" and must be "met by united action." Unless definitive united action be taken, Dulles warned, "The situation would be much worse in three or four years and might lead to a world conflict."[28]

Dulles also took the message public. On March 29 the secretary of state delivered an address on "The Threat of a Red Asia" before the Overseas Press Club of America at New York City and outlined the position of the Eisenhower administration. Dulles explained in sweeping terms the urgency of U.S. action in Indochina. Repeating many of the same points made to foreign government officials, Dulles affirmed that communist aggression "should not be passively accepted" but be "met by united action"; and while this "might involve serious risks," these risks were "far less" than those the U.S. might face in the coming years "if we dare not be resolute today."[29] As was typical with so many decisions surrounding America's intervention in Indochina, the so-called united action was ill-defined. When asked directly by Gaganvihari Mehta, the Indian ambassador to the United States, what "united action" meant, Dulles was noncommittal. "I informed him I did not wish [to] specify what I had in mind," Dulles explained. "I said I hoped military activity would not spread but that this possibility was not excluded." However, Dulles underscored that he did not consider a peaceful settlement could be acceptable if it meant giving away Indochina to the communists. Dulles concluded that it was "important for tactical reasons that at present we should not make plain our intentions in suggesting united action." On this point, Dulles was not simply being coy, for as he acknowledged, "In any case [the] nature of such action [was] still under consideration."[30]

Privately, Eisenhower continued to harbor doubts. In large part, the president's uncertainty stemmed from the lack of support forthcoming from London and Paris. However, Eisenhower also seemed to equivocate on the overall importance of Indochina. During an April 6 NSC meeting, Eisenhower "expressed his hostility to the notion that because we might lose Indochina we would necessarily have to lose all the rest of Southeast Asia."

Here, Eisenhower appeared to hold out hope that the tumbling of allied states to the communist onslaught could be halted and cautioned that the domino theory was exaggerated, although the United States could not afford to let the Soviets "gain another bit of territory." To that end, the president "expressed the opinion that the thing to do was to try to get our major allies to recognize the vital need to join in a coalition to prevent further Communist imperialism in Southeast Asia," that is, to form a regional coalition.[31] On the following day, however, Eisenhower appeared to change his mind. During an April 7 press conference, the president was asked to clarify the strategic importance of Indochina to the free world. In response, the president answered in explicitly geographical terms. "You have, of course, both the specific and the general when you talk about such things," Eisenhower explained. He elaborated: "You have the specific value of a locality in its production of materials that the world needs. Then you have the possibility that many human beings pass under a dictatorship that is inimical to the free world. Finally, you have broader considerations that might follow what you would call the 'falling domino' principle." Simply put, Eisenhower said, "You have a row of dominos set up, you knock over the first one, and what will happen to the last one is the certainty that it will go over very quickly." Turning to the strategic importance of Indochina at the local scale, Eisenhower again highlighted tin, tungsten, and rubber among the region's valuable resources. Eisenhower then detailed that Asia had "already lost some 450 million of its peoples to the Communist dictatorship, and we simply can't afford greater losses." Notably, Eisenhower underscored how the loss of one territory would have a multiplier effect on neighboring states. "But when we come to the possible sequence of events," the president said, "the loss of Indochina, of Burma, of Thailand, of the [Korean] Peninsula, and Indonesia . . . now you begin to talk about areas that not only multiply the disadvantages that you would suffer through loss of materials, sources of materials, but now you are talking about millions and millions and millions of people." Finally, Eisenhower discussed the "geographical position" of Indochina as a whole. Here, the loss of control of the region "takes away, in its economic aspects, that region that Japan must have as a trading area or Japan, in turn, will have only one place in the world to go—that is, toward the Communist areas in order to live." Eisenhower repeated in stark economic terms the fundamental importance of Indochina and the containment

68 / Bracketing War

of communism, concluding that "the possible consequences of the loss are just incalculable to the free world."[32]

Eisenhower's grand strategy for the Cold War was in fact established several months earlier with the release of NSC 162/2, the "Basic National Security Policy." Warning of the mounting Soviet threat, NSC 162/2 affirmed that the "assumption by the United States, as the leader of the free world, of a substantial degree of responsibility for the freedom and security of the free nations is a direct and essential contribution to the maintenance of its own freedom and security." NSC 162/2 clarified that "the United States must maintain a sound economy based on free private enterprise as a basis both for high defense productivity and for the maintenance of its living standards and free institutions." This required, in turn, an expansive foreign policy to meet the Soviet threat. However, as noted by the report, many allies "tend to see the actual danger of Soviet aggression as less imminent than the United States does." In addition, throughout the "underdeveloped areas . . . forces of unrest and resentment against the West are strong." On this point, NSC 162/2 identified the dangers of "racial feelings, anti-colonialism, rising nationalism, popular demand for rapid social and economic progress, over-population, the breakdown of static social patterns, and, in many cases, the conflict of local religious and social philosophies with those of the West." As such, "The general unreliability of the governments of these states and the volatility of their political life complicate the task of building firm ties with them, of counteraction neutralism and, where appropriate and feasible, of responding to requests for assistance in solving their problems." Accordingly, the strategy adopted by the United States "is one of collective security" whereby alliances "must be rooted in a strong feeling of community of interests and firm confidence in the steadiness and wisdom of U.S. leadership." In concrete terms, this requires the U.S. government to "furnish limited military aid, and limited technical and economic assistance . . . according to the calculated advantage of such aid to the U.S. world position." And in the event of hostilities, the United States could respond with armed intervention, including the use of nuclear weapons.[33]

Eisenhower's approach to the siege of Dien Bien Phu conformed with the policy prescriptions articulated in NSC 162/2, notably the necessity of a collective alliance in support of France. Moreover, the deliberations within the U.S. government—including the serious consideration of deploying

U.S. combat forces—brought further clarity to the presumed importance of Southeast Asia as a whole. On January 16, 1954, the National Security Council issued NSC 5404, clarifying the U.S. position on Southeast Asia. The report cautioned that "Communist domination, by whatever means, of all Southeast Asia would seriously endanger in the short term, and critically endanger in the longer term, United States security interests." In addition, the loss of Southeast Asia would have serious economic consequences for many nations of the free world, notably Japan, and conversely would add significant resources to the Soviet bloc. Echoing previous policy pronouncements, Indochina was singled out as a cornerstone of U.S. strategy in Southeast Asia, as the war *clearly* represented a struggle between communist and noncommunist forces. To fail to respond to the communist threat in Indochina placed the entire spatial order in jeopardy, for the loss of Southeast Asia would lead to the loss of India, the Middle East, and ultimately Europe.[34] And yet, as Jeffrey Kimball writes, the Eisenhower administration's policy remained puzzling. As repeated policy documents, including NSC-162/2, affirmed, Indochina was vital to America's national security, but officials also acknowledged that the region lay on the periphery of the global struggle against the Soviet Union.[35] In the words of Army Chief of Staff Matthew B. Ridgway, intervention in Indochina was a "dangerous strategic diversion of limited United States military capabilities" in a "non-decisive theater to the attainment of non-decisive objectives."[36] Eurasia remained the real prize; and Indochina's importance was more often than not qualified by geopolitical relations between the United States and other European powers. Thus, while U.S. national interests in Southeast Asia were, as Kimball concludes, too great to abandon, they were not always sufficiently palpable to expend strategic and political assets.[37] In the end, Eisenhower refused to commit U.S. ground forces to Vietnam without guaranteed allied support. As Secretary of State John Foster Dulles detailed in March 1954, "If the United States sent its flag and its own military establishment—land, sea or air—into the Indochina war, then the prestige of the United States would be engaged to a point where we would want to have a success." He explained, "We could not afford thus to engage the prestige of the United States and suffer a defeat which would have worldwide repercussions."[38]

On May 7, 1954, America's geopolitical calculus changed and the reality of Indochina "being lost" to communism set in. With the defeat of French

70 / Bracketing War

forces at Dien Bien Phu, the Eisenhower administration resolved, at least temporarily, the paradox and recentered Indochina. No longer was Southeast Asia geographically peripheral to the main theater of the Cold War, but instead, the region was seen as a key actor in the unfolding political drama of the Cold War. As Secretary of State John Foster Dulles explained a month prior to France's defeat, Indochina was the key to Southeast Asia and that if the communists gained Indochina, it was only a question of time until all of Southeast Asia fell, thus imperiling America's western defensive perimeter.[39] From this point forward, a litany of U.S. officials, including the next four presidents, would confront Vietnam in unambiguous territorial terms. Success was defined not by the defeat of the enemy but by the survival of an ally: the State of Vietnam. For America's involvement in Indochina, Dien Bien Phu was an inflection point—not because any U.S. combat troops were committed but because the political response to the battle committed U.S. officials to a path future decision makers were unable or unwilling to deviate from.[40]

A State Is Created

With the defeat of French forces at Dien Bien Phu and the subsequent signing of the Geneva Accords, U.S. officials reassessed their diplomatic and military options while holding true to the overall grand strategy of an American spatial order. On this point, Soviet expansionism remained the gravest threat to U.S. interests. And yet, Washington wanted to avoid a protracted ground war against the Soviet Union or its perceived underling, China. What followed, therefore, was an attempt to bracket war through limited military interventions located predominantly in the Global South. Indeed, out of the spatial disorder of nationalist movements and anticolonial wars, U.S. advisors attempted to impose a spatial order on the world in the form of communist and noncommunist spaces. *Selective* engagement was *elective* engagement; and in 1954, Indochina remained at or near the top of possible U.S. intervention. It is still noteworthy, however, that not all members of Eisenhower's cabinet were supportive of making a stand in Vietnam. Secretary of Defense Charles Wilson, for example, believed that "it was hopeless to try to save South Vietnam, and that further expenditures were wasted money."[41] During an NSC meeting with Eisenhower in October, Wilson was more forthright, advising that "the only sensible course of action was for the U.S. to get out of Indochina completely as soon as possible." In his view, "The situation there was utterly hopeless, and [those] people should be left to stew in their own juice." For Wilson, he could "see nothing but grief in store for us if we remained in this area." Eisenhower disagreed. According to the president, "What we [are] doing in Indochina [is] being done for our own purposes. . . . If we continued to retreat in this area the process would lead to a grave situation from the point of view of our national security."[42] America was committed to hold the line against communism in Southeast Asia.

The Geneva Accords of 1954 partitioned Vietnam into northern and southern halves, pending national elections to reunify the country in 1956. However, the United States had no intention of abiding by the accords but instead wanted to construct a pro-Western, anticommunist ally in Southeast Asia, vibrant and vital enough to survive and withstand competition from Ho Chi Minh's Democratic Republic of Vietnam.[43] Indeed, rather than signing the accords, U.S. officials drafted their own proviso. As Young explains, the statement established a legal basis for future American actions disregarding the accords themselves.[44] And on that point, the Eisenhower administration intended to make the partitioning of Vietnam permanent.[45] This posed two immediate problems: "The establishment of a military line which could not be crossed by the enemy" and the "prevention of internal and creeping subversion." Effectively, Washington recognized that the State of Vietnam (South Vietnam) required its own national security, manifest precisely in the defense of its territorial integrity from foreign invasion and domestic insurgencies. As such, the United States committed itself "to build up indigenous forces, and to give some economic aid."[46] This, in fact, aligned with Eisenhower's preference for bracketing potential wars in Southeast Asia. In April, for example, the president explained "there are plenty of people in Asia, and we can train them to fight well. I don't see any reason for American ground troops to be committed in Indo China, don't think we need it, but we can train their forces and it may be necessary for us eventually to use some of our planes or aircraft carriers off the coast and some of our fighting craft we have in that area for support."[47]

In no uncertain terms, as George Kahin explains, the Eisenhower administration "sought to rationalize their policies at home by advancing for an American audience the myth that those Vietnamese who happened to dwell

72 / Bracketing War

below the seventeenth parallel had their own sense of nationhood and patriotism, distinct from whatever sentiments were possessed by those living under the communist regime in the North."[48] However, the State of Vietnam remained an ill-defined political entity, lacking the institutions of an independent government and the means to translate popular aspirations into a viable political organization.[49] What emerged was an amalgam of civilian and military initiatives, Vietnamese and American, built upon an edifice of programs established under the French. Indeed, the subsequent state was something of a Frankenstein's monster, assembled bit by bit with disparate pieces. And at the heart of this monster was Ngo Dinh Diem.

Much has been written on Diem yet he remains an enigmatic figure.[50] Indeed, as Philip Catton writes, "Staunch patriot or bumbling stooge, farsighted statesman or blinkered reactionary—Diem has always elicited sharply defined, and divergent, judgements of his character and leadership."[51] Diem was not unknown to the Eisenhower administration. Having spent considerable time in the United States, Diem had developed a loyal following of supporters, including Senator Mike Mansfield and then Senator John F. Kennedy. Diem, a Catholic in a predominantly Buddhist country, was perceived by many U.S. officials as an ardent nationalist and a staunch opponent of communism.[52] These qualities no doubt contributed to the initial support forwarded by U.S. officials when, in June 1954, the United States acquiesced to Bao Dai's invitation to Diem to form a new government in South Vietnam. However, many other U.S. officials harbored serious doubts. As Richard Immerman writes, "Diem had a well-earned reputation for intransigence, an almost mystical belief in his infallibility, and an egotism that bordered on megalomania." In addition, Diem had limited government experience and his "administrative abilities were highly suspect because he appeared not only to favor Vietnam's Catholic minority, but also to trust few individuals beyond his own family."[53] Despite these reservations, the reality was that in 1954 U.S. officials had few options other than Diem.

Over the following nine years, U.S. financial and material aid would keep the Diem administration afloat. In October 1955, just months before the scheduled national elections prescribed by the Geneva Accords were set to take place, Diem staged a referendum in order to replace Bao Dai as chief of state.[54] Washington was aware of the fraudulent tactics employed by Diem; however, by this point the consensus opinion in the White House

Bracketing War / 73

was, as journalist Homer Bigart wrote, to "sink or swim with Ngo Dinh Diem."[55] The decision was indeed a watershed moment. Within months of Diem's assumption of office, French officials abandoned any pretense of shared Franco-American responsibility for the security of a noncommunist Southeast Asia.[56] This event was neither unexpected nor unwelcomed by many officials in the Eisenhower administration. While Eisenhower was not opposed to a continued albeit circumscribed French presence in Vietnam, contradictory objectives among U.S. and French officials obviated government-building efforts. With the departure of French authorities, Seth Jacobs concludes, Diem's reign marked the U.S. crossover point from advice and support to active cobelligerency in the build-up to war.[57]

In March 1956 Diem orchestrated the election of a "representative" assembly to write the constitution for a new Republic of Vietnam (RVN) to replace the French-constructed State of Vietnam.[58] In doing so, two states vied for control: Ho Chi Minh's Democratic Republic of Vietnam and Diem's renamed Republic of Vietnam. It is inaccurate, however, to conceive of these political entities as two separate *sovereign* states—although this was the myth forwarded by U.S. officials. Since 1945 Ho Chi Minh had declared the independence of a unified Vietnam; French and U.S. officials, however, manipulated the international legal order to present the fiction of two legitimate, territorially defined states. For this reason, from 1956 onward, a key objective of U.S. policy in Vietnam was to realize the *national and international* legitimacy of the Republic of Vietnam.

Eisenhower, while wanting to limit communist expansion, was determined to not embroil U.S. ground forces in small wars or insurgencies on the grounds that such conflicts were difficult to win and would place undue burdens on U.S. resources. Instead, Eisenhower preferred that U.S. advisors train allies to fight for themselves under the general protection of America's nuclear umbrella.[59] Thus, in an effort to project U.S. power without the wholesale commitment of U.S. ground forces, the Eisenhower administration insisted that the development of a strong, modern South Vietnamese army was an essential first step in promoting a stable government. Consequently, U.S. officials through MAAG began the arduous task to organize, equip, and train Diem's Army of the Republic of Vietnam (ARVN)—to the tune of approximately $85 million per year. In addition, beyond the rebuilding of the ARVN, scores of U.S. civilians arrived in Saigon to create a civil

74 / Bracketing War

society ostensibly capable of meeting the needs and aspirations of the South Vietnamese population in terms of both security and prosperity. The chief priorities were land reform and land development, both geared toward improving the citizenry's financial well-being, protect them from Viet Minh insurgents, and to prevent the Viet Minh from recruiting peasants in South Vietnam to join their cause.[60] These latter components were given added impetus in 1959 following a decisive shift in North Vietnam's approach to reunification.

In Hanoi, following the Geneva Accords, Ho Chi Minh forwarded a "North-first" policy. After decades of colonial rule and years of armed conflict, the country and its people were exhausted. Indeed, as Pierre Asselin explains, conditions in northern Vietnam were particularly troubling; the departing French took with them everything they could of value, including factory machines and hospital equipment; they destroyed whatever they left behind and sabotaged power and water purification plants.[61] As such, several ranking members of the Politburo set aside temporarily the objective of national reunification and initiated efforts instead to rehabilitate and rebuild the North's economy and infrastructure.[62] In doing so, however, the decision to delay the struggle for national unification revealed a deep division within the Communist Party, notably between moderates, such as Ho Chi Minh and Vo Nguyen Giap, and hardliners like Le Duan and Le Duc Tho, who wanted to pursue an aggressive strategy of "total war" in the South.[63] The American support of the Diem regime confirmed, for these members, that the United States wanted to occupy Indochina in place of the French colonialists. In addition, the decision to prioritize reconstruction in the North and to delay the struggle for national reunification was met with disappointment by the revolutionaries in the South, many of whom harbored deep feelings of betrayal. With the signing of the Geneva Accords, southern insurgents felt that Hanoi effectively abandoned the South; especially difficult to swallow was the surrender of areas that had been "liberated" during the war. As Asselin remarks, the tradeoff of concrete assets for the promises of a political process in which they had no faith was not an exchange that revolutionaries in the South made willingly.[64]

Revolutionaries in the South faced an even greater danger, for Diem embarked on a brutal campaign to purge South Vietnam of its communist elements. In 1955 Diem launched the "Denounce the Communist" campaign in an effort to completely eradicate the communist movement in the South. Over the following years, thousands of actual or suspected communists were killed, captured, or otherwise neutralized, along with their sympathizers.[65] Officials in the United States were aware of the negative impacts resulting from Diem's repression. According to a CIA intelligence report prepared in October 1955, "Considerable discontent has developed among various groups in South Vietnam with the regime of President Ngo Dinh Diem."[66] The briefing explains further that "criticism of Diem's authoritarianism is being heard increasingly among influential Vietnamese, including members of his cabinet. . . . Other factors working against the regime's popularity in commercial, labor, and professional circles, as well as among the masses, are bureaucratic red tape, heavy-handed control measures, curtailment of press and civil liberties, and venality among civil servants." Simply put, civil opposition to Diem was widespread as members of all classes voiced their dissatisfaction with the regime. Effectively, support for the southern insurgency intensified not necessarily because the populace supported communism but instead because the populace opposed Diem and his administration. The CIA assessment observed, however, that "there is no alternative strong leader to hold divisive forces in check, and Diem's sudden removal from office would probably lead to political chaos."[67] On this point Logevall concurs, explaining that, over time, "Diem's defects as a leader—his obduracy, his political myopia, his easy resort to repression—became increasingly obvious to the American people. American officials were fully cognizant of these limitations but could find no one better, and so they stuck with him, their influence sagging with each passing year despite the regime's complete dependence on U.S. aid."[68]

By 1958 members of Hanoi's more hardline faction were beginning to alter the balance of power. The demand for armed struggle among the communists in the South increased daily; in turn, many party members in Hanoi believed that political struggle was no longer adequate.[69] Debate swirled within the Politburo to authorize the resumption of armed insurrection against the Diem government. Subsequently, during the Fifteenth Central Committee Conference, held in January 1959, a resolution was adopted that called for the initiation of armed struggle in the form of sustained attacks against Diem's armed forces. "Resolution 15," as the document was known, called also for the formation of a broad united front in the South to bring

76 / Bracketing War

together opponents—both communist and noncommunist—of Diem's regime in an organization controlled by Hanoi. Neither of these recommendations was implemented by the Communist Party, as the moderate wing continued to advocate caution. However, the tenor of the Party was unmistakably changing. In response to Resolution 15, Hanoi issued instructions to their counterparts in the South to create "armed propaganda brigades," a tepid but positive move to intensify subversive activities against the Diem regime. In addition, while the orders expressly prohibited the conduct of military operations against Saigon's military forces, Hanoi did dispatch to the South small arms and contingents of Southern combatants who had regrouped to the North in the immediate aftermath of the Geneva Accords.[70] Within months, however, the pendulum swung even further toward armed intervention, with the establishment of the National Front for the Liberation of Southern Vietnam (NLF). Ostensibly neutralist in political orientation, the NLF was to centralize and facilitate Hanoi's ability to more effectively control the escalating southern insurgency.[71] Consequently, in May 1959 Hanoi commissioned Group 559, a special unit charged with moving people, weapons, and supplies overland from the North to the South; in July, Group 759 was established to facilitate sea infiltration; and in September Group 959 was formed to supply the Laotian People's Liberation Army and "Vietnamese volunteers" fighting in Laos.[72]

Kennedy's Resolve

On April 4, 1959, Eisenhower delivered a convocation speech at Gettysburg College. During his address, he implored the audience to answer a fundamental question: "Why should America, at heavy and immediate sacrifice to herself, assist many other nations, particularly the less developed ones, in achieving greater moral, economic, and military strength?" A principal reason, the president explained, was the "implacable and frequently expressed purpose of imperialistic communism to promote world revolution, destroy freedom, and communize the world." Eisenhower elaborated that "if aggression or subversion against the weaker of the free nations should achieve successive victories, communism would step-by-step overcome once free areas. The danger, even to the strongest, would become increasingly menacing." Reaffirming that "the self-interest of each free nation impels it to resist the loss to imperialistic communism of the freedom and independence of any other nation," Eisenhower presented the case for America's growing commitment to Vietnam. Conceding that the country was located halfway around the world, Eisenhower made the case that South Vietnam's geopolitical importance far surpassed its distal geography. Strategically, he described, "South Vietnam's capture by the Communists would bring their power several hundred miles into a hitherto free region. The remaining countries in Southeast Asia would be menaced by a great flanking movement." Were this to happen, the president warned, "the freedom of twelve million people [in South Vietnam] would be lost immediately, and that of 150 million others in adjacent lands would be seriously endangered." Simply put, "the loss of South Vietnam would set in motion a crumbling process that could, as it progressed, have grave consequences for us and for freedom." And behind this peril, the president cautioned, was the "continuing effort of the Communist conspiracy to attain one overriding goal: world domination." Drawing parallels with the years leading up to the Second World War, Eisenhower reminded his audience that "the course of appeasement is not only dishonorable, it is the most dangerous one we could pursue. The world paid a high price for the lesson of Munich—but it has learned the lesson well." "We have learned," Eisenhower detailed, "that the costs of defending freedom—of defending America—must be paid in many forms and in many places. They are assessed in all parts of the world—in Berlin, in Vietnam, in the Middle East—here at home. But wherever they occur, in whatever form they appear, they are first and last a proper charge against the national security of the United States." To that point, Eisenhower declared, "Mutual security and American security are synonymous." Accordingly, the president counseled, "A free America can exist as part of a free world, and a free world can continue to exist only as it meets the rightful demands of people for security, progress, and prosperity. That is why the development of South Vietnam and Southeast Asia is important." Thus, framing America's venture in South Vietnam as one of mutual security, Eisenhower concluded that "by helping one another build a strong, prosperous world community, free people will not only win through to a just peace but can apply their wonderful, God-given talents toward creating an ever-growing measure of man's humanity to man."[73]

For Eisenhower, world peace required a world free from communism; this, in turn, required a decidedly unpeaceful confrontation with "communist

78 / Bracketing War

challenges" the world over. So conceived, the military defense of South Vietnam's territorial integrity was paramount. Three years earlier, a young senator from Massachusetts—and the next president of the United States—had come to the same conclusion. Speaking before the American Friends of Vietnam, Kennedy warned of a fire "smoldering in Indochina." Vietnam, Kennedy declared, "represents the cornerstone of the Free World in Southeast Asia, the keystone to the arch, the finger in the dike. Burma, Thailand, India, Japan, the Philippines and obviously Laos and Cambodia are among those whose security would be threatened if the Red Tide of Communism overflowed into Vietnam." Certainly the specter of a communist-dominated Vietnam posed a military threat to regional and global stability. But the senator added that "the independence of Free Vietnam is crucial to the free world in fields other than the military." According to Kennedy, Vietnam's "economy is essential to the economy of all of Southeast Asia; and her political liberty is an inspiration to those seeking to obtain or maintain their liberty in all parts of Asia—and indeed the world." Indeed, Kennedy went so far as to assert that "Vietnam represents a proving ground of democracy in Asia" and that "Vietnam represents the alternative to Communist dictatorship." Were this "democratic experiment" to fail, Kennedy warned, the United States would be "directly responsible." Effectively, Kennedy framed South Vietnam's political survival as a test of the American nomos, for it was the United States that created South Vietnam. "If we are not the parents of little Vietnam," Kennedy said, "then surely we are the godparents. We presided at its birth, we gave assistance to its life, we have helped to shape its future. . . . This is our offspring—we cannot abandon it, we cannot ignore its needs. And if it falls victim to any of the perils that threaten its existence—Communism, political anarchy, poverty and the rest—then the United States, with some justification, will be held responsible; and our prestige in Asia will sink to a new low."[74]

Kennedy's ascension to the White House in 1961 heralded a new approach to military doctrine—a change that would have an immediate bearing on events in Indochina.[75] Eschewing former president Dwight Eisenhower's doctrine of "Massive Retaliation," the incoming administration favored a military capable of addressing the "spectrum of warfare" likely encountered in the unfolding new nomos, including the shifting contours of conflict in Indochina.[76] Kennedy articulated his vision—coined "flexible response"—

early in his presidency when, on March 28, 1961, he informed the U.S. Congress that "the strength and deployment of our forces in combination with those of our allies should be sufficiently powerful and mobile to prevent the steady erosion of the Free World through limited roles; and it is this role that should constitute the primary mission of our overseas forces." Kennedy explained that nonnuclear wars and guerrilla warfare since 1945 constituted the "most active and constant threat" to the security of the free world and, as such, the United States required "a greater ability to deal with guerrilla forces, insurrections, and subversion."[77]

The Kennedy administration was brimming with adherents to the president's penchant for limited war strategies and counterinsurgency operations.[78] Indeed, Robert McNamara (secretary of defense), McGeorge Bundy (national security advisor), and Dean Rusk (secretary of state), were ardent supporters of unconventional military operations geared toward the elimination of the southern insurgency in Vietnam. The man most insistent and most influential to U.S. counterinsurgency doctrine, however, was a former economics professor and Kennedy's deputy national security advisor, Walt Rostow.[79] Ideologically, Rostow believed that communism was "a disease of the transition to modernization."[80] In a June 1961 speech delivered to graduates of the U.S. military's counterinsurgency program at Fort Bragg, North Carolina, Rostow described communists as "the scavengers of the modernization process."[81] He explained that communists prey on the "weakest nations" as the "international Communist movement" operated to "exploit the inherent instabilities of the underdeveloped areas of the non-Communist world."[82] The United States, "as leader of the free world," had an obligation to uphold these nations' right to "fashion, out of [their] own culture and [their] own ambitions, the kind of modern society" they wanted.[83]

No grand strategy can provide leaders with ready-made solutions to existing or impending crises. However, performing the intellectual tasks involved in doing grand strategy—defining and prioritizing goals and threats, understanding the extent and limits of a state's capacities and capabilities—can provide policymakers with a framework in which to formulate an appropriate response.[84] Days into his presidency, Kennedy approved a "Basic Counterinsurgency Plan for Viet-Nam" drafted weeks earlier in Saigon by advisors from MAAG, the U.S. Operations Mission (USOP), the U.S. Information

80 / Bracketing War

Services (USIS), the Office of the Special Assistant to the Ambassador in Vietnam (OSA), and the U.S. Embassy in Vietnam.[85] Chaired by Joseph Mendenhall, counselor for political affairs of the embassy in South Vietnam, the committee worked from the assumption that the "Communist-inspired insurgency in [South Vietnam], aimed at the destruction of [the] authority and prestige of [an] established government, is a prelude to further inroads designed ultimately to absorb [South Vietnam] into the Communist bloc." In other words, it was a foregone conclusion that the continual political unrest in South Vietnam was external in origin and not, evidence to the contrary, an Indigenous anticolonial conflict waged by the Vietnamese. Thus, proponents of the counterinsurgency plan (CIP) within the Kennedy White House identified communist insurgents—not conventional military forces—as "clearly the major immediate threat to the stability of [South] Vietnam." That said, the CIP accentuated the dual threat confronting the Diem regime, namely that South Vietnam was "the only country in the world which is forced to defend itself against a communist internal subversion action, while at the same time being subject to the military supportable threat of a conventional external attack from communist North Viet-Nam." Consequently, the CIP forwarded three objectives: to "suppress and defeat disruptive Communist activities in South Viet-Nam and concurrently maintain a capability to meet overt aggression"; to "establish and maintain political and economic control and stability"; and to "interdict aid flowing to insurgents across Vietnamese borders, to include both police and military action in coordination with the adjacent nations of Laos and Cambodia."[86] On January 28, Kennedy approved the CIP and directed his staff to develop a comprehensive approach to combatting the NLF insurgency.[87] These plans, in turn, provided the foundation for Kennedy's expansion of America's so-called advisory role in South Vietnam.

Against this background, in April 1961 Kennedy authorized the formation of a Presidential Task Force on Vietnam.[88] Programmatically, the Task Force was directed to develop plans to "counter the Communist influence and pressure upon the development and maintenance of a strong, free South Vietnam." Four broad areas of study were identified: political, military, economic, and psychological. Notably, the Task Force operated under the assumption that restrictions imposed by the Geneva Accords on the number of U.S. military personnel operating in Vietnam should be eliminated;

Bracketing War / 81

this was necessary both to "assist the Vietnamese government with special ideas to make it more responsive to the needs of the people" and to assist the South Vietnamese government in the conduct of counterguerrilla operations. As such, a principal objective was the implementation of "effective measures . . . to deny the use of Cambodian territory for the transit or safe haven of Communist armed forces operating in South Vietnam."[89] Soon thereafter, a series of draft reports and action plans were developed, disseminated, and discussed among senior members of the military establishment and the Kennedy administration. Concern coalesced around several key issues, notably the support and cooperation of Diem, tax and foreign exchange reforms by the Diem administration, necessary organizational reforms of the South Vietnamese military, the popular support of the Vietnamese, and cooperative relations with both the Laotian and Cambodian governments. On this latter point, Robert Komer, staff member of the National Security Council, underscored the importance of "sealing off the borders" with Cambodia and Laos, something that was "a lot easier said than done."[90]

On April 29, 1961, members of the NSC discussed and approved in part the recommendations forwarded in the draft "Program for Action on Vietnam" and, as follow-up, Kennedy authorized "specific military actions" to be carried out in accordance with the approved plan.[91] In addition, a "Program of Action to Prevent Communist Domination of South Vietnam" was presented to Kennedy on May 3.[92] In its scale and scope the document illustrates the unfolding strategies toward South Vietnam within the White House. The report underscored how Hanoi's support of the newly formed NLF "significantly increased their [Hanoi's] program of infiltration, subversion, sabotage and assassination" to overthrow the Diem government. On that point, the report detailed, "the internal security situation in South Vietnam has become critical" such that "a state of active guerilla warfare now exists throughout the country." If conditions continued, the very survival both of the Diem regime and South Vietnam as a sovereign nation was at risk. Of particular importance was the increased movement of enemy forces through both Laos and Cambodia. Among the proposals forwarded, a key condition was "the cooperation of other free nations in the area in support of regional measures designed to inhibit the transit or safe haven of Communist subversive or guerrilla forces operating in South

82 / Bracketing War

Vietnam." Specific recommendations included the expansion of South Vietnam's radar surveillance capability, the establishment of an effective border intelligence and patrol system, and the use of military forces to interdict enemy personnel infiltrating South Vietnam.[93] Increasingly, the security of America's vital interests was tied to the physical and territorial security of South Vietnam.

That said, despite the recommendations forwarded in the "Program for Action on Vietnam," neither civilian nor military advisors could agree on the security measures needed to defend the territorial integrity of South Vietnam. Since the mid-1950s, for example, both the Pentagon and MAAG officials advocated defensive measures in the event of a massive onslaught of North Vietnamese or Chinese forces. Indeed, based on recent events on the Korean peninsula, for MAAG advisors, the specter of large-unit campaigns weighed heavily on their minds. The consensus opinion of MAAG remained that insurgency alone was insufficient to overthrow the South Vietnamese government; consequently, less thought and planning went into counterinsurgency strategy or tactics.[94] The first two commanders of MAAG, Lt. General John W. O'Daniel and Lt. General Samuel T. Williams, proposed to build a lightly equipped South Vietnamese army that, supported by a smaller air force and coastal navy, could delay a North Vietnamese or Chinese invasion until U.S. or allied reinforcements could arrive; both commanders assumed also that these same units could effectively counter any guerrilla activities marshalled by insurgents in the South. This approach tended to run counter to the long-standing opinion of CIA analysts who early on determined that "the Viet Minh capability to infiltrate personnel and arms into South Vietnam, and to reinforce Communist and potential dissident elements will remain the most serious threat to the establishment of a viable and stable national government in the south."[95] Kennedy leaned toward the assessments of his civilian advisors, as evidenced by his authorization of National Security Action Memorandum No. 52, issued on May 11.[96] Here, Kennedy affirmed that America's objectives were "to prevent Communist domination of South Vietnam; to create in that country a viable and increasingly democratic society, and to initiate, on an accelerated basis, a series of mutually supporting actions of a military, political, economic, psychological and *covert* character designed to achieve this objective."[97] Broadly, NSAM 52 reaffirmed the need to support the Diem regime,

Bracketing War / 83

build rapport among the Vietnamese population, and promote economic programs throughout the country.

Notably, NSAM 52 also underscored the need to secure South Vietnam's porous borders with Laos and Cambodia. By this point, NLF insurgents had been active in the South for several years and had developed into a highly organized and formidable political and military force. Administered by the Central Committee Directorate for the South, with significant though not complete oversight by Hanoi, the NLF and its military wing, the People's Liberation Armed Forces (PLAF), exercised influence or control over an estimated 60 percent of South Vietnam's rural population.[98] Markedly, U.S. officials transliterated the Central Committee as COSVN (Central Office for South Vietnam) and imagined the command structure "as a Viet Cong Pentagon, a place that could be found and smashed." In time, Isaac Arnolds explains, COSVN "was to occupy a bizarre place in the evolution of America's Cambodia strategy. It was offered, like Eve's apple, every time the military leadership sought to expand American actions there."[99] In 1969, for example, the Joint Chiefs of Staff would describe COSVN as occupying "a tract of land approximately 9 square kilometers in size," which contained "COSVN headquarters and support elements, consisting of an estimated 1,600 enemy personnel."[100] However, in reality COSVN was a leadership group, not a fixed headquarters, and it functioned as an extension of the Central Committee in Hanoi, which was in charge of the overall direction of the struggle in the South.[101] This misperception would play a decisive role in Richard Nixon's expansion of the war into Cambodia in subsequent years.

In an effort to provide further clarity to America's rising financial and military commitment to South Vietnam, preparations were made throughout the summer of 1961 for a critical fact-finding mission to Saigon led by General Maxwell Taylor and accompanied by Rostow.[102] Numerous subjects warranted attention, including relations with Diem, the attitudes of South Vietnamese troops and local officials, existing land reform policies and agrarian reform, and the use of "exotic" weapons such as the Lazy Dog unguided missile.[103] Of critical importance was a determination whether military intervention was required, including unconventional approaches, to halt the deteriorating political, economic, and military conditions in Vietnam. "I suspect there are many unconventional forms of assistance,"

84 / Bracketing War

Kennedy affirmed, "which we might bring to this situation if we apply all our initiative and ingenuity." To that end, the president instructed Taylor to "see that we are not overlooking any possibilities which fall outside of strictly orthodox measures."[104]

On November 3 Taylor submitted his report to the president and, essentially, called for a substantial increase in America's commitment to prevent the fall both of Vietnam and of the entirety of Southeast Asia "into Communist hands." Specific military recommendations proposed by Taylor were sweeping, addressing both organizational structures and operational and tactical concerns. For example, the report called for the reorganization of MAAG, Vietnam and for the insertion of U.S. advisors at all levels of civilian and military governance. In addition, the report called for the introduction of three helicopter squadrons and the provision of more light aircraft to counter the growing insurgency; these material additions would complement proposed counter-infiltration operations in Laos and increased covert offensive operations in the North. Notably, recommendations also included the deployment of eight thousand ground combat troops disguised as a "humanitarian task force" to assist with flood relief.[105]

The subsequent Taylor-Rostow report generated intense debate within the White House. On the one hand, more hawkish members, including McNamara, Bundy, and Rusk, supported many of the recommendations, including an immediate, decisive military commitment.[106] McNamara, for example, explained that the basic issue was whether the United States would "commit itself to the clear objective of preventing the fall of South Vietnam to Communism, thus holding the non-Communist areas of Southeast Asia" and "to support this commitment by necessary immediate military actions and preparations for possible later actions." Responding in the affirmative, McNamara determined that the "strategic implications worldwide" to prevent the spread of communism in Vietnam and the rest of Southeast Asia would be "extremely serious." That is, nothing short of the American nomos was at risk. McNamara thus supported "the introduction of a U.S. force of the magnitude of an initial 8–10,000 men—whether in a flood relief context or otherwise." However, he warned also that an eventual commitment of about 220,000 men was likely.[107] Rusk concurred, noting that nothing short of the introduction of U.S. forces "on a substantial scale" would prevent the fall of South Vietnam. The risk of a wider war was possible—

Bracketing War / 85

the struggle might be prolonged, and North Vietnam or China might overtly intervene; however, for Rusk, "the ultimate possible extent of our military commitment in Southeast Asia must be faced."[108] Rostow, predictably, was among the most vocal for an expanded U.S. military presence. "We must be prepared," he warned, "to do whatever we believe necessary to protect our own and the Free World's interest."[109]

On the other hand, several staff members, such as Abram Chayes (State Department legal advisor) expressed reservations. Chayes premised that the conclusions rightfully drawn from the Taylor Report demonstrate that the "basic causes of deterioration and threatened collapse of non-Communist authority" in South Vietnam "are not military but political." And yet, Chayes reflected, "the remedies proposed would undertake to cope with the situation principally by military and semi-military means." Steering clear of an increased military commitment, Chayes believed that "a more promising course of action would be to seek to internationalize the problem with a view to a negotiated settlement or a United Nations solution." Otherwise, the prospects appeared grim. Chayes concluded: "The central feature of the [Taylor recommendations] would be the initial introduction of substantial numbers of United States troops to help in pacifying the country. It is said that to embark on this course we must be prepared to escalate. . . . In assessing the prospects for this course the long history of attempts to prop up unpopular governments through the use of foreign military forces is powerfully discouraging. . . . The drawbacks of such intervention in Viet-Nam now would be compounded, not relieved, by the United States penetration and assumption of co-responsibility at all levels of the Vietnamese government as suggested in the Taylor Report."[110]

The president's final decision on the report, according to Marilyn Young, reflected both his hesitations and his determination to act.[111] Kennedy did not authorize the deployment of U.S. combat troops; he did, however, consent to increasing the number of U.S. military advisors currently active in South Vietnam. Consequently, the number of U.S. military personnel increased from a few hundred to over sixteen thousand. In addition, the president authorized the reorganization of the American advisory apparatus. Here, Kennedy's decision reflected more than just the recommendations contained within the report. Since the Geneva Accords in 1954, the American bureaucratic commitment to South Vietnam had become unwieldly,

86 / Bracketing War

plagued by internecine battles and redundancy: two autonomous CIA stations were operating in Saigon; added to these were myriad other agencies, including the U.S. Agency for International Development (USAID) and the U.S. Information Agency (USIA).[112] Accordingly, McNamara facilitated the establishment of a new command structure, Military Advisory Command, Vietnam (MACV), to replace the ineffective MAAG. Under this new structure, the head of MACV was to direct U.S. military activities and to advise the Saigon government on internal security and on the organization, deployment, and operations of the armed forces. However, MACV was never wholly a military entity. In fact, military operations often required authorization from the U.S. ambassador to South Vietnam and, by extension, the secretary of defense. And while a coequal relationship in theory existed between the commander of MACV and the White House, the latter retained significant oversight and frequently had the final say on all operations.[113]

When General Paul D. Harkins assumed command of a reorganized and reinvigorated MACV on February 13, 1962, U.S. strategy was still oriented primarily toward theater- and regional-wide conventional warfare.[114] Under the guidance of McNamara and other like-minded advisors in the Kennedy administration, however, both pacification programs and covert operations geared toward the securement of South Vietnam's territorial borders began to assume prominence.[115] In 1961, for example, a joint U.S. military-civilian program, the Civilian Irregular Defense Group (CIDG), was launched. U.S. Army Special Forces teams, employed by the CIA, recruited, organized, and trained ethnic minorities located in the strategically important Central Highlands and the Mekong Delta. Both regions were highly vulnerable to enemy infiltration, and the plan was to use the Indigenous, non-Viet peoples to conduct offensive antiguerrilla activities and border surveillance.[116] Within two years, U.S. Special Forces were in control of fifty-one thousand paramilitary troops.[117] As Harkins recalled years later, while the possibility of an invasion from the North remained constant, "the main thing was the infiltration from Laos and Cambodia. That was the thing that was bothersome."[118] Equally bothersome was the fact neither the CIDG nor any of the other military and pacification operations initiated under MACV in tandem with the Diem regime throughout 1962 and 1963 were successful in conclusively stemming the insurgency in the South. Corruption, incompetence, and an overall lack of leadership within the Army of the Republic of Vietnam (ARVN) impeded the execution of many programs, and insufficiently trained personnel combined with inadequate resources contributed to the lack of progress.[119]

Avoiding War, Making War

When Kennedy entered the White House, it was not Vietnam but instead Laos that quickly occupied center stage, the repercussions of which would later inform U.S.-Cambodian relations.[120] The threat was not so much the conditions on the ground in Laos as it was that the likelihood of a communist-controlled Laos threatened the security of South Vietnam. An impoverished, land-locked country, Laos held little political or economic importance to U.S. policymakers. For American military planners, though, the country held tremendous strategic value, not least because it served as a key conduit in the reprovisioning of communist insurgents in South Vietnam. In turn, for Kennedy, Laos would serve "as a test bed for the development of relevant military doctrines, local political deals, and superpower diplomacy."[121]

The chaos in Laos was a by-product of the 1954 Geneva Accords. When Vietnam was arbitrarily divided, both Laos and Cambodia were in theory guaranteed their independence and neutrality. And while plans were developed in each case for internal political settlements, to be overseen by the International Control Commission, the procedures were ill-defined and proved impossible to implement.[122] In an attempt to bring peace and stability to his country, Laotian Prince Souvanna Phouma established a neutralist government, joined by his half-brother and leader of the communist Pathet Lao, Prince Souphanouvong. However, Eisenhower was opposed to neutrality and rejected the proposed coalition government. Sensing a political opportunity, in 1959 the right-wing general Phoumi Nosavan, assisted by the CIA, staged a coup, forcing the Pathet Lao and Souvanna's neutralists to retreat. Armed conflict ensued, with the communist-neutralist coalition receiving support from the Soviets, Chinese, and North Vietnamese governments while Phoumi received support from the United States.[123] A series of additional clandestine CIA operations authorized by Eisenhower failed and, by the end of 1960, the situation appeared dire.

As the Kennedy administration prepared to take office, Eisenhower expressed his hope that the incoming president would continue backing the

88 / Bracketing War

beleaguered Phoumi government, even to the point of deploying U.S. combat forces—an option, it should be noted, Eisenhower himself did not use. During conversations with Kennedy, though, Eisenhower described Laos as "the cork in the bottle." The loss of Laos, the outgoing president explained, would mark "the beginning of the loss of most of the Far East." When asked directly by Kennedy if the United States should intervene, Eisenhower answered affirmatively, justifying that the risk of war "was preferable to a communist success in Laos." Eisenhower cautioned, however, that "unilateral action on the part of the United States would be very bad for our relations in that part of the world and would cause us to be 'tagged' as interventionists."[124]

Kennedy accepted the argument forwarded by Eisenhower on the centrality of Laos to U.S. geopolitical interests in the region. Kennedy also was not opposed to military intervention; however, the president feared that the United States lacked the strength to intervene unilaterally with conventional forces in Southeast Asia while retaining sufficient forces to secure Europe.[125] On this point, Kennedy approached the Laotian crisis from a decidedly broader vantage point, ever mindful that the specter of World War III almost always loomed on European soil. In addition, Kennedy recognized that landlocked Laos provided crucial logistical problems. As detailed in a report prepared by Kennedy's Inter-Agency Task Force on Laos, "The geography of Laos, particularly its isolation and lack of access to the sea, its mountainous-jungle terrain, absence of railroads, inadequate roads and airstrips" made the country "a most undesirable place in which to commit U.S. forces to ground action."[126]

Wanting to avoid a major ground war in Southeast Asia, but cognizant of the importance of the Ho Chi Minh Trail, Kennedy continued and intensified the use of counterinsurgency operations in Laos. Simultaneously, Kennedy also explored a diplomatic solution to the crisis. Specifically, Kennedy directed his advisors to affect a negotiated settlement that might result in a neutralist government in control of Laos. As detailed in a State Department telegram, "We conceive of Laos as a neutral state, unaligned in her international relations but determined to preserve her national integrity. In order to exist in this special status, enjoy independence and retain territorial integrity, some temporary international machinery to guard this neutrality will have to be devised. Neutralized status would envisage . . .

no foreign military bases, no foreign troops and no military alliances."[127] Essentially, U.S. officials hoped to neutralize Laotian territory so as to prevent the infiltration of Vietnamese personnel and materiel into South Vietnam. Indeed, as outlined in the Inter-Agency Task Force report, a coalition government that included members of the Pathet Lao could be acceptable if it facilitated the overall "objective of creating Laos as an independent *buffer* state."[128] U.S. efforts to contain communism were *always* bracketed in practice, despite rhetoric to the contrary.

On July 23, 1962, the International Conference on the Settlement of the Laotian Question in Geneva came to a close with the formal signature of a Declaration on the Neutrality of Laos and a Protocol to the Declaration.[129] In reality, Laos was far from a neutral state, in the sense that it provided a buffer to the ongoing crisis in South Vietnam. North Vietnam continued to utilize the Ho Chi Minh Trail, and the Pathet Lao resumed their guerrilla war. In turn, the United States expanded its covert warfare in Laos to attack enemy supply lines, sabotage military and civilian targets, and engage in numerous other psychological campaigns against communist forces both in Laos and North Vietnam.[130]

The Laotian crisis underscored the U.S. commitment to bracket armed conflict in Southeast Asia and, through diplomatic channels, establish a legal-spatial order that would safeguard the security of South Vietnam and thus curtail the expansion of communism. Indeed, U.S. Ambassador at Large Chester Bowles proposed a "Charter for a Free and Independent Southeast Asia."[131] Bowles's proposal marked the culmination of a series of reports he prepared, urging the Kennedy administration to clarify its "political-economic" objectives in Southeast Asia.[132] Recognizing the "maintenance of an effective but unprovocative military presence capable of deterring an overt attack by Communist forces," Bowles did not "deny the importance of the US military role" in nonaligned states. However, he cautioned that "the failure of the Lao and South Vietnamese governments, with almost unlimited U.S. support, to create viable societies which their people are prepared vigorously to defend had led to a direct U.S. confrontation with Communist forces in Southeast Asia." For Bowles, these events "raised far-reaching questions about the political framework" in which U.S. military forces could most effectively be deployed.[133] Bowles explained that "as long as we lack a political 'grand design' for Southeast Asia, the initiative will

90 / Bracketing War

continue to rest with our adversaries and with our allies and camp followers, whose parochial views often ignore the global forces with which American policy must contend." Bowles warned, "We may find ourselves forced to choose between an escalating war or a humiliating retreat in an area where the strategic conditions are disadvantageous to us." Thus, urging Kennedy to "go beyond Mr. Eisenhower's famous 'falling dominoes' analogy to explain U.S. objectives in Southeast Asia," Bowles called into question "the profound confusion" among American allies and the "200 million Southeast Asians" most directly concerned. Drawing a geopolitical parallel with the Marshall Plan and the rebuilding of Europe, Bowles premised that "what we want for the people of [Southeast Asia] is almost precisely what the people want for themselves: guaranteed national independence, more rapid economic development, and maximum freedom of choice within their own cultures and religions." These objectives, according to Bowles, "not only coincide with our own interests; they are wholly compatible with our present undertakings."[134]

According to Bowles, "peace throughout Southeast Asia" could be achieved through the formation of an "independent belt" in Southeast Asia, a reconstituted political geography that would include Laos, Burma, Thailand, South Vietnam, Cambodia, and Malaya. Effectively, Bowles proposed a monumental regional bloc that would bracket potential armed conflict with China and the Soviet Union. As Bowles explained, "In the absence of a stabilizing development of this kind, a massive Chinese intrusion into this area is likely sooner or later with the strong possibility of a major war into which the Soviet Union might be drawn." Bowles conceded that a "United States policy for an independent and neutral Southeast Asia" might "deeply disturb our relations with [South] Vietnam, the Philippines, and Taiwan" but "in view of the ugly nature of the alternatives" he concluded it was a risk worth taking.[135] Finally, Bowles argued, "in a political sense an 'American bastion' in Southeast Asia is a dead end street even if it were feasible militarily. Our best hope for stability in this area lies in the development of a buffer concept."[136]

In the end, Bowles's proposal fell on deaf ears, as neither Secretary of State Dean Rusk nor Assistant Secretary of State W. Averell Harriman found the plan practical. Instead, the Kennedy administration refocused efforts on retaining South Vietnam as an independent, pro-Western state secured by

U.S. military force. In so doing, the call for extending the "neutrality model" to other parts of Southeast Asia disappeared. The prevailing sentiment among members of the Kennedy administration was that America's spatial order held little room for nonaligned states. As U.S. Ambassador J. Kenneth Galbraith remarked, "If in Laos or in any other country neutralism becomes merely a stage which precedes a communist takeover then the whole concept of neutralism will become a stench in the nostrils."[137]

Johnson's War

On November 1, 1963, Diem was deposed by a military coup and executed. The coup itself was not unexpected. For several months CIA operatives had been working to facilitate the ouster of South Vietnam's head of state. Still, U.S. officials were ill-prepared to deal with the political fallout that followed.[138] Diem's assassination placed the United States in a difficult geopolitical position, one that struck at the core of the American nomos. In spreading "freedom" and "democracy," how should the U.S. government respond to authoritarian governments, military juntas, and other forms of totalitarianism? Such concern was far from academic. In 1962–63, for example, representative governments fell to military coups in Argentina, Peru, Guatemala, Ecuador, Honduras, and the Dominican Republic. Ambassadors, consular generals, and foreign area officers were well aware of the intricacies—and charges of hypocrisy—involved in recognizing or condemning any given coup. In fact, on November 1, as the coup against Diem was underway, Lodge received a telegram from the State Department.[139] Rusk informed the ambassador in Saigon, "If coup succeeds, recognition problem will be urgent." That is, the question of officially recognizing the newly installed government was necessary—but the timing was critical. As Rusk explained, under normal conditions "you would expect to deal in friendly and cooperative fashion with effective authorities from the outset." However, with regime change in Saigon, the ambassador could expect that the timing of America's "announcement of formal recognition might be delayed for a brief period." The coup, Rusk feigned, was "wholly Vietnamese" and that the South Vietnamese generals "should understand that false recognition by the United States *in advance of other governments* would falsely brand their action as American-inspired and manipulated." Rusk notified the U.S. embassy in Saigon to convey to the generals that formal recognition

92 / Bracketing War

would be forthcoming, but it would be postponed for a few days.[140] To further clarify its position—and to make clear its concerns—the State Department sent a follow-up telegram to Lodge, explaining that "if current trends are continued we should move promptly toward support and recognition, but this move will require careful justification in light of danger of misleading comparisons in Latin America. Our thought is to emphasize failings of Diem regime in repression, loss of popular support, inability to continue effective prosecution of war, and even signs of desire to negotiate with enemy."[141] Lodge responded in the affirmative: "Agree we should move promptly to support and recognize. We should decide to resume commercial import payments but on a periodic and selective basis without public announcement so as to avoid appearance of blank check or pay-off. We should not be first to recognize but should assure other friendly Embassies that this is our attitude that we will recognize as soon as a few others have done so. We should, of course, give unmistakable signs of our satisfaction to the new leadership."[142]

The formal recognition of the newly installed military junta in South Vietnam remained a source of contention within the White House for several days after. On November 4, for example, Bundy acknowledged that the United States would recognize the new government in the next day or two; he also emphasized the need for that to be transmitted to "the American Republics Section of the State Department because . . . cables were already coming in from Latin American countries which pointed up how our recognition policy in Vietnam appeared to differ from that in Latin America." Notably, Chester Cooper, a CIA official, suggested that "this might be a good time to spell out U.S. recognition policy." Bundy demurred, explaining that "he was enough of a diplomatic historian to know that if a government did this it would certainly be in trouble, because the approach to recognition changed with circumstances."[143] Effectively, discussion surrounding Diem's assassination brought to light the geopolitics of the formal recognition of state sovereignty. The American mission to spread freedom and democracy globally was necessarily contingent upon U.S. political and economic interests. As Bundy privately acknowledged, the ouster of Diem was an example of an acceptable type of military coup.[144]

Weeks later, America faced its own violent transfer of power when Kennedy was assassinated on the streets of Dallas, Texas. Lyndon B. Johnson,

Kennedy's successor, vowed to continue many of the slain president's programs and to retain most of his cabinet. In the months following the assassination, for example, Johnson explained, "I constantly had before me the picture that Kennedy had selected me as executor of his will, it was my duty to carry on and this meant his people as well as his programs. They were part of his legacy."[145] This approach would circumscribe but not dictate Johnson's approach to the newly installed government in Saigon.[146]

By the time Johnson assumed the presidency, America was committed to the sovereignty and territorial integrity of South Vietnam, irrespective of democratic principles. Two days into his presidency, on November 24, Johnson met with McNamara, Ball, Bundy, John McCone (director, CIA), and Henry Cabot Lodge, recently appointed as U.S. ambassador to South Vietnam, to discuss the "South Vietnam Situation."[147] Lodge expressed optimism in the aftermath of the elimination of Diem. Indeed, he floated the idea that perhaps Hanoi would be interested in some political arrangement that would bring an end to the growing conflict. McCone disagreed. Viet Cong activity was on the rise. Bundy agreed, noting also that the South Vietnamese military continued to have difficulties. Throughout the meeting, Johnson listened intently to the arguments before interjecting that he approached the situation in Vietnam with some misgivings. The president explained that he had never been happy with U.S. operations in Vietnam nor did he support the removal of Diem. However, all that was in the past. What mattered was moving forward. And on that note, Johnson made clear he wanted "no more divisions of opinion, no more bickering" over policy in South Vietnam. In addition, Johnson underscored his contention that the United States need not "reform every Asian into our own image." He cautioned that "all too often when we engaged in the affairs of a foreign country we wanted to immediately transform that country into our image." For Johnson, this was a mistake. Instead, Johnson was "anxious to get along, win the war" and not place so much effort "on so-called social reforms." To that end, Johnson expressed "little tolerance" with "spending so much time being 'do-gooders.'" Johnson thus set the course to achieve America's objectives in South Vietnam *not* primarily through economic development programs or social programs but instead through military action: to "win the war."[148] As such, the securement of South Vietnam's borders remained critical. Government-building was important only insofar as the sitting

94 / Bracketing War

government remained securely in America's orbit and free from communist influence or dominance.

Johnson wasted little time in rearticulating America's grand strategic objectives in South Vietnam.[149] Within hours of the November 24 meeting, Johnson issued National Security Action Memorandum (NSAM) 273, declaring that "it remains the central object of the United States in South Vietnam to assist the people and Government of that country to win their contest against the externally directed and supported Communist conspiracy." Markedly, this affirmation carried the vestiges of Rostow's counterinsurgency doctrine, that is, that the communist revolution in South Vietnam was external in origin, dictated and supported by Hanoi and Moscow. NSAM-273 reiterated also the need to "concern our own efforts, and insofar as possible we should persuade the Government of South Vietnam to concentrate its efforts, on the critical situation in the Mekong Delta. This concentration should include not only military but political, economic, social, educational and informational effort. We should seek to turn the tide not only of battle but of belief, and we should seek to increase not only the control of hamlets but the productivity of this area, especially where the proceeds can be held for the advantage of anti-Communist forces."[150] At this point, state-building had supposedly been accomplished; still needed were programs and military operations to secure and defend South Vietnam's territorial integrity. This task required, in turn, renewed efforts to seal off the country's porous borders with Laos and Cambodia, whether by diplomacy or military force.

In December 1963 McNamara departed on another fact-finding mission to South Vietnam. According to McNamara, "The situation [in South Vietnam] is very disturbing" and that current trends, unless reversed in the next two to three months, would "lead to neutralization at best and more likely to a Communist-controlled state." McNamara characterized the recently installed government as "indecisive and drifting"; of the existing U.S. advisory structure, "It lacks leadership, has been poorly informed, and is not working to a common plan"; and of the insurgency, "the Viet Cong now control very high proportions of the people in certain key provinces, particularly those directly south and west of Saigon." Infiltration remained a problem. McNamara highlighted that enemy personnel and materiel continued to arrive from the North using land corridors through Laos and Cambodia, the Mekong River waterways from Cambodia, and some entry points along the coast. However, based on his assessment, "The infiltration problem, while serious and annoying, is a lower priority." Instead, McNamara advocated the continuation of covert actions, including both sabotage and psychological operations, into North Vietnam. Such operations, the secretary of defense believed, "Should aim to select those that provide maximum pressure with minimum risk."[151] The secretary concluded with the admission that his "appraisal may be overly pessimistic" but that the administration should prepare for "more forceful moves if the situation does not show early signs of improvement."[152]

McNamara's assessment of communist infiltration warrants some attention. For U.S. officials, the existence of the Ho Chi Minh Trail and its tributaries was well known. Indeed, for many policymakers, including Rostow, the trail complex confirmed that the insurgency in South Vietnam was wholly external. This presumption, also, was used in diplomatic circles, as U.S. officials attempted to shape world opinion against Hanoi and to justify U.S. operations as fully in support of an imperiled ally, that being the Saigon government. The problem was that U.S. intelligence analysts had little firm knowledge of the scale and scope of communist infiltration. On December 27, 1963, six days after McNamara concluded that infiltration from the North was "serious and annoying," William Jorden drafted a memorandum on the subject of "Viet Cong Infiltration into South Viet Nam."[153] Based on his assessment of available intelligence, Jorden counseled that the "infiltration of men and material from outside South Viet Nam in support of the Viet Cong is continuing" although "this is but one factor among many in the situation." In line with McNamara's report, Jorden agreed that "to regard [infiltration] as the decisive element in explaining Viet Cong successes over the past year would be an error." That said, Jorden did single out Cambodia as a key source of supplies, including chemicals for the production of explosives, in support of the insurgency in the South. From a practical standpoint, Jorden underscored the need "to take steps to halt or slow infiltration than to merely complain about it." In other words, in light of the evidence that a substantial amount of supplies from the North continued to infiltrate the South, Jorden concluded that "any public diagnosis of this particular disease should be accompanied by a prescription for cure or at least amelioration."[154]

96 / Bracketing War

Success in late 1963, however, appeared more illusory than attainable. A December CIA report concluded that "a satisfactory reduction of the Communist insurgency will be a long and arduous process given the tenacity and strong position of the Viet Cong in many areas." The report explained that "the prolonged political crisis in Saigon has tended to obscure a gradual intensification of Viet Cong guerrilla activity since mid-1963" and that by the time of the coup, the insurgency "had regained momentum and was approaching levels of activity sustained prior to the increased US intervention."[155] Faced with this prospect, Johnson was not content to sit and wait. Even prior to McNamara's report the president had already committed the United States to prepare plans for increased "covert operations by South Vietnamese forces, utilizing such support of U.S. forces as is necessary, against North Vietnam." For Johnson, possible military operations would "include varying levels of pressure all designed to make clear to the North Vietnamese that the U.S. will not accept a Communist victory in South Vietnam and that we will escalate to whatever level is required to insure their defeat."[156] On the basis of McNamara's recommendation, Johnson approved Operation Plan 34-A (OPLAN-34A). Broadly, the program had as its premise that North Vietnam directed and supported the insurgency in the South through a radio network (for propaganda purposes) and through infiltration of cadres, weapons, and materiel from Laos and Cambodia. More concretely, the drafters of OPLAN-34A forwarded a program of covert operations directed against North Vietnam, the objective being to convince Hanoi that it was in their economic self-interest to refrain from supporting the armed struggle in South Vietnam.[157] Through OPLAN-34A, for example, the Special Operations Group (SOG) (later renamed "Studies and Observations Group") came into existence.[158] First activated on January 24, 1964, SOG combined special forces from all the services—Army Green Berets, Navy SEALS, Air Force's Air Commandos, and Marine Corps Force Recon—and, in time would become the largest clandestine military unit since the OSS. Although housed under the command of MACV, the SOG was not subordinate to MACV nor to its commander, William Westmoreland. Rather, the program head answered directly to the Joint Chiefs of Staff (JCS) in the Pentagon, often with explicit White House–level input.[159]

Only a few voices in the Johnson administration or Congress spoke out against the escalation of U.S. military intervention in South Vietnam;

even fewer expressed their reservations publicly.[160] The consensus viewpoint among Johnson's closest advisors, notably McNamara and Bundy, was consistently hawkish. Indeed, as David Barrett finds, "McNamara was a true believer in the righteousness, the feasibility, and the necessity of the growing American presence in Vietnam."[161] On March 16, 1964, for example, McNamara informed Johnson that unless an "independent non-Communist South Vietnam" is achieved, "almost all of Southeast Asia will probably fall under Communist dominance." Were this to occur, effective U.S. and anticommunist influence in Burma, Malaysia, Thailand, the Philippines, India, Australia, New Zealand, Taiwan, South Korea, and Japan would be lost. McNamara thus forwarded several recommendations; and while these fell short of the deployment of U.S. combat forces, the overall thrust was to increase an American presence in South Vietnam.[162] Significantly, McNamara recommended also that the U.S. Navy expand its longstanding Desoto Patrol operations off the coast of North Vietnam.[163]

In early August 1964, the destroyer U.S.S. *Maddox* was patrolling in the Gulf of Tonkin, opposite North Vietnam, gathering intelligence. However, unknown to the commander of the *Maddox,* South Vietnamese and U.S. forces were also participating in covert activities as part of OPLAN-34A. When Hanoi retaliated against South Vietnamese patrol boats on August 2, North Vietnamese forces targeted the *Maddox.* The U.S. destroyer was unharmed, but Johnson and his military command determined that the U.S. needed to step up operations in the Gulf. Two days later, the U.S.S. *Turner Joy* also reported that it came under attack by North Vietnamese forces.[164] In turn, Johnson ordered retaliatory air strikes against military targets in North Vietnam. However, Johnson also used the suspected attacks to garner political and popular support for armed intervention in Vietnam. On August 7 Johnson asked for and received a congressional mandate to take whatever actions necessary and required to repel any future attack against U.S. forces in the region. In short order, Congress consented, with the Senate voting 88 to 2 in support of the Gulf of Tonkin Resolution; the House passed the bill without dissent. As Herring writes, "U.S. prestige was now publicly and more firmly committed not merely to defending South Vietnam but also to responding to North Vietnamese provocations."[165]

By early December, the president and his aides agreed to initiate a two-phase escalation of military operations. The first would involve "armed

98 / Bracketing War

reconnaissance strikes" against infiltration routes in Laos as well as retaliatory air strikes against the North in response to PLAF attacks. The second phase would entail "graduated military pressure" against the North, in the form of aerial bombing and, potentially, the deployment of U.S. ground troops to the South.[166] This escalation, however limited in scale and scope, was met with armed assaults launched by the PLAF, thus establishing a dangerous pattern of attacks and counterattacks. In February 1965, in response to PLAF raids on a U.S. military installation at Pleiku, Johnson authorized the initiation of Operation Rolling Thunder, a sustained air campaign against North Vietnam. Senator Mansfield again urged caution and expressed concern about a possible large-scale conflict with China. Johnson, however, was adamant. Johnson stated that for too long "he had kept the shotgun over the mantel and the bullets in the basement." Now, "the enemy was killing his personnel and he could not expect them to continue their work if he did not authorize them to take steps to defend themselves."[167] Thus, in March and April Johnson approved additional requests forwarded by Westmoreland for the deployment of U.S. combat forces and logistical support personnel to protect U.S. military installations throughout South Vietnam and to undertake operations within fifty miles of their base areas.[168]

By this point "a decision either to increase the American role in Vietnam or to disengage was becoming necessary."[169] The collapse of South Vietnam appeared all but inevitable without an increased U.S. military response; and for those advisors within the Johnson administration advocating an escalation of war, the current piecemeal, reactionary approach was not working. A hardening of policy objectives was also becoming more apparent. In March 1965, for example, John McNaughton, assistant secretary of defense for international security affairs, provided an action plan in which he calculated in percentages the desired aims of U.S. policy toward South Vietnam: "to avoid a humiliating US defeat" (70 percent); "to keep [South Vietnam] (and then adjacent) territory from Chinese hands" (20 percent); and "to permit the people of [South Vietnam] to enjoy a better, freer way of life" (10 percent). McNaughton concluded that it was essential to "avoid harmful appearances which will affect judgements by, and provide pretexts to, other nations regarding how the U.S. will behave in future cases of particular interests to those nations—regarding U.S. policy, power, resolve and competence to deal with their problems."[170]

Notably, even those advisors opposed to increased military intervention were in agreement with the political end point. In May 1965, Undersecretary of State Ball developed a plan for a political resolution in South Vietnam. Ball explained that "we have, from the beginning, made clear that our objective in Southeast Asia is to bring about a political solution that would assure the independence of South Viet-Nam." However, Ball counseled, "We have so far assumed that we could achieve an acceptable political settlement only when our military pressure had reached the point where the North Vietnamese and Viet Cong were ready to give up the struggle." This path, Ball warned, would most likely lead to "a situation where each side will be led to accept more dangerous and onerous expedients in an effort to achieve its major objectives."[171]

On June 5, 1965, Westmoreland and Ambassador Maxwell Taylor reported to Washington that if "the military situation continues seriously to deteriorate" the most appropriate course of action would be "a more active military involvement" including the commitment of "US ground forces to action."[172] Westmoreland followed up with a request to the Joint Chiefs of Staff for thirty-four U.S. battalions, plus an additional ten battalions from South Korea, to "take the fight to the [Viet Cong]."[173] Up to this point, U.S. ground forces in South Vietnam were engaged in predominantly defensive operations as part of a so-called enclave strategy. The options of withdrawal and a massive air war against North Vietnam had long since been rejected; however, the limited bombing campaign undertaken since February was not producing the expected results.

McNamara concluded that there were only three options Washington could pursue in Vietnam. The first was to "cut our losses and withdraw under the best conditions that can be arranged—almost certainly conditions humiliating the United States and very damaging to our future effectiveness on the world scene." A second was to "continue at about the present level." Such a course of action, however, "almost certainly would confront [the United States] later with a choice between withdrawal and an emergency expansion of forces." In other words, to do nothing at this point would delay the inevitable, perhaps at a point when it would be "too late to do any good." The third option—which McNamara favored—was to "expand promptly and substantially the U.S. military pressure against the Viet Cong in the South and maintain the military pressure against the North Vietnamese in

100 / Bracketing War

the North." And while not disregarding political means, for McNamara an increased military strategy "would stave off defeat in the short run and offer a good chance of producing a favorable settlement in the longer run." McNamara did concede that an increased military response "would imply a commitment to see a fighting war clear through at considerable cost in casualties and materiel and would make any later decision to withdraw even more difficult and even more costly than would be the case today."[174]

On July 28, following several days of intense meetings with his top civilian and military officials, Johnson announced his decision during a midday news conference. Speaking in support of Westmoreland's request, the president committed himself—and the United States—to an expanded military strategy in South Vietnam. And while falling short of Westmoreland's initial demands, Johnson did approve the immediate deployment of an additional 50,000 U.S. troops to Vietnam; he privately agreed to send another 50,000 before the end of the year.[175] In addition, the president authorized Westmoreland to adopt an aggressive search-and-destroy strategy and to increase dramatically the bombing of North Vietnam.[176] Johnson essentially made an open-ended commitment to deploy U.S. military forces as the situation demanded—just as McNamara foretold. Conspicuously, Johnson made this commitment without consulting the South Vietnamese government, thus belying the public rhetoric about saving a sovereign ally from foreign aggression.[177]

Although Johnson committed the United States to an eventual ground war in Vietnam, he continued to circumscribe the scale and scope of military operations. Johnson informed Westmoreland that he would send additional forces only if conditions warranted it. Also, Johnson made clear that he would not authorize the deployment of U.S. combat troops into North Vietnam, Laos, or Cambodia. Given these parameters, Westmoreland was compelled to formulate a strategy designed to defend and secure South Vietnam without explicitly defeating North Vietnam. His eventual strategy comprised three elements. In the initial phase of the war, the first task was to "stem the tide" of the southern insurgency. Once conditions stabilized—and additional U.S. combat troops arrived—Westmoreland planned to initiate the second phase of the war: the commencement of large-scale operations to destroy major enemy units and bases. During this phase, the South Vietnamese military would clear and pacify designated high-priority areas, thereby further strengthening the Saigon government and weakening the enemy. Full restoration of government control throughout the countryside, the progressive withdrawal of U.S. combat troops, and the solidification of state building would occur in the final phase.[178]

Westmoreland's strategy also entailed three operational components, each designed to meet a particular aspect of his conduct of the war.[179] The first one included "search-and-destroy" operations. These missions were a mainstay of the anticipated conventional war; as such, search-and-destroy operations were not designed to hold ground or establish any type of permanent presence. Instead, they were planned most often to attack the enemy's major combat formations and base areas. A second type of operation, dubbed "clearing" or "clear and hold," was intended to disrupt enemy guerrilla forces in areas slated for pacification. Here, U.S. combat troops would enter a targeted area, establish a base camp, and create a liaison with Indigenous civil, military, and intelligence agencies. Smaller units would conduct myriad patrols, raids, and ambushes, eschewing the previous enclave strategy of simply defending base areas. When a patrol detected PLAF or PAVN forces, numerically superior armed troops would rush to the location to destroy them. Lastly, U.S. troops would assist in localized pacification efforts in an attempt to strengthen the South Vietnamese government's presence in the area. Operating in tandem, clearing operations would be expected to transition into securing operations. Ultimately, as U.S. combat forces reduced the fighting capacity of the PLAF and PAVN, South Vietnamese forces— both military and paramilitary—would assume greater responsibility for local defense. Remnant insurgents would be rooted out, thereby cementing the government's hold over the region's people and resources.[180]

Johnson was wary of dragging the United States into war in Vietnam. However, he understood the risks of being seen as soft on communism. To that end, Johnson hoped that a strategy of limited armed force would deter Hanoi from further aggression and, ultimately, lead to a negotiated settlement that would secure South Vietnam. This strategy, however, required the defense of South Vietnam's borders, including its exposed western border with Cambodia.

[3]

BORDERING WAR

> If Cambodia were to fall completely under Communist influence,
> her geographic position would endanger the security of friendly
> Southeast Asian countries.
>
> —Inter-Agency Study Group Report

As America's military footprint in South Vietnam deepened throughout the summer of 1965, Secretary of Defense Robert McNamara clarified U.S. policy and detailed his general assessment of the war's early progression. McNamara reaffirmed America's objectives in South Vietnam, specifically, to "create conditions for a favorable outcome" by demonstrating both to the North Vietnamese and the National Liberation Front [NLF] that "the odds are against their winning." For McNamara, a "favorable outcome" comprised nine fundamental elements; these centered in part on the perpetuation of a stable government in South Vietnam—hopefully pro–United States but possibly neutralist; the withdrawal of North Vietnamese forces in the South; and the cessation of insurgent attacks in the South. McNamara acknowledged the possibility that a token force of U.S. ground troops would remain in South Vietnam for the foreseeable future, not unlike the geopolitical situation on the Korean peninsula.[1]

For McNamara, however, the short-term prospects for South Vietnam appeared bleak. The secretary of defense explained that the situation in the South was worse than it had been the year before: the South Vietnamese government was unable to provide security in the rural areas, and pacification efforts were making little progress. Of paramount concern was that there were no indications that extant efforts to "throttle" the inflow of supplies to southern insurgents was making an impact. Hence, McNamara recommended that Johnson "expand promptly and substantially the U.S. military

103

104 / Bordering War

pressure against the Viet Cong in the South and maintain the military pressure against the North Vietnamese in the North while launching a vigorous effort on the political side to lay the groundwork for a favorable outcome by clarifying our objectives and establishing channels of communication." In addition, McNamara emphasized the need to "make quiet moves through diplomatic channels" to open a dialogue with both Moscow and Hanoi. To this end, it was necessary also to make clear U.S. objectives vis-à-vis the American public and America's allies and friends. That said, McNamara concluded that the number of U.S. military personnel killed in action might approach five hundred a month within the year and, over the long term, even if successful, it was not obvious how the United States would be able to disengage its forces from Vietnam.[2]

Four months later, McNamara expanded his assessment of the political and military situation in South Vietnam in explicitly geopolitical terms. That is, McNamara made explicit the particular spatial order at stake. According to McNamara, the ongoing courses of action in Vietnam made sense "only if they are in support of a long-run United States policy to contain Communist China." Drawing parallels both with Germany and Japan in the 1930s and 1940s, McNamara counseled that China looms as the "major power threatening to undercut our importance and effectiveness in the world." Beyond a mere security concern, McNamara stressed that "we have our view of the way the US should be moving and of the need for the majority of the rest of the world to be moving in the same direction if we are to achieve our national objective." For McNamara, this entailed a move toward "economic well-being, toward open societies, and toward cooperation between nations." McNamara explained that "the role we have inherited and have chosen for ourselves for the future is to extend our influence and power to thwart ideologies that are hostile to these aims *and to move the world, as best we can, in the direction we prefer.*" Ultimately, according to McNamara, "our ends cannot be achieved and our leadership role cannot be played if some powerful and virulent nation . . . is allowed to organize their part of the world according to a philosophy contrary to ours."[3]

In support of America's spatial order, McNamara presented and commented upon a catalogue of military and nonmilitary options; notably, he underscored that military actions are "essential to success in Vietnam, but they are not sufficient." Rather, McNamara concluded that "the heart of South Vietnam will begin to beat and the body to breathe only when [South Vietnamese] militia, police, intelligence and administrative personnel have been introduced in sufficient strength to saturate [the countryside], destroy the VC infrastructure and reestablish the agencies of Government." Alongside economic aid initiatives and psychological warfare campaigns, McNamara accentuated the need to minimize or eliminate the infiltration of enemy forces and materiel into South Vietnam. "The pattern of infiltration and VC force augmentation," McNamara explained, "strongly implies that Laos is being heavily used both as a channel and as a staging base for operations in South Vietnam." Consequently, McNamara proposed the "creation of a 175-mile-long anti-infiltration 'barrier' to run near the 17th Parallel from the sea to Thailand." McNamara added that "any such barrier would of course have to be complemented by effective measures countering infiltration by sea and from Cambodia."[4] Essentially, for the secretary of defense, Cambodia was important insofar as it formed the soft underbelly of South Vietnam.

According to Hal Brands, the prioritizing function of grand strategy is essential. If practitioners of statecraft are to avoid strategic exhaustion—including military overstretch—they must maintain a firm conception of core interests and deploy their resources accordingly.[5] The logical corollary is that practitioners must also have a firm conception of those areas peripheral to national interests. Such geopolitical calculus, however, always retains an element of uncertainty. Brands clarifies that states, and especially superpowers such as the United States, "often have interests in nearly every region of the world, and find themselves dealing with dozens of foreign policy issues from day to day. Even if it were possible to address all of these issues case by case, the various solutions would inevitably come into conflict with one another."[6] America's support of the coup against Ngo Dinh Diem is a case in point. While appearing to be of momentary benefit to the United States, America's involvement would subsequently limit diplomatic efforts in Cambodia. In addition, the determination of strategic importance may shift rapidly in response to changed political, economic, or military conditions. Effectively, not only is grand strategy inherently marked by a degree of spatial uncertainty, but policymakers are often placed in a reactionary role, responding to unanticipated events that threaten to undermine their intended aims and aspirations. In light of McNamara's concerns, in this

106 / Bordering War

chapter I detail how Cambodia, a sovereign state formally recognized both by the United States and the United Nations, moved from the periphery to center stage in America's war in Indochina. In so doing, I highlight how ancillary events impose themselves on the articulation of grand strategy.

The Cambodian Conjunction

Although French forces in Indochina were defeated by Japan in the early months of the Second World War, under the Vichy government French officials continued to make policy in Cambodia. As such, when Cambodia's longtime monarch, King Sisowath Monivong, died in 1941, it was the French who determined his successor. By lineage, the rightful heir was Prince Monireth, Monivong's eldest son. French officials, however, determined that the younger and less experienced Norodom Sihanouk would best serve their interests.[7] Initially, the French were correct. Throughout the duration of the war, Sihanouk idled away his time in Phnom Penh and offered no visible resistance to French colonial rule.[8] However, Sihanouk quickly matured into a skillful politician. After the Second World War, Sihanouk bargained concessions from the French, including a written constitution that allowed for a democratically elected assembly in 1947 and, two years later, powers to administer Cambodia's foreign policy.[9] Under his guidance, a newly formed government promulgated over 150 laws and nearly 400 administrative decrees.[10]

Sensitive to the ever-present power politics of his country, Sihanouk worked to solidify the independence of his country and, in so doing, his own position. Under the pretext of a national emergency, Sihanouk marginalized political opposition and dissolved the national assembly.[11] Most publicly, though, in 1953 Sihanouk embarked on a whirlwind global tour in an effort to regain sovereignty for his kingdom. Keenly sensitive to the ongoing conflict in neighboring Vietnam, Sihanouk devised a strategy to retain power for himself while keeping Cambodia out of the crosshairs of war. In Paris, Sihanouk declared that he alone could establish a genuinely neutral and independent Cambodia. French officials were not impressed; but Sihanouk was not finished. Sensing the virulent anticommunism in the West, Sihanouk affirmed his pro-Western and pro-democratic credentials in Canada, Japan, and the United States. In the United States, for example, Sihanouk met with Vice President Richard Nixon, Secretary of State John

Foster Dulles, and Ambassador Donald Heath.[12] The meeting was cordial, although Sihanouk was disappointed that the United States did not promise to support his demands for further concessions from the French. Sihanouk had underscored the need for complete independence from French colonial rule, stressing that the loyalty of the Cambodian people was in peril. Indeed, when meeting with U.S. representatives in Japan, Sihanouk cautioned that "most Cambodians did not regard the Communists as their enemies as much as the French" and that "the majority of his people would no doubt fold their arms and let the Communists move in if worse came to the worst."[13] From the U.S. perspective, however, a wholly independent Cambodia could only work to the Viet Minh's advantage, for without French economic and military support, Sihanouk's government would surely collapse. The response of Dulles is illustrative of most responses. Cambodian independence, Dulles explained, was meaningless without French economic and military support; for if left alone, communist forces would swallow Cambodia.[14] That said, U.S. officials conceded—among themselves—that it was essential that the French make clear that their intention to give the people of the Associated States of Indochina maximum freedom to choose their own form of government, that is, once internal security throughout the region had been established.[15]

Soon enough, the geopolitical winds shifted. Mired in a steadily worsening war against the Viet Minh, in October 17, 1953, French officials granted Sihanouk authority over judicial and foreign affairs, as well as authority over Cambodia's armed forces. Sihanouk welcomed these overtures but saw an opportunity to push the envelope further. France retained an economic hold on the kingdom, especially the all-important rubber industry. Consequently, Sihanouk upped the ante and called for mass demonstrations throughout the country. Sihanouk's gambit paid off, and on November 9, 1953, Paris assented to the king's demands.[16] Cambodia's promising political future appeared even brighter when, in 1954, the Geneva Accords affirmed Cambodia's sovereignty and territorial integrity.

And for the citizens of Cambodia, the future did appear promising. Nearly everyone had enough to eat, almost all peasants owned the land they tilled and—importantly—there was an abundance of land to cultivate; and for nonfarmers, towns offered employment.[17] A foreign observer captured some of this optimism, writing in 1955 that "Cambodia seems to stand at the

108 / Bordering War

extended new road to life among the many nations. She has passed several tollgates and is entering the main highway. . . . In certain places in the world, there are unspoiled places awaiting training and education for the new era; Cambodia is one of those places."[18] In Washington, also, Cambodia appeared as a potential bastion of strength and stability in an otherwise unstable region. Just one year earlier, for example, U.S. officials worried that Sihanouk failed to appreciate the severity of the "Chinese and Communist menace," but now the situation was different.[19] As Robert McClintock, then serving as the U.S. chargé d'affaires in Cambodia, wrote, "There is a new awareness (for Cambodia) of the seriousness of purpose of the Communists in planning world-wide domination." Now, McClintock, explained, "The Cambodian government is particularly grateful to the United States for its support of the Cambodian thesis that the Viet Minh in Cambodia are foreign invaders and their evacuation from Cambodian soil is the only acceptable solution." On this point, McClintock happily reported, "The leaders of the country unanimously look to the United States for the salvation for their country from Communism. They know that the United States has no vested interest to protect in this Kingdom and they intuitively trust not only our motives but our ability to protect weak peoples." For McClintock, "The United States now has in staunchly anti–Viet Minh Cambodia a potentially important supporter in the struggle against Communism in Southeast Asia. By proper handling and tactful diplomatic negotiation, the manpower resources of this country will be [a] real asset to US foreign policy."[20]

McClintock's optimism, however, was tempered by the entangled geopolitics of U.S.-French relations. Crucially, France's defeat at the hands of the Viet Minh and the subsequent loss of Tonkin and Annam impelled French officials to extend their influence over Cambodia, Laos, and the State of Vietnam.[21] Essentially, the position of France was to maintain suzerainty over its former possessions. This maneuver, however, pitted France and the United States in a contest of wills over effective governance of the country and the practical work of building up Cambodia's Armed Forces (Forces Armées Nationales Khmères, or FANK). Simply put, U.S. officials viewed the Cambodian government as unable to withstand the likelihood of communist subversion and infiltration. In 1950, the Eisenhower administration had authorized the formation of the Military Assistance Advisory Group, Indochina; and in the months subsequent to the Geneva Accords, it was

Bordering War / 109

this apparatus that featured prominently in the struggle to advise, train, and equip Cambodia's armed forces. Initially, Cambodian officials welcomed the assistance of MAAG personnel and especially military aid. Concurrently, however, these officials also balked at the possible loss of French assistance. Indeed, representatives of both France and Cambodia concluded a secret agreement on the continuance of French support.[22] Washington was not unaware of these machinations. On January 6, 1955, for example, U.S. Ambassador to France C. Douglas Dillon informed the State Department that the reduction of France's military and political influence in Vietnam "has made them more than ever determined [to] maintain and if possible increase it in Cambodia and Laos. They are unwilling [to] concede to [the] US in Cambodia and Laos to the same extent as in South Vietnam."[23] French officials reasoned that while South Vietnam would ultimately fall to the Viet Minh, the same was not true for either Cambodia or Laos. Dillon cautioned that France was actively working to solidify its hegemonic role in the remnants of its former colony, especially in Cambodia.

Dillion's assessment was in fact well known among U.S. officials. Robert McClintock, now ambassador to Cambodia, reiterated that "our reporting of current French plans for dominance in Cambodia has been so extensive that little additional comment seems necessary." In fact, the administration of President Dwight D. Eisenhower understood that France continued to use Cambodia as a "compulsory dumping ground for high cost exports" as part of its outdated "mercantile colonial policy." As McClintock affirmed, these policies "which became extinct so far as [the] US was concerned in [the] 18th Century" were antithetical to the opening of Indochina's markets to free competition.[24] From Washington's point of view, the economic restructuring of Indochina was jeopardized both by France's antiquated colonial revanchism and a subversive communist threat controlled by Moscow through its Vietnamese puppets. The American problem was such that defense against the latter threat required the buildup of Cambodia's military capabilities, ideally through the establishment of a U.S. Military Assistance Advisory Group, Cambodia. This, however, required the removal of the French—a condition many Khmer officials were unwilling to support.

In a memorandum to the Joint Chiefs of Staff, Admiral Arthur Davis succinctly laid out the problem from a military standpoint. "As long as the French remain in Cambodia," Davis counseled, "there will be only token

110 / Bordering War

compliance on the part of the Cambodians, due to French influence, in reference to the acceptance of U.S. doctrinal guidance." As such, the "effectiveness of a U.S. military aid program for Cambodia will be negligible." Davis concluded, "Either prior to or concurrent with the negotiation of a MAAG, Cambodia, bilateral agreement, the U.S. must obtain from the Government of Cambodia, an agreement in writing providing for the ultimate withdrawal of French instructors and technicians."[25] From a strategic standpoint, however, U.S. officials recognized that Cambodia "was not an isolated problem, but was related to others, importantly, to the role of France in our over-all coalition strategy." Indeed, as described by Assistant Secretary of State Walter Robertson, "However much of an anchor around our necks the French might be in Cambodia . . . we need them in Europe."[26] The challenge for the Eisenhower administration was to establish a viable U.S. military training program in Cambodia without unduly disturbing U.S.-French relations.

Throughout the first part of 1955, U.S. officials entered into delicate diplomatic discussions both with French and Cambodian officials to achieve their short-term objectives.[27] On this point, the Eisenhower administration wanted "to provide, in addition to political and economic stability, those military forces which are required to maintain the internal security of Cambodia and which will also provide a limited capability for its defense."[28] Cambodia was a sovereign state; but it neighbored South Vietnam. And it was this latter state that, from the vantage point of the United States, always held precedence. Ideally, Phnom Penh would serve as a reliable pro-American government, a necessary bulwark on South Vietnam's western border. The worst-case scenario was that Phnom Penh would align with the Soviet bloc and thus pose a significant threat to the survival of South Vietnam. At the moment, this latter scenario seemed remote but still possible. According to McClintock, of all the countries in Southeast Asia, Cambodia was probably "least vulnerable to immediate Communist subversion." Unlike South Vietnam, in Cambodia there was no appreciable communist movement; indeed, "Indigenous communists [were] limited to intellectuals largely in [the] capital city and to students returning from France where Communists [had] made skillful and successful play to capture their imaginations and loyalty."[29] In other words, communist ideology was purely external in origin; and in accordance with Rostow's theory of modernization, massive injections of economic and military aid should be sufficient to retain the loyalty of Cambodia's people. However, the biggest danger to Cambodia's stability and, in turn, to America's state-, nation-, and government-building activities in South Vietnam was the frontier between the two states. McClintock underscored that the forested and mountainous areas of northeastern Cambodia, in particular, could be used by communists to infiltrate South Vietnam. Herein was the core rationale for U.S. military assistance to Cambodia: to hold "Cambodia immune from Communist penetration."[30]

On May 16, 1955, the United States and Cambodia signed a Military Defense Agreement (MDA) that provided for the establishment of MAAG, Cambodia; it would become operational in November of that year. Remarkably, Cambodia was the only professedly neutral country in the world where the United States established a MAAG.[31] Not surprisingly, international reaction to the MDA was highly critical of American intentions, with Burma, China, France, India, and North Vietnam voicing strong opposition to the agreement.[32] The United States was accused of violating the Geneva Accords and, in doing so, raising tensions in the region. U.S. officials, for their part, maintained they were simply "answering repeated Cambodian requests for military assistance."[33] This would not be the last time Washington feigned innocence in its diplomatic relations with Cambodia.

Sihanouk capitalized on these events to further consolidate his own power. As mandated by the Geneva Accords, Cambodians in 1955 were to participate in free and open democratic elections. And on paper, the slated political contestation appeared to offer a wide range of options for the citizenry. On the political left stood both the Pracheachon and the Democrat Party.[34] A stalwart platform of this latter party was its opposition to foreign (namely, U.S.) influence; increasingly, members of the Democrat Party assumed also a more hardline, anti-Royalist position. On the political right stood members of the Liberal Party and an assortment of other groups formed in the early 1950s.[35] However, in February 1955, just months before the scheduled elections, Sihanouk initiated a nationwide referendum, asking voters to approve his Royal Crusade for Independence from two years earlier. Pointedly, anyone who wanted to vote against the king was required to discard a ballot adorned, not by chance, with his likeness. In a monarchy such as Cambodia, the discarding of the king's image constituted an act of lèse-majesté and grounds for arrest. Not unexpectedly, 95 percent of the

112 / Bordering War

electorate voted to support Sihanouk, who was now positioned to participate in national politics more actively.[36] However, Sihanouk then did something entirely unexpected: he abdicated the throne. This was a shrewd move on Sihanouk's part because according to the constitution, the king was not allowed to participate in politics. As prince, though, Sihanouk was able to contest the 1955 National Assembly elections as head of his newly formed party, the Sangkum Reastr Niyum (People's Socialist Community) all the while retaining a figurative hand on the throne.[37]

Sihanouk's Sangkum party predictably swept to victory on September 11, 1955, claiming 83 percent of the vote and winning every seat in the national legislature.[38] The election was clearly rigged, but U.S. officials were initially untroubled by Sihanouk's undemocratic consolidation of power. Conditions soon changed, however, as Sihanouk moved from a professed pro-Western position to a more neutralist stance, marked by his 1955 participation at the Bandung Conference and his pledge to support a nonaligned political-economic agenda. In addition, U.S. officials expressed concern when Sihanouk announced that he would extend formal recognition to the People's Republic of China and reject membership in the American-led South East Asian Treaty Organization (SEATO).

But where U.S. policymakers saw a tilt toward communism, Sihanouk's moves were more nuanced. Above all, Sihanouk maintained a neutral foreign policy because he discerned, correctly, that Cambodia's sovereignty and territorial integrity were threatened by all of his neighbors, regardless of ideology. Indeed, Sihanouk repeatedly described Cambodia as "a sheep surrounded by three wolves with long teeth."[39] In Washington, officials and officers rarely understood Sihanouk's national security concerns. William Sebald, for example, warned that "Cambodia will develop along lines unsatisfactory to attainment of our political objectives unless Norodom Sihanouk returns to the throne and having done so takes actions which in the past he has been unwilling to do."[40] In short, Sihanouk as potential communist supporter worried U.S. officials more than Sihanouk as authoritarian.

Sihanouk in fact was not a communist, although he did adhere to an ideology of Khmer socialism, which later modulated into what he termed "Buddhist socialism." In this context, however, the term "socialism" acquired a particular meaning, in that it denoted "a society mobilized to perpetuate the status quo."[41] As Michael Vickery explains, it was not Marxist socialism but rather a "Royal Buddhist Socialism," an ideology predicated on the traditional Cambodian practice of the sovereign always providing for the welfare of its people.[42] Far from a radical or revolutionary ideology, socialism for Sihanouk was conservative in orientation. This form of doctrinal nuance was lost on many U.S. policymakers. In response to Sihanouk's apparent leftward shift, for example, Admiral Felix Stump, commander-in-chief, Pacific Command, warned that Sihanouk was "promoting pro-Communist policies." If these assessments were accurate, Stump concluded, Sihanouk's "antagonistic attitude [would] threaten [to] damage [the] entire U.S. assistance program, particularly [in] Southeast Asia."[43] For Stump, the time had come "for the US to make some reaction other than turning the other cheek when neutralists and others spit in our face." This was a matter of national security. "Aid to neutralist countries and anti-American countries," the admiral premised, "make our Allies wonder what is the best policy to get more aid." In short, he questioned, why should any government uphold U.S. policies if America continued to authorize scarce resources to countries plainly not in line with U.S. interests? Indeed, acknowledging that "foreign aid money is not sufficient to do the job we need to do," Stump cautioned, "we cannot afford to throw any of it down the rat hole but should place it where it will do the most good to strengthen the democratic world." Stump recognized the geopolitical significance of Cambodia and agreed that "we should endeavor to do all we can to strengthen Cambodia if strengthening that country will strengthen the democratic world." If not, he declared, then "we ought to place the money where it will do more good . . . against the Chinese and Russian Communists." Better to make an example of Cambodia, Stump argued, as that would demonstrate that the United States provides aid "entirely for the benefit of the US and the free world." In the end, the admiral believed, the American taxpayer was "sick and tired" of providing aid "for the pussyfooters."[44]

Stump's position was pervasive among U.S. officials but not undisputed. Other policymakers maintained that Sihanouk—although not expressly pro-Western—was still ardently anticommunist. In response to Stump's concerns, for example, George Lodoen, U.S. Army general and director of MAAG, Cambodia, countered that any "recommendation for reduction in United States assistance would not serve [the] best interests [of the] United States in Cambodia or [Southeast Asia]." Lodoen explained that "Cambodia

114 / Bordering War

is still politically solid, solidly anti-Communist, and [a] potential strong spot in [Southeast Asia]." Better to view Sihanouk's escapades, the general allowed, "as nothing more than [his] desire [to] advertise his naïve neutralist policy." Lodoen concluded that Sihanouk was "well-aware [of] disastrous results if he permits Communism [to] gain [a] foothold in his country."[45] McClintock concurred, noting that "if we hold steadfast and continue our present policies we will be acting in [our] true strategic interests." The U.S. ambassador to Cambodia reaffirmed that U.S. policy toward Cambodia was to "assist Cambodia [to] remain independent," that is, to "deny this area of [the] Mekong Basin to Communist penetration." Thus far, McClintock rationalized, "Cambodia is still without Communist taint." As such, any deviation from current policy might prove disastrous. The danger, McClintock cautioned, was not to be found among Cambodia's peasantry but its military. According to McClintock, "We can stop economic aid tomorrow and amounts of rice and fish placed in [the] stomachs of Cambodian peasants will remain the same." However, he continued, any "sudden 'let's show them' stoppage of aid would have sweeping political repercussions both here and in Asia." More precisely, he premised, "If we should stop military assistance we would find [an] army of 35,000 vigorous and highly principled young men with guns in their hands suddenly placed out of [a] job." McClintock was convinced that if military aid was withdrawn from Cambodia, Washington would be in short order handing over a strategic area to the communists, thereby enabling them to control all land routes between Thailand, Laos, and South Vietnam. For McClintock, the basic issue was "not whether Cambodia is neutralist or more positively in [the] Western bloc, but whether Cambodia [could] be denied to communism."[46] This was in fact the message Nong Kimny, Cambodian ambassador to the United States, delivered to the U.S. State Department. According to the ambassador, Cambodian neutrality was a matter of state but Cambodia recognized also "the evil of Communism." He affirmed that if "Cambodia states that she is prepared to fight to defend her independence against outside interference, Cambodia recognizes that a threat comes only from Communism."[47]

On the whole, however, Washington's national security concerns transcended Sihanouk. Cambodia was important in the abstract only insofar as it bordered South Vietnam; consequently, U.S. concerns toward the country were clearly secondary to the state-, nation-, and government-building efforts in South Vietnam. Apart from the provision of limited military equipment and training, there was less consideration given to any form of economic development in Cambodia, certainly not compared to America's support of South Vietnam. That said, Cambodia did serve to potentially bolster American credibility and prestige in the region. As State Department official Kenneth Young explained, "There is more at stake for the U.S. than just our relations with the Cambodians. What we do there is being carefully watched in Asian capitals. If we can improve the situation, it will enhance our reputation and standing in Southeast Asia. If we act suddenly and drastically because of the Prince's provocations and without going through an attempt to set the matter right, the U.S. will be criticized in Asia."[48] On that point, diplomacy was strongly favored among those U.S. officials serving in Phnom Penh. McClintock, again, underscored that "the U.S. must, and can, deny the lower basin of the Mekong occupied by Cambodia to Communist penetration" and that this could be achieved "by a judicious economic and military aid program to maintain its independence."[49] The determination expressed by McClintock and other State officials would be severely tested in the coming months, however. In June Cambodia and China signed an aid agreement giving Cambodia $22.8 million over two years in economic assistance primarily to build factories, irrigation systems, and other forms of infrastructure; by year's end, Sihanouk would also travel to the Soviet Union and several other communist-bloc states, including Poland, Yugoslavia, and Czechoslovakia.[50]

As Sihanouk's foreign policy vacillated between the Western and communist blocs, Eisenhower's National Security Council (NSC) conducted a comprehensive reevaluation of America's national security interests in Southeast Asia.[51] Notably, and in light of recent events in Cambodia, much debate centered on "the U.S. attitude toward neutralist countries on the one hand, and toward countries which joined with [the United States] in collective security arrangements on the other hand." As expressed by John Foster Dulles, the State Department's position was one of maximum flexibility. The secretary explained that the "State did not wish to lay down as a fixed policy statement the principle of preferential treatment for countries formally aligned with the United States. It might well happen that some country aligned with the United States in some kind of collective security pact

116 / Bordering War

would not actually be in need of military or economic assistance; whereas some other countries which were in a neutralist position might need our help to prevent itself from being absorbed into the Communist orbit." Acting Secretary of Defense Reuben Robertson countered that "it was his experience, when he visited the Southeast Asian countries, that it would be a very great help if these countries could be convinced that the United States would really come to their assistance in the event that they were threatened by Communist bloc countries." According to Robertson, those governments were "not so convinced, and if we proceed to give military assistance to neutral nations . . . nations allied with us will assume that this assistance will be given" to others. Admiral Radford agreed. He stressed that "we would never be able to retain our allies in Southeast Asia if our allies felt that other countries were in a position to obtain U.S. assistance without ever joining any kind of alliance with the United States." In the end, Eisenhower sided with the argument forwarded by Dulles; however, the president also clarified that any military intervention "should be qualified by a clear reference to the fact that our vital interests were deemed to be at stake."[52]

On September 5, 1956 Eisenhower approved a "Statement of Policy on U.S. Policy in Mainland Southeast Asia," otherwise known as NSC-5612/1. From the outset, the document underscored the complex geopolitics of the region: "Since mainland Southeast Asia does not represent a unified area, courses of action must generally be determined in the light of widely varying country situations." That said, the document continued, the "basic objectives and directions" of U.S. national security policy should be established on a regional basis. In other words, the NSC recognized the interconnectivity of policymaking and that, broadly conceived, "the national security of the United States would be endangered by Communist domination of mainland Southeast Asia, whether achieved by overt aggression, subversion, or a political and economic offensive." More concisely, "The loss to Communist control to any single free country would encourage tendencies toward accommodation by the rest" and that "the loss of the entire area would have a seriously adverse impact on the U.S. position elsewhere in the Far East." This, in turn, would "have severe economic consequences for many nations of the free world, add significant resources to the Communist bloc in rice, rubber, tin and other minerals, and could result in severe economic and political pressures on Japan and India for accommodation to the Communist bloc." Given the region's importance, therefore, it was concluded that "U.S. policies must seek to build sufficient strength in the area at least to identify aggression, suppress subversion, prevent Communist political and economic domination, and assist the non-Communist governments to consolidate their domestic positions." Notably, NSC-5612/1 forwarded America's willingness to act unilaterally, even toward neutral governments, in defense of its national security interests. Thus, while the United States would "make clear its own devotion to the principle of collective security" and, in the event of communist aggression, "the provisions of the UN Charter or the SEATO Treaty" would be invoked, the United States would "not forgo necessary action [on] behalf of such a state or states because of the possibility that other allies might be loath to participate or to furnish more than token military forces." The United States effectively positioned itself as the exception to the geopolitical norm, that is, to assume prerogative to both side-step international treaties and subvert the territorial integrity of sovereign states if American interests abroad were threatened. Sihanouk implicitly was targeted. As specified in the document, it would be U.S. policy "to encourage individuals and groups in Cambodia who oppose dealing with the Communist bloc and who would serve to broaden the political power base in Cambodia." With a pledge to "provide modest military aid for indigenous armed forces capable of assuring internal security," the Eisenhower administration affirmed its objective to "maintain Cambodia's independence and to reverse the drift toward pro-Communist neutrality."[53] In short, the United States declared its openness to support dissident armed movements in Cambodia deemed to be anticommunist in orientation.[54]

This is not to suggest that the Eisenhower administration was actively seeking to depose Sihanouk; rather, a coup against the prince remained one option among many to achieve America's regional and global objectives. Sihanouk, for the moment, remained for many U.S. officials the best means to particular ends. Consequently, several attempts were made to bring Sihanouk back into the pro-Western fold. In February 1957, for example, Carl Strom, who replaced McClintock as U.S. ambassador to Cambodia, acknowledged that "there can be no question but that the Communists have made considerable headway with Sihanouk by inviting him to [Beijing], Warsaw, Moscow, Prague, and also Belgrade." And while Sihanouk had made state visits to noncommunist countries, the balance was decisively tipped in

118 / Bordering War

favor of the Soviet bloc. However, Strom explained, "We cannot in the long run sulk and refuse to compete to a certain extent with our enemies. While we cannot flatter him the way they do, there are many things we can do, and have failed so far to do, to impress him with our desire for peace, our economic strength, our democratic institutions and our friendship for his country."[55] Such overtures would include formal state visits and the provision of military assistance.

Ironically, the need to oust Sihanouk was articulated most strongly by Ngo Dinh Nhu, brother of South Vietnam's President Ngo Dinh Diem. For several years relations between Cambodia and South Vietnam had deteriorated and, with Washington's support firmly behind Saigon, the moment for political action seemed opportune. In mid-November 1958 Ngo Dinh Nhu spoke with U.S. officials, including the U.S. ambassador to South Vietnam, Eldridge Dubrow, on the possibility of replacing Sihanouk. Dubrow rejected the South Vietnamese overture, though, on the grounds that the removal of the popular prince would "probably be unsuccessful and would only enhance his prestige." That said, Dubrow conceded that "we had been thinking about the matter quite seriously."[56]

Perhaps it was this latter admission that propelled the South Vietnamese to move forward, as two attempts to remove Sihanouk were made in early 1959. First up was an ill-fated challenge by Sam Sary, a longtime member of the Sangkum and a close advisor to Sihanouk. The proximate cause was apparently personal. Since 1957 Sam Sary served as Cambodian ambassador to the United Kingdom. However, in 1958 he was accused of beating a Cambodian woman who had been his mistress; in light of the scandal, Sihanouk recalled the ambassador. On his return, Sam Sary conspired to remove Sihanouk. The plot involved establishing an opposition party, an armed insurrection near the borders, efforts to produce insecurity in the countryside, and an uprising in Phnom Penh. With foreknowledge of the attempted coup, Sihanouk was able to stop the effort. In turn, Sihanouk accused both the South Vietnamese and Thai governments of supporting the "Bangkok plot," as the incident became known. Also suspected, both by Cambodian and French officials, was U.S. involvement; the Eisenhower administration, predictably, denied any knowledge of the conspiracy.[57] A second attempt to remove Sihanouk materialized on February 20 when Dap Chhuon, a warlord in northwest Cambodia, declared his intent to overthrow

Sihanouk. Similar to Sam Sary, Dap Chhuon was not acting alone. He had been provided with money, arms, and radio equipment by both South Vietnam and Thailand. In response, Sihanouk deployed troops to Siem Reap and captured Dap Chhuon's forces. Initially, Dap Chhuon escaped but was captured on March 3 and apparently died of wounds inflicted during his capture.[58] U.S. officials, once again, denied any knowledge or culpability.

On February 21 U.S. Undersecretary of State Christian Herter sent a telegram to the American embassy in Phnom Penh, counseling officials to underscore that the United States was "not in [the] slightest degree involved [in any] alleged Cambodian coup plots." In addition, all officials were to maintain that the "US position against foreign interference [in the] domestic affairs of other countries [was] well known and [a] matter of record." On that point, Herter emphasized that the "US [was] not in [a] position [to] obtain accurate information [of] foreign meddling, in any, in coup plots [in] Cambodia" and that the United States was "not privy [to] intrigue [of] this nature" given the United States' well-known practice of noninterference. As such, it was America's contention that any rumors of U.S. complicity in the coups were "inspired by efforts [of] our enemies to destroy [the] mutual confidence between Cambodia and [the] US."[59] In Phnom Penh, however, the swift denial by the Eisenhower administration rang hollow. Sihanouk was suspicious of American complicity and duplicity. Indeed, Sihanouk instructed his ambassador to the United States, Nong Kimny, to inform U.S. officials that the Cambodians had in their possession documents "proving that a plot against the government and the Throne existed." Tactfully, in his dealings with American officials, Nong Kimny downplayed U.S. involvement but did express Sihanouk's concern that if U.S. authorities were aware of the plot, they should have passed this information to the Cambodian government.[60]

U.S. officials were in fact aware of the plots against Sihanouk. That they failed to prevent these attempts or even to inform Sihanouk were based in part on practical geopolitical considerations. As Strom relayed to the U.S. State Department on February 16—four days *prior* to the Dap Chhuon plot—the "question of relative worthiness of Vietnam and Cambodia to receive U.S. support has beclouded [the] real issue for months." And while the general consensus was that South Vietnam was "clearly the more worthy," U.S. officials also recognized that "the Western objective of denying

120 / Bordering War

all of Southeast Asia to Communist control cannot be achieved without [the] establishment of some modus vivendi among Thailand, Cambodia, [South] Vietnam, but particularly between [South] Vietnam and Cambodia." It was well understood, however, that both the Thai and the South Vietnamese governments suspected Sihanouk of procommunist leanings; as such, the prospect of a communist-controlled Cambodia posed a significant threat to America's security interests in Southeast Asia. Against this backdrop, Strom explained, the United States was in possession of information regarding the plots against Sihanouk but did not support these operations. Strom reaffirmed that any move against Sihanouk by Thailand or South Vietnam would almost certainly be matched by "a flood of protest notes from [Beijing], Moscow and Afro-Asian capitals." In addition, Strom stressed that the "threat of Red Chinese military intervention" remained "lurking in the background." Accordingly, the U.S. ambassador recommended that Washington "insist in a most categorical manner that [the South Vietnamese government] break off all relations with [the] Dap Chhuon conspiracy . . . and that [South Vietnam] take positive steps for settlement of its principal differences with Cambodia."[61]

By September, U.S. involvement in the repeated coups against Sihanouk was undeniable, and the fallout would, as David Chandler details, cast a shadow on U.S.-Cambodian relations for years to come. On the one hand, any attempt by U.S. officials to place an anticommunist ally inside Cambodia lost momentum, while on the other hand, Sihanouk became permanently distrustful of American intentions. His suspiciousness would later play into the hands of the Vietnamese communists.[62] The Eisenhower administration, however, never publicly or formally acknowledged having intelligence on or complicity in any of the coup attempts. Moreover, the United States was unwilling to actively restrain the South Vietnamese in their dealings with Sihanouk. As Herter explained following the Dap Chhuon attempt, "We frankly doubt US capacity to stop all [South Vietnamese] action against Sihanouk over [an] indefinite period of time unless we are prepared to use sanctions such as aid reduction to force Diem [to] accept our position [on] this matter." This was not possible, though, as any reductions in economic or military aid would weaken the Diem government and "lay the ground work for increased Communist influence in South Vietnam." Strom conceded also that Sihanouk's attitude and willingness to work with the communist bloc "completely undermines [the] efforts of [the] US and others to promote friendly relations between Cambodia and [its] neighbors."[63]

Since NSC-5612/1 had been adopted, all U.S. military operations in Cambodia were to be conducted in the context of broader objectives, namely "to prevent the countries of Southeast Asia from passing into or becoming economically dependent upon the Communist bloc; to persuade them that their best interests lie in greater cooperation and stronger affiliations with the rest of the free world; and to assist them to develop toward stable, free, representative governments with the will and ability to resist Communism from within and without, and thereby to contribute to the strengthening of the free world." Consequently, in support of a noncommunist Cambodia, "U.S. military aid should be continued as long as Cambodian leaders demonstrate a will to resist internal Communist subversion and to carry out a policy of maintaining Cambodian independence." On that point, America's "purpose" was to "deny Cambodia to Communism" while "not expecting a greater show of gratitude or even substantially improved cooperation on the part of the Cambodian Government."[64] Notably, U.S. officials recognized that Cambodia, in addition to its important geostrategic position in Southeast Asia, was a bellwether for America's dealings with peripheral states. As McClintock described it in 1957, "The application of U.S. policy to a neutralist state of seeking to aid it to obtain its sovereign independence has a scope much wider than Cambodia." "In this small country," McClintock explained, "there is found in microcosm all the elements with which the Free World must deal in adjusting its policies to the great anti-colonial revolution which in varying degrees has been completed or is in the process of occurrence in the zone from Southeast Asia through the continent of Africa, and including the Middle East." Thus far, McClintock concluded, in Cambodia "we have been able to apply a policy which although perhaps not as desirable as that of perfecting systems of collective security, has at least demonstrated the advantage of utilizing the inert weight of neutrality as a counterpoise to communism."[65] In the aftermath of the ill-fated coup attempts, however, America's credibility both within Cambodia and beyond was very much in jeopardy. Consequently, the recurring political frictions between Phnom Penh and Saigon forced U.S. officials to recalibrate the basic American policy toward Cambodia.

122 / Bordering War

In March 1960 U.S. officials grudgingly accepted that "Sihanouk was a much more astute politician and had much greater control over the country than when our policy on Southeast Asia was written." Indeed, it was concluded that "we must direct our policy toward getting along with Sihanouk, who has survived a number of attempts to unseat him."[66] During a meeting of the National Security Council held in July, Allen Dulles echoed this assessment, noting that "in Cambodia we continue to have to deal with Sihanouk who is a difficult character." The problem was exacerbated by the fact that South Vietnam was "still planning anti-Sihanouk activities." Markedly, the Diem government expressed its own frustrations with Sihanouk's apparent procommunist proclivities, inasmuch as South Vietnam accused the prince of allowing Vietnamese communists to use "Cambodia as a staging area." As Dulles warned, both South Vietnam and Thailand were watching intently how the United States extended support, including military aid, to Sihanouk. Indeed, as Herter explained, both Saigon and Bangkok worried that any military equipment the United States provided to Cambodia would be used against them instead of against communist China.[67]

On July 25 the National Security Council adopted NSC-6012, its "Statement of Policy on U.S. Policy in Mainland Southeast Asia." Much of this document resembled previous statements, notably NSC-5612/1 and NSC 5809. U.S. diplomacy toward any individual state would remain regional in scope; this aligned with the long-standing presumption that the geopolitics in the region were inextricably interconnected. Thus, while South Vietnam remained the central focus of U.S. national security concerns, it was not possible to support Saigon without focusing on political conditions in neighboring Cambodia and Laos. Consequently, "In order to assist in maintaining Cambodia's independence and in curbing its tendency to increased orientation toward the Sino-Soviet Bloc," it was necessary to "demonstrate continued friendly U.S. support for Cambodia's independence, understanding of its policy of neutrality, and concern for its economic and social progress." To that end, "in shaping [any] particular course of action in Cambodia," it was U.S. policy to "devote special efforts toward developing Sihanouk's understanding of U.S. policies and of the U.S. position in Southeast Asia." This, in turn, required substantial effort to "impress on the governments of neighboring countries the importance of repairing their relations with Cambodia."[68] Effectively, policymakers in Washington neither favored nor trusted Sihanouk; their concerns centered on whether Sihanouk would open the door to external communist agitators. Indeed, few officials in Washington gave any credence to the prospect of a localized communist movement flaring up inside Cambodia. They were wrong.

Seeing Red

The Khmer communist movement has its origins not in the writings of Karl Marx or the persona of Joseph Stalin. Rather, the movement traces its beginnings to the Second World War. Under Vichy French colonial rule, numerous Khmer Issarak (Free Khmer) groups formed to challenge both French authority and Japanese occupation.[69] Unbounded by ideology, liberation was the common goal. Where these disparate groups differed mostly was in practice, not purpose. Some Khmer revolutionaries, for example, agreed to collaborate with their Vietnamese counterparts, while others were opposed; some supported Sihanouk, while others sought to eliminate the monarchy as a whole. Later, when the Franco–Viet Minh War broke out in 1946, Vietnamese communists turned to Cambodia's revolutionaries for assistance. Strongly influenced by Soviet advisors, the Vietnamese concluded that only the total defeat of the French and their expulsion from the entirety of French Indochina could assure their independence. To that end, Viet Minh officials told their Khmer counterparts that they could play a small but vital part in liberating Indochina, as part of a greater international movement capable of delivering equity and justice among the downtrodden nations.[70] Soon, Vietnamese communists gained greater influence among the Khmer liberation movement and began to use Cambodian territory in their own war against the French.[71]

In 1951, Vietnamese communists helped establish the Khmer People's Revolutionary Party (KPRP).[72] Modeled after the Vietnamese Communist Party, the KPRP would later form the nucleus of the Communist Party of Kampuchea (CPK), derided by Sihanouk as the "Khmer Rouge," or "Red Khmer." In the early 1950s, however, the fledgling movement struggled both to find its identity and to chart its own path. Hanoi did not support revolutionary movements in the abstract but instead viewed these with an eye toward its own national security. As such, the Vietnamese communists denounced Cambodian ideas of nationalism and local ways of organizing

124 / Bordering War

society as "feudal."[73] In practice, therefore the KPRP was subservient to both Hanoi and to the overall Vietnamese communist movement, as the KPRP's mandate was to fight imperialism broadly and *not* to wage communist revolution in Cambodia.

When Sihanouk secured independence in 1953, the future of the Khmer communist movement was unclear. Sihanouk's crusade for independence had obviated, in the minds of many Khmer resistance fighters, the need for revolution. During the war against the French, most Khmer—including several members of the KRPR—were not fighting *for* communism; rather, they were fighting *against* French colonialism. The subsequent Geneva Accords dealt a further blow to the Khmer communists. Whereas Vietnam was divided following the convention, the Accords specified that Cambodia remain unified; in other words, unlike the artificial division of Vietnam, there was no recognition of any formal communist element in Cambodia. In addition, neither the Soviet Union nor China extended recognition to the KRPR. And, in fact, there was no Cambodian communist representative allowed to participate at the conference. This meant, in practical terms, KRPR cadres had no territory to seek safety in or a base from which to regroup. Instead, Cambodian communists had two options. On the one hand, they could lay down their arms and participate in the national elections scheduled for 1956: and in fact, many men and women did, forming the Pracheachon Party to challenge, through democratic means, Sihanouk's rule. Notably, many of these men and women would also secretively recruit and train potential party members. On the other hand, Khmer communists could travel to North Vietnam, where they would receive military and political training in anticipation of a return to Cambodia when conditions warranted. Eventually, between one thousand and two thousand Khmer communists chose this path and would remain in North Vietnam until the early 1970s, to return only following Nixon's incursion into Cambodia and the start of the Cambodian Civil War.[74]

Cambodia would remain a central factor in Hanoi's approach to the anticipated struggle against the United States. In particular, the North Vietnamese leadership understood that the struggle was regional in scope and would most certainly encompass—at a minimum—the neighboring states of Laos and Cambodia. To that end, the leadership in Hanoi required the support of communist parties in Laos and Cambodia.[75] In practice, this meant that communist activities in these two countries remained deferential to the primary cause of Vietnamese unification. Indeed, North Vietnamese support for both Laos and Cambodia would pivot on their geostrategic importance insofar as political or military conditions necessitated. Paradoxically, for Hanoi, the value of Cambodia rested in its neutrality. This seemingly contradictory conclusion was derived from two interconnected determinations. In support of their southern counterparts, the NLF, Hanoi required access through Cambodia's eastern territories—the Ho Chi Minh and Sihanouk Trails. This objective was best achieved through Cambodian neutrality. If, for example, Sihanouk aligned with the West, it was possible that the United States would establish a sizeable military presence in support of its defense of South Vietnam. Conversely, if Sihanouk aligned with the communist bloc, the United States might intervene militarily in Cambodia to prevent Cambodia toppling as the first domino. Thus, in an ironic twist of geopolitical reasoning, Sihanouk's adherence to neutrality played into the strategic calculus of the North Vietnamese. Communist expansion into Cambodia, for Hanoi, was never the objective. For U.S. officials, as detailed earlier, Sihanouk's neutrality appeared to threaten their objectives in South Vietnam.

The Khmer Rouge, strangely, was caught in the middle. Many Khmer Rouge cadres wanted to overthrow the Sihanouk regime and establish their own government. To do so, however, they required the material and logistical support of their Vietnamese counterparts. This support, though, was not forthcoming, for Hanoi assessed that the Khmer Rouge was ill-prepared and ill-equipped to exert control over the country. In the event Sihanouk was deposed, Vietnamese officials surmised that swift U.S. military intervention would follow and, with it, the imposition of a pro-Western government in Phnom Penh. It was imperative, therefore, that Sihanouk remain in power. For Hanoi's leadership, the Khmer Rouge were expressly prohibited from challenging or subverting Sihanouk's authority.[76] In hindsight, Sihanouk's geopolitical appraisal was correct. His most immediate threat was not from Moscow, Beijing, or even Hanoi; nor did the budding communist movement in Cambodia pose a significant threat. And while it remains speculative whether Sihanouk had much firsthand knowledge of Hanoi's strategy, it is true as Sihanouk surmised that the pro-Western governments in South Vietnam and Thailand, both supported militarily and financially

126 / Bordering War

by the United States, constituted more pressing risks both to his rule and to the stability and security of his country.

Since the late 1940s, most U.S. officials held firm to their conviction that the global communist threat was monolithic and that the Soviet Union was a masterful puppeteer manipulating weak and vulnerable states on the global stage. Within the communist bloc, of course, officials from Beijing to Hanoi to Moscow were exceptionally sensitive to the numerous fault lines that threatened to undermine any solidarity in purpose and action. The Cambodian communist movement, underappreciated at the time even by Hanoi, was greatly splintered. In part, disagreements among the Khmer communists resulted from differences in personal experiences and, by extension, in their expectations moving forward. Some Khmer, for example, were long-standing veterans of the communist movement; they had trained and organized with their Vietnamese counterparts and were, accordingly, more receptive to the strategy promoted by Hanoi: namely to align at least temporarily with Sihanouk. Other members were adamantly opposed to Sihanouk and distrustful of their Vietnamese counterparts. Beyond these considerations, Khmer communists had internal disagreements both in ideology and in strategy; effectively, the early years of the communist movement in Cambodia were beset by myriad factions and alliances that severely curbed its expansion and effectiveness.[77]

That the movement was beset by factionalism and ideological differences enabled a small but determined group of individuals to steadily take control.[78] On this point, U.S. Ambassador Trimble was prescient. When, in March 1962, Trimble made reference to a "steadily growing group of 'young intellectuals'—French-educated, leftist-oriented and personally ambitious," he was spot on.[79] From the late 1950s onward, more radical members of the fragmented movement, including Pol Pot, Son Sen, Khieu Samphan, Ieng Sary, and Ieng Thirith, strategically placed themselves in positions of power. Unlike other veteran revolutionaries who for years struggled against the French for Cambodia's independence, these men and women were political upstarts and revolutionary novices. Recently returned from university studies in Paris, many harbored dreams of the purity of revolution. Indeed, as May Ebihara explains, the Khmer Rouge did not emerge out of the grass roots—like many revolutions elsewhere it was organized by educated leaders from urban or upper-peasant backgrounds—but it obviously required control over much of the rural population.[80] Simply put, the Khmer Rouge was composed mainly of peasants, but it was not a peasant-led revolutionary movement.

In 1960, delegates of the moribund KPRP met secretively in a Phnom Penh railway yard to elect new leaders and to draft a political agenda. The meeting marked the first convention of the KPRP in nine years and also the first concerted effort of a group of Khmer communists to step outside Hanoi's considerable shadow. Cadres agreed upon a platform that openly departed from Hanoi's position by declaring Sihanouk and the "ruling feudal class" to be "the most important enemy of the Kampuchean revolution."[81] Subsequently, veteran revolutionary Tou Samouth was elected as party secretary, with Nuon Chea and Pol Pot elected, respectively, as the second and third highest-ranking members. Within two years, however, Tou Samouth was dead, killed apparently by Sihanouk's secret police while detained and tortured under the authority of Defense Minister Lon Nol. Tou Samouth's death opened the door for Pol Pot and his allies to assume greater control of the movement, and sometime in late February or early March 1963, Pol Pot was formally installed as secretary general.[82] Civil war against Sihanouk was not imminent; but it was in the air. Pol Pot's vanguard, known simply as Angkar, was formed.

An Uneasy Geopolitical Relationship

In the Kennedy White House, U.S. objectives in Cambodia vis-à-vis Vietnam remained very similar to those of the previous administration and, oddly, conformed to those of Hanoi. Under Kennedy, U.S. foreign policy was "based on a simple precept—to assist Cambodia to remain independent."[83] This did not mean that Cambodia should be pro-Western; rather, U.S. objectives could be met so long as Cambodia was not procommunist. A major stumbling block impacting U.S.-Cambodian relations, however, centered on the use of Cambodian territory by Vietnamese communist insurgents, South Vietnamese armed forces, and increasing numbers of U.S. covert operatives. The Diem administration maintained that substantial numbers of enemy personnel—coupled with voluminous amounts of military supplies—were moving across Cambodia to infiltrate South Vietnam; in addition, these enemy forces, when threatened by the South Vietnamese military, would find sanctuary across the border. Sihanouk, for his part,

128 / Bordering War

agreed that *some* Vietnamese communists were active in Cambodia but countered that the main threat to the stability of his government was South Vietnamese forces operating illegally inside Cambodian territory. These widely divergent positions were mirrored within the American intelligence community. Overall, there was a general recognition among both U.S. civilian and military analysts that the Ho Chi Minh Trail traversed Cambodian territory and that a separate offshoot, the so-called Sihanouk Trail, was being utilized. Beyond this agreement, however, there remained a considerable chasm between those analysts who concluded that Cambodia was a key sanctuary and logistics conduit for communist activities and those who downplayed its importance. Trimble, for example, held that South Vietnamese claims were "grossly exaggerated." For Trimble, the argument that the Vietnamese communist use of Cambodia was of a "significant scale" to account for the "growing insecurity" of South Vietnam was simply an excuse forwarded by Diem to hide his inability to "effectively cope" with the communist insurgents. Indeed, for Trimble, "Sihanouk's detestation and fear of [the] Vietnamese and in particular [the] Viet Minh" obviated any outright support by the prince. Thus, while the ambassador could "not deny [the] existence of some limited Viet Cong activity in Cambodia," he affirmed that he had "yet to see convincing evidence that [the] type and scale of such activities are responsible to any significant degree for [the] growing insecurity" in South Vietnam. Consequently, Trimble counseled, it was unlikely "that new border control measures would succeed in curbing such activities to any appreciable degree."[84]

Several key advisors within the U.S. military establishment also downplayed the threat Cambodia posed to South Vietnam. On November 15, 1961, General Edward Scherrer, chief of MAAG, Cambodia, sent a telegram to Admiral Henry Felt, commander-in-chief, Pacific Command, that "with the limited means available, the US Ambassador and his agencies, including MAAG, have continuously investigated, to include ground and aerial reconnaissance, allegations of Viet Cong bases and training areas in Cambodia." "We have found none," he concluded, "we believe there are none." That said, the general added: "In border areas where surveillance is extremely difficult due to rugged heavily forested terrain and where FANK is very thinly spread because of limited forces, there are undoubtedly cases of clandestine infiltration of individuals or small groups; but these are not with the consent or approval" of the Cambodian government or military. He cautioned, though, that "such violations are likely to increase as the Viet Cong build up and increase operations into [South Vietnam] from southern Laos."[85]

Unsurprisingly, Walt Rostow was of the opinion that Cambodia's porous borders posed a significant risk to South Vietnam. "We are quite confident," the national security advisor informed Kennedy, "that Cambodia is being used as a safe haven for [the] Viet Cong."[86] General Edward Lansdale, likewise, concluded that enemy operations in Cambodia posed a significant threat to the security of South Vietnam. In response to Scherrer's telegram, for example, Lansdale quipped, "What is disturbing is that we used to get similar reports from Laos." He pondered, "There was a time, not long ago, when nobody could find a Pathet Lao in the country and it became rather popular around town to poo-poo the idea that there were any Communist guerrillas in Laos. Now we get a similar poo-pooing from Cambodia." The general continued, "I wonder if these folks who go looking really know what a Communist guerrilla looks like? In Cambodia, I feel certain that he looks, talks, and claims to be just like the other folks on rubber plantations, in villages, and in the rice paddies." He concluded, "Wouldn't it be a good thing for the Chief of MAAG-Vietnam, who has access to Viet Cong prisoners, to provide some clues to Chief of MAAG-Cambodia? It might be okay for American civilians to be lulled into a real lotus-land picture, but our military need to look at the scene with hard realism."[87]

Sihanouk, understandably, was suspicious of U.S. intentions. Indeed, while U.S. officials warned of the evils of communism, Sihanouk continued to worry about his proximate neighbors, Thailand and South Vietnam, and their military patron, the United States. During the early months of the Kennedy administration, for example, Sihanouk renewed his public criticisms of the United States and threatened to sever diplomatic and economic ties between the two countries. Indeed, in October 1961 Sihanouk pronounced, "The U.S. is too stupid; they try to buy other people with money, but they have always failed. This is because they are stupid and are cheated by such [leaders] as [Thai Prime Minister] Sarit [Thanarat] and Diem." In turn, NSC staff member Robert Johnson retorted that Sihanouk was simply reviving "the old allegations that the U.S. was using Thailand and Vietnam in an effort to overturn him."[88] Days later, Johnson mocked the

130 / Bordering War

Cambodian leader, charging that Sihanouk "is terribly sensitive to criticism and to the possibility that the traditional enemies of Cambodia, Thailand and Vietnam, are plotting against him."[89] The reality was that conversations to overthrow Sihanouk were ongoing, especially in Saigon, and U.S. officials were aware of many of these plots.

As the communist insurgency in South Vietnam intensified and Diem proved ineffective in meeting this development, the question of Cambodia's territory became more pressing. By March 1962, Trimble acknowledged that the "Communist threat in Cambodia, in terms of pressures operating within the country, is limited at the present time" but there was a local communist front group (discussed in greater detail below) and there was the "steadily growing group of 'young intellectuals'—French-educated, leftist-oriented and personally ambitious." For the moment, Sihanouk commanded the "loyalty of the overwhelming portion of the Cambodian population" but what would happen, Trimble asked, "if Sihanouk should disappear from the scene?" This was, in fact, the problem that plagued U.S. policymakers from the mid-1950s onward: Sihanouk was volatile, impulsive, and unpredictable; but he also was hugely popular among the Cambodian people. Any effort to overthrow Sihanouk would likely make a bad situation worse. To that end, it was better to support the prince—however unpalatable—and attempt to align U.S. foreign policy with Sihanouk's brand of neutrality. Trimble clarified that "as Sihanouk sees it, the present balance of power in Southeast Asia safeguards Cambodia's independence." On the one hand, Sihanouk agreed that communist China posed an existential threat to Southeast Asia but, on the other hand, he believed also that the pro-Western countries of Southeast Asia posed an imminent threat to Cambodia. Thus, while Sihanouk remained anticommunist in practice, he was unwilling to align Cambodia "defensively with its non-Communist neighbors to forestall a Communist victory."[90]

In November 1963 Sihanouk renounced U.S. military and economic aid and, in 1965, he severed diplomatic relations. These were remarkable moves. Between 1955 and 1963, Cambodia received approximately $400 million from the United States, comprising 30 percent of Sihanouk's defense budget and 14 percent of its total budget.[91] In fact, the amount of U.S. aid surpassed the combined amount of aid provided by China and the Soviet Union.

However, Sihanouk worried—rightfully so—that U.S. aid programs were creating a military class in Cambodia dependent on the United States and, more broadly, that Cambodia was becoming an American client state.[92] Even more pressing, Sihanouk feared that Washington was supporting right-wing guerrillas. Formed from the remnants of the Khmer Issarak in the 1950s, the Khmer Serei (also meaning "Free Khmer") comprised paramilitary units made up of ethnic Khmer who were recruited, paid, and armed by the Thai and the South Vietnamese to overthrow Sihanouk.[93]

Sihanouk's long-held suspicions were correct. When the CIA and U.S. Army Special Forces initiated the Civilian Irregular Defense Group (CIDG) program in 1961, they enlisted the aid of the Khmer Serei to patrol South Vietnam's borders to prevent infiltration from Cambodia and Laos.[94] Sihanouk claimed, however, that he held evidence that the Khmer Serei also actively working to undermine his government and to replace him with someone more pliable to Bangkok, Saigon, and Washington. The Kennedy administration, in turn, downplayed or denied any U.S. support of the Khmer Serei, going so far as to conclude that the paramilitary group posed "no significant military or political threat to [the] Cambodian government."[95] Indeed, it was the determination of the Kennedy administration that any anti-Sihanouk activities on the part of the Khmer Serei actually threatened America's position. Sihanouk adhered to a policy of neutrality and, for the moment, that satisfied U.S. objectives in South Vietnam. As detailed in a telegram from the State Department to the U.S. Embassy in Vietnam, Khmer Serei activities "represent at best pinpricks against Sihanouk, but he reacts to them in [a] manner which may create serious world crisis in [Southeast Asia]."[96] To that end, U.S. officials ostensibly worked to curb Thai and South Vietnamese support of the Khmer Serei.[97]

The degree of American involvement with the Khmer Serei in 1963 remains murky.[98] In a State Department telegram, for example, U.S. officials acknowledged that the United States had "of course given a variety of arms and communications equipment to the [South] Vietnamese and Thai Governments just as it has to the Cambodians." As such, when confronted with accusations that the United States was supporting the Khmer Serei, the State Department bemoaned that "evidence must be specific—exactly when and where did the Americans give the arms and radios as alleged?"[99]

132 / Bordering War

Months later, however, all doubts were removed. The U.S. Embassy in Saigon would confirm (secretly) that "as many as 1,000 of the 1,677 ethnic Cambodians receiving training in Vietnamese Special Forces—which were supervised by U.S. officials through the CIA-funded CIDG program—were probably members of the anti-Sihanouk Khmer Serei dissidents."[100] Moreover, U.S. officials acknowledged that Americans were actively sanctioning military raids on Cambodian border villages.[101]

Until his own death at the hands of an assassin on November 22, 1963, Kennedy and his staff hoped to resolve the seemingly insurmountable issues separating the United States and Cambodia.[102] In private conversations, several officials reflected on the steadily deteriorating conditions and the implications for U.S. national security concerns in the region. Averill Harriman, then serving as undersecretary of state for political affairs, worried that they had "messed things up." As such, in an effort to mend bridges, plans were developed for Acheson to visit Phnom Penh. As NSC staff member Michael Forrestal explained to McGeorge Bundy, "It seems to me imperative that we make some personal gesture toward [Sihanouk] soon. If we do not, we may have to make some very much more expensive gestures to salvage the West's position."[103] Kennedy was killed, and the planned visit never happened.

Kennedy's death marked a transition in U.S. policy toward South Vietnam and, by corollary, toward Cambodia. On November 23 and 24, newly sworn-in President Lyndon Johnson convened a series of meetings with his cabinet to discuss the situation in Vietnam. Conversations explicitly related to Cambodia were minimal and considered mostly in relation to their effect on the new South Vietnamese government. State Department officials, for example, informed Johnson that "Cambodian-Vietnamese relations remain[ed] poor" and that Sihanouk was "upset about the activities of Cambodian dissidents in Vietnam and Thailand." For its part, the Saigon government was "concerned about Viet Cong use of Cambodian territory."[104] In time, Johnson would have to address both of these diplomatic problems. His approach, however, would continue to center almost entirely on military conditions in South Vietnam and less on the political situation in Cambodia. As Johnson explained in a memorandum to General Maxwell Taylor, chair of the Joint Chiefs of Staff, "The more I look at it, the more it is clear to me that South Vietnam is our most critical military area right now." A similar memorandum was sent to John McCone, director of the CIA, in which Johnson reiterated that "the more I look at South Vietnam, the more I think we must be very quick and firm in getting the best possible men on the job."[105] Cambodia would remain in the shadows of U.S. policymaking but would also cast a dark shadow on America's defense of South Vietnam.

[4]

ATERRITORIAL WARS

Given the likely intensity of the conflict in the weeks and months ahead along the Cambodian frontier, we shall not be able to live with this sanctuary.

—Walt Rostow, Memorandum to President Johnson

Throughout the Cold War, the overall direction of American foreign policy was that of containment: to limit, if not roll back, the geographic expansion of Soviet-led communism.[1] Explicitly formulated in spatial and territorial terms, this geopolitical doctrine had a particular military counterpart. As Simon Dalby explains, the Second World War was marked by the continuous front line, and success in military campaigning was related to the conquest of territory. "Liberation" from the Axis powers of Germany, Japan, and Italy was a spatial process of the advance of U.S. and allied military power. However, Dalby expounds that this understanding of the representation of U.S. power led to the formulation of "national security" in terms of forward military defense, understood in territorial terms. Simply put, according to Dalby, "The relations of space and power came to be understood in terms of distance providing security, and influence requiring the military occupation of territory."[2]

America's war in Indochina was not a conventional territorial war. Unlike the Second World War, there were no front lines; nor was the objective to secure and occupy territory. Indeed, from a tactical standpoint, territory was held or relinquished seemingly on an ad-hoc basis. Victory, as defined by U.S. officials, was never dependent upon the capture of Hanoi. This is not to imply, however, that the war was not territorial. In fact, America's military strategy was explicitly territorial, although this cannot be fully appreciated without placing military planning within the overall scope of America's

135

136 / Aterritorial Wars

grand strategy during the Cold War. As noted, U.S. foreign policy was predicated in large part on the territorial containment of communism; by extension, American objectives *in South Vietnam* were to prevent communism from crossing the borders of South Vietnam. In other words, America's strategy in South Vietnam was decidedly territorial, in the sense that U.S. objectives were fundamentally about securing the territorial integrity of South Vietnam. For U.S. planners, internal operations inside South Vietnam, including the various pacification programs launched throughout the 1960s, were doomed to failure until and unless South Vietnam's borderlands were secured. As explained by the U.S. Joint Chiefs of Staff in October 1966, it was necessary to "continue to press the enemy militarily, improve pacification programs, and attain a military posture" that could be maintained indefinitely. Of vital importance was the necessity to install, expand, and defend barriers to impede enemy infiltration.[3] Paradoxically, though, American objectives *in Cambodia* were *aterritorial,* marked by a geopolitical logic not confined to territorial aggrandizement. For U.S. policymakers, the objective vis-à-vis the government in Phnom Penh was never to control, occupy, or secure Cambodian space; instead, the intent was always and necessarily to secure the borders of South Vietnam. As Walt Rostow cautioned Johnson in December 1967, more aggressive military action against the Vietnamese communist use of Cambodian territory was required. "It is essential," the special assistant to the president explained, "that we make it clear to Sihanouk that we cannot live with these arrangements and he had better do something about them."[4] Accordingly, in this chapter I detail the geopolitical reasoning of U.S. policymakers under the presidential administration of Lyndon B. Johnson as they struggled to devise a military strategy that could effectively compel Sihanouk into compliance without risking an expanded war in Indochina.

Hidden Wars

From the start of overt U.S. military operations, U.S. military advisors voiced their concern about South Vietnam's porous border with Cambodia. On November 12, 1965, the Joint Chiefs of Staff (JCS) informed Secretary of Defense McNamara of their concern that the People's Liberation Armed Forces (PLAF) were using "Cambodia for a source of supply, for a sanctuary, and for temporary military facilities." For example, as detailed in their memorandum, "Supplies in the form of weapons, ammunition, medicine, and chemicals used in munitions [had] been captured during actual infiltration into South Vietnam (SVN) from Cambodia." In addition, reports from U.S. Special Forces advisors—who had been active in Cambodia for over a year—indicated that the PLAF had "established temporary military facilities, such as rest camps, training areas, hospitals, workshops, and storage depots on Cambodian soil." The JCS report explained further that "although the Cambodian government has been careful not to provide the VC [Viet Cong] military support and has asserted its neutrality . . . Cambodians do permit the use of their territory and resources by the communist insurgents." The memorandum did not indicate that Sihanouk actively collaborated with the Vietnamese communists; however, the JCS did indicate that the use of Cambodian territory was made possible by "some active cooperation with the VC at lower Cambodian Government and military levels, an indifferent attitude by other officials, and the inability or failure of the Government to control or even patrol its frontiers." Notably, in contemporary parlance, the JCS premised that Cambodia was a "failed state"; as such, from their vantage point, conventional rules of engagement were called into question. Based on their understanding, the "Cambodian sanctuary provides the VC with a decided military advantage and has a detrimental effect on the war effort in SVN." And yet, the report continued: "Cambodia is the only contiguous source of VC support against which no action is being taken. Since control of the insurgency [in South Vietnam] involves seeking out and destroying the VC/PAVN [People's Army of Vietnam] forces and their sources of support, the reasons for taking action in this remaining area are militarily clear." Operationally, nine "courses of action" were detailed, including the expansion of covert surveillance missions in Cambodia, diplomatic pressure on the Cambodian government, and over air and/or ground cross-border operations into Cambodia.[5] Essentially, the JCS memorandum underscored the dilemma that marred U.S. policy from the beginning: the disconnect between political objectives and military solutions. Over the next four years, this would plague the Johnson administration.

For members of the JCS, the "military requirements [were] of paramount importance and that forceful action must be taken to stop the use of Cambodian territory for VC logistics and sanctuary despite possible adverse

138 / Aterritorial Wars

political and military reaction."[6] Key individuals within the government agreed also that decisive action in Cambodia or against the Cambodian government was necessary. In response to fighting along the Cambodian–South Vietnamese border near Plei Me, Ambassador Henry Cabot Lodge on November 20 requested that U.S. and ARVN troops be given authorization to "fire on the Viet Cong and the North Vietnamese forces in self-defense, even though they might be on the Cambodian side of this ill-defined border area."[7] During a subsequent telephone conversation with the president, McNamara recommended authorization, noting also that George Ball, McGeorge Bundy, William Bundy, and James Wheeler supported the move. In addition, McNamara recommended that pressure be applied to the United Nations to assemble a coalition force to patrol the border; this had been attempted the previous year, only to be scuttled by Sihanouk.

Johnson consented on both recommendations and two hours later Ball informed the U.S. embassy in Saigon of the decision. Accepting the urgency of "immediate operations into Cambodia," Ball relayed that the White House agreed that both U.S. and South Vietnamese forces "must have all authority necessary for self-defense." Ball also acknowledged the difficulties in drawing hard distinctions between "self-defense" and other military activities. However, the undersecretary of state emphasized that "these distinctions might be most difficult to preserve, but from [a] political standpoint it is essential that this be done." Accordingly, when dealing with the "handling of any press announcement of operations" that might extend into Cambodia, Ball laid out several guidelines. Foremost among these, Ball explained, was the need for plausible deniability. "While location of action should not be stated incorrectly," Ball allowed, "we should avoid as long as possible any express statement that GVN and U.S. forces have been in Cambodia. This might involve stating that exact locations [are] being checked further." In addition, he underscored that "stress should be placed on [the] theme that GVN and/or US forces were under attack and that measures taken were in self-defense. [The] term 'self-defense' should be driven home, and terms such as 'immediate pursuit' or 'hot pursuit' should not be used." Lastly, Ball stressed the need for sensitivity when dealing with Sihanouk; as such, "evidence of physical installations would of course be particularly useful."[8] In other words, material proof of enemy activity should be provided so that U.S. officials could justify their covert military operations.

The decision to authorize covert action into Cambodia under the pretense of self-defense substantially expanded the geography of U.S. military operations. Certainly, limited cross-border operations preceded this moment; indeed, covert teams had been active along the Cambodian border for several years. The difference was that now U.S. combat forces were actively fighting in South Vietnam. Previously, covert operations were motivated by the need to gather intelligence; now, there was a perceived need to aggressively strike at the enemy. Notably, Johnson did not authorize offensive operations into Cambodia, but the implications were clear. As Ball explained, the distinction between "self-defense" and "offense" was a fine line, a line that could be moved easily if required.[9] William Bundy echoed this approach in conversation with Arthur Goldberg, U.S. Representative at the UN on November 21. If (or when) military action extended into Cambodia, Bundy explained, it would be crucial to "stress above all the rationale of self-defense, since our lawyers tell us that any 'hot pursuit' justification does not have, for ground forces, explicit support in international law." In other words, U.S. forces would not cross the border in hot pursuit but instead were "maneuvering . . . into Cambodian territory . . . to defend themselves."[10]

For both U.S. military and civilian officials, the unfolding military strategy in South Vietnam was increasingly mediated by diplomatic relations with Sihanouk. Even in the best of times, relations between the two countries had been strained. In 1963, for example, Sihanouk signed a treaty of friendship with China and cut diplomatic ties with South Vietnam. The prince also terminated all U.S. assistance programs in Cambodia. Concurrently, however, Sihanouk authorized his military to eliminate known or suspected Khmer communists in the country. For many members of the U.S. intelligence community, Sihanouk's actions were both chaotic and contradictory; and indeed, many of his policies were. On that point, the professed neutrality of Sihanouk frustrated U.S. officials who often viewed the prince as mentally unstable in his diplomacy. An intelligence memorandum distributed in December 1965 opined that "the often unfathomable, sometimes senseless and frequently amusing fluctuations which have characterized the day to day conduct of Cambodia's foreign policy over the past 12 years have obscured what, in fact, has been a remarkable coherent and consistent policy." According to this report, "The discrepancy lies in the fact that Cambodia's policy has Prince Sihanouk as both its author and chief

140 / Aterritorial Wars

practitioner. The confusion between style and substance, between neurotic fantasies and logically reasoned arguments . . . has put into question the credibility of Cambodia's foreign policy." Remarkably, U.S. analysts conceded that "the primary motivation of Cambodia's foreign policy is the preservation of Cambodia as a nation state" and that "survival is, in the final analysis, the root policy of all nations." However, in Sihanouk they saw something *different*. According to these experts, "The difference is that Cambodia feels that its continued existence is in real and constant jeopardy" and that "in recent years this preoccupation has been in part an expression of Sihanouk's emotional response to factors beyond his control." U.S. intelligence agents concluded instead that Sihanouk's neutralism was "practical rather than theoretical," in short, motivated less by the principles forwarded by the Non-Aligned Movement than by neurotic prudency. Sihanouk was "no ideologue" but simply attempting to avoid "entanglement in the cold war."[11]

By 1965 relations between Phnom Penh and Washington strained to the point of breaking. The final straw was a border incident that occurred on April 28 when four planes bombed the villages of Phum Chantatep and Moream Tiek in Kompong Cham province. The villages were approximately four kilometers from the South Vietnamese border. A thirteen-year-old boy was killed with several other villagers wounded. In the aftermath, U.S. military attachés confirmed both the attack and the casualties. At first, however, U.S. officials publicly blamed the South Vietnamese air force. In reality, the planes were American. "One of our aircraft dropped bombs on a Cambodian village," Bundy admitted to Johnson, explaining that the only question was "whether we admit it to the Cambodians who are now accusing us of it." Bundy noted that several advisors within the White House believed that the United States should take responsibility and that "there is no real alternative" and "we can't get anyone else to take the responsibility." The entire situation, Bundy bemoaned, was "very irritating." Moving forward, Bundy counseled that "we could, of course, pretend it never happened." Failing that, other responses would be to accept responsibility and offer compensation; or say nothing publicly and wait to see how events played out. In the end, Johnson elected to wait. No apology would be forthcoming and three days later Sihanouk broke diplomatic relations.[12] For Bundy, the break was predictable but inconsequential. He counseled the president:

"We will deal with the air matter by saying that it is still under investigation. . . . More generally, if we get any flak on this air incident, now or later, we will point out in reply that Cambodia has provided a variety of facilities for the Viet Cong over a long period of time and is therefore in a poor position to criticize a single Air Force error, however tragic it is for those who were hit."[13] The accidental bombing of a Cambodian village, the needless death of a young boy, the deliberate disinformation campaign: It all captured in stark relief America's malfeasant attitude and actions toward Sihanouk and Cambodia. From both a moral and legal standpoint, the sovereignty of Cambodia was irrelevant; the premature death of Cambodians an irritant to U.S. national security concerns.

In December the JCS requested that U.S. and South Vietnamese forces be authorized "to take extensive counteraction against VC/PAVN forces in Cambodia." Specifically, they called for authorization to "strike 'known or suspected' troops, lines of communication and bases inside Cambodia by ground forces, including close air support, and by air attacks using B-52." As understood by Assistant Secretary of State William Bundy the proposed escalation of military operations went "considerably beyond the authority requested" and, as such, caution was warranted. Indeed, Bundy explained to Secretary of State Rusk, "In view of the lack of convincing evidence that Cambodian territory is being used as a major base or major infiltration route, the requested authority would be difficult to justify." On that point, Bundy emphasized that the actions requested would effectively constitute "acts of war against Cambodia." Bundy was hardly a dove, but his reservations struck at the core element in the military's continual requests to expand operations into Cambodia, namely the paucity of concrete evidence that Cambodia was a *significant* component of the Vietnamese communists' infiltration routes or base of operations. Bundy recommended that authorization be "limited only to major operations in which it is clear that the U.S./GVN armed forces involved required such authority for their adequate self-defense" and that "decisions to confer such authority be taken in Washington."[14]

Westmoreland unsurprisingly voiced his frustration with the cautious Johnson administration. On December 9 the MACV commander sent a telegram to his superior, Admiral Ulysses Sharp, outlining his plans to engage in cross-border combat operations in Cambodia. Based on reported observations and collected intelligence—derived from ongoing covert surveillance

142 / Aterritorial Wars

missions—Westmoreland explained that "it is perfectly clear to us that the border areas of Cambodia now contain motorable infiltration routes, command centers, base, training and supply areas." It was vital, the general stressed, to face "the facts of life and recognize that we face a major threat." Amazingly, the general admitted that "we will not be able to produce the kind of evidence which would stand up in court against those who insist on such proof." However, for Westmoreland the intelligence was sufficient and "perfectly clear" to wage war on a sovereign state. Noting that Sihanouk was unable or unwilling to control his border, Westmoreland determined that "it is in our national interest to draw the obvious conclusion and take what measures are necessary to reduce the utility of this area to the PAVN/VC and to mount offensive air attacks against them as necessary." In support of his military strategy, Westmoreland wanted to use overt military action in Cambodia in support of planned operations in South Vietnam, notably in Darlac, Pleiku, and Kontum provinces along the Cambodian border. Specifically, "in order to foresee and forestall the problems which stem from the use of a Cambodian sanctuary," Westmoreland requested authorization to use artillery and airstrikes against enemy positions ten kilometers into Cambodia; to permit ground troops to "maneuver into Cambodia" up to two kilometers if deemed necessary for the preservation of the force or the attainment of the objective within South Vietnam; to utilize observation aircraft to fly reconnaissance and surveillance missions within a ten-kilometer strip inside Cambodia in support of U.S. operations; and to deploy ground reconnaissance teams five kilometers into Cambodia. Most importantly, Westmoreland requested that these authorizations "be granted as standard operating procedures whenever U.S. troops operate in areas adjacent to the Cambodian border in Darlac, Pleiku, and Kontum provinces."[15] Despite Westmoreland's request, the White House refused to grant authorization. Rusk reaffirmed Johnson's position that "we are not seeking a wider war." That said, Rusk indicated that military planning could proceed on the assumption that action beyond "self-defense" may arise and, if future conditions warranted a change in policy, authorization would be granted.[16]

Throughout the Johnson presidency, the debate for expanded military operations in Cambodia would remain a sticking point between the military establishment and civilian advisors. The crux was not that the latter were opposed to armed intervention; indeed, most members of Johnson's staff were hawkish on the war. The problem was that of optics. Could the White House justify widening the war in Vietnam? Unlike the pacification and counterinsurgency operations conducted within South Vietnam, efforts to interdict enemy troops, supplies, and other resources in Cambodia border crossing into South Vietnam required the semblance of international legitimacy.

That NVA/PLAF forces were crossing into Cambodia was widely recognized. At issue was the long-standing question of the scale and scope to which enemy forces were moving into South Vietnam. And on this vital question, the intelligence remained inconclusive. In December 1965, for example, CIA analysts concluded that "the Viet Cong have procured supplies in and through Cambodia but shows that the volume of such supplies has been small in comparison with Viet Cong requirements and in comparison with what they have received through Laos, by direct sea infiltration, and from within South Vietnam." In addition, intelligence indicated that the "Communists have also established small but useful clandestine facilities on Cambodian territory." However, sources suggested also that "these facilities have played only a small part in the over-all Communist effort in South Vietnam." In short, CIA analysts concluded that "although it is clear that the Viet Cong have used Cambodian territory since the early days of the insurgency in South Vietnam, the magnitude of that use and its relative importance to the guerrillas have never been clear."[17] Ball was equally blunt in his appraisal: more "convincing evidence" of the use of Cambodian territory by NVA/PLAF forces was needed.[18]

For Westmoreland, civilian calculations missed a vital element, namely that the use of sanctuaries on foreign soil, especially Cambodia, undermined strategically his conduct of the war. As discussed earlier, from 1964 onward, U.S. military officials through MACV dictated the grand strategy of the conflict.[19] Westmoreland, in particular, advocated a protracted war of attrition that would reduce Hanoi's capability to wage war and to sustain the southern insurgency. On paper, the objective was to lure the enemy into large set-piece battles where superior American firepower could be brought to bear. On the ground, however, the enemy refused to play its assigned role, electing instead to retreat into Laos or Cambodia. For MACV, officials it was the inability to sustain offensive combat operations that assumed

144 / Aterritorial Wars

importance, arguably less so than the reprovisioning of insurgents operating in South Vietnam.

The White House was not unresponsive to Westmoreland's concerns. However, faced with conflicting intelligence, prudence was the order of the day. McNamara held firm that "unless there is a sudden, significant increase in either use of Cambodian territory by the PAVN/Viet Cong or step-up in logistical support from [Cambodia], a gradual response by the U.S. Government and certain other friendly governments is both appropriate and desirable."[20] Johnson, especially, admitted his concerns about Cambodia but hoped that diplomacy could impel Sihanouk to better enforce his borders.[21] In addition, U.S. officials sought to enlist third-party governments to better impress upon Sihanouk the gravity of the situation. In January 1966, for example, U.S. representatives collaborated with their Australian counterparts to push Sihanouk "to adopt a more realistic position." Working through the Australian embassy in Phnom Penh, Dean Rusk wanted Sihanouk to understand that Washington could not tolerate the use of Cambodian territory by Vietnamese communists; and that the Cambodian government should not actively support or collaborate with the Vietnamese communists. Rusk wanted Sihanouk to know that while U.S. officials were "aware that exaggerated claims have been made regarding VC use of Cambodia" the fact remained that "the Americans are convinced that the VC have abused Cambodian territory."[22] In turn, the U.S. government was prepared to help stabilize Cambodia's border in any way possible.

Three weeks later, McNamara provided Johnson with a more detailed appraisal of enemy movement into South Vietnam. Newly acquired intelligence indicated that "the infiltration from the North was mainly by truck. It is on greatly improved routes—routes, some of which are new and some of which have been widened, or upgraded for truck use, or all-weathered, or built to by-pass points vulnerable to choke-point bombing, or constructed under jungle canopy and bamboo-trellised camouflage to prevent aerial observation." As such, anti-infiltration tactics required "a cumulative and sustained effort" capable of targeting "the supplies en route into North Vietnam from the outside world, inside North Vietnam, en route from the North by sea or through Laos and Cambodia to South Vietnam, or inside South Vietnam." That said, with respect to ongoing efforts, McNamara allowed that it was not clear that aerial bombing alone would "cut the flow of men and material from the North to the South" in sufficient numbers to make any appreciable difference in the course of the war.[23]

Sihanouk was in a difficult position. In an effort to preserve Cambodia's sovereignty and territorial integrity, the prince was compelled to balance the geopolitical threats posed by all foreign parties. Sihanouk understood also that loyalty and friendship only went so far; the assassination of Diem two years earlier underscored that point. As such, Sihanouk repeatedly denied or downplayed the use of Cambodian territory by the Vietnamese communists. To do otherwise would risk expansion of the war into Cambodia, as the United States would almost certainly deploy combat forces into his country.[24] In Washington, U.S. officials were not completely indifferent to Sihanouk's plight. Apart from cross-border movements, Cambodia remained to a degree peripheral to the main objective of securing South Vietnam. Sihanouk was important only insofar as the prince helped or hindered America's overall strategy.

Over the course of the Johnson administration, efforts to influence Sihanouk continued. Many U.S. officials, however, bemoaned the futility of diplomatic overtures. In April 1966, William Bundy expressed doubt that any diplomatic "mission to Sihanouk would produce any useful result." He also doubted the success of having a multinational coalition patrol the border—even if authorization from the international community was granted. "A genuinely effective control operation," Bundy concluded, "would require some thousands of men with helicopters, bases and good communications, and a willingness to engage" PAVN and PLAF troops.[25] Other officials developed more unconventional plans.[26] To take one example, on May 28, Robert Komer—serving as special assistant to the president—explained that "Requests from our embattled field commanders that we bomb Cambodia or at least drop leaflets leave me cold—they would have far too little effect to outweigh the political uproar they would cause." In an attempt to counter "these 'gung ho' suggestions," Komer reasoned "there ought to be imaginative ways of putting a quiet squeeze on Sihanouk via economic means and psywar." Noting the deepening economic crisis in Cambodia, Komer pressed for a "quick study of other means of quiet economic warfare against Cambodia," specifically a "rice strategy." Komer acknowledged such efforts

146 / Aterritorial Wars

"will take time but we'll keep the needle in."[27] In the interim, the White House remained at an impasse, and the armed struggle within South Vietnam continued.

In early 1966, bolstered by U.S. combat troops in excess of 184,000, Westmoreland tried to seize the initiative against the Vietnamese communists. Modifying his earlier strategy, Westmoreland authorized his troops to "find, fix, and destroy" the enemy.[28] Subsequently, several military operations were initiated, including both Operation Marauder and Operation Crimp in the Mekong Delta and Operation Matador in the Central Highlands. Strategically, these military actions underscored for Westmoreland the depth of enemy infiltration in South Vietnam as well as the benefits the enemy derived from sanctuaries in neighboring Cambodia.[29] In addition, limited covert cross-border missions into Cambodia were planned under the code name "Daniel Boone."[30] Initially, Operation Daniel Boone had a restricted geographic area of operation. By 1967, however, covert missions were underway all along the South Vietnamese border, penetrating about twelve miles inside Cambodia.

An Unconventional War

In early 1966 Sihanouk made political overtures to Beijing. For U.S. officials, this was not surprising. Sihanouk was public in his conviction that America could not win in Vietnam and, in the event of a North Vietnamese victory, Sihanouk anticipated that Chinese patronage would deter possible Vietnamese encroachments on Cambodian territory. However, in a diplomatic move that did surprise Washington, in April Sihanouk formally recognized the Democratic Republic of Vietnam. Prior to this move, the Phnom Penh government had recognized South Vietnam but had only extended "commercial representation" to the North. Now, Cambodia's representation of Hanoi and Saigon was on an equal level. For U.S. policymakers, this represented a significant change in the geopolitical playing field. William Trueheart, director of the Office of Southeast Asian Affairs, reasoned that Cambodia's recognition of North Vietnam confirmed that "Sihanouk [had] not changed his assessment of the final outcome of the struggle in South Vietnam." However, for Trueheart, the "legal consequences" of Sihanouk's diplomatic move were unclear, with three scenarios possible: to establish de facto relations with Hanoi; to recognize the existence of two separate governments, while maintaining political relations with only one; or to recognize the DRV as the sole government of Vietnam. Trueheart premised that "Sihanouk is likely to preserve the ambiguity in order to retain maximum flexibility."[31]

For some U.S. officials, Sihanouk's diplomatic overtures to both Beijing and Hanoi seemed to confirm their long-held suspicions that the prince was a committed communist. If so, Cambodia's position on America's Cold War calculus required a fresh look. As such, in June 1966, the CIA prepared the report "Cambodia and the Vietnamese Communists" in an effort to provide a modicum of clarity on an uncertain situation. To begin, the CIA did not conclude that Sihanouk was a communist, although his political loyalties remained enigmatic. Sihanouk's "swing to the left" was "more apparent than real." Sihanouk, for example, maintained cordial relations with other noncommunist governments. That said, it was "no accident that the reorientation of Cambodia's foreign policy coincided with the recrudescence of Communist activity in South Vietnam." In short, "the key factor behind Sihanouk's current erratic course" was "the growing impact of U.S. military forces on the war in South Vietnam, an impact which has caused Communist troops to make greater use of Cambodian territory." On that point, the CIA reasoned, "Sihanouk clearly knows what the Communists are doing in Cambodia, although he is probably not aware of all the details nor of the magnitude of their incursions." Either way, the CIA affirmed, "the increasing Vietnamese communist use of Cambodian territory poses, in the final analysis, the gravest problems for Phnom Penh. Acquiescence— the course which Sihanouk has thus far followed—opens Cambodia to a very real threat of U.S. and South Vietnamese retaliation. The immediate alternative, a determined effort to limit the Vietnamese presence in Cambodia, is just as unpalatable to Phnom Penh. Such a course would necessitate a major realignment of Cambodia's foreign policy away from the Communists—a move which Sihanouk undoubtedly considers premature at this juncture." Regardless, the report concluded, Sihanouk's "fundamental objectives—to prevent the war from spreading to Cambodia and to ensure Cambodia's existence as a nation state no matter what the future political organization of Indochina—will remain the same."[32]

Johnson was in agreement that the war should not expand into Cambodia and favored a diplomatic solution in dealing with Sihanouk.[33] Members

148 / Aterritorial Wars

of his cabinet agreed also in principle but warned the president not to be sidetracked by a country largely inconsequential to America's national security interests. George Ball, for example, yielded that improved foreign relations with Phnom Penh could be advantageous but that the president was "dealing with someone [Sihanouk] who is not only proud and sensitive but also highly mercurial and temperamental." For Ball, Johnson needed to remain focused on the bigger picture. "At the present time," Ball explained, "the most important aspect with regard to Cambodia is the use of its territory by the Viet Cong."[34] Cambodia remained central only to the degree its territory was used by Vietnamese communists. As far as America's geopolitical commitment to Cambodia, nothing else mattered. Roger Hilsman, an official in the U.S. State Department, concurred, remarking that "our fundamental objective is to cope with [the] problem of Cambodia in such a way as to meet [the] security interests of [the] Free World in Southeast Asia."[35]

For Johnson, something had to be done. Diplomacy appeared to be a nonstarter, and the president remained adamant that U.S. combat forces were not to cross into Cambodia. All that seemed to remain was the continued use of covert operatives, including the Khmer Serei. This option, though, was highly controversial. The U.S. State Department, for example, held that support for the Khmer Serei was counterproductive and had urged the Thai and South Vietnamese governments to cut their ties with the dissidents. In addition, the State Department advised against the recruitment of *any* ethnic Cambodians in South Vietnam, including those not affiliated with the Khmer Serei. On this point, State Department officials believed that the Cambodian minority population in South Vietnam was already strongly influenced by the Khmer Serei and, if Sihanouk learned that a force of Khmer was being formed for cross-border operations into Cambodia, the prince would interpret this as a serious threat to his regime. The logical outcome would be Sihanouk aligning even more closely with Beijing and Hanoi. Conversely, both MACV and the JCS were supportive of the proposal, noting that "Cambodians who have lived in border regions are ideal for use in this type of operation due to their familiarity with the area, language, and customs of the people."[36]

As civilian and military officials debated the merits of recruiting ethnic Khmer, Westmoreland continued to press for greater latitude in securing the border regions with Cambodia. Claiming that both PAVN and PLAF

Aterritorial Wars / 149

cross-border activities were on the increase, Westmoreland warned that military inaction would lead to increased U.S. casualties, force diversions, and generally prolong the war. In addition, the general warned that South Vietnam's geography posed a multitude of challenges that all required unique solutions. In the southern provinces surrounding Saigon, for example, Vietnamese communists made considerable use of Cambodian territory as sanctuary when fleeing U.S. combat forces. For Westmoreland, this use of Cambodian space was merely a hindrance to his overall strategy. The Central Highlands, but specifically Pleiku and Kontum provinces, posed a greater threat. According to Westmoreland, an estimated 140 tons of rice per day were being transshipped into South Vietnam via Cambodia; arms, ammunition, explosives, medical supplies, equipment and materiel were also being delivered; and at least six NVA regiments, four battalions, and eight infiltration groups were known to have entered South Vietnam from Cambodia. Additional units remained in base areas and staging grounds inside Cambodia. To counter enemy operations, Westmoreland subsequently proposed six options, ranging from a "continuation of current U.S. policy of accommodation with respect to Cambodia" to "the seizure and occupation of selected NVA-VC base areas in northeast Cambodia." His recommendation fell between the extremes: "a simultaneous expansion of current U.S. policy towards (1) amity and the restoration of diplomatic relations and (2) conflict within current parameters to establish the base for more militant actions to eliminate the sanctuary."[37]

Westmoreland's request was followed with a demand by the JCS that Johnson abandon his "gradual and cautious approach."[38] Since November 1965 both MACV and the JCS "recommended that forceful action be taken to stop the use of Cambodian territory by enemy forces as a logistics base and sanctuary." And while Johnson did authorize the military to expand and intensify covert intelligence-gathering missions in Cambodia, including the conduct of surveillance activities along the Mekong and Bassac waterways, more was needed. Indeed, the JCS warned "VC/NVA exploitation of the pseudo-neutrality of Cambodia has increased to serious proportions." After months of intransigence, the enemy's use of the Cambodian sanctuaries constituted "a clear and present danger." The JCS reprimanded the White House, declaring that "actions authorized under current policy have proven inadequate to counter the growing threat imposed by VC/NVA use

150 / Aterritorial Wars

of Cambodia. An impasse exists wherein the collection of convincing intelligence is prerequisite to changes in policy, while adequate intelligence cannot be obtained until this policy is changed." As such, the JCS concluded that the persistent threat "requires a continuous commitment of sizeable friendly forces to the border area, impedes progress of the land campaign, and results in unnecessary US and friendly casualties." In response, the JCS affirmed that "current national policy with respect to Cambodia must again be reviewed in light of overall US objectives in Southeast Asia and the continued use of the Cambodian sanctuary by the VC/NVA." Echoing Westmoreland, the JCS proposed that Johnson authorize the immediate intensification of intelligence collection programs—the existing Daniel Boone missions—through expanded ground reconnaissance operations inside Cambodia, the use of high-altitude U-2 photography over Cambodia on a continuing basis, and the circumscribed continued use of medium- and low-altitude day/night photography in Cambodia; in addition, the JCS recommended authorization for the immediate pursuit of actively engaged VC/NVA forces when withdrawing into Cambodian territory. In support of these more aggressive operations, the JCS acknowledged the need also for a more extensive coordinated public affairs and information program and supporting psychological operations.[39]

Unconvinced that Cambodia posed a clear and present danger, the State Department distributed a national intelligence estimate on the scale and scope of PAVN/PLAF use of Cambodian territory. Released on January 26, 1967, the report was the collective effort of the major U.S. intelligence agencies operating in Vietnam, including the CIA, the intelligence sections of the Departments of State and Defense, and the National Security Administration (NSA). Also participating were members of the Atomic Energy Commission (AEC). The conclusions contained in this report differed substantially from that prepared by the JCS, as apparent in the report's first line: "Denying the Communists the use of Cambodian territory and supplies would make life more difficult for them; it would not constitute a decisive element in their ability to conduct military operations in South Vietnam." The report continues: "The availability of Cambodian territory is of considerable psychological and military advantage to the Communists. They use it as a sanctuary to evade allied forces and more permanently as a refuge for rest, training, medical care, storage of supplies, and as a convenient and secure route for the infiltration of personnel from North Vietnam." In short, the intelligence report agrees with the position forwarded by MACV and the JCS regarding the benefits accrued by the PAVN/PLAF in their military operations. However, the report differed with respect to the magnitude of those benefits, which must be balanced against the political risks. Strikingly, "no evidence of large-scale diversions of . . . arms or of any substantial clandestine movement of arms into Cambodia and then forward to the Communists in Vietnam" was identified. And with regard to other materiel shipped through Cambodia, the report stated that "the quantities involved are not critical to the overall Communist effort."[40] In a follow-up memorandum, State Department representative George Denny explained that the "CIA has concluded that the MACV study (1) failed to discriminate sufficiently in the use of raw intelligence reports and (2) overstated the significance of Cambodia to Communist military operations in South Vietnam."[41]

The January 26 report did not, however, provide sufficient clarity—certainly not for the JCS—and so the question of Cambodia's centrality to the war effort in South Vietnam remained. Consequently, a Joint Study Group under Department of State chairmanship was established to consider further "the problem of Viet Cong-North Vietnamese use of Cambodia." Unlike the previous study group, this committee included both civilian and military analysts, with representatives from the Department of Defense, the JCS, CIA, and the United States Information Agency (USIA). In practice, the study group approached their task with the presumption that "efforts to deal with this problem should continue to be primarily in the political sphere." However, the study group also affirmed that "those actions which are clearly required in terms of self-defense of our forces in South Vietnam should continue to be authorized as necessary." And after months of deliberation, they released their report on May 1. Foremost, the study group recommended that "Daniel Boone-type operations in the border zone of Northeastern Cambodia be authorized on a case-by-case basis." In addition, the group recommended "measures designed to expand air intelligence collection programs" and expanded psychological operations. Other proposals, notably those involving military operations conducted by U.S. forces on Cambodian territory, were deferred pending further diplomatic overtures to Phnom Penh.[42]

152 / Aterritorial Wars

On the recommendation of the Joint Study Group, on May 22 presidential authorization was granted for limited cross-border intelligence gathering and verification operations in northeastern Cambodia. Secrecy was paramount, and not just for military reasons. Conducted without the knowledge or consent of the Phnom Penh government, these missions were in violation of Cambodian sovereignty. Consequently, both geographic and operational restrictions were imposed in an effort to conceal the presence of U.S. personnel operating inside Cambodia. Reconnaissance teams, for example, were restricted in size to include not more than twelve men—with no more than three U.S. advisors present on any team. Helicopters were not permitted for team infiltration or exfiltration. No more than three missions could be carried out at one time, and the duration of any given mission was to be kept to a minimum. Teams were also to take precautions to avoid contact with Cambodians. If caught, the U.S. government would deny any knowledge of the mission.[43]

Westmoreland and the JCS welcomed the authorization to expand covert operations into Cambodia although they continued to chafe at the restrictions imposed by the White House. Throughout 1967 and 1968, Westmoreland made repeated requests to extend the operating area along the entire frontier from Laos to the Gulf of Siam; authorize the infiltration and exfiltration of personnel by helicopter; and increase the number of authorized missions from five to thirty each month. Concurrently, U.S. officials continued to debate the legality of the missions. In September 1967, George Aldrich, a legal advisor, provided an extensive review of the problem. Conceding that "Cambodia may not have taken all the measures which reasonably can be expected of it to enforce its neutrality . . . the remedy for such shortcomings is diplomatic, or legal, not military."[44] In other words, the apparent abrogation of Cambodian neutrality by Sihanouk's refusal or inability to prevent the use of Cambodian territory by the Vietnamese communists did not justify U.S. military intervention. Aldrich did concede, in part, that "armed [U.S.] reconnaissance patrols [operating] on Cambodian territory can be defended" but only on the grounds that these patrols were operating in Cambodia in order to defend American and allied forces; moreover, the threat posed by the enemy had to be "so serious that it must be countered." Aldrich also weighed in on the use of enemy activity in Cambodia. He agreed

Aterritorial Wars / 153

that PAVN/PLAF forces were in violation of Cambodia's neutrality; however, he noted that "the extent and significance of their use [of Cambodian territory] is uncertain." Contrary to the military's position, Aldrich concluded that cross-border "activity is not believed to be a 'decisive element' in the enemy effort." For Aldrich, consequently, the legal risks of expanded covert operations within Cambodian territory greatly outweighed the potential military gains. He clarified his reasoning: "In view of the enemy's limited use of Cambodian territory to date, and the limited capacity of the Cambodian government to protect its territory from all abuse, Cambodia cannot be said to have abandoned or substantially compromised its policy of non-involvement in the conflict." Aldrich therefore agreed with existing U.S. policy precisely "to avoid extending the Viet Nam war to Cambodia." This meant, from a tactical standpoint, that combat operations not be authorized in Cambodia "except as necessary to suppress hostile fire from Cambodian territory and to preserve U.S. forces engaged on the South Vietnamese side of the border. Immediate pursuit of enemy ground forces into Cambodia is not otherwise permitted."[45]

More concretely, in his evaluation of the Daniel Boone program, Aldrich explained that proposed revisions "would be fundamentally different from the small, covert operations now authorized in a remote corner of Cambodia." He noted that "increased frequency, operation in more populous areas, and the use of helicopters would greatly increase the risks of disclosure and of direct confrontation with Cambodian forces." Even more troubling was Aldrich's warning that "expanded Daniel Boone operations in Cambodia cannot be viewed as an isolated step. Once authorization is granted for expanded military activities in Cambodia, the pressure for taking the next step—use of force against [PAVN/PLAF] positions in Cambodia—would be very difficult to resist." Aldrich stated bluntly, "We should be fully aware now of where the end of this road is likely to lead and not begin to go down it unless we are prepared to travel to the end."[46]

For Aldrich, the geopolitical repercussions of U.S. military operations were clear. "From a legal point of view," Aldrich counseled, "Cambodia is not a party to the conflict in Viet Nam. It has not intervened in South Viet Nam and has not become a co-belligerent with North Viet Nam. It retains its status as a neutral. *Abuse of Cambodian neutrality by NVA/VC forces does*

154 / Aterritorial Wars

not automatically justify corresponding violations of Cambodian territorial integrity by U.S. or friendly forces." Further, to the extent that enemy forces in Cambodia posed a threat to South Vietnam or to U.S. personnel in South Vietnam, Aldrich explained that "Article 33 of the United Nations Charter obligates the 'parties to any dispute, the continuation of which is likely to endanger the maintenance of international peace and security' to seek 'first of all' a peaceful solution to the dispute. Article 37 provides that, should they fail to obtain a peaceful settlement, they are required to refer the dispute to the Security Council." For Aldrich, any proposed expansion of Daniel Boone would be in violation of international norms. Indeed, even if concrete evidence existed to demonstrate the Vietnamese communists' infringement of Cambodia's territorial integrity, the legal response would be to take the matter to the United Nations, not to sanction covert military operations into Cambodia. Aldrich concluded that while "military force may legitimately be used by one state on the territory of another state in self-defense . . . when hostile actions threatened the first state in such a significant way that their suppression is not merely desirable but necessary," with respect to Cambodia "it is far from clear that an impartial observer would decide that the demonstrable facts of its use by NVA/VC forces are sufficiently threatening to South Viet Nam and to our forces in South Viet Nam to justify direct military action based upon the right of self-defense." And finally, for Aldrich, "The advantages of countering the threat posed by misuse of Cambodian territory must be balanced against the disadvantage of prejudicing the chances of a constructive role for Cambodia in the future political and economic development of Southeast Asia."[47]

Aldrich's legal opinion did little to resolve the issue, and the debate of Cambodia's centrality to America's mission in South Vietnam raged on.[48] All the while, Westmoreland continued to press for permission to expand military operations into Cambodia beyond the limited reconnaissance patrols approved by Johnson. With time, these demands far surpassed the lifting of existing restrictions. In December, for example, Westmoreland proposed a seventy-two-hour period of B-52 and other tactical airstrikes to be conducted on sanctuaries in Cambodia. The general admitted that "B-52 strikes will leave a clear signature in Cambodian territory"; however, he argued it was necessary to "strike the concentration expeditiously and [in] full force if we are to gain maximum advantage."[49]

On receiving Westmoreland's request to carpet-bomb Cambodia, both McNamara and Rusk were taken aback. Rusk was exceptionally forthright. "The action which General Westmoreland is proposing," he explained, "would be a significant act of war against Cambodia. This would change the entire character of the war. If Cambodia is attacked, they may ask the Chinese to side with them. Then we will really have a new war on our hands." McNamara concurred: "I believe . . . that it is most unwise to expand the war beyond the South Vietnamese borders." Indeed, McNamara admitted, "I am scared to death. I am scared of a policy based on an assumption that by going somewhere else we can win the war."[50] Westmoreland did have his supporters. Wheeler, for example, countered that "the Joint Chiefs do not want to widen the war either. We only wish Cambodia would be neutral—honest to God neutral, too."[51] McNamara remained unconvinced. At this point, McNamara had already announced his departure from the Defense Department to serve as president of the World Bank. Since first being appointed secretary of defense in January 1961 McNamara was a stalwart supporter of America's war in Vietnam. McNamara was certain in his anticommunist convictions and agreed it was necessary for the United States to take a stand. Six years later McNamara expressed deep reservations. "We have poured more bomb loads onto North Vietnam, than in the whole of World War II," the secretary of defense told David Lilienthal, "and yet we have no sign that it has shaken their will to resist, none."[52] As such, and in stark contrast to his earlier beliefs, McNamara told Johnson that the "war cannot be won by killing North Vietnamese. It can only be won by protecting the South Vietnamese so they can build and develop economically for a future political contest with North Vietnam." Of B-52 strikes against Cambodia, McNamara explained, "While I recognize this is a good way to fight a conventional war, this is not a conventional war." On this point, incoming Secretary of Defense Clark Clifford agreed: "General Westmoreland's recommendation does not make sense to me. You have a certain number of square miles in which 5,000 men are located. The General asked for a B-52 strike. The enemy are scattered all over the countryside when the first bomb hits the ground."[53] Curiously, as the conversation continued, Rusk did not rule out the possibility of expanding the war into Cambodia. He clarified that "if we take this action it would be absolutely essential to consult the Congress and our allies."[54] Presciently, McNamara noted that "the U.S. cannot run B-52s

156 / Aterritorial Wars

around the clock without public knowledge of that."[55] In the end, Johnson declined to make a firm decision on Westmoreland's request but did ask for additional information.

With U.S. troop levels in South Vietnam surpassing the half-million mark at the beginning of 1968, most members of the Johnson administration counseled against any geographic expansion of the war. Even the hawkish Rostow expressed reservations on the possible expansion of war into Cambodia; he did, however, imply that future authorization may be necessary in the event of intensified enemy action.[56] From a practical standpoint, Rostow agreed that the "basic U.S. policy toward Cambodia remains recognition of its sovereignty, independence, neutrality and territorial integrity." Rostow explained, "We do not seek to engage Cambodia in the war in Viet-Nam, nor do we seek to expand the war to Cambodian territory." That said, Rostow conceded that "it has been increasingly difficult for the United States to maintain a policy of respect for Cambodia's position in the face of continuous and intensified violation of Cambodia's sovereignty by the VC and NVA forces." In the end, Rostow warned, "We wish to make it clear that we do not seek to take military action in the border areas" of Cambodia; however, the US position was clear, precisely "the prevention of enemy use of Cambodia's territory."[57]

The often-acrimonious debates over the size and composition of enemy forces—both in Cambodia and beyond—encapsulated starker divisions within the overall politico-military conduct of the war. As Graham Cosmas explains, these debates also affected the broader evaluation and assessment of U.S. progress in attrition and pacification. Johnson and his civilian advisors were particularly concerned about the impact of enemy strength figures on U.S. public opinion.[58] In fact, by late 1967 several of Johnson's closest advisors were disillusioned both with the conduct of the war and with the war itself. The outgoing McNamara was the most outspoken. No longer in favor of a war he helped fabricate, McNamara argued that the "continuation of our present action in Southeast Asia would be dangerous, costly in lives, and unsatisfactory to the American people."[59] As such, McNamara advised Johnson to "level out," if not actually decrease, troop levels in South Vietnam. Several other members of the White House, including Rusk, Rostow, and McGeorge Bundy agreed. The consensus was to keep the pressure on Hanoi through sustained aerial bombardments; the deployment of additional U.S.

combat troops was unlikely to result in decisive success and would most certainly raise the human, economic, and political costs to an unsustainable level.[60] Concurrently, as Johnson and his advisors moved toward leveling off the American war effort in Vietnam, their counterparts in Hanoi were completing preparations for an expansion of military operations.[61]

Throughout 1967 the more hardline leaders in Hanoi proposed a new initiative, a "general offensive" throughout the entirety of South Vietnam that would, if successful, result in the collapse of the Saigon government and the hastened departure of the Americans. Composed of both political and military elements, the plan involved concerted attacks by main force units and local guerrillas on urban settlements in the South; the main targets were South Vietnam's major cities—Saigon, Huế, and Da Nang. Diversionary strikes against isolated U.S. military installations throughout the country, but especially in the Central Highlands, would effectively render the South Vietnam military impotent in their ability to counterattack. In the ensuing chaos, Hanoi anticipated a "general uprising" of the population in the South, thereby facilitating the collapse of the government. The operation was set to commence on January 30 to coincide with the Tet Mau Than holiday, the Vietnamese lunar New Year.[62]

Endings and Beginnings

For the dry season campaign of late 1967 and early 1968, Westmoreland remained committed to the threefold strategy developed by MACV since the start of U.S. combat operations in mid-1965: to wear down the PAVN/PLAF conventional main force units through combat operations, anti-infiltration programs, and the destruction of the enemy's logistical network; to help the South Vietnamese government regain control over the territory and people dominated by the enemy's shadow government (pacification); and to train and modernize the South Vietnamese forces so they could eventually handle the threat of internal insurgency and external invasion without the need for significant U.S. combat forces.[63] In consideration of the first objective, Westmoreland hoped both for increased combat troops and authorization to extend military operations into Cambodia. Neither was forthcoming, circumscribing the options available for MACV's planners. Regardless, Westmoreland and his officers were optimistic. Hoping to take advantage of the logistical network established over the preceding two years, Westmoreland

158 / Aterritorial Wars

directed his commanders to initiate division-sized operations west of Saigon to target three key infiltration routes that entered South Vietnam from Cambodia. In so doing, Westmoreland anticipated sharply reducing the amount of supplies reaching PLAF base areas in South Vietnam and exacting heavy losses on units under the command of the communist's Central Office for South Vietnam (COSVN).[64]

In late December and early January MACV gathered sufficient intelligence to indicate a major enemy offensive was imminent. However, Westmoreland determined that Hanoi's main target was in the Central Highlands, most likely an attempt to cut South Vietnam in half. Only belatedly, after the first wave of attacks began on January 30, did U.S. officials fully appreciate the scale and scope of the North Vietnamese strategy.[65] In the early morning hours, approximately 84,000 PAVN and PLAF troops struck Saigon and 36 of 44 provincial capitals throughout South Vietnam; numerous smaller villages and hamlets also fell to the onslaught. The anticipated civilian uprising, however, did not materialize and in the course of intensive fighting, the attacking forces were driven back. Between the end of January and March 31, combined PAVN/PLAF losses were estimated to exceed fifty thousand, or roughly 60 percent of the forces committed to battle.[66]

In the aftermath of Tet, citing the high body count of enemy forces, Westmoreland and members of the JCS declared victory. Indeed, for many military advisors and planners, the apparent defeat of the PAVN/PLAF forces called for a swift counteroffensive. Subsequently, both CINCPAC and the JCS reopened the issue of further U.S. troop deployments to South Vietnam and broader authority to attack the enemy's Cambodian and Laotian bases and supply routes. General Wheeler and Admiral Sharp, in particular, encouraged Westmoreland to deploy substantial reinforcements.[67] Initially, though, Westmoreland's requests were surprisingly modest, compelling his senior commanders to underscore the urgency to seize the initiative. Coming around, Westmoreland submitted a request to the White House on February 12. Noting that "the enemy [had] changed his strategy," Westmoreland explained that America's strategy must also change. Indeed, the entire context of the war shifted with Tet, as Hanoi was no longer "fully mobilized to achieve a quick victory." "Time is of the essence," Westmoreland argued, for "exploiting this opportunity could materially shorten the war."[68]

Johnson harbored doubts but still authorized the mobilization of an emergency contingent of reinforcements—and only for a limited duration.[69] For Wheeler and the JCS, this was still insufficient; so Johnson dispatched the general to Saigon on a fact-finding mission. On his return, not unexpectedly, Wheeler recommended an additional 206,000 troops to be sent to South Vietnam as well as the removal of all restraints on military operations in Cambodia, Laos, and North Vietnam.[70] Wheeler's report was met with skepticism by the White House but, nevertheless, Johnson—increasingly despondent over the war—directed the new secretary of defense, Clark Clifford, to undertake a thorough review of the request.[71] On March 4, Clifford replied to the president: "There is a deep-seated concern by your advisors. There is a concern that if we say, yes, and step up with the addition of 206,000 more men that we might continue down the road as we have been without accomplishing our purpose—which is for a viable South Vietnam which can live in peace." Clifford continued, "There are grave doubts that we have made the type of progress we had hoped to have made by this time. As we build up our forces, they build up theirs. We continue to fight at a higher level of intensity. Even were we to meet this full request of 206,000 men, and the pattern continues as it has, it is likely that by March he [Westmoreland] may want another 200,000 to 300,000 men with no end in sight." Clifford warned also that "if we continue with our present policy of adding more troops and increasing our commitment, this policy may lead us into Laos and Cambodia." Gravely, the secretary of defense concluded, "I see more and more fighting with more and more casualties on the U.S. side and no end in sight to the action."[72]

Ultimately, Johnson concurred with Clifford's recommendation to deny Westmoreland's request for an additional 206,000 troops. In fact, instead of increasing U.S. troop levels, on March 22 Johnson announced his decision to scale back the authorization of "emergency" reinforcements, from an anticipated 30,000 to only 13,500.[73] Moreover, Johnson "promoted" Westmoreland from commander of MACV to the position of chief of staff of the army, effectively removing him from oversight of the Vietnam War. General Creighton Abrams, Westmoreland's deputy commander, would assume the helm of MACV. Nine days later, during a televised broadcast to the American people, Johnson also announced that the United States would cease air attacks on all but the southernmost portion of North Vietnam,

160 / Aterritorial Wars

thus effectively concluding Operation Rolling Thunder.[74] The president explained that such a move was necessary, in the hopes that a sign of military deescalation would open a path toward peace through negotiation. Then, unexpectedly, Johnson revealed that he would not run for reelection.

Twice more in 1968 Hanoi launched substantial military offensives against the Saigon government; and each time, PAVN and PLAF forces were driven back. Abrams had reason to believe that Allied fortunes were on the rise.[75] As Cosmas writes, "Abrams' immediate battlefield situation was favorable. He possessed a balanced American combat force and a completed logistical base, as well as a vastly expanded intelligence system. A unified American organization for promoting pacification was in place. The South Vietnamese government and armed forces had withstood the shock of Tet and seemed to be improving in stability and effectiveness. The enemy had come into the open in his repeated offenses and was suffering severe, possibly crippling, losses."[76] In March Clifford had described South Vietnam as a "sinkhole."[77] Now, a growing sense of optimism was becoming apparent. Following a brief trip to South Vietnam in mid-July, Clifford reported, "Our field commanders from General Abrams on down are confident that the enemy can be turned back and defeated."[78]

Despite the renewed optimism expressed by Clark Clifford and Creighton Abrams, a potential dark spot continued to cast a shadow over U.S. state-, government-, and nation-building efforts in South Vietnam. As both civilian and military officials in Washington gradually accepted the necessity of putting the South Vietnamese military in a position to conduct the war on their own, the problem of enemy infiltration remained paramount.[79] Indeed, for many intelligence analysts, notably those within MACV, Tet clearly demonstrated the threat posed by Cambodia's permeable borders.[80] According to MACV, in the lead-up to Tet, an estimated 31,700 personnel entered South Vietnam during 1967, more than twice the number that infiltrated during the previous year. In addition, approximately 6,500 tons of weapons and supplies were carried into South Vietnam, including thousands of automatic rifles, machine guns, and handheld antitank rocket launchers.[81] On this point, an intelligence memorandum of March 7, 1968, determined that the "Communists continue to use Cambodian territory for tactical sanctuary, for base areas, for the infiltration of personnel, and as a source of rice, medicines, and sundry supplies." Moreover, there was no indication that "the step-up in military activity since the Tet offensive has taxed the capability of the established supply route from North Vietnam via Laos and the trail system along the Cambodian border." In fact, this report concluded that "there is a growing body of circumstantial evidence . . . that the Communists may have stepped up the acquisition of supplies through southern Cambodia."[82]

Throughout the remainder of Johnson's tenure as president, Abrams, like Westmoreland before him, argued relentlessly for authority to strike the enemy's Cambodian and Laotian bases with artillery, airpower, and ground forces.[83] Johnson, however, refused to authorize any military operations that would expand the war geographically, especially into Cambodia. Instead, members of the Johnson administration continued to spar diplomatically with Cambodia's unpredictable prince.[84] Ultimately, however, the Cambodian problem would rest with the incoming administration of Richard M. Nixon and his national security advisor, Henry A. Kissinger.

[5]

A WIDENING WAR

Do you think there's a prayer for Vietnamization if Cambodia is taken over?

—HENRY KISSINGER to WILLIAM ROGERS

On January 21, 1969, the newly elected U.S. president, Richard Nixon, assembled his National Security Council (NSC) to discuss how to achieve victory in South Vietnam.[1] The president emphasized that while he did not believe in changing policy for change alone, he believed that with respect to Vietnam it was necessary to rethink existing policy to determine if the United States was still on course to meet its objectives. In addition, Nixon counseled that it was unwise for the enemy to assume American political and military efforts were "locked on the same old tracks." On that point, Kissinger stated that the most difficult problem on Vietnam could be traced to "fundamental disagreements on facts."[2] Consequently, under National Security Study Memorandum (NSSM) 1, Nixon directed his advisors to "develop an agreed evaluation of the situation in Vietnam as a basis for making policy decisions." The U.S. ambassador in Saigon, Ellsworth Bunker, the Joint Chiefs of Staff (JCS), and Military Advisory Command, Vietnam (MACV) were to prepare separate responses to questions posed by Nixon. Questions were grouped under six main areas of concern: diplomatic negotiations, enemy strength, South Vietnamese military preparedness, pacification operations, the South Vietnamese government, and U.S. military operations.[3] In addition, the Central Intelligence Agency (CIA) would provide additional information and in tandem with both the Departments of State and Defense if necessary.[4]

In a follow-up meeting, Nixon reiterated his appeal to "seek ways in which we can change the game." The president believed that the "best course of

164 / A Widening War

action would be to hang on" in Saigon and to continue with military pressure on Hanoi. Another possible route was to persuade the Soviet Union to pressure Hanoi into agreeing to a negotiated settlement that would leave the South Vietnamese government intact. These measures, however, would take time, and Nixon had pledged on the campaign trail to end, not prolong, the war. "While I am optimistic that it can be done," the president stated, "I am worried about our ability to sell it to the American people." On that point, Secretary of State Rogers speculated, "I think we can expect more from the American people, especially if we could at some point reduce our commitment by perhaps 50,000." In other words, token troop withdrawals, even if done unilaterally without immediate reciprocation from Hanoi, could, as Nixon mused, "buy time and perhaps some support."[5]

For Nixon, an immediate resolution of the conflict was not on the table. Instead, he believed that "about six months of strong military action, combined with a good public stance which reflects our efforts to seek peace" were needed. Nixon explained, "I feel we must not lose our nerve on this one. We should buy time with negotiations and continue to push the enemy." The president then summarized his position:

> The south must know that we are with them. The north thinks they are going to win anyway. We must leave some hope on both sides. When you lose your nerve, you can lose the basket. The mix of actions should be something like this. We talk hard in private but with an obvious peaceful public stance, seeking to gain time, initially giving the South Vietnamese a chance to strengthen the regime and add to the pacification effort while punishing the Viet Cong. Within three or four months bring home a few troops unilaterally as a separate and distinct action from the Paris negotiations, and as a ploy for more time domestically, while we continue to press at the negotiating table for a military settlement.[6]

Toward the end of the meeting, almost as an afterthought, the subject of Cambodia surfaced. Nixon asked if it would be appropriate to reestablish diplomatic relations with Cambodia. Nixon had once met Norodom Sihanouk and now believed "we can do business" with Cambodia's leader. General Andrew Goodpaster, deputy commander of MACV, supported the idea. With improved relations, the general counseled, officials could better approach Sihanouk about the movement of North Vietnamese arms through Cambodia. Kissinger's response was more tempered, quipping that "Sihanouk's main value is the fact that he mirrors the attitudes of the Asians. He is a sort of barometer. You can be sure he will never stick his neck out."[7] Nixon, however, understood that Cambodia was central to his evolving Vietnam policy. As Graham Cosmas writes, Nixon early on agreed with General Creighton Abrams, commander of the MACV, on the salience of Cambodia. Since assuming his command months earlier, Abrams constantly argued to expand U.S. and South Vietnamese military operations into Cambodia.[8] An expanded war in Cambodia was not inevitable in January 1969, but the currents were plainly shifting.

Both Nixon and Kissinger would, long after the war, claim that they had come belatedly to the decision to launch military operations on Cambodian territory; that it was North Vietnamese violations of Cambodia's neutrality that forced Washington's hand to act decisively and forcefully. In reality, Nixon long harbored a desire to strike at Cambodia.[9] In this chapter I trace the practical geopolitical reasoning surrounding Nixon's authorization to launch a secret but brutal bombing campaign against Cambodia. In doing so, I detail *why* Cambodia remained central to Nixon's foreign policy in Indochina while Vietnam became relegated to the periphery. Markedly, U.S. foreign policy under Nixon demonstrated a more nuanced scalar politics than was evident under previous administrations. Within the wider Indochina conflict, Cambodia was central to possible success in South Vietnam; and yet, paradoxically, Vietnam writ large was deemed peripheral to America's spatial order. From Truman to Johnson, Indochina was portrayed as the geopolitical cornerstone of democracy in Southeast Asia, and Southeast Asia was key to the territorial defense of a communist-free Europe. Under Nixon, a different Cold War calculus emerged, with Cambodia a key spatial variable.

Asia for the Asians

Nixon was committed to winning the war in Vietnam. Indeed, during the opening months of his presidency, Nixon repeatedly confessed (often in private) his fear of becoming the first U.S. president to lose a war. However, Nixon was also a political realist and, as such, was shrewd enough not to place all his eggs in one basket. Tentative at first, Nixon and his most trusted advisor, Kissinger, would soon begin to rhetorically distance the importance

166 / A Widening War

of Vietnam to American national security concerns.[10] In part, both men understood that they had to address the limits of U.S. power; that it was neither economically nor militarily feasible to defend every piece of ground threatened by communism.

Beginning in January 1969, the Nixon administration developed a two-track policy of diplomatic negotiation and "Vietnamization"—that is, unilateral withdrawal of U.S. combat troops combined with a major effort to strengthen Saigon's armed forces.[11] Broadly stated, the endgame of Vietnamization was to bolster South Vietnam's military capacities and capabilities in order to defend the Saigon government both from domestic insurgencies and North Vietnamese aggression. As Cosmas describes, at most, this policy would give a noncommunist South Vietnam a chance to survive—the preferred result from Nixon's point of view. At minimum, the Nixon administration could disengage on acceptable terms without appearing to betray an ally that was still trying to carry on the fight.[12] Thirty-two months later, Kissinger would say the quiet part out loud. In a September 1971 memorandum to Nixon, Kissinger reflected, "The underlying assumption remains what it has been from the outset of your Administration: the manner in which we end the war, or at least our participation, is crucial both for America's global position and for the fabric of our society." The national security advisor continued: "A swift collapse in South Vietnam traced to precipitate American withdrawal would seriously endanger your effort to shape a new foreign policy role for this country. The impact on friends, adversaries and our own people would be likely to swing us from post-World War II predominance to post Vietnam abdication." In short, nothing less than the future of the American nomos was at stake. Kissinger surmised that "rather than run the risk of South Vietnam crumbling around our remaining forces, a peace settlement would end the war with an act of policy and leave the future of South Vietnam to the historical process. There would be a clear terminal date rather than a gradual winding down. We could heal the wounds in this country [the U.S.] as our men left peace behind on the battlefield and a healthy interval for South Vietnam's fate to unfold."[13]

Diplomacy was crucial to Nixon's Vietnam policy; but diplomacy, as practiced by Kissinger, was best conducted from a position of power and military superiority. Thus, when Nixon and Kissinger initiated secret discussions with Hanoi and continued the open sessions in Paris that had started under the Johnson administration, they did so with the understanding that more aggressive military operations were in the offing.[14] Indeed, the diplomatic strategy was to compel Hanoi into accepting a negotiated settlement that was most advantageous to the United States. Here, the verb form *to compel* has a distinct meaning. Following Thomas Schelling, "compellence" refers to a "threatening action that is intended not to forestall some adversarial action but to bring about some desired action, through 'fear of consequences.'"[15] In other words, "the power to hurt is bargaining power."[16] And, unlike deterrence, compellence is an active strategy. Schelling explains, "The threat that compels rather than deters often requires that the punishment be administered *until* the other acts, rather than *if* he acts. This is because often the only way to become committed to an action is to initiate it. This means, though, that the action initiated has to be tolerable to the initiator and tolerable over whatever period of time is required for the pressure to work on the other side."[17] Compellence required, for Nixon and Kissinger, a willingness to tolerate unrestricted warfare against the enemy—including the use of "diplomatic violence" against a neutral country.

Vietnamization, the second component of Nixon's strategy, is best described as an assemblage of policies and practices oriented toward the transfer of military operations from the United States to South Vietnam.[18] In April 1969, the U.S. military presence peaked, with over 540,000 personnel stationed throughout South Vietnam. If U.S. military forces stationed offshore and in neighboring Thailand were included, the total approached 626,000.[19] Nixon knew that he could not increase the number of U.S. troops in South Vietnam; but he also grasped that the immediate withdrawal of forces would threaten South Vietnam's survival and thus potentially weaken America's credibility as an ally. The intent, therefore, was to effect a gradual drawdown, in part to buy time to build up South Vietnam's Armed Forces of the Republic of Vietnam (ARVN) but also to placate an American populace tired of war.

Conceptually, Vietnamization did not appear fully formed; there is no singular document that detailed Nixon's strategy. Instead, Vietnamization marked a geopolitical conjunction of myriad reports, speeches, and memorandums. In March 1969 Secretary of Defense Melvin Laird met with both U.S. and South Vietnamese military and civilian officials in Saigon. Laird's purpose, in his words, was "to determine how we could achieve our

168 / A Widening War

objectives in Southeast Asia, consistent with our vital national interests." On his return to Washington, Laird informed Nixon that his appraisal of the war was based on four critical assumptions: (1) no breakthrough in Paris is likely in the near future that would achieve a political resolution of the conflict; (2) no U.S. military escalation beyond the limited objective of achieving and maintaining South Vietnamese sovereignty; (3) that sovereignty for South Vietnam required forces capable of self-defense; and (4) that North Vietnam would not voluntarily abandon their aim to secure political control of South Vietnam. Laird emphasized, also, the demands of the American public to "bring the war to a satisfactory conclusion" which, to most Americans, meant "the eventual disengagement of American men from combat." To the South Vietnamese leaders, specifically, Laird had stressed that "the key factor in sustaining the support of the American people is to find the means by which the burden of combat may promptly, and methodically, be shifted to the South Vietnamese." This necessitated a strategy that balanced "the safety and security of our own and allied forces . . . while working towards the objective of self-determination for the South Vietnamese." In short, Laird underscored that "substantial de-Americanization of the war is an indispensable precondition" of moving forward.[20]

Laird's assessment of the politico-military situation did not presume the termination of war in South Vietnam. Indeed, as the defense secretary conceded, Hanoi would not voluntarily give up its ultimate objective of national unification. For Laird, the path forward meant "the orderly replacement of United States Forces as the armed forces of South Vietnam take over a steadily increasing share of the war effort." Thus, when all facets of America's intervention in Indochina were phased out, U.S. policymakers intended "to leave the South Vietnamese forces with the equipment necessary for them to cope with the residual insurgency and to help deter any renewal of aggression by North Vietnam." Thus, Laird recommended the accelerated and unilateral withdrawal of U.S. forces, in order to not only satisfy demands of the American public but also to demonstrate to the South Vietnamese government the pressing need to assume the military burden.[21]

On March 28, Nixon convened his NSC to discuss the prospects of deescalation. On this critical issue, the president asked, "How do we de-Americanize this thing in such a way as to influence negotiations and have them [Saigon] move along quicker?" Nixon explained, "The reality is that we are working against a time clock. We are talking 6 to 8 months. We are going to play a strong public game but we must plan this. We must get a sense of urgency in the training of the South Vietnamese." Essentially, for Nixon, everything hinged on the need "for improvement in terms of supplies and training" of the South Vietnamese military. To this, Laird responded, "I agree, but not with your term de-Americanizing. What we need is a term Vietnamizing to put the emphasis on the right issue."[22] From that point, Vietnamization served as a touchstone for Nixon's approach to the war. Crucially, Vietnamization did not imply that the United States was any less committed to a military solution to a political problem. Indeed, as secret negotiations with the North Vietnamese continued and MACV worked to bolster the South Vietnamese armed forces, Nixon remained focused on trying to compel Hanoi to meet U.S. demands. The challenge for Abrams and other military officials was to force Hanoi's hand with a steadily dwindling number of U.S. combat forces.

Seven weeks later, Nixon delivered his first speech to the American public on the topic of the Vietnam War. The president explained that he wanted to end the war; and the easy thing would be to immediately withdraw all U.S. troops. To do so, however, would "betray" his responsibility as president, and military defeat would damage America's credibility. Nixon framed America's "essential objective in Vietnam" as the "opportunity for the South Vietnamese people to determine their own political future without interference." Surprisingly, Nixon next declared, "We are prepared to accept any government in South Vietnam that results from the free choice of the South Vietnamese people themselves."[23] This was a remarkable statement. For years, U.S. officials underscored the need to maintain a pro-Western, noncommunist government in Saigon. Neutrality was never an option. With this singular declaration, Nixon changed the political objective for U.S. intervention in Indochina from guaranteeing a free and independent South Vietnam to creating the opportunity for South Vietnam to determine its own political future.[24] In one fell swoop, Nixon transformed America's grand strategy, effectively negating the domino theory and the accompanying specter of global domination by the communists. South Vietnam was important because U.S. policy and practice in the region demonstrated America's resolve to sustain U.S. global hegemony and credibility.[25] Beyond that, Vietnam's geopolitical importance was less important.

170 / A Widening War

On July 25, 1969, Nixon spoke before a group of reporters on the island of Guam. "The United States," he announced, "is going to be facing . . . a major decision: What will be its role in Asia and in the Pacific after the end of the war in Vietnam?" This was not a question posed only by U.S. officials, Nixon explained, for "the Asian nations will [also] be wondering about what that decision is." Nixon expounded that, through personal conversations he had with other world leaders, "they all wondered whether the United States, because of its frustration over the war in Vietnam, because of its earlier frustration over the war in Korea—whether the United States would continue to play a significant role in Asia . . . [or] whether we would withdraw from the Pacific and play a minor role." The Asia-Pacific region, Nixon added, remained of vital importance; and he was "convinced that the way to avoid becoming involved in another war in Asia is for the United States to continue to play a significant role." The president said, "As we look at Asia today, we see that the major world power which adopts a very aggressive attitude and a belligerent attitude in foreign policy, Communist China, of course is in Asia." Therefore, Nixon cautioned, "As we look at Asia, it poses, in my view, over the long haul, looking down to the end of the century, the greatest threat to the peace of the world, and, for that reason the United States should continue to play a significant role." And yet, Nixon clarified, Asia also posed "the greatest hope for progress in the world—progress in the world because of its ability, the resources, the ability of the people, the resources physically that are available in this part of the world." For Nixon, the resolution of Asia's contradictions—the greatest threat and the greatest hope—required a sustained American presence but a presence mediated by a rapidly changing world. Nixon maintained that "Asia" should be "for the Asians" and he alluded to the emergence not only of countless Asian nationalisms but also of a regional pride. The Asian people, Nixon suggested, increasingly saw themselves in geographic terms; and this would form the basis of U.S. foreign policy moving forward. "Asia for the Asians," Nixon repeated, "is want we want, and that is the role we should play. We should assist, but we should not dictate. . . . We must avoid that kind of policy that will make countries in Asia so dependent upon us that we are dragged into conflicts such as the one that we have in Vietnam." And with that pronouncement, the president articulated what became known as the Nixon Doctrine. Nixon asserted:

I believe that the time has come when the United States, in our relations with all of our Asian friends, must be quite emphatic on two points: One, that we will keep our treaty commitments . . . ; but, two, that as far as the problems of internal security are concerned, as far as the problems of military defense, except for the threat of a major power involving nuclear weapons, that the United States is going to encourage and has a right to expect that this problem will be increasingly handled by, and the responsibility for it taken by, the Asian nations themselves.[26]

The Nixon Doctrine was not a clarion call for isolationism. Nixon was not pulling back America's hegemonic position in the world but instead was forwarding a more efficient means to fulfill the American nomos. Channeling the ghost of Kennan, Nixon argued for a return to selective engagement. Once an ardent Cold Warrior and fervent anticommunist, Nixon now saw political wisdom in exploiting the deep interstices of the communist bloc and commit his troops on a case-by-case basis. America would retain a global military footprint, certainly, but would no longer zealously push back communism wherever it emerged out of the shadows. Future interventions would be selective. America's failure in Vietnam, to this point, demonstrated for Nixon the wisdom of such an approach. Cambodia would demonstrate its malfeasance. Where South Vietnam—albeit increasingly marginal to Nixon's geopolitical imagination—remained exemplary of America's credibility, Cambodia was central but expendable.

The "Menu" Bombings

As the Nixon administration engaged in parallel open and secret negotiations with Hanoi and simultaneously implemented its Vietnamization program, a third option was considered early on: escalation of the war by massive air strikes on North Vietnam or large-scale air and ground attacks on the infiltration routes, sanctuaries, and staging areas on Cambodian and Laotian territory.[27] This third option was considered for several reasons. First, an aggressive military option—even as U.S. combat troops were being withdrawn—would support diplomatic efforts to win the war, namely to demonstrate Nixon's resolve to the North Vietnamese. Second, disruption of the enemy's capability supported the broader effort of transferring the fighting to the South Vietnamese military. This would, in turn, help the Saigon

172 / A Widening War

government to gain further legitimacy in the eyes of the South Vietnamese. Lastly, there always remained a glimmer of hope that somehow the U.S. military could find the elusive "tipping point": that fabled inflection point where Hanoi would conclude that fighting was no longer worthwhile. In short, an expansion of the war offered a potential final path to ending the war with the United States emerging as the ostensible victor.

During the waning months of the Johnson administration, the resolve of the U.S. military establishment stiffened on the need to take a more aggressive stance against enemy forces in Cambodia. Both MACV and the JCS repeatedly forwarded requests for authorization to expand military operations, especially into Cambodian territory, in an effort to interdict the infiltration of soldiers and supplies and to eliminate enemy sanctuaries and bases operating with impunity. The political border separating Cambodia and South Vietnam extended from near the South Vietnamese village of Dak To in the Central Highlands southwest to the Gulf of Thailand. Far from a straight boundary, the border meanders, giving rise to several distinct projections, including a salient known as the Parrot's Beak, formed by the tip of the Cambodian province of Svay Reing intruding approximately forty miles into South Vietnam. At its apex, the Parrot's Beak was about thirty miles from Saigon. To the north of this projection was an irregular formation, designated by U.S. officials as Angel's Wing and, on the south, the Crow's Nest. North of the Parrot's Beak, in Kompong Cham province, were two smaller salients, Dog's Head and Fishhook, which extend into South Vietnam.[28] Based on intelligence gathered predominantly from covert aerial and ground reconnaissance missions, military analysts identified these geographic locations as base areas for both PAVN and PLAF forces.

In an attempt to work within international legal rules and conventions, diplomatic overtures to Sihanouk failed repeatedly, and the delays from fruitless negotiations allowed the enemy time to recover and regroup. In September 1968, for example, the JCS provided an extensive review of "the current threat posed by VC/NVA uses of Cambodian territory as a sanctuary and source of supply" and recommended several "political and military measures to cope with this threat or to induce the Cambodian government to take more effective counter-measures against VC/NVA forces in Cambodia."[29] In response, the Joint State-Defense-CIA Study Group for Cambodia (operating on an ad hoc basis since its establishment in December 1966) underscored—again—the lack of "consensus on the extent, the significance to the Communist cause, or the physical routes used in channeling Communist supplies through Cambodia." William Bundy especially voiced his frustration with "what he viewed as a failure of the intelligence community to pursue this problem with sufficient vigor and purpose."[30]

Two days after Nixon won the presidential election, General Earl Wheeler, chair of the Joint Chiefs of Staff, sent a telegram to Admiral John McCain, commander-in-chief, Pacific Command. Wheeler affirmed that there was "general agreement on the extent of VC use of Cambodia for base areas, sanctuary, training, supply, command and control, etc." but there remained "a difference of opinion on the extent to which arms and ammunition [were] imported through Cambodian ports and distributed with Cambodian complicity." On this latter point, Wheeler was unconcerned, stressing the "general agreement on the existence and importance of those base areas." In other words, the ongoing debates regarding the magnitude of use were less important than the simple fact that Cambodian territory was being used. Any reviews should be placed within "its proper context as it relates to the policy questions involving actions against Cambodia." Moving forward, Wheeler proposed thinking about "offensive action against Cambodia" from two different positions, the first being a "direct attack against base areas and enemy forces located in Cambodia," and the second being "political and military operations to neutralize the logistic system within Cambodia supporting those enemy forces." This was a crucial distinction, Wheeler concluded, in that "the rationale for attacking the base areas is not directly dependent on the extent of Cambodian logistic support."[31]

McCain was largely in agreement. In a series of telegrams sent in December 1968, McCain upheld "the fundamental importance of viewing Laos and Cambodia as integral parts of the overall problem of containing Communist aggression in Southeast Asia." Observing that the "North Vietnamese design for eventual domination of the Indochina area [had] been set back" by U.S. military operations, he warned that "the problem of VC/NVA use of Cambodia" remained a "constant concern."[32] The logistical routes in Cambodia were crucial to the overall U.S. strategy in support of South Vietnam, McCain explained, adding that upward of 60 percent of PAVN/PLAF supplies moved through Cambodia. Accordingly, for the admiral, "denial of the Cambodian logistic base would have significant adverse effects on

174 / A Widening War

[Hanoi's] military capability in the southern part of [South Vietnam]."[33] And of Sihanouk, McCain scoffed that the prince was "of more value to the Communists as a 'neutralist' than as a declared ally." McCain believed that the United States "should apply maximum military pressure against the enemy wherever and whenever tactically feasible, including Cambodian border areas, with a view towards causing the greatest impact possible on the Communist overall strategic plans for the Indo-Chinese area."[34] McCain did, almost as an afterthought, admit that any military operations were "subject to political considerations."

Under the Nixon administration, Cambodia moved to center stage. During a cabinet meeting convened on January 30, Kissinger asked "whether or not there was some type of planning activities that could be initiated which would signal to the North that we might be considering a step-up or escalation of operations." Several possibilities were raised that could *signal* U.S. escalation but fall short of actual on-the-ground operations, including increased aerial reconnaissance and the movement of additional aircraft carriers into the region. Wheeler however raised the ante, suggesting "that perhaps some additional offensive operations in Laos or Cambodia would be appropriate." Specifically, Wheeler proposed that "a foray by ground forces into North Vietnamese base areas, sanctuaries or logistics installations might prove very effective." In fact, the general noted, an operation had already been planned that would include attacks on base areas in the Fishhook region of Cambodia. Laird, unwilling to commit to an expanded war, cautioned that increased military operations in Cambodia would pose a difficult political problem, a concern that neither Wheeler nor Kissinger shared.[35]

Laird was not alone in seeking nonmilitary solutions. On February 5, for example, the White House considered several diplomatic courses of action with respect to Cambodia. Secretary of State Rogers favored this option, seeing that "an eventual resumption of relations, and easing of the atmosphere in the meantime, is to our advantage." He explained that "even a small U.S. representation would give us some intelligence and information gains. If it progressed to the point where we had good military attachés there, with freedom to travel, we might in the end learn a great deal more—while the fact that we were watching might operate to tone down the supply activities now taking place through Cambodia." Rogers, consequently, recommended that a first step "be a declaration of respect and recognition of the sovereignty, independence, neutrality and territorial integrity of Cambodia within its present frontiers." This was a prudent move, Rogers counseled, in that "Sihanouk [had] repeatedly stated that such a statement, along lines issued by more than 40 countries, [was] the only pre-condition to improvement and resumption of relations."[36]

Predictably, staff at MACV continued to press for expanded military operations on Cambodian territory. On February 9, Abrams asked Wheeler for authorization to conduct B-52 raids over Cambodia.[37] Abrams based his request on a proposal forwarded by General Walter Kerwin. Based on recently obtained intelligence, Kerwin asserted that the elusive Central Office for South Vietnam (COSVN) had been located in the Fishhook area along the Cambodian border. As such, Kerwin proposed a single "short-duration, concentrated" strike of forty-two B-52s against COSVN, coupled with a similar attack against North Vietnamese forces operating in the area. Kerwin advised that while the operation could be conducted without harming Cambodian citizens, it should be conducted in secrecy. After a review of the proposed operation, Abrams supported the idea of bombing COSVN and it was this component of the plan that the general forwarded to Wheeler.[38] However, the operation could not appear to be a preemptive action. Abrams, as such, advised that the massive aerial bombardment on Cambodia soil be staged to appear as a retaliatory strike following a North Vietnamese attack on South Vietnam.

As the Abrams-Kerwin proposal solidified, it came to the attention of Ellsworth Bunker, U.S. ambassador to South Vietnam. Hawkish on the war, Bunker agreed to the operation and cabled to the State Department his approval. Clearly aware of the possible diplomatic fallout, Bunker added, "I realize fully the political implications of such a strike on Cambodian soil, but notwithstanding I support General Abrams in his request for authority to mount a strike. If Sihanouk complains, our rejoinder must be that COSVN is located on his territory and has been for years. He has done nothing about it although his forces in the area are fully aware of COSVN's presence. Preparations are being made for new attacks on South Vietnam and Saigon and we cannot permit these attacks to be planned and mounted from Cambodia." Bunker added, erroneously, that "no Cambodians live in [the] immediate area."[39] Bunker's endorsement, ironically, prevented the operation from being immediately implemented. By alerting the State Department to

176 / A Widening War

the plan, Nixon and Kissinger feared that leaks from the department would make denial of the bombing impossible to sustain.[40] As such, in an act of internal subterfuge, Kissinger instructed Rogers to inform Bunker that the matter should be tabled in anticipation of a presidential trip to Europe. Concurrently, Kissinger told Abrams to establish a back-channel communication in order to bypass both the U.S. embassy in Saigon and the State Department.[41]

Four days later Kissinger met with several key advisors, including Laird, Wheeler, Haig, Pursley, and Deputy Secretary of Defense David Packard. Discussion of possible B-52 strikes over Cambodia centered on two basic options: (1) an overtly deliberate strike or (2) a covert strike officially categorized as a mistake. Furthermore, each option contained three alternatives: (a) an attack without provocation; (b) an attack in response to a strategic provocation, that is, a large-scale enemy attack against a major South Vietnamese population center not near the suspected location of the COSVN Headquarters; or (c) an attack in response to a tactical provocation in the vicinity of the Cambodian border. The pros and cons of the resultant 2 × 3 matrix of possible B-52 strikes were then discussed. For example, "Option 2, Alternative 3" would constitute a "covert strike officially categorized as a mistake in retaliation for a tactical provocation." In this scenario, the United States would strike back against NVA forces active in South Vietnam but "accidentally" bomb targets inside Cambodia. From a diplomatic standpoint, this option provided the "most reasonable and credible circumstances internationally for acceptance of [a] U.S. cover story." In addition, this option had the advantage of demonstrating U.S. resolve both to Hanoi and Moscow, a key consideration given Nixon and Kissinger's strategy to compel Hanoi into accepting a negotiated settlement. In the end, it was recommended that "in order to set the stage for a possible covert attack" a message be sent to Abrams "authorizing him to bomb right up to the Cambodian border in the Fish Hook area" and that Abrams also "be authorized to continue planning for execution of the strike on a contingency basis." In other words, if the NVA launched a military operation *in response to U.S. military operations*, U.S. officials could reframe Hanoi's response as a military provocation. In the event Hanoi did not immediately retaliate, U.S. military operations would wait until such a response was provoked. Either way, Hanoi's counterattack to U.S. provocation would be used as justification for U.S. retaliation against North Vietnamese aggression. On the following day, Nixon signed his approval. Operation Breakfast was underway.[42]

On February 22, Kissinger began putting the pieces in place. Kissinger instructed Laird to relay Nixon's authorization to Abrams to "conduct B-52 strikes right up to the Cambodian border on the South Vietnamese side in the Fish Hook area." In addition, "a strictly back channel, eyes only message for General Abrams should be dispatched advising General Abrams to continue planning for execution of the strikes on a contingency basis." Abrams was to "be advised to maintain a continual appraisal of the tactical situation" in the designated zone with "the view towards advising us as soon as the military situation might arise which would justify the contingency strike in accordance" with the recommendations developed on February 19. Kissinger concluded that "I contemplate that should a sizeable enemy attack develop . . . in the vicinity of the Fish Hook that highest authority will approve the COSVN strike based upon the recommendations of General Abrams and an overall assessment of the military situation elsewhere in Vietnam." It was critical, therefore, that Laird "stand ready . . . to execute this attack option with minimum prior notice."[43]

All that remained was a suitable "provocation" initiated by Hanoi so that the United States could justifiably retaliate and "accidentally" bomb Cambodia. The wait was not long. On February 22 the PAVN and PLAF launched offensive operations against 125 locations throughout South Vietnam, although most targeted military installations near Saigon and Da Nang. For U.S. military analysts, the concentration of attacks in the vicinity of Saigon was a clear indication that the attacks were coming from sanctuaries inside Cambodia, to the west of Saigon. Nixon, en route to Brussels on a state visit, ordered an immediate execution of the proposed B-52 strikes on Cambodian territory. Kissinger balked, however. Believing the plan incomplete, he recommended a forty-eight-hour postponement. Nixon agreed.[44]

Of the proposed bombing campaign, Laird continued to voice his reservations. As plans were being refined, the defense secretary relayed to Nixon "some facts of the matter which continue[d] to bother" him. Laird explained that he had asked Wheeler "to put the operational machinery in motion that [was] necessary if the mission [was] to be carried out on the currently outlined schedule." And on that point, the secretary of defense conceded that he had no doubt "that the proposed strikes [could] be executed effectively."

178 / A Widening War

However, Laird raised the likelihood that some people might "not look with favor upon this mission" and that it was reasonable to believe that this was politically fraught. In particular, given the "presumed widespread knowledge of this possible mission, it would be difficult to claim, and make credible, an operational error." Laird anticipated significant pushback both from Congress and the media. Equally difficult, Laid reasoned, was the justification of B-52 strikes "against an alleged enemy headquarters in a neutral nation" given the "moderate scale [of enemy operations] thus far and the currently diminishing level of enemy activity." Laird counseled that "it would be better to hold this attack for a period in which the scope, intensity, and duration of enemy-initiated activity [were] at more pronounced levels."[45]

Nixon was determined to see through the carpet-bombing of Cambodia but conceded that diplomatic entanglements continued to pose a problem.[46] Publicly, the White House maintained that the political future of South Vietnam rested with the Saigon government. U.S. diplomacy would facilitate contact between Saigon and representatives of the National Liberation Front. Behind the scenes, however, secretive talks *without* the participation of Saigon or the NLF would take place. Crucially, private bilateral talks between Hanoi and Washington would only address the possibility of mutual withdrawal of military forces from South Vietnam. Political matters, including the future of South Vietnam, were off the table. In a March 10 memorandum, Kissinger outlined the challenges ahead, foremost of which was to compel Hanoi to enter into private talks. If handled wrongly, the United States would look weak. Hanoi might infer that America's overture to reach a settlement stemmed from a weakened military position or because of domestic opposition to the war.[47] America's credibility was at stake and the Nixon White House required some *forcible action* that would induce Hanoi to comply with their objectives. The threat or actual bombing of North Vietnam served as a compellent; so too did the targeting of Vietnamese communists forces in Cambodia. In the interim, however, diplomatic talks between officials at the U.S. State Department and their Soviet counterparts threatened to undermine Nixon's strategy. Regarding a recent conversation between Rogers and Soviet Ambassador Anatoly Dobrynin, for example, Kissinger warned that comments made by the U.S. secretary of state "seriously cut across our strategy."[48] Nixon fumed. "We cannot," the president complained, "have this thing running in every direction!"[49]

A Widening War / 179

In principle, Nixon and Kissinger agreed that diplomacy and military operations were inseparable. However, to be effective, both components needed to be framed as autonomous, at least initially as negotiations were being planned. On this point, Kissinger premised that "if you hit Cambodia after the private talks start it can break them, and you will be accused of insincerity." It was better to be preemptive, Kissinger believed. "Hit them," Kissinger told the president, "and then ask for private talks." Nixon questioned if other members of his cabinet agreed with Kissinger. The national security advisor explained that Packard was in support but Rogers believed the bombings would be bad for negotiations. Kissinger acknowledged, "I don't believe it will be easy for you to attack Cambodia while private talks are going on and not much is being done in South Vietnam." Nixon retorted, "My point is if, while the private talks are going on and they are kicking us, we are going to do something." The president stressed, "There is not going to be any de-escalation. State [Department] has nothing to do with that. We are just going to keep giving word to Wheeler to knock [the] hell out of them." In light of recent enemy activity, Nixon explained, "We cannot tolerate one more of these without hitting back. We have already warned them. Presumably they have stopped. If they hit us again, we hit them with no warning. That is the way we are going to do it. I can't tolerate argument from Rogers on initiating private talks with the North Vietnamese in Paris 'to see how they behave.'" Nixon concluded, "In the future, we will have to keep more close control. I think that Bill [Rogers] did not realize the tremendous significance of tying political with military matters."[50]

Laird's ongoing efforts to halt the proposed bombing campaign went for naught as Nixon was determined to let Hanoi know "who is boss around here."[51] On March 18 the first B-52 bombing raids against Cambodia were carried out.[52] Wheeler was ecstatic. The "secondaries [secondary explosions] were about 4 to 7 times the normal bomb burst," the general marveled. For Wheeler, "this was significant" in that it seemed to confirm reports of massive supplies of armaments stored inside Cambodia. Kissinger reflected on the diplomatic side of the bombing. If Hanoi responds militarily "without any diplomatic screaming," Kissinger mused, "we are in the driver's seat."[53]

In the event the B-52 strikes did become public, the White House was prepared to treat the missions as routine military operations within the

180 / A Widening War

framework of ongoing military operations in Cambodian territory. Kissinger, for example, clarified that "BREAKFAST Plan would be announced routinely by Saigon as a normal B-52 operation against targets along the Cambodian border. The targets would not be specifically identified." In addition, "Press briefings and backgrounders would in no way directly identify the action as the 'appropriate response' to the Saigon/Hue shellings" and that "all press queries [would] be referred to the Saigon spokesperson who [would] neither affirm nor deny reports of attacks on Cambodia but state that this [was] under investigation." Indeed, "with respect to any attacks against Cambodia," Kissinger stressed, the administration would "take the same public position of 'no comment' as in the case of bombing attacks on Laos." Should Phnom Penh protest, the United States would neither confirm nor deny knowledge of the attacks but indicate that investigations would be forthcoming. If, however, Sihanouk became too vocal in his protests, the White House would apologize and offer compensation. If this still did not satisfy the Cambodian leader, the White House would "acknowledge responsibility, offer compensation [but] explain that incidents along the Cambodian border [occurred] due to the extensive VC use of military exploitation of Cambodian territory" and that the Nixon administration would request an international investigation of the territory in question.[54] Effectively, the last recourse was to fix blame on Sihanouk himself for allowing the Vietnamese communists access to Cambodian territory.

Of course, neither Nixon nor Kissinger anticipated the Cambodian bombings to become public. Well aware of Cambodia's neutral status, Nixon directed that all information on Menu operations be closely guarded. Knowledge of both the strategic and tactical dimensions was limited to those individuals essential to the operation; and to ensure secrecy, an elaborate procedure was devised to conceal the bombings. MACV was the driving force of the campaign. Abrams, assisted by a few staff officers, nominated Menu targets through McCain to the JCS for final approval by Laird, Kissinger, and Nixon. Initially, Abrams submitted each target individually; beginning in late August, however, the White House allowed him to propose weekly packages, each including three or four attacks. Under a system developed by MACV staff officers, each Menu raid began with the launching of a regularly requested ARC LIGHT strike against targets within South Vietnam. However, Abrams concurrently submitted the actual

Menu strike requests, by special security communication channels, through CINCPAC to the JCS, who obtained the approval of the secretary of defense. In this way, the cover missions allowed inclusion of the Menu sorties in the regular statistical summaries of air activity. From a tactical standpoint, Menu sorties were conducted at night and directed by ground control radar. All missions were flown so that the aircraft passed over or near the targets in South Vietnam, although the ordnance was dropped on the Menu targets in Cambodia. To further conceal the actual bombing locations, even from U.S. military personnel, the B-52 crews were briefed on the South Vietnam targets and received instructions to avoid Cambodia. In-flight, pilots and navigators received new target coordinates; all other crew members remained unaware that their aircraft was being guided beyond the designated target in South Vietnam to strike locations in Cambodia. Upon returning, as crew members filed routine reports as though the strikes had been carried out on the Vietnamese targets, separate and highly classified reports were submitted through a secret channel for the Menu strikes. Effectively, the Menu operations were included in overall statistical totals for the war effort but were not identified with Cambodia. After each strike, MACV used aerial reconnaissance and, wherever and whenever possible, deployed SALEM HOUSE teams to assess bomb damage.[55]

The original scope of the operation was for a single B-52 raid.[56] However, both MACV and the Nixon administration were so pleased with the initial results that authorization for the continuance of covert B-52 strikes on Cambodian territory was given. The overall campaign was now designated as Operation Menu. Subsequent missions, code-named Lunch, Dinner, Dessert, Snack, and Supper, targeted based areas along the Cambodian–South Vietnamese border.[57] Operation Menu continued, in secret for fifteen months until it was terminated on May 26, 1970. In total, 3,875 sorties were flown, dropping 180,823 tons of munitions onto Cambodia.[58]

The Coup against Sihanouk

In November 1963 Sihanouk had renounced U.S. military and economic aid, and in 1965 the prince broke all diplomatic relations with Washington. These were bold moves, both from a political and military vantage point. Sihanouk's renunciation of diplomatic ties with the United States only deepened the suspicions of many civilian and military analysts of the

182 / A Widening War

Cambodian leader's "leftist" turn to Beijing and Hanoi. However, there were several domestic consequences of Sihanouk's decision. Between 1955 and 1963, for example, Cambodia received approximately U.S.$400 million from the United States, comprising 30 percent of Sihanouk's defense budget and 14 percent of its total budget.[59] In fact, the amount of U.S. aid surpassed the combined amount of aid provided by China and the Soviet Union. This worried Sihanouk, though, and for good reason. Progressively, U.S. aid programs were creating a military class in Cambodia dependent on the United States and, as such, Sihanouk feared that Cambodia was becoming an American client state. Consequently, to cope with the loss of U.S. assistance, Sihanouk nationalized major sectors of the economy.[60] By way of illustration, in early 1964, foreign trade, including rice exports, was placed under the control of a new state corporation given monopoly control, the Société nationale d'exportation et d'importation (SONEXIM). In turn, the existing Royal Cooperative Office became responsible for the purchase and processing of the rice export crop, which was then sold through SONEXIM, which subsequently controlled the import of agricultural inputs, including fertilizers, pesticides, and farm equipment, which were distributed for sale through the Royal Cooperative Office.[61]

Initially, Sihanouk's strategy appeared to be working. Cambodia exported 500,000 tons in both 1964 and 1965, with total rice production levels in excess of 2.5 million tons. By 1966, however, the economy took a downward turn, thus contributing to societal unrest. The nationalization of rice, for example, maintained state profits through the suppression of the domestic price of rice. This came at the expense, however, of smallholder farmers who could no longer pay their debts after selling their crops at the government-fixed price.[62] Compounding the government's problem was the fact that large portions of rice exports were being sold on the black market, depriving the state of tax revenue.[63] With armed conflict intensifying in neighboring South Vietnam—and the significant presence of PAVN and PLAF operating within Cambodian territory—Chinese merchants in Phnom Penh and other urban centers were anxious to sell rice and other goods directly to the Vietnamese communists because the latter paid in American dollars at international rates. Dependent on its heavy taxation of rice exports, the government was running short of legitimate sources of income.[64] This impelled Sihanouk to launch a campaign, known as *ramassage du paddy*, to force farmers to sell their rice to the government at artificially low prices.[65] Farmers caught selling rice illegally were severely punished.

The struggle over land rights, coupled with government campaigns to forcibly collect rice from recalcitrant peasants, proved volatile. Beginning in March 1967 localized uprisings flared up around Samlaut in western Battambang province; by the end of the year, these rebellions had developed into armed conflict throughout much of the country.[66] Villagers seized arms, destroyed government property, and killed government officials, sparking unrest in other provinces among the disaffected rural poor.[67] Sihanouk responded in force, ordering the Cambodian military to wage a bloody counterattack on the Khmer Rouge, a derogatory term he coined in reference to the protestors. Convinced that the Vietnamese communists were behind the uprisings—a premise that carried some validity—Sihanouk offered a bounty for the severed head of any captured insurgent. Retribution became spectacle with the public execution of suspected leaders and the screening of graphic films of the killings throughout the country. Sihanouk reportedly claimed to have put to death fifteen hundred Khmer Rouge during the rebellion.[68]

Social unrest and discontent were not limited to rural Cambodia. Sihanouk's nationalization policies angered Cambodia's small but vocal commercial class. Likewise, a growing mass of high school and university graduates were unable to find jobs commensurate with their education, and members of the Cambodian armed forces resented budgetary cuts following Sihanouk's decision to cut ties with the United States.[69] Sihanouk was accumulating enemies along a broad spectrum of Cambodian society with a diminishing set of options with which to respond. In a desperate attempt to stabilize his regime, on August 12 Sihanouk named General Lon Nol as prime minister and minister of defense. Prince Sisowath Sirik Matak, a cousin and rival of Sihanouk, was appointed deputy prime minister. Soon thereafter, Lon Nol and Sirik Matak commenced a program of economic reforms and a policy of denationalization. Sihanouk initially agreed to these policies but, by October, he began to voice his opposition. In addition, both Lon Nol and Sirik Matak turned their attention to the use of Cambodian territory by PAVN and PLAF forces. Sihanouk, who retained oversight of foreign affairs, viewed this as a foreign policy matter; Lon Nol and Sirik Matak considered it a domestic problem.[70]

184 / A Widening War

In early March 1970 public protests between pro- and anti-Sihanouk factions and several anti-Vietnamese demonstrations erupted in Phnom Penh and along the Cambodian–South Vietnamese border. These were neither spontaneous nor incidental but instead marked a concerted effort by Lon Nol and his followers to foment discord among the Cambodian population and used as the backdrop for more sweeping geopolitical changes. On the diplomatic front, Lon Nol and Sirik Matak canceled Sihanouk's trade agreement with North Vietnam and the NLF that had permitted them to purchase supplies in Cambodia and to use the port at Sihanoukville; in addition, the two collaborators ordered Vietnamese communist troops to leave the country.[71] Then, on the morning of March 18, General Lon Nol, Prince Sirik Matak, and their coconspirators in the Cambodian legislature deposed Sihanouk in absentia and seized governmental power.[72]

The roots of the coup are deep and intimately entangled with U.S. foreign policy: the sustained B-52 bombings of Operation Menu, repeated cross-border operations conducted by U.S. Special Forces and/or South Vietnamese forces, and recurrent intimations that Washington would welcome the removal of Sihanouk. That said, much remains hidden, including the degree of U.S. complicity and culpability in the coup. In the immediate aftermath, officials from Beijing to Hanoi to Paris quickly blamed the Nixon administration for orchestrating the coup. On April 4, for example, Le Duc Tho, North Vietnam's chief negotiator with Kissinger at the Paris peace talks, accused Washington of organizing the coup in Cambodia in an attempt to "put pressure on the resistance fight of the Vietnamese people and to threaten the Democratic Republic of Vietnam."[73] Both Nixon and Kissinger remained steadfast in their denials of U.S. involvement in the action; indeed, to date, no direct link between the U.S. government and Sihanouk's usurpers before the coup has been established.[74] Regardless of American complicity, the coup against Sihanouk irrevocably altered the geopolitical terrain of the war in Vietnam. In the words of a CIA analyst, "The move against Sihanouk . . . opened a Pandora's box."[75]

Widening the War

In the immediate aftermath of the coup, Nixon called on his top advisors to assess the situation. With the overthrow of Sihanouk, Kissinger asked if a communist insurgency might develop in Cambodia. Thus far, the Khmer

Rouge were considered little more than a "nuisance."[76] Would the coup alter this calculation? Thomas Karamessines, deputy director of plans at the CIA, thought this scenario possible but not probable. CIA intelligence suggested that "the strength of nationalist sentiment against the Communists" was quite strong in Cambodia. Could Hanoi capitalize on the coup? Undersecretary of State Alexis Johnson was doubtful: the North Vietnamese would not want to get involved in a war on two fronts in the South. Karamessines added that "the North Vietnamese would have no reason to mount an insurgency since they could continue to use Cambodia territory. Even if the Cambodians stopped cooperating with the communists, the latter would find it difficult to retaliate because the Cambodians might enlist South Vietnamese assistance in suppressing communist insurgents." In a separate report, State Department official Theodore Eliot submitted a suite of possible scenarios for Cambodia. He suggested, in general, that the United States continue to support Cambodian neutrality and territorial integrity and "not trying to force Cambodia into our camp." If the new regime asked for military assistance or U.S. troops, Nixon should react cautiously and "avoid getting sucked into a major role."[77] Given the uncertainty, Nixon directed Richard Helms, director of the CIA, to "develop and implement a plan for maximum assistance to pro U.S. element in Cambodia." All planning, Nixon insisted, was to be completely secret: "Handle like our air strikes."[78]

Following the meeting, Kissinger provided Nixon with a more extensive update on the situation in Cambodia. Kissinger began with a brief comment on what was known, that Cheng Heng, chairman of the National Assembly, was entrusted with the functions of chief of state; effectively, however, both Lon Nol (prime minister) and Sirik Matak (deputy prime minister) appeared to be in control. Lon Nol, notably, had the backing of the military and also reputedly controlled much of the "lucrative smuggling trade with the Communists." Kissinger counseled that, publicly, Lon Nol was vehemently opposed to communism; however, the general's previous "dealing[s] with the Communists do not suggest that he is a fervent anti-Communist or anti-Vietnamese patriot." Kissinger guessed that the situation would probably take one of three courses: a Lon Nol–Sirik Matak government supported by the Cambodian military; a compromise between Lon Nol, Sirik Matak, and Sihanouk; or a Sihanouk victory. Regardless,

186 / A Widening War

Kissinger believed, any future government in Phnom Penh would "probably have to be more circumspect and covert about its cooperation with the Vietnamese."[79]

An immediate decision centered on recognition of the new government. Kissinger, for example, understood that the constitutionality of the regime change was "doubtful." Rogers, likewise, voiced his caution. He suggested to Kissinger, "I think we should be very careful not to say anything until we know more about it." Kissinger replied, "All we are saying [now] is that we respect their neutrality and not another word."[80] Two days later, Kissinger informed Nixon, "We have taken the line that the U.S. Government has not taken any action to alter the status of its diplomatic relations with Phnom Penh. We have not explicitly recognized the new regime. . . . They claim to be the continuing legal Government of Cambodia, and we have simply not challenged that claim."[81] Frankly, recognition of the new regime by the Nixon White House would be nothing more than window dressing. For several months the United States had waged a covert aerial campaign on Cambodian while publicly declaring its respect for Cambodian sovereignty, neutrality, and territorial integrity. Diplomatic formalities, in practice, mattered little in the conduct of war.

As U.S. officials vacillated on the appropriate course of action, senior leaders in Beijing made overtures to the new government in Phnom Penh in an effort to solidify North Vietnamese access to base areas and supply routes in Cambodia. As Isaacs explains, this was no trivial offer, for it meant that China would not sponsor Sihanouk as head of a rival Khmer government or support a Cambodian liberation war.[82] Lon Nol, however, balked at the Chinese offer and decided instead to forge a relationship with the Americans, built on the assumption that they were joined in a fight against a common enemy, that is, communism.[83] Rebuffed in their proposal, Chinese officials did subsequently encourage Sihanouk to form a government-in-exile and, on March 23, the prince announced the formation of the National United Front of Kampuchea (Front Uni National du Kampuchea, or FUNK). Two months later Sihanouk established the Royal Government of National Union of Kampuchea (Gouvernement Royal d'Union Nationale du Kampuchea, or GRUNK). Sihanouk would serve as head of state, and Penn Nouth was picked to serve as prime minister.[84] In outward appearances, Sihanouk and Penn Nouth provided legitimacy to the government; in reality, the government was nothing more than a façade. Behind the scenes, in the tropical rainforests of northeastern Cambodia, real power was exercised exclusively by Pol Pot, Ieng Sary, Nuon Chea, and a few other key cadres.

Sihanouk recognized his Faustian bargain, but he also understood the wider geopolitical game Nixon was playing. Writing in the journal *Foreign Affairs,* Sihanouk disparaged the Nixon administration. Sihanouk was convinced that the United States had valid reasons for fighting against communism in Southeast Asia but that "it would be pure hypocrisy to assert that the United States is defending the highest interests of the Indochinese peoples . . . from falling to communism, using for that purpose bombs and napalm, and an apocalyptic destruction of the countries and peoples concerned." Sihanouk was no communist. But he understood that, in the eyes of the oppressed, "communism can only be, now and in the future, a deliverance." Sihanouk was prophetic in his conclusions: "The longer the United States insists on maintaining unpopular and pro-imperialist regimes in our countries, the more it will draw upon itself the hatred of our peoples and will, in consequence, build up both their revolutionary movements and their fighting solidarity."[85]

Hanoi likewise responded to the coup after an initial delay. Militarily, PAVN and PLAF forces in Cambodia began an offensive to secure the border region and to isolate Phnom Penh, while simultaneously starting to organize and arm the communist insurgents in the Khmer Rouge.[86] At this point, the Khmer Rouge—MACV's "nuisance"—probably had little more than three thousand members within its ranks. However, a CIA intelligence brief warned that prior to the coup, Hanoi was attempting to "foster a revolutionary movement and take control" of Cambodia. Specific objectives included a long-range program of subversion, the establishment of Cambodian front groups, and the support of the Khmer Rouge; these would all be aided by "VC/NVA military forces." The report expounded that "Cambodia [had] always occupied an important place in Vietnamese Communists goals to gain hegemony over Southeast Asia." As such, CIA analysts determined that communist sympathies in Cambodia were external in origin, that is, orchestrated by Hanoi. Indeed, the report concluded, "Hanoi's long-range goal of controlling the whole of Indochina must have been the most compelling reason for the emergence of the Khmer Rouge insurgency."[87] On this point, Hanoi's objectives in Cambodia mirrored Washington's. For

188 / A Widening War

both belligerents, Cambodian territory was violated in an effort to gain a strategic military advantage in South Vietnam. The coup and Sihanouk's subsequent "defection" to the communist side threatened to tilt the pendulum to Hanoi's benefit.

Incursions into Cambodia

With Sihanouk's formation of a Chinese-backed government-in-exile, the Nixon administration saw little choice but to support the Lon Nol regime. On March 23, Helms submitted a series of proposals in response to Nixon's directive four days earlier. Helms believed that "the core of any strategy devised to maintain the present government in power should consist of two elements." Overtly, the U.S. government's goal was to help the Cambodian government to maintain a stance of neutrality. This had the added benefit of gaining the "maximum of international sympathy" in that the United States could not be accused of converting Cambodia into a puppet state. Covertly, however, the United States was to "work to support and sustain the present Cambodian Government by supporting its military effort against the Viet Cong in Cambodia and shoring up its position by the provision of covert economic and political support." In other words, the United States would treat Cambodia as a puppet state to achieve its more pressing objectives in South Vietnam.[88]

Helms conceded that current information on "the exact balance of forces in Cambodia" was "thin." He noted that "some covert channels" were available and could be used "to develop detailed plans for clandestine assistance." In addition, the director advised, the United States should "send a senior CIA official on a discreet trip to Cambodia to make clandestine contact with our better placed agents." This would, Helms explained, "yield not only immediate intelligence on the situation there but would also reassure the leaders of the present government that the U.S. intends to provide them with discreet assistance." That said, Helms affirmed that "the most immediate pressing need of the Cambodian Government will almost certainly be military assistance." Under Sihanouk, both China and the Soviet Union provided arms to the Cambodian military; following the coup, these countries would presumably halt any shipments. Thus Helms reasoned that "the Cambodian leadership will need desperately an alternative supply of military weapons." As for the covert delivery of weapons and munitions, Helms

A Widening War / 189

noted, "There are Cambodian airfields to which deliveries could be made clandestinely by aircraft flying out of Thailand and South Vietnam."[89]

Having made the decision to support, both overtly and covertly, the Lon Nol government, Nixon authorized MACV to assist the Cambodian Army (FANK—Forces Armées Nationales Khmères), whose poorly equipped and ill-trained thirty-two-thousand-man army was little match for the Vietnamese communist forces.[90] Initially, both the CIA and the South Vietnamese military would provide AK-47 rifles, ammunition, and other communist materiel captured in South Vietnam to the Cambodians. In addition, the Nixon administration sought other means of equipping the Cambodian military with arms and ammunition without direct U.S. involvement. Consequently, U.S. diplomats were instructed to solicit the help of other governments, notably Australia, France, and Indonesia, in providing weapons. The CIA, lastly, was authorized to explore the possibility of the Lon Nol government "making open purchases from Belgian arms dealers with covert U.S. funds provided for this purpose."[91]

It would take time to build up Lon Nol's army. In the interim, Nixon demanded an expansion of Operation Menu to support military operations in Cambodia. Initially, after the coup, Laird suspended the Menu bombings. He was concerned that some faction in Phnom Penh might discover and publicize the attacks.[92] Six days later, however, members of Nixon's cabinet—including Laird—agreed on the "usefulness of B-52 strikes against base camps used by the North Vietnamese and Viet Cong in Cambodia." Laird remained mindful of the "political risks involved" but aligned with Bunker and Abrams who believed Menu to be "one of the most telling operations in the entire war."[93] Soon thereafter, Menu operations resumed and increased both in scale and scope. On April 18 Abrams called for authorization of tactical aircraft to be used for a thirty-day period along a narrow eight-mile strip of territory in northeastern Cambodia near the South Vietnam border. McCain granted MACV the requested authority, giving the operation the name Patio. The first Patio attacks took place on April 24 when U.S. F-100s struck enemy columns in Cambodia. The following day Abrams received additional authority to extend the Patio operation along the entire Cambodian border to a depth of eighteen miles. Similar to the Menu operation, Patio was conducted covertly, with all requests, approvals, and reports transmitted by special security channel communications; cover

190 / A Widening War

targets in Laos were announced and route reports of those false missions recorded with the Department of Defense. Reports of the actual attacks in Cambodia were provided only to a select few individuals.[94]

From a strategic standpoint, Abrams directed Menu strikes also in anticipation of future ground campaigns launched either by U.S. or South Vietnamese forces, or in some combination. On March 25, even before the B-52 strikes resumed, Nixon directed MACV to develop plans for both unilateral and combined cross-border offenses.[95] As the fighting in Cambodia intensified, Nixon's resolve only hardened. On April 1, Kissinger declared Hanoi's "ultimate objective in Cambodia" was to "have that country controlled by a government subservient or at least friendly to Hanoi." Kissinger explained that Lon Nol's stance against the communists complicated Hanoi's prospects in South Vietnam. According to Kissinger, Hanoi could not "win the war in South Vietnam under its current strategy without making use of Cambodia." Far from a sideshow, Cambodia was the pivot upon which both U.S. and North Vietnamese strategies appeared to hinge. In a separate memo, NSC staff member John Holdridge conceded the "problems of escalation and U.S. involvement" but feared more "the specter of a Communist-dominated Sihanouk government providing a secure sanctuary and logistics base for the VC/NVA." Kissinger referred to this scenario as "our nightmare."[96]

Abrams had long anticipated the possibility of unilateral or combined military ground operations on Cambodian territory. Wary of the danger posed by the North Vietnamese use of Cambodian territory, in January 1970 he had set his staff the task of planning U.S.-supported ARVN cross-border operations into Cambodia. Consequently, when Nixon requested on March 25 plans for ground actions against enemy sanctuaries along the South Vietnam–Cambodian border, General William Rosson, deputy commander of MACV, was able to submit the requested plan the next day.[97] Then, following subsequent rounds of revision, initial plans eventually coalesced around two main options. One plan comprised an attack utilizing elements of the U.S. First Cavalry Division and the ARVN Airborne Division into Base Areas 352/353. Military intelligence reports indicated that this area harbored "large supply storage and headquarters." Tactically, a series of B-52 strikes would target the areas, followed by ground attacks. The duration of the operation was expected to last three to four weeks. A second plan called for simultaneous attacks against Base Area 704, suspected to be a "major storage area and transshipment point," and Base Area 367/706, an "extensive logistics base and sub-regional headquarters." Attacks against the first area would be accomplished by an ARVN armored brigade with U.S. riverine support; attacks on the second area would be conducted by three brigades of U.S./ARVN forces in a combined air mobile and ground operation. This plan would last approximately two weeks. Kissinger was satisfied with both recommendations; however, he also instructed MACV to "develop alternative plans for attacking sanctuary areas in Cambodia where the operations could be successfully [conducted] entirely by South Vietnamese armed forces."[98]

Kissinger's request marked a critical juncture of U.S. strategic planning. As consensus formed around the necessity to launch an invasion of Cambodia, key differences among Nixon's advisors became readily apparent. Both Laird and Rogers expressed deep reservations, not necessarily about military operations against PAVN/PLAF base areas in Cambodia; they were more concerned about the level of U.S. involvement. On the one hand, they worried about the domestic political fallout in the United States if Nixon appeared to widen the war. On the other hand, they worried also about the impact such operations would have on the war in Vietnam. Laird, for example, believed that progress was being made in the Vietnamization program. He felt that "the political climate remain[ed] obscure following the removal of Sihanouk" and that both the "short and long term prospect for survival [of the present regime] are unclear at this time." On that point, Laird suggested the administration "take a balanced approach . . . supporting Cambodian neutrality and avoiding direct involvement." He saw merit in "encouraging the type and level of cooperation between Cambodian and South Vietnamese units" but would "not advocate a step-up in border operations beyond that which has seemed to work to good advantage in the past." In conclusion, Laird recommended that "any military activities we might consider should be limited and tightly controlled to avoid widening the Southeast Asia conflict and inciting US anti-war sentiment."[99]

Bunker and Abrams were in full support of expanded U.S. military operations. Certainly, they recognized the potential political fallout. This possibility, however, simply justified the need that all operations be conducted covertly, hidden from the American public. Convinced that Cambodia was

192 / A Widening War

key to ultimate victory in South Vietnam, Bunker and Abrams agreed that "some selected and judicious help should be given to Cambodia." They recognized that "cross-border operations and other forms of cross-border cooperation are a very delicate business" and conceded that "such operations create problems in the U.S. whether conducted by [South Vietnamese] or U.S. forces." However, they maintained that the "purpose of cross-border operations" was to "induce uncertainty and worry in the enemy that we may take advantage of his exposed position if he commits himself too deeply into Cambodia in actions against the Cambodian forces." As such, they recommended authorization for "cross-border operations which could be undertaken with military profit" in order (1) to signal to the enemy that America would not stand idle if Hanoi pursued military operations or insurrectionary pressure against the Lon Nol government; (2) to avoid serious strains in relations with Saigon if Thieu is committed to carry the fight into Cambodia; and (3) to give encouragement to the Lon Nol government at a time when they were most in need of support.[100]

On April 19, Nixon attended a CINCPAC briefing in Hawaii held by McCain and other military advisors. Nixon asked about the forces required to cut the Ho Chi Minh Trail. Analysts with CINPAC responded that it would require upward of eight divisions and, as such, it was not practical to conduct such an operation with conventional forces; air strikes and irregular forces were more effective. With respect to cross-border operations in Cambodia, Nixon questioned if joint operations conducted with ARVN and U.S. forces were preferable to an invasion conducted primarily by the ARVN, with the United States providing air and artillery support from bases within South Vietnam. McCain informed Nixon that plans were being prepared that could satisfy either option. Following the briefing, Nixon relayed to Kissinger that "Cambodia is important and we will have to do it fast. I need to know how soon the [South Vietnamese] can get going over there." On that point, Nixon wanted confirmation that Cambodia formally requested South Vietnamese assistance. The president stressed, "Aiding Cambodia with arms is useless—they cannot use them. Get the money to Lon Nol." Nixon suggested that he wanted to make clear to McCain that while he was not ordering U.S. troops to take part in any operation, he also didn't want the South Vietnamese "to get in there and then get the hell kicked out." Kissinger later recalled that McCain "brought home to Nixon the danger to Laos and Cambodia" and "gave focus to his inchoate anxieties about Cambodia." At this point, Nixon, Kissinger, and McCain were in agreement: "the United States could not stand by and watch Cambodia collapse and ultimately cause the collapse of the US effort in South Vietnam."[101]

General William Westmoreland, now serving as acting chairman of the JCS, offered his opinion with regard to possible military operations in Cambodia. In an April 21 memo, the former MACV commander agreed with intelligence reports indicating that "the enemy is moving to isolate Phnom Penh by the systematic interdiction of all the major roads and waterways leading into the city." He noted that the Cambodian military was "marginally effective" but that the United States had to do more "if we are to stem the deterioration within Cambodia." Arguing the need to "move quickly to exploit their vulnerabilities," Westmoreland recommended division-sized attacks and the rescinding of restraints placed on U.S. forces.[102]

By late April Nixon had apparently resolved to authorize combat operations inside Cambodia. Left unclear was the composition of forces, that is, the degree of U.S. forces involved. The timing of the operation was also critical. As the military situation in Cambodia worsened, Nixon feared the imminent total or near-total collapse of the country. Within a month of the coup, North Vietnamese forces occupied three of Cambodia's seventeen provinces and were operating in strength in five others.[103] Lon Nol's army had been forced to evacuate border posts in the Parrot's Beak area, and the communists had or were about to capture all major population centers in the northeast. The capital was being cut off from the rest of the country, and North Vietnamese forces controlled both the Mekong River and the major highways leading into Phnom Penh.[104] Early on the morning of April 22 Nixon told Kissinger, "I think we need a bold move in Cambodia." He continued, "I do not believe [Lon Nol] is going to survive." Nixon expressed his frustration that they "really dropped the ball on this one." By not acting sooner—for fear that U.S. actions would destroy Cambodia's neutrality—Hanoi was able to seize the initiative. Now, Nixon fumed, "They are romping in there and the only government in Cambodia in the last 25 years that had the guts to take a pro-Western and pro-American stand is ready to fall." As Nixon's resolve hardened, he considered the geopolitical implications. Nixon mused, "We are going to find out who our friends are

194 / A Widening War

now, because if we decide to stand up here some of the rest of them had better come along fast."[105]

Later that afternoon, Nixon met with select members of the National Security Council, including Kissinger, Laird, Rogers, Helms, Wheeler, and Vice President Spiro Agnew. Two operations were considered. The first, code-named Shoemaker, called for a combined U.S.-ARNV drive into the Fishhook area targeting COSVN and other installations; and the second, Toan Thang 42, was a South Vietnamese attack on bases in the Parrot's Beak region of the border, an area that posed the most immediate threat to Saigon.[106] Differences of opinion ranged widely, with disagreement centered primarily on the use of U.S. forces. Both Laird and Rogers hoped to limit military operations; indeed, both men favored only the continuation of the ongoing Menu and Patio operations. Helms and Wheeler, conversely, advocated for an all-out push to remove all enemy sanctuaries in Cambodia. At this point, Agnew blurted that either the sanctuaries were worth attacking or were not and that he did not understand "all the pussy-footing about." Siding with the military advisors, Agnew favored both the South Vietnamese attack on the Parrot's Beak *and* the combined operation in the Fishhook region. Kissinger recalled later that Nixon resented Agnew's outburst. It was not that Nixon disagreed with his vice president but that he resented being shown to be "less tough" than Agnew. For Kissinger, this incident almost certainly accelerated Nixon's eventual decision to go for the maximum option.[107]

For the moment, however, Nixon continued to forward a more restrained operation. With the issuance of National Security Council Decision Memorandum (NSCDM) 56, Nixon authorized several steps, including both diplomatic and military components. On the political front, Nixon called for the immediate step-up of U.S. military assistance to the Lon Nol government—wherever possible through third-country channels—and for U.S. officials to undertake maximum diplomatic efforts to enlist assistance by other interested governments. As for military operations, Nixon authorized limited cross-border division-size attacks against PAVN/PLAF sanctuaries in Cambodia, to be conducted by South Vietnamese forces with cross-border U.S. artillery support and, if necessary, U.S. tactical air support. In addition, Khmer Serei forces currently operating in South Vietnam were to take part in the operation.[108]

A Widening War / 195

Nixon's decision, however limited at this point, marked a significant alteration of U.S. strategy in that it was in violation of international standing. Cambodia was a sovereign state and, while Hanoi was in clear violation of breaching Cambodia's territorial integrity, such actions did not legitimate U.S. violations. When NSCDM 56 was announced, Roger Morris, Winston Lord, and Anthony Lake (all members of the NSC staff) sent a memorandum to Kissinger. Voicing their agreement, they conceded that "the situation in Cambodia demands action by the U.S." However, they also acknowledged that "the nature of our action is constrained by the facts of the situation." Specifically, it was necessary to recognize "that there is no attainable perfect solution in Cambodia." Noting the weaknesses of both the Lon Nol government and the Cambodian military, the staff members believed that "short of sending in U.S. divisions and/or of deep and long-term ARVN penetrations of Cambodia, it does not seem possible to achieve the 'best solution': an anti-Communist Cambodian government in control of its country and preventing VC/NVN use of its territory against South Vietnam." Time did not permit the building of an effective Cambodian military. In addition, South Vietnamese military operations on Cambodian territory would destroy any "pretensions to political legitimacy" for the Lon Nol government. Regardless, Morris and the others concluded, the military value of such operations was "extremely doubtful." In fact, no military operation would "alter the basic balance." This conclusion did not imply that no action be taken. Several courses of action were recommended, including efforts to prevent the return of Sihanouk and to support a neutral Cambodian government under Lon Nol or some other leader. Above all, they cautioned against committing publicly "by word or deed" the United States to the Lon Nol regime. On that point, they expounded that "any public US military involvement (whether troops or direct military assistance) in Cambodia could have the effect of tying us to Lon Nol." Underscoring this determination, they stressed that "there should be no US direct military involvement in Cambodia. We must assume that any use of US forces in Cambodia, e.g., US tactical air, gunships, military advisors, or participation in cross-border actions with [South Vietnamese] forces, will become public very quickly. These actions . . . would increase our involvement and prestige in a losing cause, limit diplomatic flexibility, and have severe political consequences in the US. And it could bog us down in another war in

196 / A Widening War

the long run." In the end, they concluded, the United States "must face squarely the basically untenable situation in Cambodia—and that no remedy in proportion to our interests may be available."[109] All three men would later resign in protest over the Cambodian incursion.

Nixon was undeterred. Preparations for cross-border operations continued, ostensibly to be conducted by South Vietnamese forces with tactical and logistical support provided by the United States. Nixon, though, continued to hold doubts—not about the merits of the military operation but about its composition. Early in the morning of April 24 Nixon met with Kissinger, acting chairman of the JCS, Admiral Thomas Moorer, CIA Director Helms, and Helms's deputy director, Robert Cushman. Rogers and Laird were conspicuously excluded from the meeting. Having committed himself to an invasion of Cambodia, Nixon wanted to discuss the feasibility of the combined U.S.–South Vietnamese attack against the Fishhook sanctuary to complement the South Vietnamese attack on the Parrot's Beak. Both Moorer and Helms remained strongly supportive, explaining that both operations in tandem would "relieve the North Vietnamese pressure on Phnom Penh and destroy enemy supplies and gain time for Vietnamization to work." Kissinger later telephoned both Wheeler and Abrams to gauge their support for simultaneous attacks; both men also supported the proposed actions.[110]

Only belatedly in the planning process was the question of informing Lon Nol raised. Thus far, military operations into Cambodia had been planned and coordinated exclusively by U.S. and South Vietnamese officials. But one would assume that the pro forma head of state, Lon Nol, would be part of the conversation. Perhaps sensing the elephant in the room, Undersecretary of State Alexis Johnson asked, "Do we tell Lon Nol?" Kissinger replied, "Yes, but about the time we launch it." Marshall Green, assistant secretary of state for East Asia and Pacific Affairs, suggested, also, that "Lon Nol should request it. If we put it to him he might agree." Pointedly, Green recognized that the legitimacy of the operation would be strengthened if it *appeared* that Phnom Penh requested U.S.–South Vietnamese military assistance in the form of cross-border attacks. In agreement, Kissinger instructed his advisors to "Tell [Lon Nol] shortly before." Kissinger was not prepared to risk the operation on the chance that Lon Nol refused permission. Johnson approved, noting that "we will have the messages ready."[111]

By this point, all that was certain was that military operations into Cambodia would take place. Indeed, so many competing plans were in circulation that many advisors seemed to be unaware of what was actually on the table. During Kissinger's meeting on April 24, for example, several of the participants were under the assumption that the Fishhook attack was a ruse. At one point, David Packard, deputy secretary of defense, stated, "It's a feint against COSVN and then they [the South Vietnamese] attack Parrot's Beak." Helms replied, "It's near Saigon; thus it's a good move for the rear in South Vietnam. It will have a psychological effect." Later, when Green asked: if there was "any U.S. involvement," Kissinger answered, "no Americans go into Cambodia." The national security advisor explained that "the one [operation] against the COSVN is a feint."[112] In a subsequent conversation, Laird advised Wheeler that it was absolutely essential that no U.S. advisors be introduced into Cambodia at any time during the operation. However, Abrams's plan—to Laird—implied that U.S. personnel would be on the ground in Cambodia; as such, the secretary wanted clarification. Wheeler relayed the secretary's concerns to MACV. Abrams responded that there would be no personnel on the ground in the first wave of the attack, although U.S. advisors were required to be in the air over Cambodian territory to direct U.S. gunship support. Adding to the confusion, Abrams on the following day informed Wheeler that the South Vietnamese commander was reluctant to attack the Fishhook without U.S. participation. On April 26 he submitted to the JCS a plan for a combined U.S.–South Vietnamese attack in that area.[113]

Adding to the confusion was Nixon's own subterfuge. The president was determined to deliver a punishing blow against Hanoi. However, he remained unsure if the operations authorized by NSDM 56 were sufficient. In all likelihood, by April 24 Nixon committed himself to expanded operations that would include U.S. ground forces. In part, Cambodia's physical geography mediated his decision. Mainland Southeast Asia's climate is marked by two dominant weather patterns: a dry winter monsoon and a wet summer monsoon. For years, both the U.S.–South Vietnamese forces and the North Vietnamese forces timed their military operations to coincide with the dry season. Now, in anticipation of a major offensive to save Phnom Penh, Nixon realized that the rainy season was fast approaching. For Nixon, he had one opportunity to destroy COSVN and was not prepared

198 / A Widening War

to risk that on the hopes that the South Vietnamese military would succeed. Nixon's thinking is apparent in a telephone conversation with Kissinger that afternoon.

As Kissinger recalls, the telephone conversation was in fact a ruse, orchestrated in part to deceive the U.S. Congress. The discussion was to be a three-way conversation, with John Stennis, chair of the Senate Armed Services Committee. Prior to Stennis joining the conversation, however, Nixon expressed his thinking clearly. Specifically, Nixon wanted to know about the onset of the monsoon and how that would impact military operations in the Fishhook area. He told Kissinger, "I want a clear answer to how long our option lasts—whether it lasts one month, one week or something else." Kissinger replied, "The rainy season lasts for three months after it starts." On that point, Nixon explained, "As I understand it, we have only three weeks to exercise this option. . . . I think we have to recognize we may not find another opportunity." "These guys," Nixon asserted, "have been talking about a protracted war. That is why last night, I had come to the conclusion you have to seize the opportunity when it is there, considering the weather, etc." In other words, Nixon apparently decided on the evening of April 23 to approve the more expansive plans for simultaneous U.S.–South Vietnamese military operations. However, when Stennis joined the conversation, Nixon demurred. "I will sum up what my views are," the president opened. He informed the senator, "I don't want us to get into a quagmire of military aid to Cambodia. Or else we will get into another situation." Nixon continued: "We are not going to give a lot—a few rifles doesn't bother you does it? You tell your colleagues we are not going to get into a big aid program for Cambodia. We will provide minimum rifles because they did opt for us." During a prior conversation Kissinger had briefed Stennis on Operation Menu; now, Nixon intimated how that operation—the "best-kept secret of the war"—factored into his grand strategy. With regard to possible U.S. military options to support Phnom Penh, Nixon feigned, "The first choice is air action including the B-52s which *only* you and Senator [Richard] Russell know about." Nixon conceded that he would consider the possibility of tactical air to follow—but that was all air action on the borders, not inside. He insisted that "there will be no ground action with relation to Cambodia. They have to save themselves. Any ground action will relate only to our troops in South Vietnam and our Vietnamization program." Nixon

A Widening War / 199

continued with his verbal sleight of hand, suggesting that "if ground action takes place, we will have the South Vietnamese to do it—we trained that army." The president then remarked coyly, "Our other option, we will not exercise unless we have to—that of having Americans helping South Vietnamese only if we consider that that will, in the long run, help reduce our casualties in Vietnam." Nixon then posed the question to Stennis, "How does that sound to you?"[114] Senator Stennis was impressed. "I will be with you on the nailhead," he informed the president. As the conversation drew down, Nixon repeated, "We are not going to get involved in a war in Cambodia. We are not going to occupy Cambodia. We do want basically to win in South Vietnam." That said, Nixon underscored the need to "hit those sanctuaries in Cambodia." He stated bluntly that if Hanoi's "actions in Cambodia, Laos and [South] Vietnam endangered our troops in South Vietnam, we are not going to sit and take it." In a roundabout way, Nixon justified his expansion of the war into Cambodia as the final option, to be undertaken only in defense of U.S. military personnel and to defend and secure South Vietnam from threats posed by enemy forces operating in Cambodia.[115] Later that day, Kissinger asked members of the Washington Special Actions Group (WSAG) a simple question: "What is the monsoon situation?" Wheeler replied, "It will begin to switch in mid-May; by June the area will be impassable in the Parrot's Beak area except on roads. It will last five months."[116]

On April 26 Nixon met with his senior advisors: Kissinger, Rogers, Laird, Helms, and Wheeler. The meeting was a charade, staged as a planning exercise merely to explore the possibility of U.S. ground forces participating in future operations in the Fishhook region. Both Rogers and Laird fell for the deception and said little. In actuality, Nixon was moving forward.[117] Later that day, under NSCDM 57, the president authorized "the conduct of ground operations by U.S. forces or by U.S./GVN forces into identified North Vietnamese/Viet Cong sanctuaries in Cambodia up to a depth of 30 kilometers. With the exception of the operation against Base Area 352/353, U.S. or combined U.S./ARVN operations against specific base areas will be submitted [to the president] for approval on a case-by-case basis." In addition, Nixon authorized the "provision of U.S. tactical air/helicopter and artillery up to a depth of 30 kilometers in all base areas north of and including 352/353."

Laird and Rogers did not remain complacent once they realized a decision had already been reached to commit U.S. ground forces to military

200 / A Widening War

operations in Cambodia. The following day, both secretaries made clear their resentment that the decision was made without full consultation.[118] Rogers, in particular, was concerned because he was scheduled to testify before Congress that afternoon and did not want to lie when asked if the White House was sending U.S. troops to Cambodia. In response, Nixon agreed to delay authorization for twenty-four hours until after Rogers's appearance before Congress. In the interim, the president asked Kissinger to confirm Abrams's assessment of the proposed operations.[119] Laird then followed up with a memorandum to Nixon that detailed his concerns. He concluded with the warning, "It seems prudent to me to defer involving US personnel on Cambodian soil, at least until the overall military and political picture in Southeast Asia is clearer, the potential US benefits from such involvement are greater, or the risks and costs attendant to such US actions are less."[120]

Kissinger, in response to the opposition voiced by Rogers and Laird, sent a back-channel message to Bunker in Saigon. Kissinger posed several questions for the ambassador and for Abrams. Of primary importance, Kissinger relayed, "the President is anxious to learn whether or not you both favor an attack on COSVN headquarters as a first choice among the base areas available or, whether you favor any attack by US forces on Cambodian sanctuaries in light of the effect such an attack would have on your overall security posture in South Vietnam." In addition, Kissinger continued, the president wanted to know if Bunker and Abrams preferred "to withhold implementation of the operation until the ARVN operation in the Parrot's Beak has been completed or to launch it now given all of circumstances, including difficulties imposed by simultaneous operations, impending rainy season, the overall military and psychological impact achieved by near simultaneous operations." Kissinger explained that Nixon wanted their "unvarnished views on the foregoing questions" and his subsequent decision would "be heavily guided by them."[121] Hours later, Bunker and Abrams communicated their overall assessment to the president. Abrams believed that a combined U.S.–South Vietnamese attack against base areas 352/353 in the Fishhook region was "most desirable in relation to any other base area." Indeed, the general believed those areas to be "relatively of greater value than other military efforts which could be made somewhere else" at the time. Furthermore, both Abrams and Bunker agreed that an "attack on this area should have maximum unsettling effect on the enemy who has considered until now his sanctuaries immune to ground attack." Concurrently, the operation "should have a beneficial effect on both our own and ARVN forces who have long felt handicapped by this restriction." Abrams also recommended that the "closer the operations in the Parrot's Beak or on Base Area 352/353 can be coordinated, the greater will be the impact on the enemy." The general noted that "there is not much time remaining before the beginning of the rainy season, consequently the operation should be initiated as soon as practicable." In conclusion, Abrams declared, "It is my independent view that these attacks into the enemy's sanctuaries in Cambodia are the military moves to make at this time in support of our mission in South Viet Nam in terms of security of our own forces and for advancement of the Vietnamization program."[122]

On April 28, Nixon met briefly with Kissinger, Rogers, Laird, and U.S. Attorney General John Mitchell. The purpose of the meeting, Nixon explained, was to advise those present of the decision he had reached based on his assessment of the military situation in Cambodia. Nixon reiterated he had decided not to change the current U.S. position with respect to military assistance to Cambodia or his authorization for the ARVN operation in the Parrot's Beak. However, Nixon was also prepared to initiate a combined U.S.–South Vietnamese operation against COSVN headquarters in the Fishhook area in order to protect U.S. forces in South Vietnam.[123] Nixon maintained that the COSVN operation was necessary to sustain the continuation of the Vietnamization program; as such, the planned military operation could possibly help (but not detract from) ongoing efforts to negotiate for peace with Hanoi.[124] For Nixon, Cambodia served as little more than a handle with which to wield a blunt instrument. Convinced that military victory was still possible in South Vietnam—and that winning the war was necessary to maintain U.S. credibility, deter future wars of national liberation, and provide leverage over the Soviet Union and China—Nixon concluded that the expansion of war into Cambodia would buy him the time needed.[125] In the final analysis, Nixon believed he could take action that Johnson had resisted—an aggressive ground campaign in Cambodia—and use it as a decisive military blow to turn the tide of war and force the North Vietnamese to accept a negotiated settlement that would serve U.S. security interests.[126]

202 / A Widening War

The die was cast. On the morning of April 29 twelve South Vietnamese infantry and armored divisions crossed into Cambodia, targeting the flanks of the Parrot's Beak. Two days later U.S. armored and heliborne units moved south and east into the Fishhook region of Cambodia from their positions in South Vietnam. Within a week of the offensive, approximately 31,000 U.S. and 19,000 South Vietnamese troops were in Cambodia, occupying a territory that stretched from Sihanoukville (now Kompong Som) along the coast to Phnom Penh in the west and Snuol in the north. Allied forces subsequently moved into Cambodian territory astride the critical east–west trending Highway 19 in northeastern Cambodia.[127] America's expansion of the war had begun. When Kissinger was later asked about the invasion, the national security advisor explained, "We're not interested in Cambodia. We're only interested in it not being used as a base."[128]

[6]

THE PERFIDY OF GEOPOLITICS

But the importance of Cambodia to the U.S. is its impact on
South Vietnam.

—GEORGE CARVER during a meeting of the Washington
Special Actions Group

On August 15, 1961, the United States' Central Intelligence Agency (CIA)
issued a *National Intelligence Estimate* on the "Prospects for North and South
Vietnam."[1] According to the CIA, "In providing the GVN [Government of
South Vietnam] a maximum of encouragement and extensive support in
its struggle against the Communists, the US will inevitably become identified with the GVN's success or failure." The report continued: "The US
will be under heavy pressure from other members of the non-Communist
world, many of whom view the Vietnam struggle in differing terms." On
this point, U.S. intelligence analysts determined that "the neighboring countries such as Thailand, Cambodia, Burma, Indonesia, the Philippines, and
Nationalist China" would "almost certainly look upon the struggle for Vietnam as a critical test of such US willingness and ability. All of them, including the neutrals, would probably suffer demoralization and loss of confidence
in their prospects for maintaining their independence if the communists
were to gain control of South Vietnam."[2] President John F. Kennedy and his
staff agreed with this assessment; so too did most members of Lyndon B.
Johnson's administration. Vietnam was central to American national security interests, and failure to support the Saigon government placed U.S.
credibility on the line. With President Richard Nixon, however, geopolitical
conditions both domestic and foreign mediated a reassessment of the centrality of Vietnam and, by extension, of Cambodia. America's credibility on
the world stage remained prominent. However, Vietnam was increasingly

203

204 / The Perfidy of Geopolitics

relegated from a keystone of the American nomos to a backwater of peripheral importance. Consequently, in the wake of America's retreat from Vietnam, Cambodia was left adrift.

Throughout the brutal Cambodian Civil War (1970–75), neither U.S. President Richard Nixon nor National Security Advisor Henry Kissinger were committed to the defense of the Khmer Republic. To be sure, U.S. officials publicly vowed their support for the Khmer Republic. Behind the scenes, however, a different mood prevailed. In this chapter I chronicle the practical geopolitical reasoning of Nixon and Kissinger as they expanded the Vietnam War into Cambodia. For both men, America's credibility and prestige were at stake. In the end, however, the American nomos was bolstered not by mutual alliances but by a betrayal of an erstwhile ally.

Nixon's Centering of Cambodia

On the evening of April 30, 1970, President Richard M. Nixon delivered a televised address to the American public that joint U.S.–South Vietnamese military operations were underway in Cambodia. The president explained that the operation was in response to continued aggression by North Vietnam. With U.S. troop withdrawals ongoing, Nixon affirmed that decisive steps would be taken if the lives of Americans remaining in Vietnam were endangered. Now, military aggression from Hanoi, particularly in Cambodia, posed such a risk. Nixon affirmed that Cambodia was a neutral country and that it had been America's foreign policy "to scrupulously respect the neutrality of the Cambodian people." Nixon added: "And for the past 5 years, we have provided no military assistance whatever and no economic assistance to Cambodia." Left unsaid was that Cambodia's head of state, Prince Norodom Sihanouk, had cut diplomatic relations with the United States amid continuing efforts by the U.S. and South Vietnamese governments to affect regime change. Nor did the president acknowledge the myriad covert operations conducted in Cambodia stretching back to Kennedy or the (more recent) secret bombing of Cambodia under Operation Menu. Instead, the president feigned innocence, claiming that "for 5 years, neither the United States nor South Vietnam has moved against . . . enemy sanctuaries [in Cambodia] because we did not wish to violate the territory of a neutral nation." Indeed, Nixon alleged that "even after the Vietnamese Communists began to expand these sanctuaries four weeks ago, we counseled patience to our South Vietnamese allies and imposed restraints on our own commanders." Charging that Hanoi willfully invaded Cambodia and thus "stripped away all pretense of respecting the sovereignty or the neutrality of Cambodia," Nixon purported that the Cambodian government "has sent out a call to the United States, to a number of other nations, for assistance." If Cambodia were to fall, Nixon warned, the country "would become a vast enemy staging area and a springboard for attacks on South Vietnam along 600 miles of frontier—a refuge where enemy troops could return from combat without fear of retaliation." In response, the president affirmed that a decision was made to launch military operations "in cooperation with the armed forces of South Vietnam" to "clean out major enemy sanctuaries on the Cambodian-Vietnam border." Nixon defended the operation on that grounds that decisive military action was "indispensable" to the withdrawal of American troops from South Vietnam and the resolution of that conflict. In fact, Nixon argued, the military offensive underway was "not an invasion of Cambodia" and America's objective was "not to occupy" Cambodian territory. Simply put, the president said, "We take this action not for the purpose of expanding the war into Cambodia but for the purpose of ending the war in Vietnam and winning the just peace we all desire." By way of conclusion, Nixon vowed that "if, when the chips are down, the world's most powerful nation, the United States of America, acts like a pitiful, helpless giant, the forces of totalitarianism and anarchy will threaten free nations and free institutions throughout the world. It is not our power but our will and character that is being tested tonight. . . . If we fail to meet this challenge, all other nations will be on notice that despite its overwhelming power the United States, when a real crisis comes, will be found wanting."[3]

During his speech, Nixon called on the American public to support his decision and for the "deep differences" confronting the United States to be set aside. Instead, as many advisors in Nixon's inner circle feared, the expansion of military operations into Cambodia was met with a volatile mixture of disbelief, disappointment, and anger. The following morning, May 1, protests erupted on college campuses across the nation as students voiced their opposition to a wider war.[4] In northeast Ohio, at Kent State University, a group of history undergraduate and graduate students—some of whom were Vietnam veterans—calling themselves World Historians Opposed to

206 / The Perfidy of Geopolitics

Racism and Exploitation (WHORE) distributed leaflets on campus encouraging students to meet at noon at the Victory Bell. In front of a crowd of about three hundred students, WHORE symbolically buried a copy of the U.S. Constitution one of the organizers had ripped from their history textbook.[5] They also called for a more organized protest to be held at noon on Monday, May 4.

Nixon railed against the student protesters and derided them as "bums . . . blowing up the campuses."[6] Undeterred, the president held firm that the "Cambodian base area operations to be the number one priority" in winning the war in Vietnam. Subsequently, as protests fanned across the country on May 1, Nixon ordered John McCain, commander in chief, CINCPAC, and Creighton Abrams, commander, MACV, "to prepare plans without restrictions on the use of U.S. or ARVN forces, including air assets, for this purpose." Military operations, Nixon determined, could if "necessary or desirable" expand beyond the geographic restrictions initially imposed. Nixon underscored his desire for "a hard hitting campaign to be carried out using imagination and boldness" so that the enemy would "receive the hardest blow we are capable of inflicting in his Cambodian sanctuary areas."[7]

At 11:15 on the morning of May 4 Kissinger met with the members of the WSAG to discuss the unfolding military operation in Cambodia. On the table was a request forwarded by Abrams to launch an attack against Base Area 704 and the use of Khmer "mercenaries" from South Vietnam.[8] Three hundred and fifty miles to the west, at approximately 12:25 p.m., members of the Ohio National Guard opened fire on students protesting Nixon's expansion of the war into Cambodia. A salvo of sixty-seven shots wounded nine students and killed four: Allison Krause, Sandy Scheuer, Jeffery Miller, and William Schroeder. Four hours later, Nixon was informed of the shootings. He was dismissive in his attitude. "At Kent State there were 4 or 5 killed today," the president acknowledged, "but that place has been bad for quite some time—it has been rather violent." Kissinger counseled that the Nixon administration would be blamed for the killings. Moreover, Kissinger continued, thirty-three university presidents were appealing to Nixon to leave Vietnam. "The university presidents," Kissinger retorted, "are a disgrace." Nixon agreed but conceded that "they still get an inordinate amount of publicity, like the students." Moving forward, the president suggested, "We have to stand hard as a rock. . . . If countries begin to be run by children,

The Perfidy of Geopolitics / 207

God help us." Subsequently, when Kissinger warned that "student disorders hurt us politically," Nixon challenged, "They don't if it doesn't appear we caused them."[9]

Throughout the first week of May, protests at colleges and universities continued to grow in response to Nixon's expansion of the war into Cambodia but also, markedly, in response to the murder of unarmed students at Kent State. Indeed, the killings at Kent State ignited more rallies and strikes. More than four hundred universities were shut down, and nearly one hundred thousand protesters descended on Washington, D.C.[10] Secretary of State William Rogers confided to Kissinger, "These student protests are greater than any of us anticipated." Kissinger agreed but dismissed the long-term consequences. "After another week or two when the troops come out," Kissinger mused, "it will be better."[11]

In practice, neither Nixon nor Kissinger were satisfied to wait and see if "it will be better." On May 6 Nixon met with six Kent State students who were against the war in Vietnam. During the course of the conversation, Nixon explained that he was the one who made the "difficult decision in Cambodia" and that he bore responsibility for its outcome.[12] That same day, Kissinger met with students and faculty at Stanford University. And similar to Nixon's April 30 justification for the operation, Kissinger was duplicitous in his remarks. Kissinger, for example, explained that the "incursion" into Cambodia was conducted to end the war "as quickly as possible." Moreover, the national security advisor clarified, the territory in question "was not controlled by the Cambodians." According to Kissinger's logic— and contravening Nixon's April 30 speech—the military operation was *not* conducted against a sovereign, neutral state but instead directed against disputed territory. Then, in response to the student protests, Kissinger reasoned that "Cambodia made it easy for some to do what they wanted to do anyway." In other words, university students were always protesting something, and the war in Cambodia was nothing more than the latest focal point. Dismissing allegations that Nixon widened the war, Kissinger lectured those in attendance that the students "confused a tactical question with a fundamental question." "The real issue," Kissinger expounded, "is that any society to survive must have a modicum of trust" and that "in order to have world order we must maintain a modicum of confidence in authority."[13]

208 / The Perfidy of Geopolitics

On May 7, Nixon convened a meeting with eight university presidents. Nixon recognized that the Cambodian action sparked considerable turmoil but felt that the military operation was necessary to end the war in Vietnam—the very goal demanded by the protestors. Nixon explained that when the Cambodian action would conclude in early June, he would have bought at least ten months more time to achieve a satisfactory conclusion to the war. On this point, Nixon stressed that "we're not going to fight in Cambodia or Laos, and that this summer should well bring the best news out of the Viet Nam War."[14]

For the Nixon administration, the protests were symptomatic of a deeper frustration with the war among a small segment of the population. That said, as Kissinger's comments suggest, with success on the ground it would be possible to regain control of the public narrative. More problematic was the response of Congress. In response to the growing antiwar movement, several members of the House and Senate worked to limit Nixon's war-making capabilities and legislate an end to the war. Within days of Nixon's announcement, Senators John Cooper and Frank Church attached an amendment to a Foreign Military Sales Act that would end funding of U.S. ground troops and advisors in Laos and Cambodia after June 30, ban air operations in Cambodian air space in support of Cambodian forces without specific congressional approval, and end U.S. support of ARVN forces outside of South Vietnam. Effectively, the Cooper-Church amendment was designed to force a true deescalation of the fighting by reversing Nixon's policy in Cambodia. Concurrently, Senators George McGovern and Mark Hatfield introduced an "end the war" amendment that would require the end of U.S. military operations throughout all of Vietnam by December 31, 1970, and a complete withdrawal of U.S. forces by the end of June 1971.[15]

The Nixon administration was predictably opposed to both amendments but astute enough to read the writing on the wall. In an attempt to mollify congress, Nixon set a June 30 deadline for the use of U.S. ground forces in Cambodia and imposed an arbitrary thirty-kilometer limit on their operations.[16] This action, however, did not deter Nixon from his ultimate objective to compel Hanoi by punishing Cambodia. Nixon clarified that "termination of U.S. ground operations in Cambodia . . . underlines the desirability of maintaining maximum pressure on the enemy in Cambodia through U.S. and allied air efforts. For this reason, I want to reaffirm until

The Perfidy of Geopolitics / 209

further notice, all authorities heretofore promulgated for the conduct of U.S. air operations over Cambodia."[17] In other words, the war in Cambodia would continue regardless of Nixon's ability to deploy U.S. combat forces. Nixon hailed the incursion as a success. On July 1, following the withdrawal of U.S. combat troops from Cambodia, Nixon informed the American public that the incursion was necessary to "win a just peace." The president explained that "by winning a just peace, what I mean is not victory over North Vietnam—we are not asking for that—but it is simply the right of the people of South Vietnam to determine their own future without having us impose our will upon them, or the North Vietnamese, or anybody else outside impose their will upon them." He continued, "If the United States, after all this effort, if we were to withdraw immediately, as many Americans would want us to do . . . it would have, in my view, a catastrophic effect on this country and the cause of peace in the years ahead." On this point, South Vietnam remained key in shaping the American nomos. Nixon clarified that the "domino theory" was anything but obsolete and that if the United States abandoned South Vietnam "in a way that we are humiliated or defeated" it would be "immensely discouraging to the 300 million people from Japan clear around to Thailand in free Asia." More importantly, Nixon averred, an American defeat in South Vietnam would be "ominously encouraging to the leaders of Communist China and the Soviet Union who are supporting the North Vietnamese. It will encourage them in their expansionist policies in other areas." Paradoxically, for Nixon, expanding the war into Cambodia was necessary to prevent the expansion of communism in Southeast Asia. For Nixon, these were the steps required to ensure that "the world will be much safer in which to live."[18]

"If statecraft flows from misperceptions of fundamental interest or flawed calculations," Hal Brands writes, "even a brilliant tactical performance may ultimately be for naught." Nixon's so-called incursion remains subject to intense scholarly debate. Notably within the military establishment, the operation is hailed as a success. However, even if the military component was successful, we must, as Brands suggests, consider the operation in its broader, strategic context. And on this count, the evidence suggests otherwise. Instead of drawing the war in Vietnam closer to any sort of resolution, Nixon's decision ignited a civil war in Cambodia, one that Washington was unable and unwilling to fully support.

210 / The Perfidy of Geopolitics

False Commitments

Nixon was far from forthright with the U.S. public. He was even less so with the Phnom Penh government. During the first days of military operations in Cambodia, Undersecretary of State Alexis Johnson asked if Lon Nol should be informed of ongoing and pending operations. Kissinger replied, "We can tell him we will do it. We can decide what we give him." CIA Director Richard Helms agreed, adding, "We don't want to scare him." Kissinger expounded, "We control the information we give." Later, Kissinger emphasized, "We don't want to give Lon Nol the idea we are using Cambodia for our purposes."[19] That said, the Nixon administration was using Cambodia to satisfy its objectives in South Vietnam. As such, Kissinger and his advisors discussed several options for supporting future military operations in Cambodia, including the supply of weapons, munitions, and military aircraft. It was widely understood, however, that most options were illegal, thereby necessitating more clandestine channels. Ideally, though, the consensus opinion among Kissinger's working group was to turn military operations over to the Cambodian Army [FANK] by June 30 and to withdraw all U.S. and South Vietnamese advisors at that time.[20] In other words, the goal was to impress the embryonic Lon Nol government to shoulder ground combat operations in Cambodia; this would parallel the Vietnamization program in South Vietnam. Effectively, Nixon would continue the war covertly against North Vietnam through the deception and manipulation of both the Phnom Penh and Saigon governments.

Nixon's ongoing subterfuge was of significant concern among several members of his administration. Such consternation, however, was motivated more by the potential political fallout of an increased U.S. commitment than by the situation in Cambodia. On May 7, for example, Secretary of Defense Melvin Laird vented his frustration to Kissinger during an early morning telephone conversation. Laird complained, "You know that the President has really come over here and given the military the greatest license they have ever had and I am going to step in on a few things because if we let this get out of hand, they will use all American troops." He cautioned: "We have got to keep the pressure on them to use South Vietnamese troops. The next thing they will be doing is requesting more Americans in South Vietnam. McCain would like to put the Marines back. We can't do that." Pointedly, Laird explained, "They [MACV and CINCPAC] have the idea

The Perfidy of Geopolitics / 211

that they have carte blanche and I have got to be a son-of-a-bitch to keep some pressure on them." Kissinger acknowledged Laird's worries. "There is no argument here," the national security advisor said, adding that "there is no question on principle in putting in new troops into Vietnam."[21]

In fact, both Nixon and Kissinger were keenly aware of the challenges they unleased and struggled to limit America's commitment to Cambodia. In a State Department telegram issued by Rogers and cleared by Kissinger to the U.S. embassy in Cambodia, the position of the White House was expressed candidly. "We have seen our problem," the telegram affirmed, "as essentially one of navigating between providing enough support and re-assurance to the GOC [Government of Cambodia] so that it will have the morale and determination, as well as enhance its capability, to cope with the enemy; while at the same time not leaving the GOC with any mislead-ing or false expectations as to the amounts and types of assistance that we are likely to provide." Effectively, the Nixon administration feigned to befriend the Lon Nol government sufficiently to ensure Cambodia's support in the war effort; simultaneously, however, the Nixon administration wanted to convey that U.S. support was not limitless. To this end, it was essential to distinguish between "expanding the war into Cambodia" and the destruc-tion of "major VC/NVA sanctuaries in the Cambodian-Vietnamese border in defense of Americans in Viet-Nam and the Vietnamization program in SVN [South Vietnam]." It was hoped that the latter operations would "indirectly support the GOC" but that such support was not the primary objective. Consequently, the White House would continue, wherever fea-sible, to provide small arms, ammunition, and similar equipment to the Cambodian Army, but it was crucial "to avoid getting ourselves into any 'advisor' role vis-à-vis the FANK or the GOC with the responsibilities that would flow therefrom." Moreover, it was "important to keep down the size of the mission to avoid the impression we are 'taking over' and commit-ting our prestige within Cambodia in a major way." Unlike efforts to build and support both the Saigon government and the South Vietnamese mili-tary, U.S. officials were unwilling to make similar commitments to Phnom Penh. The reason was twofold. On the one hand, the Nixon administration was well aware of congressional efforts to affect a legislative end to the war, precisely through the defunding of Nixon's war-making capacity. On the other hand, members of the Nixon administration expressed little interest

212 / The Perfidy of Geopolitics

in government building or state building in Cambodia and, as such, the White House was unwilling to risk its international credibility and prestige in support of the Lon Nol regime. As Rogers summarized, "We want to continue to do all possible to maintain the morale and determination of the GOC" but "at the same time we believe it will be in the best interests of the GOC and the US to discourage unrealistic expectations or requests."[22]

But unrealistic expectations were in abundance as Nixon steadily widened the war into Cambodia. Incredulously, both civilian and military officials in Washington believed that an undermanned and outgunned Cambodian Army could withstand the combined efforts of the People's Army of North Vietnam (PAVN) and the People's Liberation Armed Forces (PLAF)—something that neither the United States nor South Vietnam could accomplish after five years of fighting. In addition, the Nixon administration believed it possible to equip Lon Nol's military on the cheap. Facing a recalcitrant U.S. Congress, the White House was impelled to fund its support for the Cambodians by redirecting monies already appropriated elsewhere. Weapons and munitions, desperately in short supply throughout the ranks of the Cambodian military, were provided in the form of captured military assets in South Vietnam. To augment these paltry contributions, U.S. representatives continued to cajole allied governments throughout Asia to help support Phnom Penh.[23]

For his part, Lon Nol was understandably alarmed at the meager support offered by the United States. Mollifying yet supportive words were little match against artillery. On May 15 the U.S. chargé d'affaires in Phnom Penh, Lloyd Rives, relayed Nixon's position on U.S. assistance to Cambodia. Rives informed the prime minister that Nixon's promise to help Cambodia was sincere and that the United States would provide assistance; that said, he wanted to "dispel any doubts" about how far the United States could go in assisting Cambodia. The ongoing "incursion" was a "temporary and limited exercise" and, as such, Lon Nol "should not expect further US troop involvement in Cambodian affairs." On that point, Rives explains, Lon Nol "should not expect tanks, heavy artillery [or] aircraft from US sources."[24] Effectively, Cambodia was a showcase of the Nixon Doctrine in abbreviated form. Not only would U.S. combat troops not be forthcoming, but substantial economic or military aid would not be arriving either.

The Perfidy of Geopolitics / 213

On learning of the limited assistance offered by the White House, Lon Nol could not hide his frustration. The prime minister indicated that following the coup Cambodia "had chosen its position vis-à-vis communism" and, as such, he believed his government had the "right to expect more than token assistance from the US." He warned that if such assistance was not forthcoming, he saw little advantage risking both Cambodian lives and property in continuing the struggle against the North Vietnamese. In turn, Rives could only repeat the White House position: that the intent of the United States was to help but that he should not "expect too much or that he would be disappointed." Rives did suggest, however, that "Cambodia would probably be receiving some equipment captured during present operations." This was an offer Lon Nol readily understood as being both temporary and insufficient for a protracted struggle.[25]

Concern also was raised within the White House about the seemingly haphazard approach toward Cambodia. In the lead-up to the incursion, most attention centered on the military objectives of targeting enemy sanctuaries, base areas, and infiltration routes and how these would contribute to the policy of Vietnamization and related pacification efforts in South Vietnam. By mid-May, as military operations were ongoing, a few voices paused to consider the long-term political ramifications on Cambodia. Haig, for example, voiced concern to Kissinger that Rives conveyed Nixon's position "in stark black and white terms which cannot but have the effect of discouraging the Cambodian regime excessively." For Haig, the apparent miscommunication underlined "the necessity to develop an updated policy position with respect to the future of Cambodia within the broad parameters already enunciated." He highlighted that it was "becoming increasingly evident" that the White House was "rapidly approaching a point where a finite Cambodian policy must be hammered out."[26] Nine days later, following a visit to Phnom Penh and Saigon during which he met with Lon Nol, Sirik Matak, Nguyen Van Thieu, and several other Cambodian and South Vietnamese officials, Haig reiterated his concerns. Lon Nol, Haig observed, was "emotional and not very realistic." As such, "It would prove fatal to his government if he were to continue to expect a massive infusion of US assistance." That said, Haig concluded, "Cambodia must have the wherewithal to resist, and it can't wait too long."[27]

214 / The Perfidy of Geopolitics

In his May 15 memorandum to Kissinger, Haig thought it necessary to "have an individual on the ground in Phnom Penh who is fully abreast of the President's thinking and who would hopefully manifest a higher level of diplomatic skills than has Rives thus far."[28] Haig was partially correct. The White House was waiting for Senate confirmation of ambassador-designate Emory Swank and his posting to Phnom Penh.[29] However, Rives did capture, albeit unsubtly, the reality of the situation. Nixon did not expressly want to see Phnom Penh fall. Indeed, during the planning of the incursion, in mid-April, Nixon stated, "I want to make sure that Cambodia does not go down the drain without doing something."[30] This would be a familiar refrain over the coming months. However, not wanting to see Phnom Penh fall was not synonymous with wanting Lon Nol to stick around. Nixon was anything but committed to Lon Nol.

Two weeks into the incursion, CIA Director Helms reported that the North Vietnamese appeared to "have expanded the scope of their operations." Helms detailed that NVA/VC forces had "moved west toward Phnom Penh, cutting lines of communications, occupying strategic towns, and isolating Phenom Penh from major portions of Military Regions One, Two, Five and Six." The report continued that most large VC/NVA units were dispersed within Cambodia but were in a holding operation, that is, Hanoi appeared to be maintaining military, economic, psychological and political pressure on the Lon Nol government while building its own Cambodian power base in preparation to take over the country. However, it was "too early to attempt to judge the final effect" of the incursions into Cambodia.[31]

If Hanoi's intentions remained uncertain, the fate of Phnom Penh was almost a foregone conclusion. In the same report, Helms provided a dismal assessment of Cambodia's prospects. According to Helms, "The prospects of the Lon Nol Government surviving are really no better than they were two weeks ago. In fact, Lon Nol's problems are becoming more complex with the passage of each day, for he has not gotten the badly needed economic and military equipment or the political support which he has asked of his Asian neighbors." For Helms, the lack of international support "has weakened Lon Nol's confidence and the spread of war has started an erosion of his popular support." The CIA director concluded, "Prospects for Lon Nol's future are bleak, particularly if the VC/NVA continue to keep the current level of military pressure on his government."[32] Kissinger echoed

The Perfidy of Geopolitics / 215

these concerns. Three weeks into the operation, Kissinger relayed to Nixon that the incursion was "generating pressures upon Hanoi and also between Hanoi and its allies." In part, Kissinger explained, Hanoi "cannot now be certain what the U.S. will do under any given set of circumstances. They had not expected our move into Cambodia." More concretely, North Vietnamese forces had "lost a huge quantity of stores and valuable base areas"; these losses would "require considerable time to make up." On that point, the military operations did contribute to Nixon's overarching objective to prolong the struggle in South Vietnam with minimal U.S. casualties. However, Kissinger counseled, the Cambodian government was still very weak, and the Saigon government likewise was "beset with severe political and economic difficulties."[33] General Haig was even more cautious in his assessment of the military operations. Noting the severe limitations of the Cambodian armed forces, Haig considered the situation "grave but not altogether hopeless." He warned that within Phnom Penh, few individuals in the government realized "that the war will be long and there is false optimism that massive American help and a few months of training will allow the Cambodians to route the invaders." For Haig, the situation demanded, among other things, immediate shipments of military equipment, tactical and B-52 sorties in northeast Cambodia, convoys and patrols along the Mekong River to Phnom Penh, the introduction of South Vietnamese and Thai combat forces, and substantial military and economic assistance from neighboring Southeast Asian governments. Barring these steps, Haig concluded that the chances of the Lon Nol government surviving were "dim at best."[34]

The eventual fate of Lon Nol—or of Cambodia—mattered little to Nixon. The president's major objective was to gain time for Vietnamization to work. And for this reason alone Cambodia remained central. Under President Johnson, South Vietnam's territorial integrity was defended largely through clandestine means, notably the use of U.S. Special Forces operating covertly along South Vietnam's borders with North Vietnam, Laos, and Cambodia. Other technological fixes, such as the ill-fated "McNamara Line," also were implemented. In the end, Johnson was willing to increase America's military operations in South Vietnam; he was not prepared to expand the war overtly into neighboring Cambodia (or Laos). Nixon harbored fewer doubts and gambled that an aggressive stance in Cambodia offered untapped advantages to "win the peace" in South Vietnam. However, in the aftermath of

216 / The Perfidy of Geopolitics

the Cambodian incursion, Congress rescinded the Gulf of Tonkin Resolution and attempts to cut off funding for military operations in South Vietnam were a constant source of concern within the White House.

The military situation in South Vietnam was equally troubling.[35] Despite limited success on the battlefield, the Cambodian incursion was not the panacea promised by the military establishment. On May 31, Kissinger stated bluntly, "It seems to be that the main problem is not what is best politically but how do we keep Cambodia from collapsing in the next 3 months. We must keep them propped up and time is the crucial problem. How do we do this? Anything we can do is certainly worth the risk."[36] In this remarkably straightforward statement, Kissinger effectively summed up the endgame of America's effort to build a sovereign state in South Vietnam. Vietnamization required time; military operations to secure South Vietnam's territorial integrity promised to buy time. However, ongoing military operations along the Cambodian border depended on the stability of Phnom Penh. Ideally, the Lon Nol government would survive, thus ensuring a pro-Western buttress to South Vietnam's western border; at the minimum, a neutral government would emerge that would hinder Hanoi's use of Cambodian territory as U.S. forces withdrew from South Vietnam. This, in essence, was the message Haig had delivered to Lon Nol in late May. When the prime minister declared that Cambodia was "definitely in this anti-Communist struggle" and was prepared to "enter into your block of nations," that is, cast aside a position of neutrality, he affirmed "we will gladly do so." Haig, in response, was cautionary. He explained, "In regard to the question of joining our block of nations, as you know, it is the official position of our government to restore the neutrality of Cambodia, which may prove a myth." Nevertheless, the general continued, "it is still important that we not provide Hanoi with additional pretexts and justification for continuing their offensive against your country. We continue to hope to re-establish stability and be able to prevent further escalation or prolongation of the war. Therefore, we believe that it remains, at least for the time being, in the best interests of all parties that Cambodia continue to profess its goal of re-establishing its neutrality." Haig underscored the need to counter Hanoi's rebuilding of its logistical framework and lines of communications disrupted by the incursion; and to that point, the military operations of the Cambodian army were crucial. However, Haig counseled the prime minister, "I must be perfectly

The Perfidy of Geopolitics / 217

frank, in order not to do you any injustice. . . . The effect of undelivered promises by me could be disastrous to our planning." By way of conclusion, Haig repeated Nixon's support but stressed that Nixon "also has many problems of his own and he does not want to jeopardize our future freedom of action by making ill-conceived moves at this time. He realizes that patience, sacrifice and courage are necessary to do the job and that basically Cambodians must save Cambodia."[37]

On June 5 Laurence Lynn, director of the Program Analysis Staff of the NSC, relayed to Kissinger his assessment on the situation in Cambodia. Lynn believed that the United States "had to act in Cambodia to the extent required to protect its strategic and military interests in South Vietnam" and, in turn, was "compelled by political circumstances to act to assist the Lon Nol government." That said, in response to the altered military and political environment throughout Southeast Asia, it was necessary to "weigh carefully what US interests in Cambodia imply about the extent to which we should support the Lon Nol government." Notably, Lynn differentiated "between the necessity to assist a threatened government and the necessity to underwrite the continued existence of that Government no matter what the cost." In line with many other analysts, Lynn recognized that "Cambodia may be on the verge of collapse, military and economically, if not politically."[38] Lynn provided no firm recommendation with respect to the Lon Nol regime. However, his analysis of America's false commitments to the Phnom Penh government was accurate. From the vantage point of the White House, Lon Nol was not an ally but a geopolitical stopgap. Indeed, in late June Nixon underscored that the United States "did not want to get drawn into the permanent direct defense of Cambodia," for that "would have been inconsistent with the basic premises of our foreign policy." Instead, the president clarified, "it was the major expansion of enemy activity in Cambodia that ultimately caused allied troops to end 5 years of restraint and attack the Communist base areas" in Cambodia. "Vietcong and North Vietnamese troops have operated in Eastern Cambodia for years," the president explained, and that "the primary objective of these Communist forces has been the support of Hanoi's aggression against South Vietnam." Nixon warned that without direct intervention "the prospect suddenly loomed of Cambodia's becoming virtually one large base area for attack anywhere into South Vietnam along the 600 miles of the Cambodian frontier." From a

218 / The Perfidy of Geopolitics

strategic point of view, "the enemy in Cambodia would have enjoyed complete freedom of action to move forces and supplies rapidly across the entire length of South Vietnam's flank to attack our forces in South Vietnam with impunity from well-stocked sanctuaries along the border." Nixon reasoned that "the possibility of a grave new threat to our troops in South Vietnam was rapidly becoming an actuality." Framing the incursion in the widest terms possible, Nixon explained that "our Vietnamization program would be in serious jeopardy; our withdrawals of troops could only have been carried out in the face of serious threat to our remaining troops in Vietnam." And now, with the incursion completed, Nixon looked to the future: "With American ground operations in Cambodia ended, we shall move forward with our plan to end the war in Vietnam and to secure the just peace on which all Americans are united." Regarding Cambodia, Nixon affirmed that there would be no U.S. ground personnel other than the regular embassy staff in Phnom Penh; no U.S. advisors working with the Cambodian military; and military assistance would be provided only "in the form of small arms and relatively unsophisticated equipment in types and quantities suitable for their army." Air interdiction missions would continue—only "to protect our forces in South Vietnam."[39] Congress may have prevented the deployment of U.S. combat forces in Cambodia, but Nixon still had America's massive air power at his disposal.

Throughout the summer of 1970 both civilian and military intelligence experts continued to monitor conditions in Cambodia.[40] For some officials, early speculations of imminent collapse gave way to guarded optimism. Colonel Jonathan Ladd, tasked with coordinating U.S. military assistance to Cambodia, provided a remarkably upbeat assessment. On July 11, for example, he reported that "the enemy's hope of bringing down the Lon Nol Government quickly has now failed." Instead, Hanoi was forced to reorganize militarily, and that would require time. Ladd surmised, in turn, that the Cambodians would "be able to utilize this time to reinforce critical garrisons, distribute supplies and munitions, improve communications, coordinate defensive plans, work out South Vietnamese and Thai assistance, train troops, and gain support from other nations." Most importantly, improved conditions in Cambodia seemingly contributed to the success of Vietnamization. As Ladd detailed, "The enemy is faced with the strategic choice of either bringing more pressure to bear against Cambodians, in which case he

The Perfidy of Geopolitics / 219

cannot exert a maximum effort against [South] Vietnam and against Vietnamization, or redeploying at least some of the enemy forces now in Cambodia to Vietnam, thus relieving to some extent the current pressures against Cambodia." Kissinger was less sanguine, commenting that "we should not allow ourselves to become euphoric about Cambodia."[41]

In preparation for an NSC meeting on July 21, Kissinger reviewed the administration's diplomatic strategy and its negotiating position toward Hanoi.[42] Thus far, peace talks in Paris had stalled as Hanoi "continued to demand as the price for negotiations (1) a guaranteed and accelerated schedule for complete U.S. withdrawal and (2) an abandonment of the present South Vietnamese government."[43] Neither condition was acceptable. The White House advised that North Vietnamese troops also withdraw from South Vietnam and that the Thieu government remain in place to participate in subsequent elections to determine Vietnam's political fate.[44] Anything less almost guaranteed the loss of South Vietnam. To that end, Kissinger's three options were as follows: "Concentrate on disengagement and leave the question of political settlement entirely to the North and South Vietnamese"; "make a major effort to seek a political settlement and hinge our withdrawals on this objective"; or "continue on a middle course, withdrawing while attempting to build South Vietnamese strength and meanwhile seeking a political resolution." For Kissinger, continuation of the middle course kept open their options in the short term; however, he cautioned, "We must recognize that at some point we will face a decision to move to one or the other of the remaining courses—the point will come when our withdrawals are no longer a major bargaining card."[45]

Ever since Nixon entered the White House he had received divided counsel about troop withdrawals.[46] On one side stood Laird, the secretary of defense, who strongly advocated for unilateral troop withdrawals, believing that the war had become a political liability for the Nixon presidency. On the other side was Kissinger, concerned more that the removal of troops would deprive U.S. negotiators critical leverage in securing concessions from Hanoi essential to any agreement to end the war.[47] Indeed, three months after Nixon chose to redeploy U.S. forces from Vietnam, Kissinger warned that "withdrawal of U.S. troops will become like salted peanuts to the American public: The more U.S. troops come home, the more will be demanded." As such, Kissinger cautioned the president, "the more troops are withdrawn,

220 / The Perfidy of Geopolitics

the more Hanoi will be encouraged—they are the last people we will be able to fool about the ability of the South Vietnamese to take over from us." Effectively, for Kissinger, Vietnamization would "run into increasingly serious problems."[48] Nixon, to a degree, sided with Kissinger. From the outset, Nixon was determined not to be the "first American President to lose a war." As such, he worried that "an elegant bug-out" was tantamount to a "retreat from the world" and would "destroy the confidence of the American people in themselves."[49] However, Nixon also understood that "we buy time with troop withdrawal announcements." For Nixon, there were always three wars—"on the battlefield, the Saigon political war, and U.S. politics." Unilateral troop withdrawals could reduce U.S. casualties, buying time on the home front; as corollary, a protracted period of troop withdrawals would allow more time for Vietnamization to work.[50]

Prior to the July 21 NSC meeting, the day of reckoning was almost upon Nixon. Kissinger maintained that "withdrawal is *our* option, to play as we wish." However, the "central question . . . is whether we use it as a bargaining counter for a political settlement." He reiterated that "we can withdraw at our own pace, leaving the political future to a contest between the South Vietnamese; or we can offer a more rapid withdrawal in an effort to make a political settlement." Kissinger explained further that "we have consistently maintained that our prime objective is a rapid negotiated settlement to end the war, while our Vietnamization/withdrawal policy is a less preferred course in the absence of progress in Paris." Indeed, Kissinger reminded Nixon, "Vietnamization is designed to induce the enemy to negotiate by posing the prospect of a gradual American disengagement that maintains our domestic support while successively strengthening the South Vietnamese forces." In his final analysis, Kissinger could offer little more than a recommendation to "continue our present policy." Notably, he added, "We should see whether the longer term fallout of Cambodia" generates some movement on the part of Hanoi.[51]

During the July NSC meeting, Cambodia took center stage. Helms opened by noting that "events in Cambodia have altered the situation in Southeast Asia." According to the CIA director, "Hanoi saw opportunities—and possible gains—resulting from the fall of Sihanouk in March." However, the North Vietnamese were reportedly caught off guard by the U.S.-led military operations into Cambodia. Helms then cautioned that while "the action we took did throw them off stride" the incursion "did not alter Hanoi's determination to increase its activity in Cambodia." As such, Helms concluded that the North Vietnamese were expected to "continue their long-haul, low-profile activity" even as "their tactics in Cambodia have become bolder." Essentially, the Vietnamese communists were attempting to sow confusion in the countryside and helping the "indigenous insurgency," that is, the Khmer Rouge. Thus, while it remained uncertain if Nixon's bold move into Cambodia would delay the fall of South Vietnam, all reports indicated that Cambodia was becoming more and more unstable. Ellsworth Bunker, U.S. ambassador to South Vietnam, was more optimistic. Of the incursion, Bunker maintained that "the South Vietnamese are more confident now after Cambodia." He clarified, "Their apprehensions about U.S. redeployments have largely disappeared. They feel the war will diminish, though it may go on for a long time in a no-war, no-peace situation." Bunker concluded that "with respect to Cambodia . . . it was more difficult for the Communists to create an infrastructure there than in South Vietnam because the Cambodians don't like South Vietnamese."[52] Left unspoken was the fact that Nixon's bid to end the war in Vietnam marked the initiation of war in Cambodia. And in the event a negotiated settlement with Hanoi was forthcoming, the Nixon administration felt no compunction to defend or secure Cambodia beyond the minimum necessary in support of South Vietnam. Until that point, the White House would continue to bomb Cambodia in order to compel Hanoi into accepting a diplomatic end to the war.

Misplaced Trust

On July 29 Nixon received a letter from Lon Nol. Military operations against Vietnamese communists, the prime minister explained, were going well. However, to fully defeat the enemy, Lon Nol warned, his troops required helicopters, armored personnel carriers, and other supplies. In addition, the prime minister made a veiled request that U.S. advisors provide training to the FANK for covert operations.[53] Nixon was unmoved. Despite Lon Nol's reassurances of military progress—an assessment that aligned with reports emanating from MACV—there were signs by late summer that the drive into Cambodia fell far short of expectations. On August 6 Nixon received an intelligence estimate prepared jointly by the CIA and relevant sections

222 / The Perfidy of Geopolitics

at the National Security Administration (NSA), the Department of State, and the Department of Defense. The report detailed that in the four months since the coup against Sihanouk, Vietnamese communists had overrun half of Cambodia, taken or threatened sixteen of its nineteen provincial capitals, and interdicted—for varying periods—all roads and rail links to the capital. As such, throughout the countryside "VC/NVA forces generally continue[d] to move at will, attacking towns and villages in the south and converting the north into an extension of the Laos corridor and a base for 'people's war' throughout the country and in South Vietnam as well." In short, the Cambodian incursion seemingly backfired, with Hanoi now expanding military operations throughout the entirety of Indochina. And while the report acknowledged that "evidence on many aspects of the Cambodian situation is fragmentary and subject to conflicting interpretations," the overall assessment was that the "survival of the Lon Nol government" would "depend heavily on the extent of foreign assistance as well as on the will and ability of the people and their leaders to organize themselves for effective military resistance to the communists; on the unity and morale of the country in the face of the hardship, destruction, and death; and on the reaction to the divisive political appeals issued in Sihanouk's name." Left unresolved, however, was concrete information on Hanoi's primary objectives in Cambodia, namely "the extent to which they can bring pressures to bear on the Lon Nol government and the degree to which they are willing to allocate available resources to such an effort."[54]

Nixon was determined to support Cambodia to the degree it helped achieve his objectives in South Vietnam.[55] To that end, Nixon made sure Lon Nol's army had sufficient weapons and munitions necessary to prolong the war but nothing more.[56] On August 20 Nixon replied to Lon Nol and expressed his support for the beleaguered prime minister: "The strong and effective defense already presented by the Cambodian armed forces against this aggression and in support of Cambodia's independence, neutrality, and territorial integrity, has inspired my own admiration and that of the American people." The president added, "The fact that United States assistance has played some part in this defense is a source of deep personal satisfaction to me." Nixon then pledged his assurance "that the United States intends to continue to provide support for your country in its brave and determined struggle." On this point, Nixon relayed that he had already authorized an initial amount of U.S.$40 million in military assistance and was considering other forms of economic assistance available.[57]

On August 27 Lon Nol responded enthusiastically and professed in admiration that the United States was "playing with distinction, its important, traditional international role as the defender of small States that are unjustly treated."[58] Lon Nol's faith and trust in Nixon were misplaced. As Arnold Isaacs concludes, the Cambodian government was "sadly ignorant of the international facts of life."[59] Indeed, many Cambodian leaders by this point were voicing their frustration with the limited support offered by the White House. On August 5 Sim Var, a member of Lon Nol's National Assembly, held the United States "morally and materially responsible" for the situation in Cambodia. "The United States," Sim Var explained, "has an obligation to assist Cambodia in her worsening military situation because the American incursion into Communist sanctuaries in the spring pushed the enemy into the countryside and toward the capital." He underscored that "it should not be forgotten that the United States is to a certain degree responsible for the war in Cambodia." More presciently, Sim Var charged that "the United States was withholding aid because the American people mistakenly considered the fighting here part of the Vietnam war, from which they want to withdraw."[60] For Sim Var and several other officials in Phnom Penh, the unfolding war in Cambodia was not simply a continuation of the conflict in Vietnam but instead assumed a character unto itself. Nixon, as we have seen, was not opposed to helping Cambodia; but for political reasons he was limited in his response. The more fundamental problem was that Nixon and Kissinger "adopted the narrow perspective of their military commanders, which was that American military aims could now be pursued on Cambodian territory."[61]

The problem was that U.S. military aims could not effectively be pursued on Cambodian territory. Lon Nol's army was ineffective against the better-trained and better-armed North Vietnamese forces. At best, Nixon faced a military stalemate in Cambodia to complement the desultory results in South Vietnam. In late August military analysts concluded that "FANK does not have the capability to conduct sustained offensive operations but that it does have a limited defensive capability to defend key population centers and lines of communication." Officials at both the JCS and CIA "agreed that the Communists are practicing a protracted war strategy in

224 / The Perfidy of Geopolitics

Cambodia."[62] In turn, the White House adopted a strategic response intended to defend Cambodian territory on a limited basis. Holding firm to the belief that the preservation of Cambodia as a *noncommunist* state was essential to the success of Vietnamization, it was decided that the primary objective was to "maintain the present Cambodian Government in control of the half of the country that includes the populated area, capital, and port." To that end, the United States would attempt to provide limited military assistance and work to enlist the support of combat troops from South Vietnam and Thailand.[63] In short, a possible neutral government served U.S. interests just as well as a pro-American or anticommunist government. And neutral governments were cheaper and came with fewer strings attached.

On October 26, the White House committed itself "to capitalize on Cambodian nationalism, support Cambodian neutrality, and promote GKR [Government of the Khmer Republic] self-sufficiency." To that end, U.S. foreign policy—as articulated in National Security Decision Memorandum 89—was to "assist in the development of close working relationships between the GKR and the friendly governments of South Vietnam, Thailand, and Laos."[64] Days later, Nixon explained his reasoning to Cheng Heng, the figurehead of Lon Nol's Khmer Republic. Expressing the United States' admiration for the "courage shown by [the] Cambodian people . . . who cherish independence and are willing [to] fight and sacrifice for it," Nixon avowed "to help, to the extent possible, so that Cambodians may be independent and choose [their] own way without foreign invaders imposing their will." Sidestepping his own personal responsibility, Nixon remarked that "we know no nation can survive unless its people are willing and able to defend [them]selves." He acknowledged that the "U.S. can help" but in the "final analysis it is [the] character of [the] Cambodians that will determine their future." Invoking the Nixon Doctrine, the president reasoned that "we prefer not to go into a country and defend it ourselves, but to help it defend itself by providing U.S. assistance such as arms." He conceded that the Cambodian military lacked weapons and that his administration was "trying to cooperate" but that "certain limitations [had been] placed on us by Congress." By way of conclusion, Nixon reiterated that it was "not so much what we do but Cambodia's own determination that will keep it independent."[65] Having initiated all-out war in Cambodia, Nixon effectively cast the Phnom Penh government adrift. Asia for the Asians, indeed.

War beyond Peace

In the months leading to the presidential election of 1972, Nixon remained focused on how the current situation in South Vietnam would impact his reelection campaign. Four years earlier Nixon had campaigned on a promise to end America's involvement in the war; he now worried that failure in South Vietnam would hurt his chances in November. Since entering the White House, neither Nixon nor Kissinger contemplated simply abandoning the war; but they understood plainly that the war had to end.[66] The favored outcome, for both Nixon and Kissinger, was for a semblance of accommodation between Saigon and Hanoi, not unlike the political situation on the Korean peninsula. As Nixon explained to Vice President Spiro Agnew, "It'll be like South Korea."[67] The essence of this geopolitical strategy was equilibrium: parity between Hanoi and Saigon was necessary so that neither could impose a military solution on the other, and each would have an incentive to settle remaining differences peacefully. In this sense, a stalemate was acceptable. This meant, in turn, supporting the South Vietnamese government sufficiently to keep the North at bay; concurrently, promises of economic aid to the communists and the continued threat of U.S. air power could be used as carrots and sticks to induce Hanoi into compliance with U.S. goals.[68]

Success, however, appeared ever more fleeting, as an obstinate Hanoi government refused to countenance a divided Vietnam. Given this predicament, could South Vietnam be forfeited? Publicly, Nixon remained steadfast in his rhetoric that America's credibility was at stake; that America's commitment to South Vietnam was, by extension, a commitment to America's friends and allies in all corners of the world. Privately, though, Nixon sought another path that could salvage both America's credibility and his own political future. On August 3, 1972, Nixon admitted in private conversation with Kissinger that "South Vietnam probably is never gonna [sic] survive anyway." With an eye toward the elections, Nixon explained, "winning an election is terribly important . . . but can we have a viable foreign policy if a year from now or two years from now, North Vietnam gobbles up South Vietnam? That's the real question." Kissinger counseled that "if a year or two years from now North Vietnam gobbles up South Vietnam, we can have a viable foreign policy if it looks as if it's the result of South Vietnamese incompetence." Notably, the national security advisor underscored

226 / The Perfidy of Geopolitics

that "if we sell out in such a way that, say in a three- to four-month period, we have pushed President Thieu over the brink—we ourselves—I think, there is going to be—even the Chinese won't like that. . . . But it will worry everybody. And domestically in the long run it won't help us all that much because our opponents will say we should've done it three years ago." To that end, Kissinger acknowledged that "we've got to find some formula that holds the thing together a year or two, after which—after a year, Mr. President, Vietnam will be a backwater. If we settle it, say, this October, by January 1974 no one will give a damn."[69]

For both personal and practical matters, Nixon preferred that South Vietnam survive as a sovereign state. Barring that outcome, however, it was necessary that a semblance of peace last long enough to demonstrate the viability of the Accords in that a "decent interval" was necessary for the claim of "peace with honor."[70] Concurrently, Nixon was compelled to downplay the centrality of South Vietnam to the American nomos. Over the course of several months, both in public orations to the American populace and in private conversations with world leaders, Nixon and Kissinger would keep up the charade of gradually disassociating the United States from South Vietnam and deflecting the region's overall importance to national security concerns.[71] Indeed, as early as mid-1971 Kissinger already had downplayed the importance of South Vietnam in his diplomacy. On a secret trip to China in July of that year, Kissinger met with Chinese Prime Minister Zhou Enlai to discuss, in part, a negotiated settlement of the war in Vietnam. "On behalf of President Nixon," Kissinger informed the prime minister on July 9, "we are prepared to withdraw completely from Indochina and to give a fixed date. . . . [We] will permit the political solution of South Vietnam to evolve and to leave it to the Vietnamese alone." Markedly, as part of the effort to distance the United States from the future of South Vietnam, Kissinger reframed American national security interests. In 1954, Kissinger lectured his Chinese counterpart: "It was America's mission to fight communism all around the world and for the U.S. to be the principal force, to enlarge itself in every struggle at every point of the world at any point of time." In other words, no region was deemed so peripheral as to escape America's commitment to protecting the free world. Under Nixon, Kissinger said, the administration operated "on a different philosophy." "We do not deal with communism in the abstract," he explained, "but with

The Perfidy of Geopolitics / 227

specific communist states on the basis of their specific actions toward us, and not as an abstract crusade." Implicitly, Kissinger acknowledged that the United States would not oppose the installation of a communist government in Saigon. Indeed, the national security advisor admitted that "our position is not to maintain any particular government in South Vietnam. We are prepared to undertake specific obligations restricting the support we can give to the government after a peace settlement and defining the relationship we can maintain with it after a peace settlement."[72] The following day, July 10, 1971, Kissinger again committed the United States to the unilateral withdrawal of U.S. military forces from South Vietnam. He did, however, call out the need for "a transition period between the military withdrawal and the political evolution" so that "the people of Vietnam and of other parts of Indochina [could] determine their own fate." Kissinger nevertheless stated, "If after complete American withdrawal, the Indochinese people change their governments, the U.S. will not interfere. The United States will abide by the determination of the will of the people."[73]

Kissinger echoed these sentiments during a May 1972 meeting in Moscow with Soviet Foreign Minister Andrei Gromyko. The issue, Kissinger explained, "is not the preservation of any particular government." Ideally, South Vietnam would remain a sovereign, noncommunist state; less desirable but still acceptable would be a neutral South Vietnam. In fact, Kissinger conceded that the United States would allow whatever government happened to materialize. "All we ask," Kissinger added, "is a degree of time so as to leave Vietnam for Americans in a better perspective." In short, it was imperative for the United States to maintain its prestige and credibility, to not look as if America had betrayed its ally and lost the war. "What we mean," Kissinger made clear, "is that we will not leave in such a way that a Communist victory is guaranteed. However, we are prepared to leave so that a Communist victory is not excluded, though not guaranteed."[74]

The following month, during a subsequent meeting with Zhou, Kissinger reaffirmed his belief "that if a sufficient interval is placed between our withdrawal and what happens afterward that the issue can almost certainly be confined to an Indochina affair." Again, the White House vowed to not intervene, regardless of how imperiled South Vietnam might become following the withdrawal of U.S. forces. That said, for Kissinger it was vitally "important that there is a reasonable interval between the agreement on the ceasefire,

228 / The Perfidy of Geopolitics

and a reasonable opportunity for political negotiation." He expounded: "The outcome of my logic is that we are putting a time interval between the military outcome and the political outcome." Here, the military outcome was the signing of a peace treaty that would effectively end America's involvement in Indochina; the political outcome was the anticipated downfall of the Saigon regime. Effectively, Kissinger allowed that if any possible regime change happened in Saigon after a sufficient period had elapsed following America's departure from South Vietnam, the United States would not respond militarily in an attempt to prop up any noncommunist government. "We will agree to an historical process or a political process," Kissinger concluded, "in which the real forces in Vietnam will assert themselves, whatever these forces are. . . . [We] believe that the most rapid way of ending the war would be to concentrate on the military issues and permit us to disengage from Indochina, and after that permit the local forces to work it out, either through negotiations or other means." To underscore his point, Kissinger reiterated his belief "that if a sufficient interval is placed between our withdrawal and what happens afterward that the issue can almost certainly be confined to an Indochina affair."[75]

From mid-1972 onward, both Washington and Hanoi saw diplomacy as the best means of ending their war on the most favorable terms possible. However, as Asselin explains, both governments understood that any negotiated settlement would be highly problematic. Nevertheless, the two belligerents "acted in collusion and agreed to vague and largely unworkable positions because finalizing an agreement was more important than peace itself."[76] For its part, the Nixon administration wanted to extricate itself from an unwinnable war with its international credibility intact. Indeed, Nixon was prepared to sacrifice previous U.S. commitments to Saigon if it meant pulling America out of an unwinnable war. In doing so, however, the future of Cambodia, and of its relationship with the United States, also became less certain.

For Kissinger, the hoped-for equilibrium in South Vietnam hinged on the resolution of conflict in Cambodia. In an ideal world, Phnom Penh would remain pro-American; barring that, a neutral government could be just as effective to ensure the long-term survivability of South Vietnam. Beyond that, the particular composition of Cambodia's government was of no real concern. If Lon Nol could prove effective, so be it; otherwise, it would be necessary to seek alternatives, possibly Sihanouk or a coalition government

The Perfidy of Geopolitics / 229

with Sihanouk. On January 23, 1973, for example, Kissinger would explain to Lakshmi Jha, the Indian ambassador to the United States, that "we are not in favor of seeing Peking [Beijing] dominate Phnom Penh, because we don't want any great power to dominate Phnom Penh." He continued: "If some accommodations could be reached between Lon Nol and the Khmer Communists, with the North Vietnamese already agreed to withdraw, we could get a neutral Cambodia in which no great power exercises a dominate influence."[77] Kissinger, on this point, was not prepared to make the mistakes of previous administrations, that is, a dedicated commitment to a particular leader, such as Ngo Dinh Diem or even Thieu. Over the coming months, U.S. officials would continue to consider whether Lon Nol should be removed.[78]

By late 1972, peace negotiations between Kissinger and Hanoi's top negotiator, Le Duc Tho, had broken down. Blaming Hanoi for the deadlock, Nixon concluded his only option was to intensify the bombing of North Vietnam.[79] On December 17 Nixon authorized the commencement of a series of air strikes, including waves of B-52 sorties, to begin on the following day. Code-named Linebacker II, the operation targeted several sites in and around North Vietnam's major urban centers, including Hanoi and Haiphong.[80] From the initiation of Linebacker II until its conclusion on December 29, 200 B-52s flew 729 sorties and other aircraft flew 1,216 sorties; in total, 20,370 tons of bombs were dropped, mostly in and around Hanoi. U.S. analysts concluded that the bombing damaged or destroyed 1,600 military complexes, 372 trucks and railway cars, 25 percent of North Vietnam's petroleum stockpiles, 80 percent of its electrical power plants, and countless factories and other assets.[81] However, the bombings also destroyed innumerable schools, pagodas, markets, shops, and homes, with more than 1,300 civilians killed in Hanoi alone.[82] Civilian deaths were anticipated but summarily disregarded. As Alexander Haig told Nixon dismissively, "There'll be some slop-over casualties, but goddamnit . . ."[83]

Whether the so-called Christmas bombings forced Hanoi back to the negotiating table remains subject to debate. Less controversial is the deeper significance of the bombing as it relates to the American nomos. Stanley Karnow, while believing that the bombing accomplished little diplomatically, suggests that Nixon's main motivation was not diplomacy but instead a way to reassure Thieu of America's long-term commitment and to warn

230 / The Perfidy of Geopolitics

Hanoi that he would not hesitate to bomb North Vietnam again should the armistice break down.[84] Indeed, as Nixon explained to Kissinger in November 1972, "What really counts is not the agreement but my determination to take massive action against North Vietnam in the event they break the agreement."[85] In other words, Nixon realized that no agreement would prevent Hanoi from its ultimate objective of a unified Vietnam. However, Nixon believed—or, rather, hoped—that the continued presence of U.S. air power would serve as deterrent.[86] In similar logic, Nixon would later explain that he initiated the Christmas bombings to demonstrate his "own unilateral capability to prevent violation" and to establish "credibility in policing the agreement."[87]

Talks between Kissinger and Le Duc Tho resumed and, on January 23, 1973, Nixon announced that "we today have concluded an agreement to end the war and bring peace with honor in Vietnam and in Southeast Asia." Nixon affirmed that "the people of South Vietnam have been guaranteed the right to determine their own future, without inference" but that "the United States will continue to recognize the Government of the Republic of Vietnam as the sole legitimate government of South Vietnam." To that end, Nixon pledged "we shall continue to aid South Vietnam within the terms of the agreement, and we shall support efforts by the people of South Vietnam to settle their problems peacefully among themselves." At no point in his speech did Nixon mention Cambodia. This is not altogether remarkable. The Cambodian government had no role in the negotiations and, in fact, the resultant Paris Peace Accords—signed January 27—were notoriously vague on Cambodia's political future. That said, Cambodia *in the abstract* did factor prominently in U.S. postwar objectives, and the importance of Cambodia in Nixon's speech is found in its absence. Throughout, Nixon warns repeatedly that "the terms of the agreement must be scrupulously adhered to" and that he expected "other interested nations to help insure that the agreement is carried out and peace is maintained."[88] Nixon realized that the Accords could not effectively end the war in Vietnam; rather, they merely signaled the end of America's overt involvement. Indeed, Nixon anticipated a resumption of military operations, for it was a foregone conclusion that the terms of the agreement would be violated. Among the most promising violations would be infringements of South Vietnam's territorial integrity, particularly along its border with Cambodia.

The Perfidy of Geopolitics / 231

Following the signing of the Accords and the cessation of U.S. military operations, Agnew traveled to Saigon for a brief meeting with Thieu to demonstrate America's firm commitment to South Vietnam. Meanwhile, sporadic fighting continued, with both North and South Vietnamese forces operating in violation of the peace agreement. Agnew relayed to Thieu that Nixon was "fully aware of the need to assist the Vietnamese economy" and that "the U.S. has no intention of withdrawing its presence from Asia or retreating on its commitments." On this point, Agnew reminded Thieu of America's "air power in Thailand, the B-52s in Guam and the Pacific Fleet." Agnew and Thieu discussed also the anticipated threats to South Vietnam. Of particular importance was that peace be maintained in Laos and Cambodia. If that was assured, Thieu reasoned, "problems in South Vietnam would be greatly lessened and would be manageable."[89]

The Bombings of 1973

The Paris Peace Accords did little to resolve the growing civil war in Cambodia. Article 20 called for the parties to respect Cambodia's independence, sovereignty, territorial integrity, and neutrality, as had been delineated in the Geneva Accords of 1954. More precisely, it required all foreign governments to withdraw their forces and to end their military activities in Cambodia. Foreign countries, moreover, were not permitted to use Cambodia to encroach on the sovereignty of security of other countries. For U.S. officials, the inclusion of this latter clause was designed to deter Hanoi from using Cambodian territory to sneak troops and supplies into South Vietnam. Notably, the Accords did not provide for a ceasefire in Cambodia. Rather, the Lon Nol government and the Khmer Rouge were to settle their conflict without foreign intervention.[90] Aware of the vagueness of the Accords, U.S. negotiators also read an additional statement into the record, informing Hanoi that the Lon Nol government would halt offensive operations as soon as the ceasefire in Vietnam took effect; in turn, a de facto truce in Cambodia could result if the insurgents reciprocated. The statement warned, however, that if the communists continued military operations, the United States and the Cambodian government would take "necessary countermeasures" and, specifically, the United States "would continue to carry out air strikes in Cambodia as necessary until such time as a ceasefire could be brought into effect."[91] In essence, U.S. policymakers tacitly

232 / The Perfidy of Geopolitics

understood that Hanoi would continue to exercise influence in Cambodia (and Laos) and that any semblance of military activity could be used as a pretext to renew fighting.[92]

Such was the context for a back-channel message to Bunker sent by Haig in the days leading up to the signing of the Accords. Now serving as vice chief of staff of the U.S. Army, Haig instructed Bunker to forward operational guidance to Generals Fred Weyand and John Vogt.[93] These included that carrier-based air operations continue south of the demilitarized zone into Laos and Cambodia during the post-ceasefire period "even though this requires overflight of South Vietnam." However, there were to be "no sorties flown over Cambodia and Laos from US air bases in South Vietnam." Guidelines specified also that "during the 72 hours following the initiation of the ceasefire in South Vietnam we should plan to withhold U.S. air action over Cambodia unless a serious tactical emergency develops." The expected suspension of air operations was to "assess the effect of Lon Nol's [expected] unilateral declaration of the cessation of all offensive operations by Khmer forces."[94] Publicly, therefore, as U.S. officials proclaimed that peace was at hand, preparations were underway in anticipation of resuming the aerial bombing of Cambodia.

On January 23 Haig informed Admiral Thomas Moorer, chair of the JCS, that when a ceasefire in Vietnam goes into effect, "Lon Nol will announce unilaterally that he is also terminating all offensive operations in Cambodia. He will do that to put the pressure on the other side for a de facto ceasefire." Haig explained that the Khmer Rouge and the Vietnamese communists "may not want to abide" by the ceasefire, "so what we have to do is cut down on our air activity in Cambodia as soon as the ceasefire which might go into effect in [South Vietnam]." In other words, the White House expected that fighting would quickly flare up in Cambodia, and U.S. officials would wait to take advantage of any action that could be construed as a violation of the settlement. This aligned with Nixon's demand to "lay on a heavy effort in Cambodia which is the least stable area of all." By way of conclusion, Haig stressed that "the onus is not on us of escalating the war" but that at the slightest provocation "we are going to start pouring it in there."[95] In actuality, the United States had not stopped "pouring it in" on Cambodian targets. Until Lon Nol announced a ceasefire, U.S. air operations, including B-52 strikes, continued over Cambodia.[96]

The Perfidy of Geopolitics / 233

In Washington, Kissinger met with members of the WSAG on January 24 to discuss the anticipated resumption of military operations. When the awaited ceasefire took effect, the national security advisor reiterated, all tactical air and B-52 strikes would be suspended for seventy-two hours, but with U.S. forces ready to "react to any offensive actions launched by the enemy during that period." When asked if operations would resume after seventy-two hours, Kissinger admitted, "It depends on what happens. You understand the rules; we don't launch any offensive actions during the 72 hour period, but we can react to any offensive actions they launch. We don't stand by and do nothing if they launch an attack." It remained unclear, however, how U.S. officials would determine whether Hanoi was in violation of the ceasefire. When Moorer inquired about "who will make the determination that the enemy is launching a new attack," Haig responded that "the people on the ground are the only ones who can do that." Kissinger agreed, noting that "our local commander should be ready to assist if the Cambodians are attacked. However, he has to understand that we want to show restraint, but not to the extent of endangering FANK units."[97] In other words, air combat operations in Cambodia would be suspended until such time U.S. officials could charge Hanoi to be in violation of a ceasefire agreement of which the Cambodians were not signatories.

On January 28 Lon Nol delivered his much-anticipated speech calling for a unilateral ceasefire. He announced, "We Cambodian people request that the North Vietnamese aggressors and their Viet Cong lackeys lay down their weapons and immediately pull out of Cambodian territory. We forbid all arms caches and sanctuaries and all military bases or other strategic installations on our land." However, he asserted also that "by virtue of the 1954 Geneva agreement, we are legitimately and entirely entitled to reoccupy our territory which has been illegally controlled by the North Vietnamese and the Viet Cong." As such, the president affirmed that on the following morning all military operations would be suspended to "permit the North Vietnamese and Viet Cong troops to withdraw from our territory with the shortest delay." Lon Nol warned that his forces would move into the disputed territories "to contact the people and assure their security. Any impediment against this move of our armed forces can occur only from infringements upon these rules. Whosoever does so must bear complete responsibility for all consequences. We will always maintain the rights of

234 / The Perfidy of Geopolitics

legal self-defense by continuing our self-defense operations across the country."[98] As Isaacs writes, if this was a ceasefire offer in any sense, it was so qualified that a suspicious enemy could hardly be expected to embrace it. Effectively, Lon Nol was demanding that all enemy forces surrender their arms and allow government forces to reoccupy communist-held territory. Conversely, Lon Nol asserted his right to resume military operations if his forces met any resistance.[99]

Over the subsequent days, Nixon and his staff closely monitored events in Cambodia for any sign that Hanoi was in violation of the accords.[100] On January 29, Kissinger requested that analysts working with the JCS provide a "list of the most serious violations thus far." Of special interest was any indication of widespread enemy movement out of Cambodia.[101] The wait was not long. Within days of the ceasefire it was clear that the North Vietnamese had no intention of withdrawing their forces from Cambodia or Laos, and by February 9 fighting had continued to escalate.[102] More troubling were the activities of the Khmer Rouge.

U.S. officials, but especially Kissinger, struggled to make sense of the unfolding situation. For years, U.S. intelligence experts were baffled by the Khmer communists. That myriad factions within the Khmer Rouge existed was well understood; the geopolitical loyalties of these factions, and their ultimate objectives, were less clear.[103] Kissinger, however, remained obstinate in his conviction that the Khmer Rouge *had* to be serving a foreign master, most likely Hanoi, possibly Beijing, but maybe even Moscow. In time, Kissinger's hubris would contribute to collapse of Phnom Penh; until then, Kissinger's blinders laid the foundation for an aerial bombing campaign that surpassed the brutality of even the Christmas bombings. On February 6, as White House staff monitored ceasefire violations, Kissinger asked of his WSAG, "Who controls the insurgents of Cambodia?" Carver responded that "they are essentially controlled by North Vietnam, but there is a lot of finagling and fooling around by the Chinese and others. Various groups are frying their own fish in Cambodia." Seeking clarification, Kissinger asked, "What fish are the Chinese frying there?" Carver explained (in error) that it was "reasonable to believe that many members of the Khmer Rouge have been members of the Chinese Communist Party rather than the Communist parties of Cambodia or North Vietnam, and therefore their loyalties may lie in that direction." Not satisfied with this response, Kissinger

The Perfidy of Geopolitics / 235

demanded, "What I want to know is what the Chinese want the Cambodian Communists to do. Are they in favor of a ceasefire in Cambodia or not?" In other words, Kissinger considered the Khmer Rouge to answer primarily to the Chinese; therefore, the operative question was China's gambit, that is, to what objective were the Chinese guiding the Khmer Rouge? When Carver explained that they didn't know if the Khmer Rouge were in favor of a ceasefire, Kissinger repeated, "I don't care who they are loyal to, I just want to know who is for what in Cambodia." He continued, "This situation in Cambodia is difficult to get on top of. Who is going to influence whom?" James Schlesinger, also of the CIA, interjected, "the old Khmer Rouge have the greatest influence among the various groups." Carver disagreed, suggesting that "the anti-Sihanouk element in the Khmer Rouge is most likely controlled by North Vietnam." On that point, both Daniel Murphy of the JCS and William Sullivan of the State Department disagreed.[104] In frustration, Kissinger called upon the CIA and other intelligence agencies to provide an assessment on the various Khmer Rouge groups, including a determination of who controlled or influenced them and an evaluation of their intentions.[105]

Despite having limited understanding of the military and political situation unfolding in Cambodia, the White House remained steadfast in its effort to compel Hanoi into compliance. On February 9, just eleven days after the Paris agreement, Nixon authorized the bombing of Cambodia.[106] And similar to his decision to order both Operation Menu and the 1970 "incursion" into Cambodia, Nixon's decision to resume military operations was made with scant regard for Cambodia itself. On February 15, Nixon informed the Joint Chiefs of Staff that "the Korean War was not about Korea, but basically about Japan." So too it was with Vietnam, the president explained. "Vietnam was important not for itself but because of what it demonstrated in terms of support for our friends and allies and in terms of showing our will to our enemies." Noting that he could have "bugged out" of Vietnam in 1968, Nixon maintained that his determination demonstrated "our commitments to our friends and our determination to our enemies." Fearful of appearing weak on the global stage, Nixon warned that "we must regain the respect for our military or we will end up with a country and a world which is unsafe."[107] Nixon reiterated these concerns three months later, conceding that America would appear as a "paper tiger" if South Vietnam

236 / The Perfidy of Geopolitics

collapsed.[108] Nixon essentially initiated the sustained bombing of Cambodia for personal and symbolic reasons: to recuperate a perceived loss of prestige and credibility in the eyes of China and the Soviet Union. It was never in support of Lon Nol. On February 10, Nixon relayed to Agnew and NSA Deputy Assistant Brent Scowcroft that he "could not guarantee any government in Cambodia and that Lon Nol must understand that."[109]

In the end, the United States unleashed an air campaign against Cambodia "with unprecedented fury."[110] In March 1973 American B-52s dropped more than 24,000 tons of bombs on Cambodia; by April the tonnage increased to 35,000 tons; and in May the total surpassed 36,000 tons—an amount almost equal to the total for the whole year of 1972.[111] The bombing of Cambodia became so intense that the Seventh Air Force faced serious logistical problems; indeed, B-52 sortie rates increased to as many as eighty-one per day. By the time the bombing campaign ended, American B-52s had dropped more than 260,000 tons of explosives on Cambodia.[112]

Toward the End

The Nixon administration premised that the sustained bombing of Cambodia was a necessary instrument in their ongoing negotiations to bring about peace in the country. On that point, Nixon warned that "a total bombing halt would jeopardize the negotiating effort on Cambodia, undermine the Paris Agreement, and threaten US credibility."[113] For Nixon, "the purpose of the bombing [was] not to get into a war in Cambodia, but to enforce the peace in Vietnam."[114] In opposition to Nixon's policy, however, was a recalcitrant Congress that, on the whole, was committed to limiting, if not ending, the president's military activities in Southeast Asia. In early May, Congress moved to pass concrete prohibitive legislation on Indochina. These efforts included legislation designed to cut off military funding for combat activities in Indochina and legislation intended to curb the president's ability to wage war.[115] In the end, Nixon agreed to a "compromise" on Indochina. In exchange for a six-week extension of the bombing campaign in Cambodia, Nixon accepted a cutoff of military funds effective on August 15. The relevant passage of the legislation specifies that "on or after August 15, 1973, no funds herein or heretofore appropriated may be obligated or expended to finance directly or indirectly combat activities by United States military forces in or over or from off the shores of North Vietnam, South

The Perfidy of Geopolitics / 237

Vietnam, Laos or Cambodia."[116] Later, in November 1973, Congress overrode a Nixon veto and passed the War Powers Resolution. In concrete terms, the resolution curbed Nixon's ability to deploy U.S. military forces abroad; symbolically, however, the resolution made clear that renewed military intervention in Southeast Asia was out of the question.[117]

For members of the Nixon administration, the writing was on the wall. In June, as the congressional machinations unfolded, Kissinger remarked to CIA Director Schlesinger, "It is getting impossible to do anything in Indochina." The consequences were grave indeed, portending for Kissinger "a total collapse in Cambodia."[118] However, Cambodia itself was of little consequence beyond its usefulness to South Vietnam. Indeed, Kissinger was forthright when he admitted that "South Vietnam is the ballgame."[119] In practical terms, the principal objective remained: to prevent the immediate fall of the Saigon government. This required a check on Cambodia's imminent collapse. George Carver, a CIA officer, described candidly "the importance of Cambodia to the U.S. and its impact on South Vietnam." "From the point of view of South Vietnam," Carter explained, "the longer Hanoi has to wait for unrestricted access in Cambodia, the more difficult it is for them to move in South Vietnam. The longer they have to wait, the less chance they have of improving their political prospects in South Vietnam, which are now fairly bleak. This argues for stretching out the Cambodian unravelling."[120]

In private, however, U.S. officials held little hope that the Lon Nol regime would survive. Indeed, several intelligence analysts portended the fall of Phnom Penh within months. And yet, the longer Phnom Penh held, the better the chance that a political arrangement similar to that of Korea could take hold. And to this end, U.S. strategists were back to where they had been years earlier: the survival of Saigon required protection from enemy infiltration along its western border with Cambodia. For South Vietnam to endure, and for its armed forces to effectively counter anticipated PAVN and PLAF offenses, Hanoi had to be denied the use of Cambodian territory. This was precisely the motivation for the 1973 bombings. With this option denied, Nixon and Kissinger were forced to find other options.

Might the removal of Lon Nol provide a necessary jolt to delay the inevitable? Could the return of Sihanouk, for example, bring some much-needed stability to Cambodia? According to a CIA memorandum, "Continuing or

238 / The Perfidy of Geopolitics

increased U.S. assistance to the GKR [Government of the Khmer Republic] might slow the rate of decay, but hardware and material aid do not of themselves affect and cannot offset the major obstacle to improvement: the Phnom Penh government's inability to pull itself together. . . . This—not hardware or other forms of quantifiable assistance—is the central issue. Unless or until the GKR can start functioning as a government, there is little hope for any significant improvement in its position—no matter what additional assistance the United States provides."[121] Kissinger, for his part, had already come to this conclusion. In a conversation in June 1973 with the South Vietnamese ambassador to the U.S., Tran Kim Phuong, Kissinger conceded that the United States didn't "really have a solution" for Cambodia. He explained, "The problem in Phnom Penh is they have never been able to form an adequate government." In turn, Phuong questioned whether the United States could deal with the various factions on the other side: that is, the Khmer insurgents. Here, Kissinger equivocated, asking rhetorically: "Which is really better, the Khmer Rouge or Sihanouk? Is it better to have the faction controlled by Hanoi or Sihanouk? We simply haven't made up our minds on this matter."[122] He remained uncertain, even as opportunities seemed to materialize. In March, Schlesinger informed Kissinger that among Cambodia's office corps, "There is some interest in a possible coup." Kissinger did not immediately discount the possibility but instead told Schlesinger, "You'd better finish your hearings before you start getting into these ideas."[123] The problem, Kissinger well knew, was that apart from Sihanouk there were few viable candidates to replace Lon Nol.[124] What was certain, however, was that neither Nixon nor Kissinger were wedded to Lon Nol and, if the opportunity presented itself, they would gladly welcome regime-change. As Kissinger stated bluntly, "I consider Lon Nol expendable."[125]

Kissinger's glib remark came into clarity in conversation with his Chinese counterparts. On May 30, Kissinger explained to Ambassador Huang Chen, chief of China's Liaison Office in Washington, D.C., that from Nixon's vantage point, "the Vietnam peace agreement removed a major irritant" in U.S.-China relations but that "there was one outstanding problem, that is Cambodia." Kissinger highlighted Nixon's position on "the importance of reaching a settlement in Cambodia similar to that in Laos." Otherwise, Kissinger said, "It would be a tragedy if we allowed Cambodia to flare up and reopen the conflict all over Indochina." The president, Kissinger added,

The Perfidy of Geopolitics / 239

"was not committed to any one man" but instead was willing to "let the warring elements live together." In the end, Kissinger reasoned that "the Cambodian people could determine which is better for their future."[126] A week later, Kissinger affirmed that the United States had "no objection" if the government in Phnom Penh was "on very friendly terms" with Beijing, on the condition that all parties concerned would "refuse to participate in great power hegemonial activities in Southeast Asia." For Kissinger, it was important that "the matter in Cambodia be ended in a way not necessarily wounding for the U.S."[127] In concrete terms, this meant that America retain its prestige and credibility; and this meant, in turn, the continued existence of an independent, sovereign South Vietnam. All that was required, for Nixon and Kissinger, was that America provide South Vietnam with just enough "breathing space" to not fall immediately.[128] And to this end, Cambodia remained central to U.S. geopolitics. On August 3, as termination of Nixon's bombing campaign neared, the president ruminated, "We'll hope the poor little Cambodians can hang on for a little longer than we think." Kissinger doggedly replied, "Well, if they can hold on for longer than we think, then we can make it."[129]

Naively, Lon Nol continued to trust the United States. "I can tell you that in the course of that conversation [with Alexander Haig]," the embattled leader announced in early 1973, "the assurance of the firm support of the United States for the just struggle of the Khmer Republic against the North Vietnamese aggression was confirmed to me."[130] And yet, the Nixon administration demonstrated no loyalty or commitment to anyone in Phnom Penh or, for that matter, to Cambodia itself. Indeed, in anticipation of Cambodia's eventual demise, Nixon and his staff worked to transfer blame onto the Lon Nol government. With only one week remaining of the bombing campaign, for example, Kissinger emphasized that "if Phnom Penh goes we want it to be absolutely clear that the U.S. was not responsible for its fall." He continued, "If the situation in Phnom Penh falls apart, we want to be sure that they did it to themselves and that there was no lack on our part." To that end, Kissinger stressed the importance of controlling the narrative in the United States. Recasting the bombing campaign, Kissinger instructed his staff "to get all departments off the wicket that we are bombing neutral Cambodia." Instead, Kissinger explained, "We are bombing North Vietnamese troops in neutral Cambodia who are killing Americans. And we are doing

240 / The Perfidy of Geopolitics

this with the approval of the Cambodian government."[131] Both assertions were fabrications but, as Kissinger admitted, Lon Nol was expendable. And so was the truth.

In 1956, then Senator Kennedy was confident that if the United States "demonstrates that it has not forgotten the people of Vietnam, the people of Vietnam will demonstrate that they have not forgotten us."[132] Sixteen years later, Nixon and Kissinger conspired to relegate Vietnam to the geopolitical backwaters, a footnote forgotten to history of which "no one would give a damn."[133] Indeed, by late 1973, both Nixon and Kissinger were essentially resigned to the fact that South Vietnam would fall. As such, they continued their efforts to distance America's national security interests from events in Southeast Asia. In practice, this geopolitical shift was remarkably easy. Following the Yom Kippur War and the oil embargo initiated by the Organization of Petroleum Exporting Countries, the Middle East was steadily assuming a central place in U.S. foreign policy concerns. As such, the Nixon administration could afford to downplay, both in diplomatic relations and in public venues, American security interests in Southeast Asia. This included the centrality of Cambodia to U.S. national security interests. In July, Kissinger conveyed to Triloki Nath Kaul, the Indian ambassador to the United States, that America was disengaging from Cambodia. Kissinger explained bluntly that "Cambodia shouldn't be settled by the United States but by the Cambodians primarily." And while Kissinger conceded that the Cambodians "want to talk to me," he added that "I don't want to do more than the framework negotiation, not the details."[134] Similar reservations were relayed by Kissinger to Anatoly Dobrynin, the Soviet ambassador to the United States. When asked about the possibility of a transitional government in Phnom Penh, Kissinger replied "we would let nature take its course."[135]

The wars in South Vietnam and Cambodia continued for two years until the fall of Phnom Penh and Saigon on April 17 and April 30, 1975, respectively. During the interim, Nixon resigned in disgrace, leaving Gerald Ford to oversee the ignominious end to America's failed intervention in Indochina. At some level, Kissinger understood that the United States betrayed Cambodia. "I don't know how dangerous we are as an enemy," Kissinger mused as the bombing campaign raged over Cambodia, "but we are murder as an ally."[136]

EPILOGUE

A vast human tragedy has befallen our friends in Vietnam and
Cambodia.
—GERALD FORD, speaking before the U.S. Congress

In 1950 President Harry Truman's National Security Council asserted that
"firm non-Communist control of Indochina [was] of critical, strategic importance to U.S. national interests."[1] A quarter-century later, as preparations
were underway to evacuate the American embassy in Saigon before the final
collapse of South Vietnam, Henry Kissinger—now serving as secretary of
state under Gerald Ford—quipped, "Vietnam will be off our backs in two
weeks."[2]

Arising from the maelstrom of the Second World War, America's grand
strategy was to promote a spatial global order dominated by the United States
economically and politically.[3] Standing in the way, however, was the Soviet
Union—the only nation, U.S. officials believed, capable of mounting an
opposition to U.S. designs. Initially, the threat posed by the Soviets was
predominantly economic; in time, the specter of World War III and nuclear
conflagration assumed paramount concern. A crucial element of America's
grand strategy, therefore, was the containment of Soviet-led communism.
Containment was not a singular doctrine within America's grand strategy
but instead was an overarching spatial logic that conditioned several distinct
approaches forwarded by U.S. policymakers during the Cold War. Recognizing that in containing the expansion of communism while promoting
the expansion of U.S.-led capitalism, U.S. officials determined that some
nation-states were more central to America's spatial order than others. The
status of centrality or peripherality, however, was always contingent and
shifted according to the geopolitical context. A state may be considered of

242 / Epilogue

primary importance one day, only to be relegated to secondary concern the next. Likewise, a state thought to be of marginal importance could rapidly rise in geopolitical value as conditions changed.

America's mission in Indochina was never about the people of Cambodia, Vietnam, or Laos; the objective was never to "save" or "defend" the citizens of Southeast Asia from the harmful "cancer" of communism. Instead, it was always about geopolitical expansion in the abstract: to protect America's national security interests and to expand American power and prestige through the region. To that end, America's intervention in Cambodia is a microcosm of the indistinct, liminal geopolitics of American Cold War strategy. In practice, officials in Washington were prone to support any individual, any group, regardless of political orientation, depending on the immediacy of any given geopolitical situation. As Kissinger conceded, the most dangerous thing a country could do was to have the United States as an ally.[4]

Richard Nixon's air war did not bring victory to either Lon Nol's republic or to the United States. It did, however, create a groundswell of support for the Khmer Rouge—a factor that was widely known but covered up by high-ranking U.S. officials. On May 2, 1973, for example, CIA director of operations provided details on a new recruiting drive launched by the CPK: "They [the CPK] are using damage caused by B-52 strikes as the main theme of their propaganda. The cadre tell the people that the Government of Lon Nol has requested the airstrikes and is responsible for the damage and the 'suffering of innocent villagers.' . . . The only way to stop 'the massive destruction of the country' is to . . . defeat Lon Nol and stop the bombing. This approach has resulted in the successful recruitment of a number of young men."[5] In 1970, Khmer Rouge forces numbered around four thousand. Within five years, they exceeded sixty thousand men and women.[6]

From 1973 onward the CPK steadily, relentlessly "liberated" Cambodia and established base areas from which to operate. In doing so, increasingly draconian policies materialized, including the prohibition of religious practice, the introduction of "moral" codes, and the conscription of forced labor. To ensure discipline, Khmer Rouge established security centers and publicly executed those deemed to be enemies of the revolution. By 1974 only the national capital, Phnom Penh, and a handful of provincial capitals remained outside the orbit of Khmer Rouge control. On April 17, 1975, Khmer Rouge

Epilogue / 243

forces entered Phnom Penh and expanded policies initiated during the war: the evacuation of towns and villages, the confiscation of private property, and forced collectivization. In time, these practices would destroy their popular base, setting in motion a violent downward spiral that culminated in lingering famine and murderous, genocidal purges.[7]

Days before the Khmer Rouge occupied Phnom Penh, on April 12, 1975, Cambodian Deputy Prime Minister Sirik Matak sent a letter to John Gunther Dean, U.S. ambassador to Cambodia. For five years, Sirik Matak and other governmental officials of the Khmer Republic had placed their faith in the United States. Now, facing the imminent collapse of the capital Phnom Penh and the subsequent withdrawal of American personnel, Sirik Matak put on paper what many Cambodians were feeling. His letter, in part, reads: "You leave, and my wish is that you and your country will find happiness under this sky. But, mark it well, that if I shall die here on the spot and in my country that I love, it is too bad, because we all are born and must die one day. I have only committed this mistake of believing in you, the Americans."[8]

Nine days later Sirik Matak would be executed by the Khmer Rouge. And as the bodies piled up on the streets of Phnom Penh, U.S. policymakers moved on. Seven months after the fall of Phnom Penh, on November 26, 1975, Chatchai Choonhaven, the foreign minister of Thailand, met in Washington, D.C., with Kissinger and Assistant Secretary for East Asian and Pacific Affairs Philip Habib.[9] During the course of their conversation, Kissinger asked about Chatchai's recent meeting with Ieng Sary, a high-ranking member of the Khmer Rouge, and more broadly of developments in Cambodia:

KISSINGER: What is the Cambodian attitude?

CHATCHAI: The Cambodians want salt and fish. They wanted to barter for these items.

KISSINGER: Did Ieng Sary impress you?

CHATCHAI: He is a nice, quiet man.

KISSINGER: How many people did he kill? Tens of thousands?

HABIB: Nice and quietly!

CHATCHAI: Not more than ten thousand. That's why they need food. If they had killed everyone, they would not need salt and fish. All the bridges in Cambodia were destroyed. There was no transportation, no gas. That's why they had to chase people away from the capital.

244 / Epilogue

KISSINGER: But why with only two hours' notice?[10]

CHATCHAI: (Shrugs)

KISSINGER: What do the Cambodians think of the United States? You should tell them that we bear no hostility towards them. We would like them to be independent as a counterweight to North Vietnam?

CHATCHAI: Are you a member of the Domino Club?[11]

KISSINGER: I am.

CHATCHAI: The outer, most exposed belt of dominos is Cambodia and Laos. Thailand is in the inner belt and is less exposed.

KISSINGER: We would prefer to have Laos and Cambodia aligned with China rather than with North Vietnam.

We would try to encourage this if that is what you want.

CHATCHAI: Yes, we would like you to do that.

. . .

CHATCHAI: The right wing is what we really have to worry about, not the left. The Chinese are 100 percent in support of Cambodia's being friends with Thailand.

KISSINGER: We don't mind Chinese influence in Cambodia to balance North Vietnam. As I told the Chinese when we last met when we were discussing the Vietnamese victory in Indochina, it is possible to have an ideological victory which is a geopolitical defeat. The Chinese did not disagree with me.

. . .

KISSINGER: It is important that we [the United States] still have a presence in Southeast Asia. . . . I am, personally, embarrassed by the Vietnam War. I believe that if you go to war, you go to win and not to lose with moderation. We are aware that the biggest threat in Southeast Asia at the present time is North Vietnam. Our strategy is to get the Chinese into Laos and Cambodia as a barrier to the Vietnamese.

CHATCHAI: I asked the Chinese to take over in Laos. They mentioned that they had a road building team in northern Laos.

KISSINGER: We would support this. You should also tell the Cambodians that we will be friends with them. They are murderous thugs, but we won't let that stand in our way. We are prepared to improve relations with them. Tell them the latter part, but don't tell them what I said before.

Epilogue / 245

The exchange between Kissinger and Chatchai captures America's strategic but apathetic approach to Cambodia during the Cold War. Although Kissinger acknowledged his belief in the domino theory and thus America's position of trying to halt the spread of communism throughout Southeast Asia, Kissinger also readily agreed that China could—and should—have a free hand in intervening in Cambodia (and Laos). In practice, this meant that the United States was supportive of China's more prominent role in supporting the Khmer Rouge—despite acknowledging that thousands of men, women, and children had already died. For years, America's objective in Southeast Asia was to keep Indochina free from communism. Now, as Kissinger admitted, the United States was prepared to support communist China and its brutal ally, the genocidal and communist Khmer Rouge.

Nixon and Kissinger were, in a way, successful in that they did transform Vietnam into a geopolitical backwater for the United States. Since the mid-1970s, the former colonies of French Indochina largely remained on the periphery of American national security concerns.[12] Unlike the Middle East or Central Asia, two regions that have increasingly become central to U.S. grand strategy, events throughout mainland Southeast Asia have mostly remained peripheral to American officials. Cambodia, especially, has receded from memory, with few people in the United States aware of America's past involvement in the former French colony.

U.S. Grand Strategy in the Post–Vietnam War Era

When Jimmy Carter entered the White House in 1977 he initiated a sweeping reappraisal of U.S. national security policy. Defeat in Indochina seemingly shattered the soundness of containment and led many officials to question the application of U.S. power anywhere.[13] Southeast Asia remained problematic. In February, Carter's National Security Council prepared a memorandum that outlined America's recent involvement and future interests in the region. Conceding the "region's obvious economic and strategic importance," the NSC warned that "Asia remains an area of baffling complexity and potential turbulence." On the one hand, the Soviet Union's military power in Asia was growing slowly; its ultimate ambitions were unclear but, on the other hand, Moscow's political, economic, and social relations throughout the region were on the wane. Offering no firm plan for

246 / Epilogue

moving forward, the NSC could only repeat a question that had bedeviled U.S. officials since the end of the Second World War: "Does the U.S. retain significant strategic and economic interest in Southeast Asia?"[14]

The Carter administration would never fully resolve the problem. Indeed, U.S. officials seemed to wash their hands of the sordid affair as Washington maintained a decidedly low profile in the region. To be sure, the region—including both Vietnam and Cambodia—continued to hold strategic value for the United States, not least because the region was central to China's interests. However, a recalcitrant U.S. Congress and public prevented anything but the most rudimentary of diplomatic and economic relations taking center stage.[15]

Unburdened with events in Southeast Asia, Carter directed his attention elsewhere. Four months into his presidency, Carter announced his hope to forward a "foreign policy that is democratic, that is based on fundamental values, and that uses power and influence, which we have, for human purposes." He explained that "for too many years, we've been willing to adopt the flawed and erroneous principles and tactics of our adversaries, sometimes abandoning our own values for theirs. We've fought fire with fire, never thinking that fire is better quenched with water." This approach failed, Carter said, "with Vietnam the best example of its intellectual and moral poverty." From the Second World War onward, Carter explained, American policy was guided, in part, by a belief that Soviet expansion was almost inevitable and therefore must be contained. However, the war in Vietnam "produced a profound moral crisis, sapping worldwide faith in our own policy and our system of life." Moving forward, Carter conceded that "the world is still divided by ideological disputes" but, he qualified, it was a "new world" where the United States was no longer guided by an "inordinate fear of communism." It remained imperative that America continue to lead but do so "based on constant decency in its values," that is, informed by a foreign policy centered on moral values and human rights.[16]

Carter's optimism and retreat from containment was short-lived. By December 1978 Zbigniew Brzezinski, Carter's national security advisor, warned of an "arc of crisis" that extended from Western Africa to Southern Asia. For Brzezinski, this geographic expanse—centered on the Middle East—constituted America's "greatest vulnerability." All at once, the national security advisor explained, difficulties were surfacing in Iran, Pakistan,

Bangladesh, Saudi Arabia, and Turkey. The "resulting political vacuum," Brzezinski said, "might well be filled by elements more sympathetic to the Soviet Union." Indeed, so grave was the situation that Brzezinski counseled that America was "confronting the beginning of a major crisis, in some ways similar to the one in Europe in the late 40s." The consequences, Brzezinski concluded, "would mean a fundamental shift in the global structure of power."[17] The overthrow of America's ally, the Shah of Iran, in February 1979 and the subsequent taking hostage of fifty-two U.S. diplomats and citizens in Tehran in November seemingly confirmed Brzezinski's panicky warning.

Initially, U.S. officials considered military action against Iran. However, when the Soviet Union invaded Afghanistan on Christmas Eve, Washington was forced to reconsider its options. For Brzezinski, the Soviet offensive posed "an extremely grave challenge" that would adversely affect U.S. interests, both domestic and foreign. More importantly, the invasion was inseparable from the ongoing crisis in Iran. "With Iran destabilized," Brzezinski reasoned, "there will be no firm bulwark in Southwest Asia against the Soviet drive to the Indian Ocean."[18] However, not all analysts in America's intelligence community agreed with the national security advisor. A preliminary assessment of Soviet intentions prepared by the CIA concluded that "it is unlikely that the Soviet occupation of Afghanistan constitutes the preplanned first step in the implementation of a highly articulated grand design for the rapid establishment of hegemonic control over all of Southwest Asia." Dismissing alarmist conclusions that the invasion marked the onset of a "premeditated strategy offensive," CIA analysts countered that the operation "may have been a reluctantly authorized response" to a rapidly deteriorating position "within the Soviet Union's legitimate sphere of influence."[19] Regardless of Soviet intentions, the invasion impelled the Carter administration to shelve plans to take military action in Iran. With the containment of the Soviet Union taking precedence, U.S. officials elected instead to avoid a military confrontation with Iran in the hope of galvanizing Islamic opposition to the Soviets.[20]

On January 23, 1980, during his State of the Union address, Carter explained that the United States faced three interrelated challenges: the growth of Soviet military power beyond its borders; the dependence of Western democracies on oil supplies from the Middle East; and social, political, economic, and religious change throughout the developing world. In response,

248 / Epilogue

the president pledged that "an attempt by any outside force to gain control of the Persian Gulf region will be regarded as an assault on the vital interests of the United States of America, and such an assault will be repelled by any means necessary, including military force."[21] The Carter Doctrine was the most far-reaching spatial extension of American commitments since the redefinition of the Pacific defensive perimeter after the Korean War.[22] Most importantly, the Carter Doctrine represented a momentous shift in U.S. geopolitical and geostrategic considerations, placing the Persian Gulf region as the second priority for resource allocation after Europe.[23]

America's geopolitical revanchism intensified later that year with the election of Ronald Reagan as president. Where Carter once spoke of an "inordinate fear of communism," Reagan vowed to "leave Marxism-Leninism on the ash-heap of history." Boldly, Reagan called for a "crusade for freedom that will engage the faith and fortitude of the next generation" and that would move "toward a world in which all peoples are at last free to determine their own destiny."[24] Reagan was true to his word. Backed by a revitalized defense budget that nearly doubled in size, U.S. foreign policy reverted to its ardent anticommunist form. Under the Reagan Doctrine, U.S. officials forwarded a more forceful policy of selective American support for noncommunist insurgencies against Soviet-supported communist regimes.[25] Indeed, guided once again by the misguided belief that American confronted a monolithic communism controlled by Moscow, Reagan authorized a series of covert and overt military operations across the globe.[26] For the Reagan administration, the aim was not simply the containment of the Soviet Union—it was the absolute defeat of communism.

For Reagan, a muscular America was as much symbolic as it was strategic. Speaking at the Veterans of Foreign Wars convention in August 1980, Reagan bemoaned that "for too long, we have lived with the Vietnam Syndrome." Portraying America's military intervention in Vietnam as "a noble cause," Reagan declared that there was "a lesson for all of us in Vietnam" and that lesson was that "If we are forced to fight, we must have the means and the determination to prevail or we will not have what it takes to secure the peace." Decrying Carter's foreign policy as "one of weakness, inconsistency, vacillation and bluff," Reagan promised to stand firm against the Soviet menace.[27] For all his bluster, though, there was another lesson U.S. officials derived from the Vietnam War. As Michael Adas writes, the one

Epilogue / 249

lesson most directly linked to the failure in Indochina was the reformulation of strategy for the projection of American power in the developing world, a lesson considered especially critical for future conflicts to check the advance of communism in areas on the "periphery" of the superpower blocs.[28]

The collapse of the Soviet Union in 1991 marked the end of the Cold War and, as Bacevich writes, an opportunity for U.S. policymakers to create a bigger and better Pax Americana.[29] During the waning days of the Cold War, under Reagan, America's military footprint deepened. With the dissolution of the Soviet Union, paradoxically, the principal rationale for garrisoning the world disappeared, but U.S. officials assumed they had no choice but to maintain a global military presence.[30] Indeed, America's forward presence was extended, albeit unevenly, across the globe. The 1991 Gulf War brought this commitment into full clarity.

Throughout the Cold War, U.S. officials saw the Middle East in much the same light as they did Southeast Asia. The region was of vital interests both for geostrategic and geoeconomic reasons. To that end, it was imperative to cultivate pro-Western alliances among the myriad states and to defend these against Soviet influence or domination. The dissolution of the Soviet Union in 1991, however, posed a dilemma for Washington. As Phyllis Bennis explains, without the Soviet threat, it was more difficult for Washington to justify its continued military presence in the Middle East; and yet, America's national interests remained: access to oil, defense of Israel, and political and economic stability to encourage foreign investments and market development.[31]

In September 1980, Iraqi forces invaded Iran, igniting a war that would enflame Persian Gulf politics for much of the following decade.[32] Out of geopolitical necessity, the United States tacitly supported the Iraqi dictator, Saddam Hussein. As Hal Brands and David Palkki explain, an Iraqi defeat would empower the vehemently anti-American government in Tehran, allowing it to dominate the Persian Gulf and the international oil market. Moreover, U.S. officials feared that Saddam, facing possible defeat, might turn to the Soviet Union, thereby allowing Moscow to extend its influence throughout the Middle East. That said, some U.S. officials counseled that a failure to support Iran—despite its antipathy to America— could also open a door to Soviet influence.[33] Consequently, the United States hedged its bet and covertly supported both Baghdad and Tehran.[34]

250 / Epilogue

In 1988 the war came to an inconclusive end; but within two years, Saddam once again initiated a war. The target this time was neighboring Kuwait. Charging economic warfare, Saddam claimed that Kuwait was deliberately manipulating oil prices in an effort to subdue his country; in addition, the Iraqi leader accused Kuwait of "slant drilling" into Iraqi oil fields. Accordingly, in August 1990 Iraqi armed forces invaded and occupied Kuwait. Ultimately, approximately 140,000 Iraqi troops would be involved. The United States, in turn, condemned the invasion and organized a global coalition to oppose Iraqi aggression.[35]

On January 16, 1991, a U.S.-led multinational coalition initiated a massive six-week air campaign against Iraq followed by a ground offensive that lasted a mere four days. In the aftermath, Kuwait was liberated, Iraq was devasted, and the United States had more power than ever in the region.[36] Coming on the heels of the collapse of the Soviet Union, the Gulf War became the precipitating event for a new spatial order. As Jordan and colleagues write, for the first time, the United States became massively involved militarily on the ground in the Middle East.[37] Equally important, however, was that America's decisive victory seemed to cleanse the country of its failure in Vietnam.[38] "By God," President George H. W. Bush declared, "we've kicked the Vietnam syndrome once and for all."[39]

America's national security landscape, however, was also at a crossroads. Unopposed by its erstwhile enemy, the Soviet Union, U.S. officials scrambled to take advantage of the opportunities that seemingly lay ahead. To do so required a reassessment of America's grand strategy. In his prefatory comments to the January 1992 *National Military Strategy of the United States,* then chair of the Joint Chiefs of Staff Colin Powell opined that "the community of nations has entered into an exciting and promising era. Global war is now less likely and the US national security strategy reflects that fact." And yet, despite the premise that global war was less likely, Americans had to remain vigilant. Powell elaborated that "future threats to US interests are inherent in the uncertainty and instability of a rapidly changing world." Even if there were to be no more major wars, Fraser Cameron writes, there were numerous smaller wars that posed difficult choices for the United States.[40] Absent the translucidity of the bipolar Cold War, however, the determination of centrality or peripherality was decidedly more difficult. In addition, the fiscal hangover of the Cold War further impaired America's options for

Epilogue / 251

diplomatic or military intervention. In part because of the massive arms expenditures during the Reagan years, the United States had moved from being a creditor nation to being the largest debtor nation in the world.[41] As such, the United States could no longer purchase international alliances as easily as it did during the early years of the Cold War.

Powell explained that before the collapse of the Soviet Union "the primary focus of America's national military strategy had been the containment of the Soviet Union, and its communist ideology."[42] Now, security threats were more nebulous and required different approaches. Powell elaborated these ideas in an article published in *Foreign Affairs*. Harkening back to the euphoric days of the post–Second World War, Powell declared that "America is still the last best hope of earth, and we still hold the power and bear the responsibility for its remaining so."[43] In practice, this meant a more judicious use of diplomacy, economic leverage, and military force. Although the United States was no longer facing "communist hordes," Powell cautioned that "danger had not disappeared from the world."[44] Highlighting the new coordinates of America's spatial order, Powell explained that "all along the southeastern and southern borders of the old Soviet empire, from Moldova to Tajikistan, smoldering disputes and ethic hatreds disrupt our post-Cold War reverie."[45] From the Balkans to Somalia, Powell warned, it was difficult to "tell where or when the next crisis will appear that will demand the use of our troops." Already, in the three years since the fall of the Berlin Wall, Powell conceded that "our troops have acted in the Philippines (twice), Panama (three times), El Salvador, Liberia, Iraq (three times), Somalia (twice), Bangladesh, Zaire, Cuba, the former Soviet Union, Angola and Yugoslavia."[46] These operations did not include those where U.S. forces were deployed as part of a United Nations operations: for example, in western Sahara, Bosnia-Herzegovina, and even Cambodia.[47]

For many U.S. policymakers the end of Cold War bipolarity and clearcut ideological confrontation had brought not peace and security but rather a world teetering on the verge of chaos.[48] Such was the "opportunity" afforded by the new world order championed by Powell—an opportunity to selectively engage in those crises most beneficial to U.S. national security interests. Gone were the days of the Truman Doctrine, where the United States pledged to support and defend "free peoples everywhere." Absent the reductive but seductive spatial determinism of the Cold War, U.S. national

252 / Epilogue

security interests seemed to be everywhere and nowhere. As detailed in the 1992 *National Military Strategy of the United States*, "The real threat we now face is the threat of the unknown, the uncertain. The threat is instability and being unprepared to handle a crisis that no one predicted or expected."[49] Where Cold War strategy was circumscribed by the containment of communism and the fear of falling dominos, grand strategy in the post–Cold War era was marred by "incoherence and inconsistency."[50]

This is not to suggest, however, that U.S. policymakers were short of purpose. Seeking to perpetuate American preeminence and to foster an international order conducive to U.S. interests, Andrew Bacevich details, the administrations of George H. W. Bush and Clinton revived the project that Truman had sketched in 1947. In an effort to "extend and perpetuate American political, economic, and cultural hegemony . . . on a global scale," U.S. officials relied primarily on America's unchallenged military superiority.[51] Since the end of the Cold War, the United States has been relentless in its use of covert and overt armed force. Between 1991 and 2002, the United States engaged in 176 military operations—a significant increase in the use of armed forces since the end of the Cold War. Indeed, between 1945 and 1991, U.S. forces were deployed *only* eighty-seven times. To be clear, not all foreign operations involved the use of armed combatants. Included in this tally are actions related to disaster evacuations, humanitarian relief, and the monitoring of ceasefires. Notably, though, when U.S. officials deploy troops abroad, nearly 80 percent are justified as "promoting democracy."[52] This beguiling rhetoric of promoting democracy and protecting freedom begins to ring hollow, however, when heard alongside the electric buzz of drones and the deafening explosions of bombs and missiles. For better or worse, the Cold War imposed an order of geographic certainty on the international system from which U.S. officials operated. After the Cold War, Washington confronted "a world of increased disorder infecting areas of acute sensitivity."[53] America's new map of the world was terra incognita.

The Clinton administration fared little better than its predecessor. Guided by the vacuous slogan "It's the economy, stupid," U.S. policymakers promoted a grand "strategy of openness."[54] The primary objective was the removal of barriers to the movement of goods, capital, people, and ideas, thereby fostering an integrated spatial order conducive to American business interests, government by American norms, and defended with American military power.[55] This required, above all else, securing America's unchallenged hegemony on the world's stage. On September 21, 1993, Clinton's national security advisor, Anthony Lake, spoke at Johns Hopkins University. He pronounced that the world stood "at an historic crossroads." For five decades, Lake explained, the United States had confronted the Soviet Union, but now, with the collapse of its former adversary, it was necessary to "think anew because the world is new." An immediate challenge, Lake conceded, was the degree of America's active engagement in the world. "Geography and history," he reflected, "always have made Americans wary of foreign entanglements." And yet, he continued, it was imperative that the United States remain engaged, lest America's national interests be threatened. Certainly, Lake allowed, the United States no longer confronted a "near-term threat" to its existence; gone were the "immediate dangers" posed by Soviet expansionism. However, he cautioned, serious threats remained: terrorism, proliferating weapons of mass destruction, ethnic conflicts, environmental degradation, and economic instability. However, for Lake, America's challenge was "to lead on the basis of opportunity more than fear." This involved the promotion of "democracy" and "market economics" on a global scale; and in doing so, the United States would "be more secure, prosperous and influential, while the broader world [would] be more humane and peaceful." To create this spatial order, however, it was necessary to substitute old-fashioned containment policies with an expansionist foreign policy. "During the Cold War," Lake reminisced, "even children understood America's security mission; as they looked at those maps on their schoolroom walls, they knew we were trying to contain the creeping expansion of that big, red blob." Now, the national security advisor said, "our security mission" was the promotion of "market democracies."[56]

America's preeminence in the global economy, Lake counseled, did not translate into unlimited resources. Cautioning against overreach, he clarified that "a strategy of enlargement must provide distinctions and set priorities. It must combine our broad goals of fostering democracy and markets with our more traditional geostrategic interests. And it must suggest how best to expend our large but nonetheless limited national security resources: financial, diplomatic and military." Crucial to these determinations, Lake said, was the strategic question of "where." Eschewing the idealism of Woodrow Wilson or the blanket guarantees of Harry Truman, Lake affirmed that

254 / Epilogue

America's purpose was "not a democratic crusade." Willing to support both democratic and nondemocratic regimes, Lake explained that America's grand strategy was "a pragmatic commitment to see freedom take hold where that will help us most." To that end, he continued, "We must target our effort to assist states that affect our strategic interests, such as those with large economies, critical locations, nuclear weapons or the potential to generate refugee flows into our own nation or into key friends and allies." Furthermore, Lake made clear, America's strategy of enlargement was to isolate diplomatically, militarily, economically, and technologically those "backlash" states that threatened America's vital interests. Ultimately, Lake declared, "We should act multilaterally where doing so advances our interests—and we should act unilaterally when that will serve our purpose."[57]

Left unclear were the precise qualifying conditions that would translate policy into practice. Any region and any state was potentially central to America's national security interests. That said, the world map drawn by the Clinton administration had a remarkably familiar look about it. Europe assumed prominence but so too did Japan and South Korea, Russia and China, and the market economies of South and Central America, North America, Southeast Asia, and the Middle East. The specific course of action, however, differed according to local circumstances.[58] In some instances, a more militarist tack was preferred; elsewhere, it was diplomacy or economic leverage. The consequence was an astonishingly spacious nomos of immense complexity. By the twenty-first century the American government maintained a force of nearly 255,000 military personnel stationed on over 725 military bases in 153 countries outside the United States. This aggressive forward presence was buttressed by a nuclear arsenal of unimaginable proportions: 5,400 multiple-megaton warheads atop intercontinental ballistic missiles based on land and at sea; an additional 1,750 nuclear bombs and cruise missiles ready to be launched from B-2 and B-52 bombers; and a further 1,670 nuclear weapons classified as "tactical." An additional 10,000 nuclear warheads were stored in bunkers around the United States.[59]

Backed by an unprecedented and largely uncontested military superiority, the Clinton administration wielded an equally powerful economic stick. Under Clinton, the United States signed more than three hundred bilateral trade agreements and initiated several multinational alliances, such as the North American Free Trade Agreement, all designed to expand and protect

Epilogue / 255

U.S. interests home and abroad.[60] Indeed, channeling the ghost of Walt Rostow, Clinton's officials surmised that economic instability—hallmarks of a *failed state*—threatened to undermine America's spatial order, thereby resulting in the loss of vital resources necessary for both the United States and its allies. To that end, the grand strategy of the Clinton presidency was typified by a geopolitical paternalism, whereby U.S. officials tried to bring in line a discombobulated panoply of rogue states, failed states, and other wayward children who lived in the margins and strayed from the fold.[61] As Lake explained in a *Foreign Affairs* article, "our policy must face the reality of recalcitrant and outlaw states that not only choose to remain outside the family but also assault its basic values."[62]

Labeling certain states as "failed," Pinar Bilgin and Adam Morton explain, "serves to facilitate different kinds of policies that are simplistically aimed at two different groups of states: 'friends' and 'foes.'"[63] As such, a similar reductive logic is in play, but a logic *seemingly* devoid of any spatial order. On the one hand, following Bilgin and Morton, when "friends" cause a threat to international security because of their "weakness," the recommended policy is one of building "strong" states. Conversely, when the "weak" states that threaten international security happen to be "foes," it is invariably constructed as a "rogue state" and containment or punishment becomes the recommended policy course.[64] Curiously, if we retroactively apply this strategic logic to the war in Vietnam, we merely re-create the befuddled reasoning that confounded U.S. officials in their Cambodian calculations. South Vietnam was plainly a friendly albeit weak state. As a self-professed neutral state, though, Cambodia was neither friend nor foe. Cambodia's geopolitical liminality upset America's vision of global spatial order and problematized the tidy partition of the world into friends and foes. America's grand strategy in the twenty-first century has repeated this geographic confusion.

When George W. Bush assumed the presidency in 2001 he promised to be more selective regarding the use of force and, accordingly, he called for a less interventionist approach with regard to the internal affairs of other countries.[65] In effect, the Bush administration operated on the assumption that "failed states" were considered to be "problems" only when the situation became acute enough to threaten the world beyond their boundaries.[66] To that end, the Bush White House called for a refocusing of U.S.

256 / Epilogue

national security policy on great power politics and concrete national interests while deemphasizing smaller-scale contingency operations.[67] Mostly, though, during the first eight months of his presidency, Bush remained aloof from foreign policy matters, content to focus his energies on domestic concerns. All this changed following the devastating September 11, 2001, terrorist attacks on Washington, D.C. and New York City.

In the weeks and months following the terrorists attacks, the Bush administration moved rapidly and somewhat carelessly toward a new grand strategy informed chiefly by a handful of bureaucratic hawks: Vice President Dick Cheney, National Security Advisor Condoleezza Rice, and Secretary of Defense Donald Rumsfeld. As Colin Dueck explained, now the administration favored a more muscular strategy that emphasized American preponderance rather than equilibrium among the great powers; in addition, the new strategy called for the worldwide promotion of democracy, by force if necessary, and the need for preemptive military action against potential enemies.[68] This new direction was expressed most clearly in the Department of Defense's *Quadrennial Defense Review Report,* released September 30, 2001. Proclaiming that "America's goals are to promote peace, sustain freedom, and encourage prosperity," the document placed U.S. national security concerns on a war footing. Thus, while America's political, diplomatic, and economic leadership contributed to global peace, freedom, and prosperity, it was America's military strength that was essential to achieving those goals. Not unlike the rhetoric that guided a succession of presidents throughout the war in Vietnam, the 2001 report affirmed that America's military superiority and commitment to project and use this force was crucial to "provide a general sense of stability and confidence" in the world. As such, the "purpose of the U.S. Armed Forces [was] to protect and advance U.S. national interests and, if deterrence fail[ed], to decisively defeat threats to those interests." However, the "global security environment" was flush with uncertainty. Whereas the "international system" during the Cold War was mediated "by the division of countries into enduring and ideologically defined geopolitical blocs," the current spatial order had "become more fluid and unpredictable." And America's physical geography—buttressed by the Atlantic and Pacific Oceans—offered little protection. Now, in the aftermath of the September 11 attacks, "the geographic position no longer guarantee[d] immunity from direct attack on its population, territory, and

Epilogue / 257

infrastructure." Certainly, the report conceded, "the United States and its overseas forces were vulnerable to Soviet missiles during the Cold War," it was now clear that "an increasing number of states would acquire ballistic missiles with steadily increasing effective ranges." Moreover, America's global interests and commitments, both home and abroad, remained vulnerable to hostile states and actors.[69]

Using the September 11 terrorist attacks as justification, the Bush administration adopted an aggressive and idealistic strategy to forward American geopolitical interests. In this sense, the shocking attacks offered a window of opportunity. In his 2002 State of the Union address, Bush explained, "After America was attacked, it was as if our entire country looked into a mirror and saw our better selves." He continued: "We have glimpsed what a new culture of responsibility could look like. We want to be a nation that serves goals larger than our self. We've been offered a unique opportunity, and we must not let this moment pass."[70] As part of the greater War on Terror, a new era of manifest destiny emerged, one that afforded "unique opportunities" to refashion the American nomos. Centered in the crosshairs were Afghanistan and Iraq. Neither state was directly involved in the terrorist attacks against the United States. However, U.S. officials had long coveted a greater presence and influence in the region.[71] As Bacevich details, the Greater Middle East was to serve as the chosen arena for honing military power into a tool that would maintain America's privileged position and, as such, provide a continuing rationale for the entire apparatus of national security.[72] In actuality, the wars in Afghanistan and Iraq both ground to stalemates and, similar to Vietnam, overshadowed the foreign policies of Bush's presidential successors, Barack Obama and Donald Trump.[73]

Since the end of the Cold War, Brands writes, every U.S. administration has aimed to maintain America's primacy, to further spread liberal institutions overseas, and to contain or to roll back the major threats to this advantageous environment. Moreover, every administration has pursued these goals through policies deeply ingrained in U.S. strategic culture, for example, by promoting democracy and free trade, maintaining and expanding U.S. alliances overseas, and preserving a military supremacy against all challengers.[74] Spatially, America's national security interests have remained fixed largely on Europe, along with the Middle East, Russia, and China. That said, a recurrent refrain in America's post–Cold War grand strategy has

258 / Epilogue

been the lament of geographic certainty. From the collapse of the Soviet Union onward, U.S. officials have decried the lack of spatial clarity in the articulation of national security interests. In part, this stems from a recognition that states no longer pose the most immediate or greatest threat to U.S. interests. Especially since the September 11, 2001, terrorist attacks, U.S. officials routinely underscore the dangers posed by nonstate actors to America's political and economic well-being—a trend that has continued through the presidencies of Barack Obama, Donald Trump, and Joe Biden. "Because hostile states have interests at stake and territories to defend," John Lewis Gaddis explains, "credible threats of retaliation will normally deter and contain them."[75] Nonstate actors, conversely, behave very differently.

Does this suggest, then, that geography in world politics is irrelevant? Has the geopolitical distinction between centrality and peripherality in grand strategy itself become a marginal criteria on which to gauge national security concerns? Certainly not. As America's ill-fated wars in Iraq and Afghanistan demonstrate, the international stage still stands on the pillars of territorial states. And depending on the perceived strategic value of the pillar under inspection, some states will be deemed load-bearing with others considered expendable.

The language of the Cold War is becoming archaic.[76] For many policymakers, the spatial metaphors of containment, core and periphery, and falling dominoes sound almost quaint. But there is a hidden geography lesson to be learned from America's grand strategic adventure in Indochina and, notably, Cambodia. For all the apparent geographic certainty of the Cold War, the determination of central or peripheral interests was never clearcut. For a quarter century, the fragments of French Indochina confounded U.S. policymakers. Cambodia *in the abstract* was important; concretely, its diplomatic or military significance was less evident. Too often we gloss over the practical geopolitics that inform diplomatic efforts and military operations in the conduct of U.S. grand strategy. It is accurate that during the Cold War many U.S. officials—and many members of the American public—saw the world in stark Manichean terms, a world neatly divided into "good" and "evil" spaces. Behind this façade of geopolitical certainty, however, grave questions loomed in the shadows. Indeed, for many individuals working in the U.S. intelligence community, from the Departments of State and Defense to the Pentagon and the CIA, the world was far from black and white.

Epilogue / 259

As a political geographer, I began this project with a deceptively simple question: Was Cambodia central or peripheral to U.S. national security interests during the early decades of the Cold War? The answer, it turns out, belies the certainty found in much geopolitical rhetoric of the period. On paper, it is easy to partition the world into strategic areas and to distinguish between areas of central importance and those of peripheral interest. In practice, beyond the hyperbole of stump speeches and political aggrandizement, policymakers struggle to make spatial sense of the world. From Eisenhower onward, the spatial dilemma of Cambodia's strategic importance remained unresolved; however, too many decisions were made with firm conviction and tragic results. The survival of South Vietnam, at the apex of the Cold War, was conceived by U.S. policymakers as crucial to the creation and maintenance of the American nomos. Not simply the product of an overly reductive theory of falling dominos, the collapse of South Vietnam, in the eyes of U.S. political and military leaders, threatened a redefined spatial order centered on the United States. In an effort to create a state in southern Vietnam where none had previously existed, U.S. officials sacrificed the lives of men, women, and children in Cambodia. To that end, the United States did not so much suspend as disregard international law. The use of sovereign violence to sustain a particular spatial order mediated America's territorial logics in its war in Vietnam and foreshadowed the legitimation of future military operations.

In a telling passage of his 1960 publication, *The Stages of Economic Growth*, Walt Rostow acknowledges that "Billions of human beings must live in the world" and that they "have the right to live their time in civilized settings, marked by a degree of respect for their uniqueness and their dignity."[77] That said, Rostow justified military operations—including those in Indochina— in defense of U.S. economic interests. In other words, the geopolitical nexus of modern capitalist economies such as the United States, and transitional societies, such as those in Indochina, warranted an aggressive posture in favor of the former. According to Rostow, "National sovereignty means that nations retain the ultimate right—a right sanctioned by law, custom, and what decent men judge to be legitimacy—the right to kill people of other nations in defense or pursuit of what they judge to be their national interest."[78] For Rostow, it was abundantly clear that the sovereign right "to kill people of other nations" was not a universal right but instead a right determined by the existing nomos, that is, the right sanctioned by *international*

260 / Epilogue

law, custom, and legitimacy. Increasingly, this right was determined by the United States, and it was this sovereign right to kill that was placed in jeopardy by a failing South Vietnam made vulnerable by a seemingly peripheral state, Cambodia. When U.S. officials warned that failure to defend South Vietnam against communism threatened U.S. credibility, a key concern was the capacity to secure the unfolding American nomos. In the end, Peter Liotta suggests that national security interests answer the fundamental but essential question: "What are we willing to die for?"[79] To this question, we must pose its corollary: What are we willing to kill for?

Acknowledgments

I will not mince words. Since the Second World War a succession of U.S. administrations have failed the people of Cambodia by repeatedly rendering their lives expendable as part of an unfolding American spatial order. Many of those U.S. officials who blithely made life-and-death decisions that impacted the men, women, and children of Cambodia—and its neighbors, Vietnam and Laos—should have been tried for war crimes and other crimes against humanity. For decades, Cambodia was centered firmly in America's geopolitical crosshairs—a dark side of the Cold War that has remained mostly opaque for far too long. This is a difficult story to tell, and I first thank Jason Weidemann for allowing me the opportunity to make my case. Jason is a remarkable editor, and I continue to learn about writing and publishing during our conversations. I express also my gratitude to Zenyse Miller and the entire staff at the University of Minnesota Press who brought this manuscript to life. In addition, I thank all those scholars who provided critical feedback as this project moved from its conceptual stage through to the final manuscript. In particular, I thank John Agnew, Trevor Barnes, Simon Dalby, Lorraine Dowler, Colin Flint, Alex Murphy, and Chris Philo. Simon especially provided critical advice at a key moment in the development of this book.

Throughout my tenure at Kent State University, I have been fortunate to work with, and learn from, countless students who sharpened my thinking and honed my writing, including Gabriela Brindis Alvarez, Sutapa Chattopadhyay, Jaerin Chung, Alex Colucci, Gordon Cromley, Christabel Devadoss, Hanieh Hajj Molana, Sam Henkin, Donna Houston,

262 / Acknowledgments

Josh Inwood, Sokvisal Kimsroy, Robert Kruse, Olaf Kuhlke, Gabe Popescue, Mark Rhodes, Stian Rice, Andy Shears, Dave Stasiuk, and Rachel Will. I also benefitted from conversations, both formal and informal, on all things geopolitical with innumerable scholars, including Oliver Belcher, Carl Dahlman, Fiona Davidson, Thom Davies, Michael Dear, Stuart Elden, Salvatore Engel-Dimauro, Jamey Essex, Jim Glassman, Derek Gregory, Joseph Nevins, Shannon O'Lear, James Sidaway, Simon Springer, and Gerard Toal. My ongoing work in political geography, including this present manuscript, would not be possible without the generosity of these scholars who, offered their wisdom and tolerated my queries that, on reflection, must appear incredibly pedantic. Any errors in this final manuscript remain mine alone.

I thank my family for their encouragement: first and foremost, my parents, Dr. Gerald Tyner and Dr. Judith Tyner, for their support and encouragement and for the sacrifices they made as I pursued my dreams. I thank also my daughters, Jessica and Anica Lyn, who are now young women, ready to tackle the world and all that it offers. I thank Carter and Bubba, our seven-year-old and five-year-old rescue dog and cat, respectively. In their own unique ways, they keep me grounded, attuned to what really matters in life: a good meal, soft pillows, and belly rubs. And keeping us all in line is my life partner, Belinda. She has been with me every step of the way— since we first met as undergraduate students in the mid-1980s. Belinda has been and remains my inspiration, and I look forward to our future journeys.

Lastly, I want to express my deepest gratitude to Michael Dear. I first met Michael when I was a doctoral student in the geography department at the University of Southern California. I wasn't expressly working on geopolitics at the time—my interests centered on international labor migration. Looking back, though, I recognize how influential Michael was in shaping my academic career. Michael provided my first real foray into social theory and, by extension, geopolitics. In addition, Michael allowed me the opportunity to teach my first course on geopolitics when he was on sabbatical. That initial course offering provided a springboard to my teaching political geography at Kent State University, a course that still remains close to my heart nearly three decades later. Over the years, Michael has remained a mentor and, I would like to think, a friend. And so I warmly dedicate this book to Michael Dear.

Notes

Introduction

1. Richard M. Nixon, "Address to the Nation on the Situation in Southeast Asia," April 30, 1970, *Miller Center,* https://millercenter.org/the-presidency/presidential-speeches/april-30-1970-address-nation-situation-southeast-asia (accessed July 12, 2022).

2. See for example Richard A. Falk, "The Cambodian Operation and International Law," *American Journal of International Law* 65, no. 1 (1971): 1–25; William D. Rogers, "The Constitutionality of the Cambodian Incursion," *American Journal of International Law* 65, no. 1 (1971): 26–37; John N. Moore, "Legal Dimensions of the Decision to Intercede in Cambodia," *American Journal of International Law* 65, no. 1 (1971): 38–75; Robert H. Bork, "Comments on the Articles on the Legality of the United States Action in Cambodia," *American Journal of International Law* 65, no. 1 (1971): 79–81; and John L. Hargrove, "Comments on the Articles on the Legality of the United States Action in Cambodia," *American Journal of International Law* 65, no. 1 (1971): 81–83.

3. See for example Timothy Guiden, "Defending America's Cambodian Incursion," *Arizona Journal of International and Comparative Law* 11, no. 2 (1994): 215–70; and Joshua Kastenberg, "Fifty Years On: The Normalization of United States Military Operations in Cambodia (1969–1973) as a Mirror of Fighting in the Law's Gaps," *Southwestern Journal of International Law* 26, no. 2 (2020): 241–63.

4. See for example Wilfred P. Deac, *Road to the Killing Fields: The Cambodian War of 1970–1975* (College Station: Texas A&M University Press, 1997); John M. Shaw, *The Cambodian Campaign: The 1970 Offensive and America's Vietnam War* (Lawrence: University Press of Kansas, 2005); Jeff Hackett, "The Cambodian Incursion: Tactical and Operational Success and Its Effects on Vietnamization," master's thesis, United States Marine Corps, Command and-Staff College, Marine Corps University,

263

264 / Notes to Introduction

2008; Peter G. Drivas, "The Cambodian Incursion Revisited," *International Social Science Review* 86, no. 3/4 (2011): 134–59; Yuichi Kubota, "Territorial Control and Recruitment in the Cambodian Civil War, 1970–75: Case Studies in Battambang Province," *Asian Security* 7, no. 1 (2011): 1–26; Yuichi Kubota, *Armed Groups in Cambodian Civil War* (New York: Palgrave Macmillan, 2013); and Jesse W. Lee, *Insurgency: The Cambodian Civil War, 1970–1975* (Fort Leavenworth: U.S. Army Command and General Staff College, 2019).

5. William Shawcross, *Sideshow: Kissinger, Nixon, and the Destruction of Cambodia,* rev. ed. (New York: Cooper Square Press, 2002).

6. Michael Haas, *Genocide by Proxy: Cambodian Pawn on a Superpower Chessboard* (New York: Praeger, 1991).

7. Simon Dalby, "Geopolitics, Grand Strategy and the Bush Doctrine: The Strategic Dimensions of US Hegemony under George W. Bush," in *Hegemony or Empire? The Redefinition of US Power under George W. Bush,* edited by Charles-Philippe David and David Grondin (New York: Routledge, 2007), 51–68; at 51.

8. John Agnew and Stuart Corbridge, *Mastering Space: Hegemony, Territory and International Political Economy* (New York: Routledge, 1995), 4–5.

9. Gearóid Ó Tuathail, "Theorizing Practical Geopolitical Reasoning: The Case of the United States' Response to the War in Bosnia," *Political Geography* 21, no. 5 (2002): 601–28; see also Gearóid Ó Tuathail and John Agnew, "Geopolitics and Discourse: Practical Geopolitical Reasoning in American Foreign Policy," *Political Geography* 11, no. 2 (1992): 190–204; Klaus J. Dodds, "Geopolitics, Experts and the Making of Foreign Policy," *Area* 25, no. 1 (1993): 70–74; Gearóid Ó Tuathail, *Critical Geopolitics: The Politics of Writing Global Space* (Minneapolis: University of Minnesota Press, 1996); Simon Dalby, "Reading Rio, Writing the World: The *New York Times* and the 'Earth Summit,'" *Political Geography* 15, nos. 6/7 (1996): 593–613; Virginie Mamadouh, "Reclaiming Geopolitics: Geographers Strike Back," *Geopolitics* 4, no. 1 (1999): 118–38; Virginie Mamadouh and Gertjan Dijkink, "Geopolitics, International Relations and Political Geography: The Politics of Geopolitical Discourse," *Geopolitics* 11, no. 3 (2006): 349–66; and Virginie Mamadouh, "The Scaling of the 'Invasion': A Geopolitics of Immigration Narratives in France and the Netherlands," *Geopolitics* 17, no. 2 (2012): 377–401.

10. Amos A. Jordan, William J. Taylor Jr., and Michael J. Mazarr, *American National Security,* 5th ed. (Baltimore: Johns Hopkins University Press, 1999), 3.

11. Charles A. Beard, *The Idea of National Interests: An Analytical Study in American Foreign Policy* (New York: Macmillan, 1934); Hans J. Morgenthau, *In Defense of the National Interest: A Critical Examination of American Foreign Policy* (New York: Knopf, 1951); Donald E. Nuechterlein, *United States National Interests in a Changing World* (Lexington: University Press of Kentucky, 1973); and Martha Finnemore, *National Interests in International Society* (Ithaca, N.Y.: Cornell University Press, 1996).

Notes to Introduction / 265

12. David Jablonsky, "The State of the National Security State," *Parameters* (Winter 2002–3): 4–20; at 4.

13. Philippe Le Billion, *Wars of Plunder: Conflicts, Profits and the Politics of Resources* (London: Hurst & Company, 2012), 10.

14. Mazen Labban, "The Geopolitics of Energy Security and the War on Terror: The Case for Market Expansion and the Militarization of Global Space," in *Global Political Ecology,* edited by Richard Peet, Paul Robbins, and Michael Watts (New York: Routledge, 2011), 325–44; at 326. See also Karen Bakker and Gavin Bridge, "Material Worlds? Resource Geographies and the 'Matter of Nature,'" *Progress in Human Geography* 30, no. 1 (2006): 5–27; Gavin Bridge, "Material Worlds: Natural Resources, Resource Geography and the Material Economy," *Geography Compass* 3, no. 3 (2009): 1217–44; Matthew Huber, "Theorizing Energy Geographies," *Geography Compass* 9, no. 6 (2015): 327–38; Matt Huber, "Resource Geography II: What Makes Resources Political?" *Progress in Human Geography* 43, no. 3 (2019): 553–64.

15. Huber, "Resource Geography II," 554.

16. John A. Williams, Stephen J. Cimbala, and Sam C. Sarkesian, *US National Security: Policymakers, Processes, and Politics,* 6th ed. (Boulder, Colo.: Lynne Rienner, 2022), 3.

17. David Jordan, James D. Kiras, David J. Lonsdale, Ian Speller, Christopher Tuck, and C. Dale Walton, *Understanding Modern Warfare* (Cambridge: Cambridge University Press, 2008), 26.

18. John M. Collins, *Grand Strategy: Principles and Practices* (Annapolis, Md.: Naval Institute Press, 1973); Paul Kennedy, *The Rise and Fall of the Great Powers* (New York: Random House, 1987); Paul Kennedy, ed., *Grand Strategies in War and Peace* (New Haven, Conn.: Yale University Press, 1991); Michael Howard, "Grand Strategy in the Twentieth Century," *Defense Studies* 1, no. 1 (2001): 1–10; Robert Art, *A Grand Strategy for America* (Ithaca, N.Y.: Cornell University Press, 2003); Colin Dueck, *Reluctant Crusaders: Power, Culture, and Change in American Grand Strategy* (Princeton, N.J.: Princeton University Press, 2008); Peter Layton, "The Idea of Grand Strategy," *RUSI Journal* 157, no. 4 (2012): 56–61; Hal Brands, *What Good Is Grand Strategy? Power and Purpose in American Statecraft from Harry S. Truman to George W. Bush* (Ithaca, N.Y.: Cornell University Press, 2014); William Martel, *Grand Strategy in Theory and Practice: The Need for an Effective American Foreign Policy* (Cambridge: Cambridge University Press, 2014); Lukas Milevski, *The Evolution of Modern Grand Strategic Thought* (Oxford: Oxford University Press, 2016); Paul D. Miller, "On Strategy, Grand and Mundane," *Orbis* 60, no. 2 (2016): 237–47; Nina Silove, "Beyond the Buzzword: The Three Meanings of 'Grand Strategy,'" *Security Studies* 27, no. 1 (2018): 27–57; and Richard K. Betts, "The Grandiosity of Grand Strategy," *Washington Quarterly* 42, no. 4 (2020): 7–22.

19. Basil H. Liddell Hart, *The Decisive Wars of History: A Study in Strategy* (London: G. Bell & Sons, 1929), 150.

266 / Notes to Introduction

20. Jordan et al., *Understanding Modern Warfare*, 26.

21. Williams et al., *US National Security*, 3.

22. B. A. Friedman, "Tactics," in *Understanding the U.S. Military*, edited by Katherine Carroll and William B. Hickman (New York: Routledge, 2022), 242–58; at 242.

23. Jordan et al., *Understanding Modern Warfare*, 27.

24. Edward N. Luttwak, "The Operational Level of War," *International Security* 5, no. 3 (1980–81): 61–79; at 61.

25. Peter D. Feaver, "What Is Grand Strategy and Why Do We Need It?" *Foreign Policy*, April 8, 2009, https://foreignpolicy.com/2009/04/08/what-is-grand-strategy-and-why-do-we-need-it/.

26. Brands, *What Good Is Grand Strategy*, 3.

27. See for example Carl Schmitt, *The Concept of the Political*, translated by George Schwab (Chicago: University of Chicago Press, 1996 [1938]); Carl Schmitt, *The "Nomos" of the Earth in the International Law of the "Jus Publicum Europaeum,"* translated by Gary L. Ulmen (New York: Telos Press, 2003 [1950]); and Carl Schmitt, *Political Theology: Four Chapters on the Concept of Sovereignty*, translated by George Schwab (Chicago: University of Chicago Press, 2005 [1922]).

28. Schmitt, *The "Nomos" of the Earth*, 42.

29. Schmitt, *The "Nomos" of the Earth*, 67, 70.

30. Layton, "The Idea of Grand Strategy," 59.

31. Kevin Narizny, *The Political Economy of Grand Strategy* (Ithaca, N.Y.: Cornell University Press, 2007), 8.

32. Nina Silove, "Beyond the Buzzword: The Three Meanings of 'Grand Strategy,'" *Security Studies* 27, no. 1 (2018): 27–57; at 36.

33. Silove, "Beyond the Buzzword," 40.

34. Williams et al., *US National Security*, 3.

35. John Lewis Gaddis, *Strategies of Containment: A Critical Appraisal of Postwar American National Security Policy* (New York: Oxford University Press, 1982), viii–ix. See also Ó Tuathail and Agnew, "Geopolitics and Discourse," 191–92.

36. Klaus-John Dodds and James D. Sidaway, "Locating Critical Geopolitics," *Environment and Planning D: Society and Space* 12 (1994): 515–24; at 517. See also Patrick O'Sullivan, "Antidomino," *Political Geography Quarterly* 1, no. 1 (1982): 57–64; Keith L. Shimko, "Metaphors and Foreign Policy Decision Making," *Political Psychology* 15, no. 4 (1994): 655–71; and Alberto Vanolo, "The Border Between Core and Periphery: Geographical Representations of the World System," *Tijdschrift voor Economische en Sociale Geografie* 101, no. 1 (2010): 26–36.

37. Daniel Yergin, *Shattered Peace: The Origins of the Cold War and the National Security State* (Boston: Houghton Mifflin, 1977); Melvyn P. Leffler, "The American Conception of National Security and the Beginnings of the Cold War, 1945–48," *American Historical Review* 89, no. 2 (1984): 346–81; Anna Kasten Nelson, "President

Notes to Introduction / 267

Truman and the Evolution of the National Security Council," *Journal of American History* 72, no. 2 (1985): 360–78; Melvyn P. Leffler, "National Security," *Journal of American History* 77, no. 1 (1990): 143–52; Melvyn P. Leffler, *A Preponderance of Power: National Security, the Truman Administration, and the Cold War* (Stanford: Stanford University Press, 1992); and Andrew Preston, "Monsters Everywhere: A Genealogy of National Security," *Diplomatic History* 38, no. 3 (2014): 477–500.

38. Emily S. Rosenberg, "Commentary: The Cold War and the Discourse of National Security," *Diplomatic History* 17, no. 2 (1993): 277–84; at 277.

39. C. Vann Woodward, "The Age of Reinterpretation," *American Historical Review* 66, no. 1 (1960): 1–19; at 2; see also Preston, "Monsters Everywhere," 482.

40. Woodward, "The Age of Reinterpretation," 2.

41. Preston, "Monsters Everywhere," 482.

42. Preston, "Monsters Everywhere," 484.

43. Quoted in Anders Stephanson, *Manifest Destiny: American Expansion and the Empire of Right* (New York: Hill & Wang, 1995), xi.

44. Stephanson, *Manifest Destiny,* xii.

45. Theodore Roosevelt, "Remarks in Waukesha, Wisconsin," April 3, 1903, *The American Presidency Project,* available at https://www.presidency.ucsb.edu/documents/remarks-waukesha-wisconsin-0.

46. H. W. Brands, "The Idea of National Interest," *Diplomatic History* 23, no. 2 (1999): 239–61; at 240.

47. Preston, "Monsters Everywhere," 484.

48. Quoted in George W. Baer, "U.S. Naval Strategy 1890–1945," *Naval War College Review* 44, no. 1 (1991): 6–33; at 9.

49. Michael S. Neiberg, "American Entry into the First World War as an Historiographical Problem," in *The Myriad Legacies of 1917: A Year of War and Revolution,* edited by Maartje Abbenhuis, Neill Atkinson, Kingsley Baird, and Gail Romano (Cham, Switzerland: Palgrave Macmillan, 2018), 35–54; at 41–42.

50. United States Congressional Record, 63rd Congress, 3rd Session, January 15, 1915, https://www.congress.gov/bound-congressional-record/1915/01/15/senate-section.

51. Barbara Salazar Torreon, "Instances of Use of United States Armed Forces Abroad, 1798–2017," *Congressional Research Service,* October 12, 2017, https://digital.library.unt.edu/ark:/67531/metadc1042375/m2/1/high_res_d/R42738_2017Oct12.pdf.

52. Brooke L. Blower, "From Isolationism to Neutrality: A New Framework for Understanding American Political Culture, 1919–1941," *Diplomatic History* 38, no. 2 (2014): 345–76; at 350.

53. "Address Delivered by the Secretary of State on 'Our Foreign Policy' at Washington on March 17, 1938," *Foreign Relations of the United States,* https://history.state

268 / Notes to Introduction

.gov/historicaldocuments/frus1931-41v01/d320 (accessed May 1, 2022) (emphasis added).

54. See for example John Agnew, "An Excess of 'National Exceptionalism': Towards a New Political Geography of American Foreign Policy," *Political Geography Quarterly* 2, no. 2 (1983): 151–66.

55. Rosenberg, "Commentary," 278.

56. Preston, "Monsters Everywhere," 494; see also John A. Thompson, "Conceptions of National Security and American Entry into World War II," *Diplomacy and Statecraft* 16, no. 4 (2005): 671–97; David Ekbladh, "Present at the Creation: Edward Mead Earle and the Depression-Era Origins of Security Studies," *International Security* 36, no. 3 (2011/12): 107–41; and Dexter Fergie, "Geopolitics Turned Inwards: The Princeton Military Studies Group and the National Security Imagination," *Diplomatic History* 43, no. 4 (2019): 644–70.

57. Fergie, "Geopolitics Turned Inwards," 644.

58. Quoted in Preston, "Monsters Everywhere," 494.

59. Spykman, "Geography and Foreign Policy, I," 29.

60. Spykman, "Geography and Foreign Policy, I," 29–30 (emphasis added).

61. Thompson, "Conceptions of National Security," 671–72.

62. Preston, "Monsters Everywhere," 492.

63. Franklin D. Roosevelt, "December 29, 1940: Fireside Chat 16: On the 'Arsenal of Democracy,'" https://millercenter.org/the-presidency/presidential-speeches/december-29-1940-fireside-chat-16-arsenal-democracy (accessed April 28, 2022).

64. Preston, "Monsters Everywhere," 492.

65. Alfred Vagts, "Geography in War and Geopolitics," *Military Affairs* 7, no. 2 (1943): 79–88; at 83.

66. Vagts, "Geography in War and Geopolitics," 84.

67. Fergie, "Geopolitics Turned Inward," 644; see also John A. Thompson, "The Exaggeration of American Vulnerability: The Anatomy of a Tradition," *Diplomatic History* 16, no. 1 (1992): 23–43.

68. Michael Cox, "From the Truman Doctrine to the Second Superpower Détente: The Rise and Fall of the Cold War," *Journal of Peace Research* 27, no. 1 (1990): 25–41; at 26.

69. Leffler, "National Security," 150.

70. Simon Dalby, "American Security Discourse: The Persistence of Geopolitics," *Political Geography Quarterly* 9, no. 2 (1990): 171–188; at 173–74.

71. Agnew and Corbridge, *Mastering Space*, 37.

72. "President Harry S. Truman's Address before a Joint Session of Congress," March 12, 1947, *The Avalon Project*, https://avalon.law.yale.edu/20th_century/trudoc.asp (accessed May 17, 2022).

73. "Memorandum by President Truman to the Canadian Prime Minister (Mackenzie King)," October 6, 1946, *Foreign Relations of the United States*, https://history.state.gov/historicaldocuments/frus1946v05/d35 (accessed May 2, 2022).

Notes to Introduction / 269

74. Brands, *What Good Is Grand Strategy*, 18.

75. "Memorandum Prepared by the Joint Chiefs of Staff," March 27, 1946, *Foreign Relations of the United States*, https://history.state.gov/historicaldocuments/frus1946v01/d589 (accessed May 1, 2022).

76. Leffler, "American Conception of National Security," 359.

77. Central Intelligence Agency, "Review of the World Situation as It Relates to the Security of the United States," September 26, 1947, https://www.cia.gov/reading room/docs/CIA-RDP67-00059A000500060004-6.pdf (accessed April 21, 2022).

78. Leffler, "The American Conception of National Security," 357.

79. Central Intelligence Agency, "Review of the World Situation as It Relates to the Security of the United States," September 26, 1947, https://www.cia.gov/readingroom/docs/CIA-RDP67-00059A000500060004-6.pdf (accessed April 21, 2022).

80. Housed within the State Department, the Policy Planning Staff was established on May 7, 1947, to consider the development of long-range policy and to draw together the myriad views of the geographic and functional offices of the department. Operating under the aegis of the National Security Act of 1947, the Policy Planning Staff undertook responsibility for the preparation of the position of the Department of State on matters before the National Security Council. See "Memorandum by the Director of the Policy Planning Staff (Kennan) to the Secretary of State and the Under Secretary of State (Lovett)," *Foreign Relations of the United States,* February 24, 1948, https://history.state.gov/historicaldocuments/frus1948v01p2/d3 (accessed April 29, 2022).

81. "Report by the Policy Planning Staff," November 6, 1947, *Foreign Relations of the United States,* https://history.state.gov/historicaldocuments/frus1947v01/d393 (accessed April 29, 2022).

82. Bruce Cronin, "The Paradox of Hegemony: America's Ambiguous Relationship with the United Nations," *European Journal of International Relations* 7, no. 1 (2001): 103–30; at 115. See also Robert Hilderbrand, *Dumbarton Oaks: The Origins of the United Nations and the Search for Postwar Security* (Chapel Hill: University of North Carolina Press, 1990).

83. "Memorandum Prepared for the Secretary's Staff Committee," November 16, 1946, *Foreign Relations of the United States*, https://history.state.gov/historical documents/frus1946v01/d582 (accessed April 29, 2022).

84. "Memorandum Prepared by the Joint Chiefs of Staff," March 27, 1946, *Foreign Relations of the United States,* https://history.state.gov/historicaldocuments/frus1946v01/d589 (accessed May 1, 2022).

85. Leffler, "American Conception of National Security," 349.

86. Paul Kramer, "Power and Connection: Imperial Histories of the United States in the World," *American Historical Review* 116, no. 5 (2011): 1348–91; at 1368.

87. Leffler, "American Conception of National Security," 349.

270 / Notes to Introduction

88. "The Joint Chiefs of Staff to the Secretary of State," March 29, 1946, *Foreign Relations of the United States,* https://history.state.gov/historicaldocuments/frus1946v01/d590 (accessed May 1, 2022).

89. "Report by the National Security Council," September 29, 1949, *Foreign Relations of the United States,* https://history.state.gov/historicaldocuments/frus1949v01/d146 (accessed May 2, 2022).

90. Fergie, "Geopolitics Turned Inward," 648.

91. Thompson, "Exaggeration of American Vulnerability," 43.

92. "Statement by President Truman in Response to First Soviet Nuclear Test," September 23, 1949, *Wilson Center,* https://digitalarchive.wilsoncenter.org/document/134436.pdf (accessed May 2, 2022).

93. "Editorial Note," *Foreign Relations of the United States,* https://history.state.gov/historicaldocuments/frus1950-55Intel/d5 (accessed June 8, 2022).

94. "Report by the Special Committee of the National Security Council to the President," January 31, 1950, *Foreign Relations of the United States,* https://history.state.gov/historicaldocuments/frus1950v01/d162 (accessed May 2, 2022).

95. "Report by the Special Committee of the National Security Council to the President," January 31, 1950, *Foreign Relations of the United States,* https://history.state.gov/historicaldocuments/frus1950v01/d162 (accessed May 2, 2022).

96. "Report by the Policy Planning Staff," November 6, 1947, *Foreign Relations of the United States,* https://history.state.gov/historicaldocuments/frus1947v01/d393 (accessed May 6, 2022).

97. "A Report to the President Pursuant to the President's Directive of January 31, 1950," April 7, 1950, *Foreign Relations of the United States,* https://history.state.gov/historicaldocuments/frus1950v01/d85 (accessed May 3, 2022).

98. "Paper Prepared by the Deputy Director of the Policy Planning Staff (Ferguson)," February 8, 1951, *Foreign Relations of the United States,* https://history.state.gov/historicaldocuments/frus1951v01/d11 (accessed May 3, 2022).

99. Thomas C. Schelling, *Arms and Influence* (New Haven, Conn.: Yale University Press, 2000 [1996]), 35.

100. "Paper Prepared by the Joint Strategic Survey Committee and Representatives of the Department of State," August 3, 1951, *Foreign Relations of the United States,* https://history.state.gov/historicaldocuments/frus1951v01/d305 (accessed May 2, 2022).

101. David Chandler et al., *In Search of Southeast Asia: A Modern History,* revised edition (Honolulu: University of Hawai'i Press, 1987), 186–87. Cochinchina, initially under the authority of the colonial and naval ministries in Paris, was the only colony in the narrow constitutional sense. Tonkin, Annam, Cambodia, and Laos were administered as distinct and autonomous protectorates under the authority of the French Foreign Ministry. Beginning in 1887 all five political entities were brought under the authority of a single governor-general headquartered in Hanoi.

Notes to Chapter 1 / 271

Five regional heads served under the governor-general: the governor of Cochinchina and the *résidents supérieurs* of Annam, Tonkin, Cambodia, and Laos.

102. Stephen Kinzer, *Overthrow: America's Century of Regime Change from Hawaii to Iraq* (New York: Times Books, 2006), 3. See also David F. Schmitz, *Thank God They're on Our Side: The United States and Right-Wing Dictatorships, 1921–1965* (Chapel Hill: University of North Carolina Press, 1999); David F. Schmitz, *The United States and Right-Wing Dictatorships, 1965–1989* (Cambridge: Cambridge University Press, 2006); and Vincent Bevins, *The Jakarta Method: Washington's Anticommunist Crusade and the Murder Program that Shaped Our World* (New York: Public Affairs, 2020).

103. Kinzer, *Overthrow*; see also Tim Weiner, *Legacy of Ashes: The History of the CIA* (New York: Anchor, 2008).

104. Walter LaFeber, "The Tension between Democracy and Capitalism during the American Century," *Diplomatic History* 23, no. 2 (1999): 263–84; at 263.

105. Robert Buzzanco, "Prologue to Tragedy: U.S. Military Opposition to Intervention in Vietnam, 1950–1954," *Diplomatic History* 17, no. 2 (1993): 201–22; at 202.

106. Latin America was not included in Kennan's report as his staff had not yet studied sufficiently the problems of that region. See "Memorandum by the Director of the Policy Planning Staff (Kennan) to the Secretary of State and the Under Secretary of State (Lovett)," *Foreign Relations of the United States,* February 24, 1948, available at https://history.state.gov/historicaldocuments/frus1948v01p2/d3 (accessed April 29, 2022).

107. "Report by the Policy Planning Staff," February 24, 1948, *Foreign Relations of the United States,* https://history.state.gov/historicaldocuments/frus1947v01/d393 (accessed April 29, 2022).

108. "Report by the Policy Planning Staff," February 24, 1948, *Foreign Relations of the United States,* https://history.state.gov/historicaldocuments/frus1947v01/d393 (accessed April 29, 2022).

1. Into the Breach

1. Hal Brands, *What Good Is Grand Strategy? Power and Purpose in American Statecraft from Harry S. Truman to George W. Bush* (Ithaca, N.Y.: Cornell University Press, 2014), 19.

2. Harold Sprout and Margaret Sprout, "Securing in the United States: How Can We Achieve It?" in *Foundations of National Power: Readings on World Politics and American Security,* edited by Harold Sprout and Margaret Sprout (Princeton, N.J.: Princeton University Press, 1945), 731.

3. Amos A. Jordan, William J. Taylor Jr., and Michael J. Mazaar, *American National Security,* 5th ed. (Baltimore: Johns Hopkins University Press, 1999), 66.

272 / Notes to Chapter 1

4. Ivo H. Daalder and James M. Lindsay, *America Unbound: The Bush Revolution in Foreign Policy* (Washington, D.C.: Brookings Institute Press, 2003), 8.

5. Michael Adas, *Dominance by Design: Technological Imperatives and America's Civilizing Mission* (Cambridge, Mass.: Belknap Press of Harvard University Press, 2006), 226–27.

6. Mark Lawrence, "Explaining the Early Decisions: The United States and the French War, 1945–1954," in *Making Sense of the Vietnam Wars: Local, National, and Transnational Perspectives*, edited by Mark P. Bradley and Marilyn B. Young (Oxford: Oxford University Press, 2008), 23–44; at 24.

7. Gary R. Hess, "Franklin Roosevelt and Indochina," *Journal of American History* 59, no. 2 (1972): 353–68; Evelyn Colbert, "The Road Not Taken: Decolonization and Independence in Indonesia and Indochina," *Foreign Affairs* 51, no. 3 (1973): 608–28; Gary R. Hess, "United States Policy and the Origins of the French-Viet Minh War, 1945–46," *Peace & Change* 3, nos. 2–3 (1975): 21–33; Walter La Feber, "Roosevelt, Churchill, and Indochina: 1942–45," *American Historical Review* 80, no. 5 (1975): 1277–95; David G. Marr, *Vietnam 1945: The Quest for Power* (Berkeley: University of California Press, 1995); Mark Lawrence, *Assuming the Burden: Europe and the American Commitment to War in Vietnam* (Berkeley: University of California Press, 2005); Fredrik Logevall, *Embers of War: The Fall of an Empire and the Making of America's Vietnam* (New York: Random House, 2013).

8. "Memorandum of Conversation, by the Adviser on Caribbean Affairs (Taussig)," March 15, 1945, *Foreign Relations of the United States*, https://history .state.gov/historicaldocuments/frus1945v01/d68 (accessed June 21, 2021).

9. "The Secretary of State to the President," September 8, 1944, *Foreign Relations of the United States*, https://history.state.gov/historicaldocuments/frus1944Quebec/d165 (accessed June 21, 2021).

10. Hess, "Franklin Roosevelt and Indochina," 354.

11. "Memorandum of Conversation, by the Secretary of State," March 27, 1943, *Foreign Relations of the United States*, https://history.state.gov/historicaldocuments/frus1943v03/d22 (accessed June 21, 2021).

12. Hess, "Franklin Roosevelt and Indochina," 354.

13. La Feber, "Roosevelt, Churchill," 1289.

14. Huynh Kim Khanh, "The Vietnamese August Revolution Reinterpreted," *Journal of Asian Studies* 30, no. 4 (August 1971): 761–82; at 763.

15. Hess, "Franklin Roosevelt and Indochina," 354–55.

16. La Feber, "Roosevelt, Churchill," 1278.

17. "Joint Chiefs of Staff Minutes of a Meeting at the White House," January 7, 1943, *Foreign Relations of the United States*, https://history.state.gov/historicaldocuments/frus1941-43/d329 (accessed June 21, 2021).

18. "Bohlen Minutes," November 28, 1943, *Foreign Relations of the United States*, https://history.state.gov/historicaldocuments/frus1943CairoTehran/d358 (accessed June 21, 2021).

Notes to Chapter 1 / 273

19. "The Secretary of State to the President," September 8, 1944, *Foreign Relations of the United States,* https://history.state.gov/historicaldocuments/frus1944Quebec/d165 (accessed June 21, 2021).

20. Marilyn B. Young, *The Vietnam Wars, 1945–1990* (New York: HarperPerennial, 1991), 10.

21. George C. Herring, "The Truman Administration and the Restoration of French Sovereignty in Indochina," *Diplomatic History* 1, no. 2 (1977): 97–117; at 99.

22. See for example Stephen Rosskamm Shalom, *The United States and the Philippines: A Study of Neocolonialism* (Quezon City, Philippines: New Day Publishers, 1986); H. W. Brands, *Bound to Empire: The United States and the Philippines* (New York: Oxford University Press, 1992); and James A. Tyner, *America's Strategy in Southeast Asia: From the Cold War to the Terror War* (Lanham, Md.: Rowman & Littlefield, 2007).

23. Herring, "The Truman Administration," 99.

24. "Statement by President Truman of France's Role in the Settlement of Questions of World and European Interest," May 18, 1945, *Foreign Relations of the United States,* https://history.state.gov/historicaldocuments/frus1945v04/d671 (accessed June 21, 2021).

25. Herring, "The Truman Administration," 99.

26. "The Acting Secretary of State to the Ambassador in France (Caffery)," May 9, 1945, *Foreign Relations of the United States,* https://history.state.gov/historicaldocuments/frus1945v06/d184 (accessed June 21, 2021).

27. "The Ambassador in France (Caffery) to the Secretary of State," August 16, 1945, *Foreign Relations of the United States,* https://history.state.gov/historicaldocuments/frus1945v04/d681 (accessed June 21, 2021).

28. "Memorandum by the Deputy Director of the Office of European Affairs (Matthews)," November 2, 1944, *Foreign Relations of the United States,* https://history.state.gov/historicaldocuments/frus1944v03/d715 (accessed June 22, 2021).

29. Quoted in William J. Duiker, *The Communist Road to Power in Vietnam,* 2nd ed. (Boulder, Colo.: Westview, 1996), 104.

30. Young, *The Vietnam Wars,* 11.

31. Herring, "The Truman Administration," 112.

32. Lawrence, "Explaining the Early Decisions," 24.

33. Herring, "The Truman Administration," 115.

34. Herring, "The Truman Administration," 105.

35. Young, *The Vietnam Wars,* 21–22.

36. Robert D. Schulzinger, *A Time for War: The United States and Vietnam, 1941–1975* (New York: Oxford University Press, 1997), 25–26. See also "The Assistant Chief of the Division of Southeast Asian Affairs (Landon) to the Secretary of State," February 27, 1945, *Foreign Relations of the United States,* https://history.state.gov/historicaldocuments/frus1946v08/d26 (accessed June 22, 2021).

274 / Notes to Chapter 1

37. Schulzinger, *Time for War,* 26.

38. Logevall, *Embers of War,* 163–64. See also Bernard Fall, *Street Without Joy: Indochina at War, 1946–1954* (Harrisburg, Penn.: Stackpole, 1961); Martin Shipway, *The Road to War: France and Vietnam, 1944–1947* (Providence, R.I.: Berghahn, 1996).

39. John Prados, *Vietnam: The History of an Unwinnable War, 1945–1975* (Lawrence: University Press of Kansas, 2009), 22.

40. Logevall, *Embers of War,* 167–68.

41. Logevall, *Embers of War,* 182; see also Lawrence, *The Vietnam War,* 33–40.

42. Logevall, *Embers of War,* 183.

43. "The Consul General at Singapore (Josselyn) to the Secretary of State," January 7, 1947, *Foreign Relations of the United States,* https://history.state.gov/historicaldocuments/frus1947v06/d63 (accessed June 22, 2021).

44. "The Secretary of State to the Embassy in France," February 3, 1947, *Foreign Relations of the United States,* https://history.state.gov/historicaldocuments/frus1947v06/d78 (accessed June 22, 2021).

45. "President Harry S. Truman's Address before a Joint Session of Congress," March 12, 1947, *The Avalon Project,* https://avalon.law.yale.edu/20th_century/trudoc.asp (accessed May 17, 2022).

46. Michael Cox, "Western Capitalism and the Cold War System," in *War, State and Society,* edited by Martin Shaw (London: Macmillan, 1984), 136–94; at 146.

47. Logevall, *Embers of War,* 184.

48. "Truman Doctrine (1947)," https://liberalarts.utexas.edu/coretexts/_files/resources/texts/1947%20Truman%20Doctrine.pdf (accessed June 23, 2021); see also "The Truman Doctrine, 1947," *Foreign Relations of the United States,* https://history.state.gov/milestones/1945-1952/truman-doctrine (accessed June 23, 2021).

49. Gaddis, *Strategies of Containment,* 65–66.

50. "President Harry S. Truman's Address before a Joint Session of Congress," March 12, 1947, *The Avalon Project,* https://avalon.law.yale.edu/20th_century/trudoc.asp (accessed May 17, 2022).

51. Brands, *What Good Is Grand Strategy,* 23.

52. "Address before the Rio de Janeiro Inter-American Conference for the Maintenance of Continental Peace and Security," September 2, 1947, *Harry S. Truman Presidential Library and Museum,* https://www.trumanlibrary.gov/library/public-papers/188/address-rio-de-janeiro-inter-american-conference-maintenance-continental (accessed July 21, 2022).

53. "The Truman Doctrine and the Marshall Plan," *Foreign Relations of the United States,* https://history.state.gov/departmenthistory/short-history/truman (accessed June 23, 2021).

54. Andrew J. Birtle, *U.S. Counterinsurgency and Contingency Operations Doctrine, 1942–1976* (Washington, D.C.: Center of Military History, United States Army, 2006), 22.

Notes to Chapter 1 / 275

55. Andrew J. Bacevich, *American Empire: The Realities and Consequences of U.S. Diplomacy* (Cambridge, Mass.: Harvard University Press, 2002), 3.

56. Brands, *What Good Is Grand Strategy*, 36.

57. "Report by the Policy Planning Staff," February 24, 1948, *Foreign Relations of the United States*, https://history.state.gov/historicaldocuments/frus1948v01p2/d4 (accessed July 21, 2022).

58. Brands, *What Good Is Grand Strategy*, 36.

59. Brands, *What Good Is Grand Strategy*, 39.

60. "The Secretary of State to Certain Diplomatic Offices," August 26, 1950, *Foreign Relations of the United States*, https://history.state.gov/historicaldocuments/frus1950v06/d266. See also "Dean Acheson's 'Perimeter Speech' on Asia (1950)," https://alphahistory.com/coldwar/dean-acheson-perimeter-speech-asia-1950/ (accessed July 21, 2022).

61. "Report by the National Security Council on the Position of the United States with Respect to Soviet-Directed World Communism," *Foreign Relations of the United States*, https://history.state.gov/historicaldocuments/frus1948v01p2/d12; see also "Memorandum by the Secretary of Defense (Forrestal) to the National Security Council," April 17, 1948, *Foreign Relations of the United States*, https://history.state.gov/historicaldocuments/frus1948v01p2/d17 (accessed June 7, 2022).

62. Lawrence, *The Vietnam War*, 33–34.

63. Gary R. Hess, "The First American Commitment in Indochina: The Acceptance of the 'Bao Dai Solution,' 1950," *Diplomatic History* 2, no. 4 (1978): 331–50; Mark Atwood Lawrence, "Recasting Vietnam: The Bao Dai Solution and the Outbreak of the Cold War in Southeast Asia," in *Connecting Histories: Decolonization and the Cold War in Southeast Asia, 1945–1962*, edited by Christopher E. Goscha and Christian F. Ostermann (Washington, D.C.: Woodrow Wilson Center Press, 2009), 15–38; and Balázs Szalontai, "The 'Sole Legal Government of Vietnam': The Bao Dai Factor and Soviet Attitudes toward Vietnam, 1947–1950," *Journal of Cold War Studies* 20, no. 3 (2018): 3–56.

64. Logevall, *Embers of War*, 198.

65. "Memorandum by the President's Special Counsel (Clifford) to President Truman," March 8, 1948, *Foreign Relations of the United States*, https://history.state.gov/historicaldocuments/frus1948v05p2/d79 (accessed May 18, 2022).

66. "The Director of the Policy Planning Staff (Kennan) to the Secretary of State," March 14, 1948, *Foreign Relations of the United States*, https://history.state.gov/historicaldocuments/frus1948v01p2/d6 (accessed May 18, 2022).

67. "Review of the World Situation as It Relates to the Security of the United States," September 26, 1947, *Central Intelligence Agency*, https://www.cia.gov/readingroom/docs/CIA-RDP67-00059A000500060004-6.pdf (accessed May 18, 2022).

68. Young, *Vietnam Wars*, 22.

276 / Notes to Chapter 1

69. Lawrence, "Recasting Vietnam," 29.

70. "Department of State Policy Statement on Indochina, September 27, 1948," September 27, 1948, *Foreign Relations of the United States,* https://history.state.gov/historicaldocuments/frus1948v06/d33 (accessed June 25, 2021).

71. "Policy Planning Staff Paper on United States Policy Toward Southeast Asia," March 29, 1949, *Foreign Relations of the United States,* https://history.state.gov/historicaldocuments/frus1949v07p1/d28 (accessed June 25, 2021).

72. Lawrence, "Explaining the Early Decisions," 32.

73. Gaddis, *Strategies of Containment,* 23.

74. Gaddis, *Strategies of Containment,* 23.

75. "The Director of the Policy Planning Staff (Kennan) to the Under Secretary of State (Acheson)," May 23, 1947, *Foreign Relations of the United States,* https://history.state.gov/historicaldocuments/frus1947v03/d135 (accessed May 6, 2022).

76. Lawrence, "Explaining the Early Decisions," 32. See also Michael Schaller, "Securing the Great Crescent: Occupied Japan and the Origins of Containment in Southeast Asia," *Journal of American History* 69, no. 2 (1982): 392–414; Michael Schaller, *The American Occupation of Japan: The Origins of the Cold War in Asia* (New York: Oxford University Press, 1985); and John Dower, *War without Mercy: Race and Power in the Pacific War* (New York: Pantheon, 1985).

77. Schaller, "Securing the Great Crescent," 394.

78. "Communist Strength in Japan," September 28, 1948, *Central Intelligence Agency,* https://www.cia.gov/readingroom/docs/CIA-RDP78-01617A003300010001-3.pdf (accessed May 18, 2022).

79. "Strategic Importance of Japan," *Central Intelligence Agency,* https://www.cia.gov/readingroom/document/cia-rdp78-01617a003200190001-5 (accessed June 25, 2021).

80. Lawrence, "Explaining the Early Decisions," 32–33. See also James A. Tyner, *America's Strategy in Southeast Asia: From the Cold War to the Terror War* (Lanham, Md.: Rowman & Littlefield, 2007).

81. Melvyn P. Leffler, "The Inevitable Tragedy. The United States Embroilment in Vietnam," *Leidschrift: Gevallen Steen* 19, no. 2 (2004): 55–74; at 62.

82. Leffler, "Inevitable Tragedy," 62.

83. Schaller, "Securing the Great Crescent," 401.

84. "Department of State Policy Statement on Indochina, September 27, 1948," September 27, 1948, *Foreign Relations of the United States,* https://history.state.gov/historicaldocuments/frus1948v06/d33 (accessed June 25, 2021).

85. Lawrence, "Recasting Vietnam," 30; Hess, "The First American Commitment," 339.

86. "Department of State Policy Statement on Indochina, September 27, 1948," September 27, 1948, *Foreign Relations of the United States,* https://history.state.gov/historicaldocuments/frus1948v06/d33 (accessed June 25, 2021).

87. Logevall, *Embers of War,* 184.

Notes to Chapter 1 / 277

88. Brands, *What Good Is Grand Strategy,* 43.

89. Logevall, *Embers of War,* 211.

90. "The Ambassador in France (Caffery) to the Secretary of State," March 16, 1949, *Foreign Relations of the United States,* https://history.state.gov/historicaldocu ments/frus1949v07p1/d11 (accessed June 25, 2021).

91. "Summary Record of a Meeting of United States Ambassadors at Paris, October 21–22," October 21–22, 1949, *Foreign Relations of the United States,* https://history.state.gov/historicaldocuments/frus1949v04/d278 (accessed June 22, 2021).

92. "The Ambassador in France (Bruce) to the Secretary of State," May 30, 1949, *Foreign Relations of the United States,* https://history.state.gov/historicaldocuments/frus1949v07p1/d31 (accessed June 23, 2021).

93. "The Secretary of State to the Consulate at Hanoi," May 20, 1949, *Foreign Relations of the United States,* https://history.state.gov/historicaldocuments/frus1949v07p1/d28 (accessed June 25, 2021).

94. Young, *Vietnam Wars,* 24.

95. "The Secretary of State to Certain Diplomatic and Consular Offices," November 9, 1950, *Foreign Relations of the United States,* https://history.state.gov/historicaldocuments/frus1950v06/d83 (accessed June 10, 2022).

96. Gaddis, *Strategies of Containment,* 41.

97. "Memorandum by the Counselor (Kennan) to the Secretary of State," January 6, 1950, *Foreign Relations of the United States,* https://history.state.gov/historicaldocuments/frus1950v01/d52 (accessed May 6, 2022).

98. Gaddis, *Strategies of Containment,* 44.

99. "Memorandum by the Counselor (Kennan) to the Secretary of State," January 6, 1950, *Foreign Relations of the United States,* https://history.state.gov/historicaldocuments/frus1950v01/d52 (accessed May 6, 2022).

100. "Memorandum by the Counselor of the Department (Kennan) to the Secretary of State," March 29, 1950, *Foreign Relations of the United States,* https://history.state.gov/historicaldocuments/frus1950v02/d330 (accessed May 6, 2022).

101. "The Secretary of State to the Consulate at Hanoi," May 20, 1949, *Foreign Relations of the United States,* https://history.state.gov/historicaldocuments/frus1949v07p1/d28 (accessed June 25, 2021).

102. "The Secretary of State to the Consulate General at Saigon," May 20, 1949, *Foreign Relations of the United States,* https://history.state.gov/historicaldocuments/frus1949v07p1/d27 (accessed June 25, 2021).

103. Hess, "The First American Commitment," 345. See also Mark Atwood Lawrence, *The Vietnam War: A Concise International History* (New York: Oxford University Press, 2008).

104. "Summary Record of a Meeting of United States Ambassadors at Paris, October 21–22," October 21–22, 1949, *Foreign Relations of the United States,* https://history.state.gov/historicaldocuments/frus1949v04/d278 (accessed June 22, 2021).

278 / Notes to Chapter 1

105. Lawrence, "Recasting Vietnam," 34.

106. Birtle, *U.S. Counterinsurgency,* 22.

107. John Agnew, "Revisiting the Territorial Trap," *Nordia Geographical Publications* 44, no. 4 (2015): 43–48; at 43. See also John Agnew, "The Territorial Trap: The Geographical Assumptions of International Relations Theory," *Review of International Political Economy* 1, no. 1 (1994): 53–80; Peter J. Taylor, "The State as Container: Territoriality in the Modern World-System," *Progress in Human Geography* 18, no. 2 (1994): 151–62; Peter J. Taylor, "Territorial Absolutism and Its Evasions," *Geography Research Forum* 16 (1996): 1–12; Jim Glassman, "State Power Beyond the 'Territorial Trap': The Internationalization of the State," *Political Geography* 18, no. 6 (1999): 669–96; Simon Reid-Henry, "The Territorial Trap Fifteen Years On," *Geopolitics* 15, no. 4 (2010): 752–56.

108. Agnew, "Revisiting the Territorial Trap," 47.

109. David Newman, "Territory, Compartments and Borders: Avoiding the Trap of the Territorial Trap," *Geopolitics* 15, no. 4 (2010): 773–78; at 773.

110. Agnew, "Revisiting the Territorial Trap," 47.

111. It should be clear that, on the Korean peninsula, the United States likewise created and defended the Republic of Korea against the equally artificial People's Democratic Republic of Korea, supported by the Soviet Union.

112. "The President to the Secretary of State," January 31, 1950, *Foreign Relations of the United States,* https://history.state.gov/historicaldocuments/frus1950v01/d56; see also "Report by the Special Committee of the National Security Council to the President," January 31, 1950, *Foreign Relations of the United States,* https://history .state.gov/historicaldocuments/frus1950v01/d162 (accessed May 2, 2022).

113. There is a vast (and contested) literature surrounding NSC-68; frequently, oppositional views are sequestered into two camps, that is, realists versus revisionists. For an informative overview, see Ken Young, "Revisiting NSC 68," *Journal of Cold War Studies,* 15, no. 1 (2013): 3–33.

114. "A Report to the President Pursuant to the President's Directive of January 31, 1950," April 7, 1950, *Foreign Relations of the United States,* https://history.state .gov/historicaldocuments/frus1950v01/d85 (accessed May 3, 2022).

115. "A Report to the President Pursuant to the President's Directive of January 31, 1950," April 7, 1950, *Foreign Relations of the United States,* https://history.state .gov/historicaldocuments/frus1950v01/d85 (accessed May 3, 2022).

116. "National Intelligence Estimate," December 11, 1950, *Foreign Relations of the United States,* https://history.state.gov/historicaldocuments/frus1951v01/d3 (accessed May 18, 2022).

117. Lawrence, "Recasting Vietnam," 16. See also George S. Eckhardt, *Command and Control, 1950–1969* (Washington D.C.: Department of the Army, 2004).

118. Graham A. Cosmas, *MACV: The Joint Command in the Years of Escalation, 1962–1967* (Washington, D.C.: Center of Military History, United States Army,

2006), 10–11. See also Gregory A. Daddis, *Westmoreland's War: Reassessing American Strategy in Vietnam* (New York: Oxford University Press, 2014), 45. Following the signing of the Geneva Accords and the departure of the French, in November 1955 MAAG, Indochina was reorganized as the Military Assistance Advisory Group, Vietnam (MAAG, Vietnam), with separate military assistance organizations for Cambodia and Laos.

119. Richard W. Stewart, *Deepening Involvement 1945–1965* (Washington D.C.: Center of Military History, 2012), 10–11.

120. Steven Hugh Lee, *Outposts of Empire: Korea, Vietnam, and the Origins of the Cold War in Asia, 1949–1954* (Kingston, Canada: McGill-Queen's University Press, 1995), 12.

121. Lee, *Outposts of Empire,* 13.

122. Lee, *Outposts of Empire,* 72.

123. "Statement Issued by the President," June 27, 1950, *Foreign Relations of the United States,* https://history.state.gov/historicaldocuments/frus1950v07/d119 (accessed June 28, 2021).

124. William Stueck, *The Korean War: An International History* (Princeton, N.J.: Princeton University Press, 1995), 43.

125. "Report to the National Security Council by the Executive Secretary (Lay)," May 17, 1951, *Foreign Relations of the United States,* https://history.state.gov/historicaldocuments/frus1951v06p1/d12 (accessed May 18, 2022).

126. Prados, *Vietnam,* 23.

127. Mark Philip Bradley, "Making Sense of the French War: The Postcolonial Moment and the First Vietnam War, 1945–1954," in *The First Vietnam War: Colonial Conflict and Cold War Crisis,* edited by Mark Atwood Lawrence and Fredrik Logevall (Cambridge, Mass.: Harvard University Press, 2007), 16–40; at 23.

128. "Memorandum by the Counselor (Kennan)," January 20, 1950, *Foreign Relations of the United States,* https://history.state.gov/historicaldocuments/frus1950v01/d7 (accessed May 6, 2022).

129. Gaddis, *Strategies of Containment,* 99.

130. Gaddis, *Strategies of Containment,* 113.

131. "Memorandum by the Secretary of the Army (Pace), the Secretary of the Navy (Matthews), and the Secretary of the Air Force (Finletter) to the Secretary of Defense (Johnson)," August 1, 1950, *Foreign Relations of the United States,* https://history.state.gov/historicaldocuments/frus1950v01/d113 (accessed May 6, 2022).

2. Bracketing War

1. Howard, "Grand Strategy," 2.

2. David Jordan, James D. Kiras, David J. Lonsdale, Ian Speller, Christopher Tuck, and C. Dale Walton, *Understanding Modern Warfare* (New York: Cambridge University Press, 2008), 26.

280 / Notes to Chapter 2

3. Bernard Brodie, *War and Politics* (New York: Macmillan, 1973); Azar Gat, *The Origins of Military Thought: From the Enlightenment to Clausewitz* (Oxford: Clarendon, 1989);

4. Jordan et al., *Understanding Modern Warfare*, 25.

5. Jordan et al., *Understanding Modern Warfare*, 10.

6. Jordan et al., *Understanding Modern Warfare*, 26–27.

7. "Report to the President by the National Security Council," July 1, 1948, *Foreign Relations of the United States*, https://history.state.gov/historicaldocuments/frus1948v01p2/d27 (accessed June 7, 2022).

8. "Memorandum by Mr. Charles S. Reed of the Division of Southeast Asian Affairs to the Director of the Office of Far Eastern Affairs (Butterworth)," August 13, 1948, *Foreign Relations of the United States*, https://history.state.gov/historicaldocuments/frus1948v01p2/d36 (accessed June 7, 2022).

9. "Memorandum by the Director of the Policy Planning Staff (Nitze)," March 5, 1952, *Foreign Relations of the United States*, https://history.state.gov/historicaldocuments/frus1952-54v12p1/d14 (accessed May 19, 2022).

10. "Memorandum by the Central Intelligence Agency," November 13, 1951, *Foreign Relations of the United States*, https://history.state.gov/historicaldocuments/frus1951v06p1/d22 (accessed May 19, 2022).

11. "Report by the Staff Planners to the Military Representatives to the ANZUS Council," November 25, 1952, *Foreign Relations of the United States*, https://history.state.gov/historicaldocuments/frus1952-54v12p1/d82 (accessed May 19, 2022).

12. "Report by the Staff Planners to the Military Representatives to the ANZUS Council," November 25, 1952, *Foreign Relations of the United States*, https://history.state.gov/historicaldocuments/frus1952-54v12p1/d82 (accessed May 19, 2022).

13. "Memorandum on the Substance of Discussions at a Department of State-Joint Chiefs of Staff Meeting," March 5, 1952, *Foreign Relations of the United States*, https://history.state.gov/historicaldocuments/frus1952-54v12p1/d13 (accessed May 19, 2022).

14. Hal Brands, *What Good Is Grand Strategy? Power and Purpose in American Statecraft from Harry S. Truman to George W. Bush* (Ithaca, N.Y.: Cornell University Press, 2014), 7.

15. "Position Paper Prepared in the Department of State," December 29, 1951, *Foreign Relations of the United States*, https://history.state.gov/historicaldocuments/frus1952-54v12p1/d1 (accessed May 19, 2022).

16. "Memorandum by the Director of the Policy Planning Staff (Nitze)," March 5, 1952, *Foreign Relations of the United States*, https://history.state.gov/historicaldocuments/frus1952-54v12p1/d14 (accessed May 19, 2022).

17. "Memorandum on the Substance of Discussions at a Department of State-Joint Chiefs of Staff Meeting," March 5, 1952, *Foreign Relations of the United States*, https://history.state.gov/historicaldocuments/frus1952-54v12p1/d13 (accessed May 19, 2022).

Notes to Chapter 2 / 281

18. David Anderson, *Trapped by Success: The Eisenhower Administration and Vietnam, 1953–1961* (New York: Columbia University Press, 1991); Thomas L. Ahern Jr., *CIA and the House of Ngo: Covert Action in South Vietnam, 1954–63* (Washington, D.C.: Center for the Study of Intelligence, 2000); Kathryn C. Statler, *Replacing France: The Origins of American Intervention in Vietnam* (Lexington: University of Kentucky Press, 2007); and Kathryn C. Statler, "Eisenhower, Indochina, and Vietnam," in *A Companion to Dwight D. Eisenhower*, edited by Chester J. Pach (Malden, Mass.: Wiley-Blackwell, 2017), 494–516.

19. Eisenhower's comments are recorded in a diary entry of then Vice President Richard Nixon. See "Editorial Note," *Foreign Relations of the United States*, https://history.state.gov/historicaldocuments/frus1952-54v13p2/d804 (accessed May 26, 2022).

20. Statler, "Eisenhower, Indochina, and Vietnam," 496.

21. "Hagerty Diary, April 26, 1954," *Foreign Relations of the United States*, https://history.state.gov/historicaldocuments/frus1952-54v13p2/d802 (accessed May 26, 2022).

22. George C. Herring and Richard H. Immerman, "Eisenhower, Dulles, and Dienbienphu: 'The Day We Didn't Go to War' Revisited," *Journal of American History* 71, no. 2 (1984): 343–63; at 346.

23. The conference initially was to determine the resolution of the Korean War.

24. Herring and Immerman, "Eisenhower, Dulles, and Dienbienphu," 345.

25. George C. Herring, *America's Longest War: The United States and Vietnam, 1950–1975*, 3rd ed. (New York: McGraw-Hill, 1996), 29.

26. Phillip B. Davidson, *Vietnam at War: The History: 1946–1975* (New York: Oxford University Press, 1991), 223–24.

27. "Memorandum of Discussion at the 192d Meeting of the National Security Council, Tuesday, April 6, 1954," April 6, 1954, *Foreign Relations of the United States*, https://history.state.gov/historicaldocuments/frus1952-54v13p1/d705 (accessed June 29, 2021).

28. "Memorandum of Conversation, by the Deputy Assistant Secretary of State for Far Eastern Affairs (Drumright)," April 2, 1954, *Foreign Relations of the United States*, https://history.state.gov/historicaldocuments/frus1952-54v13p1/d679 (accessed June 29, 2021).

29. "Editorial Note," *Foreign Relations of the United States*, https://history.state.gov/historicaldocuments/frus1952-54v16/d296 (accessed June 29, 2021).

30. "The Secretary of State to the Embassy in India," April 2, 1954, *Foreign Relations of the United States*, https://history.state.gov/historicaldocuments/frus1952-54v13p1/d680 (accessed June 29, 2021).

31. "Memorandum of Discussion at the 192d Meeting of the National Security Council, Tuesday, April 6, 1954," April 6, 1954, *Foreign Relations of the United States*, https://history.state.gov/historicaldocuments/frus1952-54v13p1/d705 (accessed June 29, 2021).

282 / Notes to Chapter 2

32. "Editorial Note," *Foreign Relations of the United States,* https://history.state.gov/historicaldocuments/frus1952-54v13p1/d716 (accessed June 29, 2021).

33. "Basic National Security Policy," October 30, 1953, *Foreign Relations of the United States,* https://history.state.gov/historicaldocuments/frus1950-55Intel/d163 (accessed June 30, 2021).

34. "United States Objectives and Courses of Action with Respect to Southeast Asia," January 16, 1954, *Foreign Relations of the United States,* https://history.state.gov/historicaldocuments/frus1955-57v22/d441 (accessed June 30, 2021); see also "Report to the National Security Council by the Executive Secretary (Lay)," January 16, 1954, *Foreign Relations of the United States,* https://history.state.gov/historicaldocuments/frus1952-54v12p1/d132 (accessed May 19, 2022).

35. Jeffrey Kimball, *Nixon's Vietnam War* (Lawrence: University Press of Kansas, 1998), 25.

36. Quoted in Herring and Immerman, "Eisenhower, Dulles, and Dienbienphu," 354–55.

37. Kimball, *Nixon's Vietnam War,* 25.

38. "Memorandum by the Secretary of State to the President," March 23, 1954, *Foreign Relations of the United States,* https://history.state.gov/historicaldocuments/frus1952-54v13p1/d628 (accessed May 19, 2022).

39. "Memorandum for the File of the Secretary of State," April 5, 1954, *Foreign Relations of the United States,* https://history.state.gov/historicaldocuments/frus1952-54v13p1/d686 (accessed May 6, 2022).

40. Frederick W. Marks III, "The Real Hawk at Dienbienphu: Dulles or Eisenhower?" *Pacific Historical Review* 59, no. 3 (1990): 297–322; and John Prados, "Assessing Dien Bien Phu," in *The First Vietnam War: Colonial Conflict and Cold War Crisis,* edited by Mark Atwood Lawrence and Fredrik Logevall (Cambridge, Mass.: Harvard University Press, 2007), 215–39.

41. "Memorandum for the Record by the Special Assistant to the President for National Security Affairs (Culter)," October 19, 1954, *Foreign Relations of the United States,* https://history.state.gov/historicaldocuments/frus1952-54v13p2/d1255 (accessed May 26, 2022).

42. "Memorandum of Discussion at the 219th Meeting of the National Security Council," October 26, 1954, *Foreign Relations of the United States,* https://history.state.gov/historicaldocuments/frus1952-54v13p2/d1281 (accessed May 26, 2022).

43. Douglas C. Dacy, *Foreign Aid, War, and Economic Development: South Vietnam, 1955–1975* (Cambridge: Cambridge University Press, 1986); Michael E. Latham, "Redirecting the Revolution? The USA and the Failure of Nation-Building in South Vietnam," *Third World Quarterly* 27, no. 1 (2006): 27–41; at 29. For extended discussions on U.S. state-building in South Vietnam, see Christopher T. Fisher, "Nation Building and the Vietnam War: A Historiography," *Pacific History Review* 74, no. 3 (2005): 441–56; James M. Carter, *Inventing Vietnam: The United States and*

Notes to Chapter 2 / 283

State Building, 1954–1968 (New York: Cambridge University Press, 2008); David Biggs, *Quagmire: Nation-Building and Nature in the Mekong Delta* (Seattle: University of Washington Press, 2010); Jessica M. Chapman, *Cauldron of Resistance: Ngo Dinh Diem, the United States, and 1950s Southern Vietnam* (Ithaca, N.Y.: Cornell University Press, 2013); Edward Miller, *Misalliance: Ngo Dinh Diem, the United States, and the Fate of South Vietnam* (Cambridge, Mass.: Harvard University Press, 2013); Jessica Elkind, *Aid Under Fire: Nation Building and the Vietnam War* (Lexington: University Press of Kentucky, 2016); and Andrew J. Gawthorpe, *To Build as Well as Destroy: American Nation Building in South Vietnam* (Ithaca, N.Y.: Cornell University Press, 2018).

44. Marilyn B. Young, *The Vietnam Wars, 1945–1990* (New York: HarperPerennial, 1991), 42.

45. Kimball, *Nixon's Vietnam War*, 26.

46. "Memorandum by the Special Assistant to the President for National Security Affairs (Cutler)," June 23, 1954, *Foreign Relations of the United States,* https://history.state.gov/historicaldocuments/frus1952-54v13p2/d990 (accessed May 19, 2022).

47. "Hagerty Diary, April 26, 1954," *Foreign Relations of the United States,* https://history.state.gov/historicaldocuments/frus1952-54v13p2/d802 (accessed May 26, 2022).

48. George McT. Kahin, *Intervention: How America Became Involved in Vietnam* (New York: Alfred A. Knopf, 1986), 103.

49. George C. Herring, Gary R. Hess, and Richard H. Immerman, "Passage of Empire: The United States, France, and South Vietnam, 1954–55," in *Dien Bien Phu and the Crisis of Franco-American Relations, 1954–1955,* edited by Lawrence S. Kaplan, Denise Artaud, and Mark R. Rubin (Wilmington, DE: Scholarly Resources, 1990), 171–95; at 171.

50. Seth Jacobs, "'Our System Demands the Supreme Being': The U.S. Religious Revival and the 'Diem Experiment,' 1954–55," *Diplomatic History* 25, no. 4 (2001): 589–624; Philip E. Catton, *Diem's Final Failure: Prelude to America's War in Vietnam* (Lawrence: University Press of Kansas, 2003); Seth Jacobs, *Cold War Mandarin: Ngo Dinh Diem and the Origins of America's War in Vietnam, 1950–1963* (Lanham, Md.: Rowman & Littlefield, 2006); and Geoffrey C. Stewart, *Vietnam's Lost Revolution: Ngo Dinh Diem's Failure to Build an Independent Nation, 1955–1963* (Cambridge: Cambridge University Press, 2017).

51. Philip E. Catton, "Ngo Dinh Diem and South Vietnam Reconsidered," in *Triumph Revisited: Historians Battle for the Vietnam War,* edited by Andrew Wiest and Michael Doidge (New York: Routledge, 2010), 29–38; at 29.

52. Herring, *America's Longest War*, 52.

53. Richard H. Immerman, "'Dealing with a Government of Madmen': Eisenhower, Kennedy, and Ngo Dinh Diem," in *The Columbia History of the Vietnam War,*

284 / Notes to Chapter 2

edited by David Anderson (New York: Columbia University Press, 2010), 120–42; at 127.

54. Immerman, "Dealing with a Government of Madmen," 130.

55. Quoted in Jacobs, "'Our System Demands the Supreme Being,'" 598.

56. Jacobs, "'Our System Demands the Supreme Being,'" 596. See also Daniel P. O'C. Greene, "John Foster Dulles and the End of the Franco-American Entente in Indochina," *Diplomatic History* 16, no. 4 (1992): 551–72.

57. Jacobs, "'Our System Demands the Supreme Being,'" 596; see also Immerman, "Dealing with a Government of Madmen," 130.

58. Immerman, "Dealing with a Government of Madmen," 131.

59. Andrew J. Birtle, *U.S. Counterinsurgency and Contingency Operations Doctrine, 1942–1976* (Washington, D.C.: Center of Military History, United States Army, 2006), 158.

60. Immerman, "Dealing with a Government of Madmen," 131.

61. Asselin, *Vietnam's American War,* 81.

62. Asselin, *Vietnam's American War,* 83.

63. Fredrik Logevall, "What Really Happened in Vietnam: The North, the South, and the American Defeat," *Foreign Affairs* 91, no. 6 (2012): 129–36; at 133. See also Lien-Hang T. Nguyen, *Hanoi's War: An International History of the War for Peace in Vietnam* (Chapel Hill: University of North Carolina Press, 2012).

64. Asselin, "Hanoi and the Geneva Agreement," 105.

65. Asselin, *Vietnam's American War,* 91.

66. Central Intelligence Agency, "Current Intelligence Weekly Summary," October 16, 1958, https://www.cia.gov/readingroom/docs/DOC_0005339974.pdf (accessed December 2, 2021).

67. Central Intelligence Agency, "Current Intelligence Weekly Summary," October 16, 1958, https://www.cia.gov/readingroom/docs/DOC_0005339974.pdf (accessed December 2, 2021).

68. Logevall, "What Really Happened in Vietnam," 131.

69. King C. Chen, "Hanoi's Three Decisions and the Escalation of the Vietnam War," *Political Science Quarterly* 90, no. 2 (1975): 239–59; at 244.

70. Asselin, *Vietnam's American War,* 95–97.

71. Asselin, *Vietnam's American War,* 102.

72. William S. Turley, *The Second Indochina War: A Concise Political and Military History,* 2nd ed. (Lanham, Md.: Rowman & Littlefield, 2009), 40.

73. "Address at the Gettysburg College Convocation: The Importance of Understanding," https://www.presidency.ucsb.edu/documents/address-the-gettysburg-college-convocation-the-importance-understanding (accessed June 29, 2022).

74. "America's Stake in Vietnam" speech, https://iowaculture.gov/sites/default/files/primary-sources/pdfs/history-education-pss-vietnam-stakes-source.pdf (accessed June 29, 2022).

Notes to Chapter 2 / 285

75. Daddis, *Westmoreland's War*, 21.

76. See especially chapter 7 of John Lewis Gaddis, *Strategies of Containment: A Critical Appraisal of Postwar American National Security Policy* (New York: Oxford University Press, 1982).

77. "President Kennedy's Special Message to Congress on the Defense Budget, March 28, 1961," https://www.mtholyoke.edu/acad/intrel/pentagon2/ps6.htm (accessed December 3, 2021).

78. Cosmas, *MACV*, 36.

79. During the Second World War Rostow served as an analyst of the Office of Strategic Services, tasked in part with the selection of enemy targets for U.S. aerial bombardment. See David Milne, *America's Rasputin: Walt Rostow and the Vietnam War* (New York: Hill & Wang, 2008), 31–34. For the importance of Rostow to Kennedy's counterinsurgency programs, see Gaddis, *Strategies of Containment*, 200.

80. Walt W. Rostow, "Guerrilla Warfare in Underdeveloped Areas," in *The Guerrilla—and How to Fight Him: Selections from the Marine Corps Gazette*, edited by T. N. Greene (New York: Praeger, 1962), 54–61; at 56.

81. Rostow, "Guerrilla Warfare in Underdeveloped Areas," 56.

82. Rostow, "Guerrilla Warfare in Underdeveloped Areas," 54, 56.

83. Rostow, "Guerrilla Warfare in Underdeveloped Areas," 56, 59.

84. Brands, *What Good Is Grand Strategy*, 8.

85. "Paper Prepared by the Country Team Staff Committee," January 4, 1961, *Foreign Relations of the United States*, https://history.state.gov/historicaldocuments/frus1961-63v01/d1 (accessed December 3, 2021).

86. "Paper Prepared by the Country Team Staff Committee," January 4, 1961, *Foreign Relations of the United States*, https://history.state.gov/historicaldocuments/frus1961-63v01/d1 (accessed December 3, 2021).

87. Daddis, *Westmoreland's War*, 49.

88. "Program for the Presidential Task Force on Vietnam," April 22, 1961, *Foreign Relations of the United States*, https://history.state.gov/historicaldocuments/frus1961-63v01/d32 (accessed December 2, 2021).

89. "Program for the Presidential Task Force on Vietnam," April 22, 1961, *Foreign Relations of the United States*, https://history.state.gov/historicaldocuments/frus1961-63v01/d32 (accessed December 2, 2021).

90. "Memorandum from the President's Special Counsel (Sorensen) to the President," April 28, 1961, *Foreign Relations of the United States*, https://history.state.gov/historicaldocuments/frus1961-63v01/d37; "Memorandum from Robert W. Komer of the National Security Council Staff to the President's Deputy Special Assistant for National Security Affairs (Rostow)," April 28, 1961, *Foreign Relations of the United States*, https://history.state.gov/historicaldocuments/frus1961-63v01/d38 (accessed December 2, 2021).

286 / Notes to Chapter 2

91. "Editorial Note," *Foreign Relations of the United States,* https://history.state.gov/historicaldocuments/frus1961-63vo1/d40; "National Security Action Memorandum No. 52," May 11, 1961, *Foreign Relations of the United States,* https://history.state.gov/historicaldocuments/frus1961-63vo1/d52 (accessed December 2, 2021).

92. "Memorandum from the Deputy Secretary of Defense (Gilpatric) to the President," May 3, 1961, *Foreign Relations of the United States,* https://history.state.gov/historicaldocuments/frus1961-63vo1/d42 (accessed December 2, 2021).

93. "Memorandum from the Deputy Secretary of Defense (Gilpatric) to the President," May 3, 1961, *Foreign Relations of the United States,* https://history.state.gov/historicaldocuments/frus1961-63vo1/d42 (accessed December 2, 2021).

94. Cosmas, *MACV,* 11; Daddis, *Westmoreland's War,* 45. This is not to say that counterinsurgency operations were neglected. Soon after Williams assumed command of MAAG, Vietnam, Williams prepared a paper that was subsequently shared with President Diem on the subject of "Guerrilla Operations" in South Vietnam. The tenor of Williams's assessment was exceptionally optimistic; he noted, "Communist guerrillas have been destroyed in Greece, Korea, the Philippines and Iran. They can be destroyed in Vietnam." That said, Williams underscored the presumption that "military operations alone are not sufficient for success as there are really two objectives: the destruction of the guerrilla force and the elimination of the Communist influence on the civil population." In other words, it was necessary to engage both in offensive-oriented campaigns to defeat the enemy and in civic actions designed to gain the loyalty of the local populace. Williams noted that "an over-all plan at Government level embracing political, psychological, economic, administrative and military action is necessary for success." In microcosm, Williams's paper encapsulated a fundamental dilemma of America's efforts of nation-, state-, and government-building in South Vietnam and, indirectly, military and diplomatic efforts directed toward Cambodia and Laos. See "Paper Prepared by the Chief of the Military Assistance Advisory Group in Vietnam (Williams)," December 28, 1955, *Foreign Relations of the United States,* https://history.state.gov/historicaldocuments/frus1955-57vo1/d285 (accessed December 3, 2021).

95. Central Intelligence Agency, "Probable Developments in Vietnam to July 1956," October 11, 1955, https://www.cia.gov/readingroom/docs/CIA-RDP79R01012A005900030001-5.pdf (accessed November 30, 2021).

96. "National Security Action Memorandum No. 52," May 11, 1961, *Foreign Relations of the United States,* https://history.state.gov/historicaldocuments/frus1961-63vo1/d52 (accessed December 2, 2021).

97. Emphasis added.

98. Cosmas, *MACV,* 72.

99. Arnold R. Isaacs, *Without Honor: Defeat in Vietnam and Cambodia* (Baltimore: Johns Hopkins University Press, 1983), 194.

100. Quoted in Isaacs, *Without Honor,* 194.

Notes to Chapter 2 / 287

101. Young, *The Vietnam Wars*, 72; Turley, *The Second Indochina War*, 46–48.

102. See, for example, "Paper Prepared in the Department of State," October 11, 1962, *Foreign Relations of the United States*, https://history.state.gov/historicaldocuments/frus1961-63v01/d155; "Memorandum for the Record by the Deputy Secretary of Defense (Gilpatric)," October 11, 1961, *Foreign Relations of the United States*, https://history.state.gov/historicaldocuments/frus1961-63v01/d156; "Draft Instructions from the President to His Military Representative (Taylor)," October 11, 1961, *Foreign Relations of the United States*, https://history.state.gov/historicaldocuments/frus1961-63v01/d157; and "Memorandum from Robert H. Johnson of the National Security Council Staff to the President's Deputy Special Assistant for National Security Affairs (Rostow)," October 14, 1961, *Foreign Relations of the United States*, https://history.state.gov/historicaldocuments/frus1961-63v01/d166 (accessed December 7, 2021).

103. The Lazy Dog was not a missile in the conventional sense, in that it contained no explosive charge. Rather, the projectile was a small, gravity-propelled projectile measuring less than two inches in length and weighing under 0.5 ounces. Designed to be dropped from an airplane, either hurled in buckets or deployed through a "cluster adapter," the Lazy Dog was an indiscriminate antipersonnel weapon. During "flight" the projectiles could attain the speed of a .50-caliber bullet, capable of smashing through dense foliage and, ultimately, human flesh. The area coverage could be exceptional, in that a single dropped cannister could hold approximately 17,500 projectiles. See "Lazy Dog," https://military-history.fandom.com/wiki/Lazy_Dog_(bomb) (accessed December 7, 2021). For more precise details on subjects to be covered during the Taylor-Rostow mission, see "Memorandum from Robert H. Johnson of the National Security Council Staff to the President's Deputy Special Assistant for National Security Affairs (Rostow)," October 14, 1961, *Foreign Relations of the United States*, https://history.state.gov/historicaldocuments/frus1961-63v01/d166 (accessed December 7, 2021).

104. "Draft Instructions from the President to His Military Representative (Taylor)," October 11, 1961, *Foreign Relations of the United States*, https://history.state.gov/historicaldocuments/frus1961-63v01/d157 (accessed December 7, 2021).

105. "Letter from the President's Military Representative (Taylor) to the President," November 3, 1961, *Foreign Relations of the United States*, https://history.state.gov/historicaldocuments/frus1961-63v01/d210 (accessed December 7, 2021).

106. Marilyn B. Young, *The Vietnam Wars, 1945–1990* (New York: HarperPerennial, 1991), 80.

107. "Draft Memorandum from the Secretary of Defense (McNamara) to the President," November 5, 1961, *Foreign Relations of the United States*, https://history.state.gov/historicaldocuments/frus1961-63v01/d214 (accessed December 7, 2021). The initial memorandum was drafted by McGeorge Bundy.

288 / Notes to Chapter 2

108. "Draft Memorandum from the Secretary of State to the President," November 7, 1961, *Foreign Relations of the United States,* https://history.state.gov/historical documents/frus1961-63v01/d222 (accessed December 7, 2021).

109. "Memorandum from the President's Deputy Special Assistant for National Security Affairs (Rostow) to the President," November 11, 1961, *Foreign Relations of the United States,* https://history.state.gov/historicaldocuments/frus1961-63v01/d233 (accessed December 7, 2021).

110. "Memorandum from the Legal Advisor (Chayes) to the Secretary of State," November 16, 1961, *Foreign Relations of the United States,* https://history.state.gov/historicaldocuments/frus1961-63v01/d261 (accessed December 7, 2021).

111. Young, *The Vietnam Wars,* 81.

112. Cosmas, *MACV,* 21; Thomas L. Ahern Jr., *Vietnam Declassified* (Lexington, Ky.: University Press of Kentucky, 2010), 9.

113. Cosmas, *MACV,* 24–29.

114. Cosmas, *MACV,* 62.

115. The most prominent pacification operation was the "Strategic Hamlet" Program. This program was itself an outgrowth of Diem's earlier and discredited "Agroville" program. Planning for the pilot project, "Operation Sunrise," began in 1961 and was limited initially to three provinces surrounding Saigon. The objective was to consolidate governmental authority in pacified areas through a defense system and administrative reorganization at the hamlet level. In theory, strategic hamlets were to form a "front line" in counterinsurgency operations, as primary responsibility for the defense of the country would rest with hamlet-based citizen militias, with the regular South Vietnamese army assuming a supporting role. In practice, the Strategic Hamlet program failed to deliver on its promises. The program was poorly implemented; as such, many hamlets were inadequately defended, quickly overrun, or infiltrated by the NLF. In addition, proposed land reforms failed to materialize and many peasants were dispossessed of their lands. See for example George C. Herring, *America's Longest War: The United States and Vietnam, 1950–1975,* 3rd ed. (New York: McGraw-Hill, 1996), 98–99; see also John C. Donnell and Gerald C. Hickey, *The Vietnamese "Strategic Hamlets": A Preliminary Report* (Alexandria, Va.: Advanced Research Projects Agency, 1962); and Philip E. Catton, "Counter-Insurgency and Nation Building: The Strategic Hamlet Programme in South Vietnam, 1961–1963," *International History Review* 21, no. 4 (1999): 918–40.

116. Cosmas, *MACV,* 78–79.

117. Birtle, *U.S. Army Counterinsurgency,* 315.

118. "Interview with Paul D. Harkins," interviewed by Ted Gittinger, November 10, 1981, *Library of Congress,* http://www.loc.gov/item/mfdipbib000475 (accessed December 7, 2021).

119. Birtle, *U.S. Army Counterinsurgency,* 319.

120. Arthur Dommen, *Conflict in Laos* (New York: Praeger, 1964); John J. Czyzak and Carl F. Salans, "The International Conference on Laos and the Geneva

Notes to Chapter 2 / 289

Agreement of 1962," *Journal of Southeast Asian History* 7, no. 2 (1966): 27–47; Norman B. Hannah, *The Key to Failure: Laos and the Vietnam War* (Lanham, Md.: Madison, 1986); Timothy N. Castle, *At War in the Shadow of Vietnam: United States Military Aid to the Royal Lao Government, 1955–1975* (New York: Columbia University Press, 1993); Edmund F. Wehrle, "'A Good, Bad Deal': John F. Kennedy, W. Averill Harriman, and the Neutralization of Laos, 1961–1962," *Pacific Historical Review* 67, no. 3 (1998): 349–77; Lawrence Freedman, *Kennedy's Wars: Berlin, Cuba, Laos, and Vietnam* (Oxford: Oxford University Press, 2000); Noam Kochavi, "Limited Accommodation, Perpetuated Conflict: Kennedy, China, and the Laos Crisis, 1961–1963," *Diplomatic History* 26, no. 1 (2002): 95–135; William J. Rust, *So Much to Lose: John F. Kennedy and American Policy in Laos* (Lexington: University Press of Kentucky, 2014); Joshua Kurlantzick, *A Great Place to Have a War: America in Laos and the Birth of a Military CIA* (New York: Simon & Schuster, 2016); and Patit Paban Mishra, "From Geneva to Geneva: A Discourse on Geo-Political Dimensions of Conflict in Laos: 1954–1962," *Journal of International Studies* 7 (2020): 103–18.

121. Freedman, *Kennedy's Wars,* 293.

122. Freedman, *Kennedy's Wars,* 293.

123. Wehrle, "'A Good, Bad Deal,'" 352.

124. "Notes of Conversation between President-Elect Kennedy and President Eisenhower," January 19, 1961, *Foreign Relations of the United States,* https://history.state.gov/historicaldocuments/frus1961-63v24/d7; and "Memorandum for the Record," January 19, 1961, *Foreign Relations of the United States,* https://history.state.gov/historicaldocuments/frus1961-63v24/d8 (accessed May 26, 2022).

125. Kochavi, "Limited Accommodation," 108.

126. "Report Prepared by the Inter-Agency Task Force on Laos," January 23, 1961, *Foreign Relations of the United States,* https://history.state.gov/historicaldocuments/frus1961-63v24/d10 (accessed July 8, 2021).

127. "Telegram from the Department of State to the Embassy in Laos," February 10, 1961, *Foreign Relations of the United States,* https://history.state.gov/historicaldocuments/frus1961-63v24/d15 (accessed July 8, 2021).

128. "Report Prepared by the Inter-Agency Task Force on Laos," January 23, 1961, *Foreign Relations of the United States,* https://history.state.gov/historicaldocuments/frus1961-63v24/d10 (accessed July 8, 2021). Italics in the original.

129. Czyzak and Salans, "The International Conference on Laos," 27.

130. Herring, *America's Longest War,* 86; Wehrle, "'A Good, Bad Deal,'" 375.

131. "Memorandum from the Ambassador at Large (Bowles) to the Secretary of State," July 12, 1962, *Foreign Relations of the United States,* https://history.state.gov/historicaldocuments/frus1961-63v02/d241 (accessed July 8, 2021).

132. "Memorandum from the Ambassador at Large (Bowles) to the President," April 4, 1962, *Foreign Relations of the United States,* https://history.state.gov/historicaldocuments/frus1961-63v02/d142 (accessed July 8, 2021); "Memorandum from

290 / Notes to Chapter 2

the Ambassador at Large (Bowles) to the President," June 13, 1962, *Foreign Relations of the United States,* https://history.state.gov/historicaldocuments/frus1961-63v02/d214 (accessed July 8, 2021).

133. "Memorandum from the Ambassador at Large (Bowles) to the President," April 4, 1962, *Foreign Relations of the United States,* https://history.state.gov/historicaldocuments/frus1961-63v02/d142 (accessed July 8, 2021).

134. "Memorandum from the Ambassador at Large (Bowles) to the President," June 13, 1962, *Foreign Relations of the United States,* https://history.state.gov/historicaldocuments/frus1961-63v02/d214 (accessed July 8, 2021).

135. "Memorandum from the Under Secretary of State (Bowles) to the Secretary of State," October 5, 1961, *Foreign Relations of the United States,* https://history.state.gov/historicaldocuments/frus1961-63v01/d145 (accessed July 8, 2021).

136. "Memorandum from the Ambassador at Large (Bowles) to the Secretary of State," August 16, 1962, *Foreign Relations of the United States,* https://history.state.gov/historicaldocuments/frus1961-63v02/d267 (accessed July 8, 2021).

137. "Memorandum of Conversation," November 7, 1961, *Foreign Relations of the United States,* https://history.state.gov/historicaldocuments/frus1961-63v19/d60 (accessed July 8, 2021).

138. Diem's immediate successor was General Duong Van Minh. He was also removed in a coup two months later, replaced by General Nguyen Khanh.

139. "Telegram from the Department of State to the Embassy in Vietnam," November 1, 1963, *Foreign Relations of the United States,* https://history.state.gov/historicaldocuments/frus1961-63v04/d264 (accessed December 8, 2021).

140. On November 2 the State Department notified all diplomatic posts around the world that the United States was prepared "to recognize new regime in Saigon early next week." Accordingly, the telegram counseled, "All missions, especially in Western Hemisphere, should be prepared to give full explanation this decision and sharp distinction between its basis and [US government] opposition to military coups against democratic regimes elsewhere." See "Circular Telegram from the Department of State to All Diplomatic Posts," November 2, 1963, *Foreign Relations of the United States,* https://history.state.gov/historicaldocuments/frus1961-63v04/d277 (accessed December 8, 2021).

141. "Telegram from the Department of State to the Embassy in Vietnam," November 1, 1963, *Foreign Relations of the United States,* https://history.state.gov/historicaldocuments/frus1961-63v04/d269 (accessed December 8, 2021).

142. "Telegram from the Embassy in Vietnam to the Department of State," November 2, 1963, *Foreign Relations of the United States,* https://history.state.gov/historicaldocuments/frus1961-63v04/d270 (accessed December 8, 2021).

143. "Memorandum for the Record of Discussion at the Daily White House Staff Meeting," November 4, 1963, *Foreign Relations of the United States,* https://history.state.gov/historicaldocuments/frus1961-63v04/d288 (accessed December 8, 2021).

Notes to Chapter 2 / 291

144. "Memorandum for the Record of Discussion at the Daily White House Meeting," November 1, 1963, *Foreign Relations of the United States,* https://history.state.gov/historicaldocuments/frus1961-63v04/d263 (accessed December 8, 2021).

145. Quoted in Brian VanDeMark, *Into the Quagmire: Lyndon Johnson and the Escalation of the Vietnam War* (New York: Oxford University Press, 1995), 10.

146. There is a voluminous secondary literature on Johnson's approach to Vietnam. Key contributions include Douglas Kinnard, *The War Managers* (Hanover: University Press of New England, 1977); Larry Berman, *Lyndon Johnson's War: The Road to Stalemate in Vietnam* (New York: W. W. Norton, 1989); David M. Barrett, *Uncertain Warriors: Lyndon Johnson and His Vietnam Advisors* (Lawrence: University Press of Kansas, 1993); and Herbert Y. Schandler, *Lyndon Johnson and Vietnam: The Unmaking of a President* (Princeton, N.J.: Princeton University Press, 2014).

147. Present at the meeting were Secretary of State Dean Rusk, Secretary of Defense Robert McNamara, Undersecretary of State George Ball, President's Special Assistant for National Security Affairs McGeorge Bundy, Director of the Central Intelligence Agency John McCone, and U.S. Ambassador to South Vietnam Henry Cabot Lodge.

148. "Memorandum for the Record of Meeting," November 24, 1963, *Foreign Relations of the United States,* https://history.state.gov/historicaldocuments/frus1961-63v04/d330 (accessed July 2, 2021).

149. Daddis, *Westmoreland's War,* 54.

150. "National Security Action Memorandum No. 273," November 26, 1963, *Foreign Relations of the United States,* https://history.state.gov/historicaldocuments/frus1961-63v04/d331 (accessed December 8, 2021).

151. "Memorandum from the Secretary of Defense (McNamara) to President Johnson," December 21, 1963, *Foreign Relations of the United States,* https://history.state.gov/historicaldocuments/frus1961-63v04/d374 (accessed December 8, 2021).

152. "Memorandum from the Secretary of Defense (McNamara) to President Johnson," December 21, 1963, *Foreign Relations of the United States,* https://history.state.gov/historicaldocuments/frus1961-63v04/d374 (accessed July 2, 2021).

153. Jorden served as special assistant to Under Secretary of State Averell Harriman.

154. "Memorandum from the Under Secretary of State for Political Affairs' Special Assistant (Jorden) to the Under Secretary (Harriman)," December 27, 1963, *Foreign Relations of the United States,* https://history.state.gov/historicaldocuments/frus1961-63v04/d378 (accessed December 8, 2021).

155. "Memorandum from the Chairman of the Central Intelligence Agency's Working Group on Vietnam (Cooper) to the Director of Central Intelligence (McCone)," December 6, 1963, *Foreign Relations of the United States,* https://history.state.gov/historicaldocuments/frus1961-63v04/d349 (accessed July 2, 2021).

292 / Notes to Chapter 2

156. "Telegram from the Secretary of Defense (McNamara) to the Ambassador in Vietnam (Lodge)," December 12, 1963, *Foreign Relations of the United States,* https://history.state.gov/historicaldocuments/frus1961-63v04/d362 (accessed July 2, 2021).

157. "Memorandum from the President's Special Assistant for National Security Affairs (Bundy) to the President," January 7, 1964, *Foreign Relations of the United States,* https://history.state.gov/historicaldocuments/frus1964-68v01/d4 (accessed December 8, 2021).

158. The formation of MACV-SOG also facilitated the expansion of psychological operations (PSYOP) conducted by U.S. forces throughout the course of the war. As Robert Kodosky explains, PSYOPs in Vietnam hardly constituted anything new; the U.S. commitment to the concept, however, did. Following the Second World War, U.S. civilian and military analysts perceived the Cold War as a contest of wills that necessitated the broad application of psychological components. Notably, the logic of PSYOPs melded effortlessly with Rostow's thesis of modernization. In theory, the widespread dissemination of propaganda was designed to win the hearts and minds of the Vietnamese peasantry, to both garner support for the South Vietnamese government and discredit the communist North. To that end, in May 1965 the Political Warfare Advisory Director was established to direct tactical PSYOP in support of military operations while other divisions within MACV orchestrated PSYOP on behalf of pacification and national development. All told, PSYOP personnel averaged between 7,000 and 9,000 total flight hours while flying approximately 2,000 sorties per month; by 1970, the United States dropped an estimated 2,000 leaflets for every man, woman, and child in Vietnam. See Robert J. Kodosky, "Leaflets, Loudspeakers and Radios, Oh My!," *Air Power History* 64, no. 3 (2017): 5–12; at 5, 6, and 8.

159. Plaster, John L. *SOG: The Secret Wars of America's Commandos in Vietnam* (New York: Simon and Schuster, 2019), 23. The day-to-day management of covert operations conducted by SOG hindered the overall effectiveness of the program. As Plaster (p. 26) explains, each proposed OPLAN-34A operation had to weave its way between the State Department, the Department of Defense, and the White House for approval, with each stop liable to change, restrict, or delay SOG plans. Effectively, both impatience and excessive oversight limited the program's success

160. Key dissenters included undersecretary of State George Ball, Senator Richard Russell, Senator J. William Fulbright, Senator Wayne Morse, Senator Ernest Gruening, and Senator Mike Mansfield.

161. Barrett, *Uncertain Warriors,* 25.

162. "Memorandum from the Secretary of Defense (McNamara) to the President," March 16, 1964, *Foreign Relations of the United States,* https://history.state.gov/historicaldocuments/frus1964-68v01/d84 (accessed July 5, 2021).

163. Established in 1962, Desoto patrols were intelligence-gathering missions involving U.S. destroyers operating in international waters off the coasts of the Soviet

Notes to Chapter 2 / 293

Union, China, North Korea and, subsequently, North Vietnam. See James A. Montgomery, "The First DESOTA Patrol," http://ussdehaven.org/first_desoto_patrol.htm (accessed July 5, 2021).

164. The attack on the U.S.S. *Turner Joy* has been fraught with controversy. It is clear now that the destroyer was not attacked by North Vietnamese forces; subject to debate, however, is whether Johnson knew this at the time.

165. Herring, *America's Longest War*, 137.

166. Fredrik Logevall, "Lyndon Johnson and Vietnam," *Presidential Studies Quarterly* 34, no. 1 (2004): 100–112; at 101.

167. "Memorandum for the Record," February 6, 1965, *Foreign Relations of the United States*, https://history.state.gov/historicaldocuments/frus1964-68v02/d77 (July 5, 2021).

168. Barrett, *Uncertain Warriors*, 26; Herring, *America's Longest War*, 146.

169. Barrett, *Uncertain Warriors*, 24.

170. "Paper Prepared by the Assistant Secretary of Defense for International Security Affairs (McNaughton)," March 10, 1965, *Foreign Relations of the United States*, https://history.state.gov/historicaldocuments/frus1964-68v02/d193 (accessed July 5, 2021).

171. "Paper Prepared by the Under Secretary of State (Ball)," May 13, 1965, *Foreign Relations of the United States*, https://history.state.gov/historicaldocuments/frus1964-68v02/d300 (accessed July 5, 2021).

172. "Telegram from the Embassy in Vietnam to the Department of State," June 5, 1965, *Foreign Relations of the United States*, https://history.state.gov/historicaldocuments/frus1964-68v02/d332 (accessed July 5, 2021).

173. "Telegram from the Commander, Military Assistance Command, Vietnam (Westmoreland) to the Joint Chiefs of Staff," June 7, 1965, *Foreign Relations of the United States*, https://history.state.gov/historicaldocuments/frus1964-68v02/d337 (accessed July 5, 2021).

174. "Memorandum from Secretary of Defense McNamara to President Johnson," July 20, 1965, *Foreign Relations of the United States*, https://history.state.gov/historicaldocuments/frus1964-68v03/d67 (accessed July 5, 2021).

175. For a detailed discussion of Johnson's decision, see Barrett, *Uncertain Warriors*, 26–46 and 51–61.

176. Logevall, "Lyndon Johnson," 101.

177. Herring, *America's Longest War*, 152–53.

178. Frank L. Jones, *Buying Time, 1965–1966* (Washington D.C.: United States Army, Center of Military History, 2015), 24.

179. Andrew J. Birtle, *U.S. Army Counterinsurgency and Contingency Operations Doctrine, 1942–1976* (Washington, D.C.: United States Army, Center of Military History, 2006), 368.

180. Birtle, *U.S. Army Counterinsurgency*, 368–69.

294 / Notes to Chapter 3

3. Bordering War

1. "Memorandum from Secretary of Defense McNamara to President Johnson," July 20, 1065, *Foreign Relations of the United States,* https://history.state.gov/historicaldocuments/frus1964-68v03/d67 (accessed September 7, 2021).

2. "Memorandum from Secretary of Defense McNamara to President Johnson," July 20, 1965, *Foreign Relations of the United States,* https://history.state.gov/historicaldocuments/frus1964-68v03/d67 (accessed September 7, 2021).

3. "Draft Memorandum from Secretary of Defense McNamara to President Johnson," November 3, 1965, *Foreign Relations of the United States,* https://history.state.gov/historicaldocuments/frus1964-68v03/d189 (accessed September 7, 2021). Emphasis added.

4. "Draft Memorandum from Secretary of Defense McNamara to President Johnson," November 3, 1965, *Foreign Relations of the United States,* https://history.state.gov/historicaldocuments/frus1964-68v03/d189 (accessed September 7, 2021).

5. Hal Brands, *What Good Is Grand Strategy? Power and Purpose in American Statecraft from Harry S. Truman to George W. Bush* (Ithaca, N.Y.: Cornell University Press, 2014), 7.

6. Brands, *What Good Is Grand Strategy,* 7.

7. Norodom Sihanouk was the son of Prince Norodom Suramarit, who was married to Monivong's daughter. See David P. Chandler, *A History of Cambodia,* 3rd ed. (Boulder, Colo.: Westview Press, 2000), 166.

8. William Shawcross, *Sideshow: Kissinger, Nixon, and the Destruction of Cambodia,* revised edition (New York: Cooper Square Press, 2002), 47.

9. Peter Manning, *Transitional Justice and Memory in Cambodia: Beyond the Extraordinary Chambers* (New York: Routledge, 2017), 42.

10. David Chandler, *The Tragedy of Cambodian History: Politics, War, and Revolution Since 1945* (New Haven, Conn.: Yale University Press, 1991), 17; Chandler, *A History of Cambodia,* 170.

11. Manning, *Transitional Justice,* 42; Chandler, *Tragedy of Cambodian History,* 65–66.

12. "Memorandum by Ambassador Donald R. Heath to the Assistant Secretary of State for Far Eastern Affairs (Robertson)," April 20, 1953, *Foreign Relations of the United States,* https://history.state.gov/historicaldocuments/frus1952-54v13p1/d226 (accessed December 10, 2021).

13. "Substance of Discussions of State-Joint Chiefs of Staff Meeting at the Pentagon Building," April 23, 1954, *Foreign Relations of the United States,* https://history.state.gov/historicaldocuments/frus1952-54v13p1/d775 (accessed December 10, 2021).

14. Chandler, *Tragedy of Cambodian History,* 68.

15. "Memorandum of Discussion at the 143d Meeting of the National Security Council," May 6, 1953, *Foreign Relations of the United States,* https://history.state.gov/historicaldocuments/frus1952-54v12p2/d392 (accessed December 10, 2021).

Notes to Chapter 3 / 295

16. Chandler, *Tragedy of Cambodian History,* 68–72; Elizabeth Becker, *When the War Was Over: Cambodia and the Khmer Rouge Revolution* (New York: Public Affairs, 1998), 76.

17. Chandler, *Tragedy of Cambodian History,* 89.

18. Quoted in David Ayers, *Anatomy of a Crisis: Education, Development, and the State in Cambodia, 1953–1998* (Chiang Mai, Thailand: Silkworm Press, 2003), 32.

19. "Memorandum by Ambassador Donald R. Heath to the Secretary of State," April 28, 1953, *Foreign Relations of the United States,* https://history.state.gov/histor icaldocuments/frus1952-54v13p1/d250 (accessed May 23, 2022).

20. "The Chargé in Cambodia (McClintock) to the Department of State," June 9, 1954, *Foreign Relations of the United States,* https://history.state.gov/historicaldoc uments/frus1952-54v13p2/d957 (accessed May 23, 2022).

21. Kenton Clymer, *Troubled Relations: The United States and Cambodia since 1870* (DeKalb: Northern Illinois University Press, 2007), 26–27.

22. "Telegram from the Department of State to the Embassy in France," January 6, 1955, *Foreign Relations of the United States,* https://history.state.gov/histori caldocuments/frus1955-57v21/d176 (accessed December 10, 2021).

23. "Telegram from the Embassy in France to the Department of State," January 6, 1955, *Foreign Relations of the United States,* https://history.state.gov/histori caldocuments/frus1955-57v21/d177 (accessed December 10, 2021).

24. "Telegraph from the Embassy in Cambodia to the Department of State," January 11, 1955, *Foreign Relations of the United States,* https://history.state.gov/his toricaldocuments/frus1955-57v21/d178 (accessed December 10, 2021).

25. "Memorandum from the Deputy Assistant Secretary of Defense for International Security Affairs (Davis) to the Chairman of the Joint Chiefs of Staff (Radford)," January 14, 1955, *Foreign Relations of the United States,* https://history.state .gov/historicaldocuments/frus1955-57v21/d179 (accessed December 10, 2021).

26. "Memorandum on the Substance of Discussion at a Department of State-Joint Chiefs of Staff Meeting," January 14, 1955, *Foreign Relations of the United States,* https://history.state.gov/historicaldocuments/frus1955-57v21/d180 (accessed December 10, 2021).

27. "Memorandum of a Conversation," February 14, 1955, *Foreign Relations of the United States,* https://history.state.gov/historicaldocuments/frus1955-57v21/d186 (accessed December 10, 2021).

28. "Letter from the Acting Secretary of Defense (Anderson) to the Secretary of State," April 6, 1955, *Foreign Relations of the United States,* https://history.state.gov/ historicaldocuments/frus1955-57v21/d198 (accessed December 10, 2021).

29. "Telegram from the Embassy in Cambodia to the Department of State," April 29, 1955, *Foreign Relations of the United States,* https://history.state.gov/histor icaldocuments/frus1955-57v21/d199 (accessed December 10, 2021).

296 / Notes to Chapter 3

30. "Telegram from the Embassy in Cambodia to the Department of State," April 29, 1955, *Foreign Relations of the United States,* https://history.state.gov/histor icaldocuments/frus1955-57v21/d199 (accessed December 10, 2021).

31. Clymer, *Troubled Relations,* 27.

32. "Memorandum of a Conversation," June 29, 1955, *Foreign Relations of the United States,* https://history.state.gov/historicaldocuments/frus1955-57v21/d208 (accessed December 10, 2021).

33. "Telegram from the Department of State to the Embassy in Cambodia," June 20, 1955, *Foreign Relations of the United States,* https://history.state.gov/histor icaldocuments/frus1955-57v21/d205 (accessed December 10, 2021).

34. Michael Leifer, "Cambodia: In Search of Neutrality," *Asian Survey* 3, no. 1 (1962): 55–60; at 55.

35. David P. Chandler, *Brother Number One: A Political Biography of Pol Pot,* revised edition (Chiang Mai, Thailand: Silkworm Books, 2000), 46.

36. Manning, *Transitional Justice,* 42.

37. In 1960, Sihanouk's father died and Sihanouk assumed the new position of head of state, which he held for the next ten years. A new king was not selected, but neither was the monarchy abolished. See Marlowe Hood and David A. Ablin, "The Path to Cambodia's Present," in *The Cambodian Agony* (London: Armonk, 1987), xv-lxi; at xxii.

38. Clymer, *Troubled Relations,* 28.

39. Leifer, "Cambodia," 59.

40. "Memorandum from the Deputy Assistant Secretary of State for Far Eastern Affairs (Sebald) to the Secretary of State," March 4, 1955, *Foreign Relations of the United States,* https://history.state.gov/historicaldocuments/frus1955-57v21/d194 (accessed December 10, 2021).

41. Chandler, *Tragedy of Cambodian History,* 87.

42. Michael Vickery, "Looking Back at Cambodia, 1942–76," in *Peasants and Politics in Kampuchea, 1942–1981,* edited by Ben Kiernan and Chanthou Boua (Armonk, N.Y.: M. E. Sharpe, 1982), 89–126; at 101.

43. "Telegram from the Commander in Chief, Pacific (Stump) to the Chief of the Military Assistance Group, Cambodia (Lodoen)," March 22, 1956, *Foreign Relations of the United States,* https://history.state.gov/historicaldocuments/frus1955-57 v21/d227 (accessed May 23, 2022).

44. "Telegram from the Embassy in Cambodia to the Department of State," March 30, 1956, *Foreign Relations of the United States,* https://history.state.gov/his toricaldocuments/frus1955-57v21/d230 (accessed May 23, 2022).

45. "Telegram from the Chief of the Military Assistance Group, Cambodia (Lodoen), to the Commander in Chief, Pacific (Stump)," March 24, 1956, *Foreign Relations of the United States,* https://history.state.gov/historicaldocuments/frus1955 -57v21/d228 (accessed May 23, 2022).

Notes to Chapter 3 / 297

46. "Telegram from the Embassy in Cambodia to the Commander in Chief, Pacific (Stump)," March 30, 1956, *Foreign Relations of the United States*, https://history.state.gov/historicaldocuments/frus1955-57v21/d231 (accessed May 23, 2022).

47. "Memorandum of a Conversation Between the Cambodian Ambassador (Nong Kimny) and the Assistant Secretary of State for Far Eastern Affairs (Robertson)," February 10, 1956, *Foreign Relations of the United States*, https://history.state.gov/historicaldocuments/frus1955-57v21/d225 (accessed May 23, 2022).

48. "Memorandum from the Director of the Office of Southeast Asian Affairs (Young) to the Assistant Secretary of State for Far Eastern Affairs (Robertson)," April 14, 1956, *Foreign Relations of the United States*, https://history.state.gov/historicaldocuments/frus1955-57v21/d233 (accessed May 23, 2022).

49. "Letter from the Ambassador in Cambodia (McClintock) to the Director of the Office of Southeast Asian Affairs (Young)," May 2, 1956, *Foreign Relations of the United States*, https://history.state.gov/historicaldocuments/frus1955-57v21/d236 (accessed May 23, 2022).

50. Clymer, *Troubled Relations*, 30.

51. "Memorandum from the Assistant Secretary of State for Far Eastern Affairs (Robertson) to the Secretary of State," August 29, 1956, *Foreign Relations of the United States*, https://history.state.gov/historicaldocuments/frus1955-57v21/d117 (accessed May 23, 2022).

52. "Memorandum of Discussion at the 295th Meeting of the National Security Council, Washington," August 30, 1956, *Foreign Relations of the United States*, https://history.state.gov/historicaldocuments/frus1955-57v21/d118 (accessed May 23, 2022).

53. "National Security Council Report," September 5, 1956, *Foreign Relations of the United States*, https://history.state.gov/historicaldocuments/frus1955-57v21/d119 (accessed May 23, 2022).

54. Clymer, *Troubled Relations*, 31.

55. "Letter from the Ambassador in Cambodia (Strom) to the Assistant Secretary of State for Far Eastern Affairs (Robertson)," February 14, 1957, *Foreign Relations of the United States*, https://history.state.gov/historicaldocuments/frus1955-57v21/d252 (accessed May 23, 2022).

56. "Letter from the Ambassador in Vietnam (Dubrow) to the Director of the Bureau of Intelligence and Research (Cumming)," November 20, 1958, *Foreign Relations of the United States*, https://history.state.gov/historicaldocuments/frus1958-60v16/d88. See also "Telegram from the Embassy in Cambodia to the Department of State," November 21, 1958, *Foreign Relations of the United States*, https://history.state.gov/historicaldocuments/frus1958-60v16/d89; and "Telegram from the Embassy in Vietnam to the Department of State," December 12, 1958, *Foreign Relations of the United States*, https://history.state.gov/historicaldocuments/frus1958-60v16/d91 (accessed May 23, 2022).

57. Clymer, *Trouble Relations*, 36–38; see also Chandler, *Tragedy of Cambodian History*, 99–101.

298 / Notes to Chapter 3

58. "Editorial Note," *Foreign Relations of the United States*, https://history.state .gov/historicaldocuments/frus1958-60v16/d97 (accessed May 23, 2022).

59. "Telegram from the Department of State to the Embassy in Cambodia," February 21, 1959, *Foreign Relations of the United States*, https://history.state.gov/ historicaldocuments/frus1958-60v16/d99 (accessed May 24, 2022).

60. "Memorandum of a Conversation," January 26, 1959, *Foreign Relations of the United States*, https://history.state.gov/historicaldocuments/frus1958-60v16/d94 (accessed May 24, 2022).

61. "Telegram from the Embassy in Cambodia to the Department of State," February 16, 1959, *Foreign Relations of the United States*, https://history.state.gov/ historicaldocuments/frus1958-60v16/d95 (accessed May 24, 2022).

62. Chandler, *Tragedy of Cambodian History*, 102, 107.

63. "Telegram from the Department of State to the Embassy in Vietnam," February 23, 1959, *Foreign Relations of the United States*, https://history.state.gov/histor icaldocuments/frus1958-60v16/d101 (accessed May 24, 2022).

64. "Paper Prepared by the Operations Coordinating Board," April 10, 1957, *Foreign Relations of the United States*, https://history.state.gov/historicaldocuments/ frus1955-57v21/d254 (accessed May 24, 2022).

65. "Memorandum from Robert McClintock of the Policy Planning Staff to the Assistant Secretary of State for Policy Planning (Bowie)," May 21, 1957, *Foreign Relations of the United States*, https://history.state.gov/historicaldocuments/frus1955 -57v21/d255 (accessed May 24, 2022).

66. "Memorandum of Discussion at the 436th Meeting of the National Security Council," March 10, 1960, *Foreign Relations of the United States*, https://history.state .gov/historicaldocuments/frus1958-60v16/d57 (accessed May 24, 2022).

67. "Memorandum of Discussion at the 452d Meeting of the National Security Council," July 21, 1960, *Foreign Relations of the United States*, https://history.state .gov/historicaldocuments/frus1958-60v16/d64 (accessed May 24, 2022).

68. "National Security Council Report," July 25, 1960, *Foreign Relations of the United States*, https://history.state.gov/historicaldocuments/frus1958-60v16/d65 (accessed May 24, 2022).

69. Ben Kiernan, "Conflict in the Kampuchean Communist Movement," *Journal of Contemporary Asia* 10, nos. 1–2 (1980): 7–74; Ben Kiernan, "Origins of Khmer Communism," *Southeast Asian Affairs* (1981): 161–80; Matthew Edwards, "The Rise of the Khmer Rouge in Cambodia: Internal or External Origins?," *Asian Affairs* 35, no. 1 (2004): 56–67; and Steve Heder, *Cambodian Communism and the Vietnamese Model: Imitation and Independence, 1930–1975* (Bangkok: White Lotus Press, 2004).

70. David Chandler, "From 'Cambodge' to 'Kampuchea': State and Revolution in Cambodia 1863–1979," *Thesis Eleven* 50, no. 1 (August 1997), 35–49; at 39.

71. Manning, *Transitional Justice*, 42.

72. Becker, *When the War Was Over*, 71.

Notes to Chapter 3 / 299

73. Chandler, "From 'Cambodge,'" 39.

74. Kiernan, "Origins of Khmer Communism," 174–75.

75. Scott Ross, "'The Masters of the Khmer Rouge': Cambodia between China and Vietnam, 1954–1975" (PhD diss., University of Missouri, 2008); see also Gareth Porter, "Vietnamese Communist Policy toward Kampuchea, 1930–1970," in *Revolution and Its Aftermath in Kampuchea: Eight Essays,* edited by David Chandler and Ben Kiernan (New Haven, Conn.: Yale University Southeast Asia Studies, 1983), 57–98; at 69–70.

76. Heder, *Cambodian Communism,* 17–18; Porter, "Vietnamese Communist Policy," 73.

77. Steve Heder, *Cambodian Communism and the Vietnamese Model: Imitation and Independence, 1930–1975* (Bangkok: White Lotus Press, 2004). For alternative readings, see Serge Thion, "The Cambodian Idea of Revolution," in *Revolution and Its Aftermath in Kampuchea: Eight Essays,* ed. David P. Chandler and Ben Kiernan (New Haven, Conn.: Yale University Southeast Asia Studies, 1983), 10–33; Craig Etcheson, *The Rise and Demise of Democratic Kampuchea* (Boulder, Colo.: Westview Press, 1984); Ben Kiernan, *How Pol Pot Came to Power: A History of Communism in Kampuchea, 1930–1975* (London: Verso, 1985); and Karl Jackson, "The Ideology of Total Revolution," in *Cambodia 1975–1978: Rendezvous with Death,* ed. Karl D. Jackson (Princeton, N.J.: Princeton University Press, 1989), 37–78.

78. Stephen Heder, "Kampuchea's Armed Struggle: The Origins of an Independent Revolution," *Bulletin of Concerned Asian Scholars* 11, no. 1 (1979): 2–23; Ben Kiernan, "Pol Pot and the Kampuchean Communist Movement," in *Peasant Politics in Kampuchea, 1942–1981,* edited by Ben Kiernan and Chanthou Boua (Armonk, N.Y.: M. E. Sharpe, 1982), 227–317.

79. "Letter from the Ambassador to Cambodia (Trimble) to the Deputy Under Secretary of State for Political Affairs (Johnson)," March 5, 1962, *Foreign Relations of the United States,* https://history.state.gov/historicaldocuments/frus1961-63v23/d83 (accessed May 24, 2022).

80. May Ebihara, "Perspectives on Sociopolitical Transformations in Cambodia/Kampuchea—A Review Article," *Journal of Asian Studies* 41, no. 1 (1981): 63–71; at 66.

81. Philip Short, *Pol Pot: Anatomy of a Nightmare* (New York: Macmillan, 2005), 137; see also Ross, "'The Masters of the Khmer Rouge,'" 46.

82. Short, *Pol Pot,* 141.

83. "Paper Prepared in the Department of State," September 22, 1961, *Foreign Relations of the United States,* https://history.state.gov/historicaldocuments/frus1961-63v23/d72 (accessed May 24, 2022).

84. "Telegram from the Embassy in Cambodia to the Department of State," June 1, 1961, *Foreign Relations of the United States,* https://history.state.gov/historicaldocuments/frus1961-63v23/d70 (accessed May 24, 2022).

300 / Notes to Chapter 3

85. "Telegram from the Chief, Military Assistance Advisory Group, Cambodia (Scherrer) to the Commander in Chief, Pacific (Felt)," November 15, 1961, *Foreign Relations of the United States*, https://history.state.gov/historicaldocuments/frus1961-63v23/d80 (accessed May 24, 2022).

86. "Memorandum from the President's Deputy Special Assistant for National Security Affairs (Rostow) to President Kennedy," September 23, 1961, *Foreign Relations of the United States*, https://history.state.gov/historicaldocuments/frus1961-63v23/d73 (accessed May 24, 2022).

87. "Memorandum from the Secretary of Defense's Assistant for Special Operations (Lansdale) to the Director for Intelligence, Joint Staff (Collins)," November 29, 1961, *Foreign Relations of the United States*, https://history.state.gov/historicaldocuments/frus1961-63v23/d81 (accessed May 24, 2022).

88. "Memorandum from Robert H. Johnson of the National Security Staff to the President's Special Assistant for National Security Affairs (Bundy)," October 31, 1961, *Foreign Relations of the United States*, https://history.state.gov/historicaldocuments/frus1961-63v23/d76 (accessed May 24, 2022).

89. "Memorandum from Robert H. Johnson of the National Security Council Staff to the President's Special Assistant for National Security Affairs (Bundy)," November 2, 1961, *Foreign Relations of the United States*, https://history.state.gov/historicaldocuments/frus1961-63v23/d77 (accessed May 24, 2022).

90. "Letter from the Ambassador to Cambodia (Trimble) to the Deputy Under Secretary of State for Political Affairs (Johnson)," March 5, 1962, *Foreign Relations of the United States*, https://history.state.gov/historicaldocuments/frus1961-63v23/d83 (accessed May 24, 2022).

91. Donald M. Seekins, "Historical Setting," in *Cambodia: A Country Study*, edited by R. R. Ross (Washington, D.C.: U.S. Government Printing Office, 1990), 3–71; at 32–34.

92. Hood and Ablin, "The Path to Cambodia's Present," xxi.

93. Craig Etcheson, "Civil War and the Coalition Government of Democratic Kampuchea," *Third World Quarterly* 9, no. 1 (1987): 187–202; at 192; Chandler, *A History of Cambodia*, 197; see also Robert L. Turkoly-Joczik, "Cambodia's Khmer Serei Movement," *Asian Affairs: An American Review* 15, no. 1 (1988): 48–62.

94. Thomas A. Bruscino Jr., *Out of Bounds: Transnational Sanctuary in Irregular Warfare* (Fort Leavenworth: Combat Studies Institute Press, 2006), 22–23.

95. "Telegram from the Department of State to the Embassy in the United States," November 13, 1963, *Foreign Relations of the United States*, https://history.state.gov/historicaldocuments/frus1961-63v23/d112 (accessed December 14, 2021). See also "Telegram from the Embassy in Cambodia to the Department of State," October 12, 1963, *Foreign Relations of the United States*, https://history.state.gov/historicaldocuments/frus1961-63v23/d108; "Telegram from the Embassy in Cambodia to the Department of State," October 21, 1963, *Foreign Relations of the United States*,

https://history.state.gov/historicaldocuments/frus1961-63v23/d109; "Memorandum from Michael V. Forrestal of the National Security Council Staff to the President's Special Assistant for National Security Affairs (Bundy)," October 28, 1963, *Foreign Relations of the United States,* https://history.state.gov/historicaldocuments/frus1961-63v23/d110 (accessed December 14, 2021).

96. "Telegram from the Department of State to the Embassy in Vietnam," November 16, 1963, *Foreign Relations of the United States,* https://history.state.gov/historicaldocuments/frus1961-63v23/d115 (accessed December 14, 2021).

97. "Telegram from the Department of State to the Embassy in Cambodia," November 16, 1963, *Foreign Relations of the United States,* https://history.state.gov/historicaldocuments/frus1961-63v23/d114 (accessed December 14, 2021).

98. Clymer, *Troubled Relations,* 59.

99. "Telegram from the Department of State to the Embassy in Cambodia," November 20, 1963, *Foreign Relations of the United States,* https://history.state.gov/historicaldocuments/frus1961-63v23/d117 (accessed December 14, 2021).

100. "President's Daily Brief," April 16, 1964, *Central Intelligence Agency,* https://www.cia.gov/readingroom/docs/DOC_0005959096.pdf (accessed December 14, 2021).

101. Clymer, *Troubled Relations,* 61.

102. Clymer, *Troubled Relations,* 59.

103. "Memorandum of Telephone Conversation Between the Under Secretary of State for Political Affairs (Harriman) and the Assistant Secretary of State for Far Eastern Affairs (Hilsman)," November 21, 1963, *Foreign Relations of the United States,* https://history.state.gov/historicaldocuments/frus1961-63v23/d118 (accessed May 25, 2022).

104. "Situation Report Prepared in the Department of State for President Johnson," November 23, 1963, *Foreign Relations of the United States,* https://history.state.gov/historicaldocuments/frus1961-63v04/d325 (accessed May 25, 2022).

105. "Memorandum from President Johnson to the Chairman of the Joint Chiefs of Staff (Taylor)," December 2, 1963, *Foreign Relations of the United States,* https://history.state.gov/historicaldocuments/frus1961-63v04/d337 (accessed May 25, 2022).

4. Aterritorial Wars

1. Simon Dalby, "American Security Discourse: The Persistence of Geopolitics," *Political Geography Quarterly* 9, no. 2 (1990): 171–188; at 173. See also John Lewis Gaddis, *Strategies of Containment: A Critical Appraisal of Postwar American National Security Policy* (Oxford: Oxford University Press, 1982).

2. Dalby, "American Security Discourse," 177.

3. "Memorandum from the Joint Chiefs of Staff to Secretary of Defense McNamara," October 14, 1966, *Foreign Relations of the United States,* https://history.state.gov/historicaldocuments/frus1964-68v04/d269 (September 7, 2021).

302 / Notes to Chapter 4

4. "Memorandum from the President's Special Assistant (Rostow) to President Johnson," December 5, 1967, *Foreign Relations of the United States,* https://history.state.gov/historicaldocuments/frus1964-68v27/d215 (accessed July 1, 2022).

5. "Memorandum from the Joint Chiefs of Staff to Secretary of Defense McNamara," November 12, 1965, *Foreign Relations of the United States,* https://history.state.gov/historicaldocuments/frus1964-68v27/d159 (accessed December 13, 2021).

6. "Memorandum from the Joint Chiefs of Staff to Secretary of Defense McNamara," November 12, 1965, *Foreign Relations of the United States,* https://history.state.gov/historicaldocuments/frus1964-68v27/d159 (accessed December 13, 2021).

7. "Telephone Conversation Between President Johnson and Secretary of Defense McNamara," November 20, 1965, *Foreign Relations of the United States,* https://history.state.gov/historicaldocuments/frus1964-68v27/d160 (accessed July 7, 2022).

8. "Telegram from the Department of State to the Embassy in Vietnam," November 20, 1965, *Foreign Relations of the United States,* https://history.state.gov/historicaldocuments/frus1964-68v27/d161 (accessed December 13, 2021).

9. "Telegram from the Department of State to the Embassy in Vietnam," November 20, 1965, *Foreign Relations of the United States,* https://history.state.gov/historicaldocuments/frus1964-68v27/d161 (accessed December 13, 2021).

10. "Note from the Assistant Secretary of State for Far Eastern Affairs (Bundy) to the Permanent Representatives at the United Nations (Goldberg)," November 21, 1965, *Foreign Relations of the United States,* https://history.state.gov/historicaldocuments/frus1964-68v27/d162 (accessed December 13, 2021).

11. "Intelligence Memorandum," December 1, 1965, *Foreign Relations of the United States,* https://history.state.gov/historicaldocuments/frus1964-68v27/d163 (accessed December 13, 2021).

12. "Telephone Conversation between President Johnson and the President's Special Assistant for National Security Affairs (Bundy)," April 30, 1965, *Foreign Relations of the United States,* https://history.state.gov/historicaldocuments/frus1964-68v27/d155 (accessed December 13, 2021).

13. "Memorandum from the President's Special Assistant for National Security Affairs (Bundy) to President Johnson," May 3, 1965, *Foreign Relations of the United States,* https://history.state.gov/historicaldocuments/frus1964-68v27/d156 (accessed December 13, 2021).

14. "Action Memorandum from the Assistant Secretary of State for Far Eastern Affairs (Bundy) to Secretary of State Rusk," December 3, 1965, *Foreign Relations of the United States,* https://history.state.gov/historicaldocuments/frus1964-68v27/d164 (accessed December 13, 2021).

15. "Telegram from the Commander in Chief, Military Assistance Command, Vietnam (Westmoreland) to the Commander in Chief, Pacific (Sharp)," December 9,

Notes to Chapter 4 / 303

1965, *Foreign Relations of the United States,* https://history.state.gov/historicaldoc
uments/frus1964-68v27/d165 (accessed December 13, 2021).

16. "Telegram from the Department of State to the Embassy in Vietnam,"
December 11, 1965, *Foreign Relations of the United States,* https://history.state.gov/
historicaldocuments/frus1964-68v27/d166 (accessed December 13, 2021).

17. "Intelligence Memorandum: Cambodia and the Viet Cong," December 28,
1965, *Central Intelligence Agency,* https://www.cia.gov/readingroom/docs/CIA-RDP
79T00472A000800030022-4.pdf (accessed December 13, 2021).

18. "Letter from Acting Secretary of State Ball to Secretary of Defense McNamara,"
January 17, 1966, *Foreign Relations of the United States,* https://history.state.gov/
historicaldocuments/frus1964-68v27/d176 (accessed December 13, 2021).

19. Hoang Ngoc Lung, *Strategy and Tactics* (Washington, D.C.: U.S. Army
Center of Military History, 1978),

20. "Letter from Secretary of Defense McNamara to Secretary of State Rusk,"
December 29, 1965, *Foreign Relations of the United States,* https://history.state.gov/
historicaldocuments/frus1964-68v27/d171 (accessed December 13, 2021).

21. "Memorandum of Telephone Conversation between President Johnson and
Under Secretary of State Ball," December 30, 1965, *Foreign Relations of the United
States,* https://history.state.gov/historicaldocuments/frus1964-68v27/d173 (accessed
December 13, 2021).

22. "Memorandum of Conversation," January 4, 1966, *Foreign Relations of the
United States,* https://history.state.gov/historicaldocuments/frus1964-68v27/d174
(accessed December 13, 2021).

23. "Memorandum from Secretary of Defense McNamara to President Johnson," January 24, 1966, *Foreign Relations of the United States,* https://history.state
.gov/historicaldocuments/frus1964-68v04/d36 (accessed September 7, 2021).

24. Clymer, *Troubled Relations,* 77.

25. "Memorandum from the Assistant Secretary of State for East Asian Affairs
(Bundy) to the President's Special Assistant (Rostow)," April 2, 1966, *Foreign Relations of the United States,* https://history.state.gov/historicaldocuments/frus1964-68
v27/d180 (accessed December 14, 2021).

26. See for example "Memorandum from the President's Special Assistant (Rostow) to Secretary of State Rusk," June 21, 1966, *Foreign Relations of the United States,*
https://history.state.gov/historicaldocuments/frus1964-68v27/d183; and "Note from
the President's Special Assistant (Rostow) to President Johnson," June 25, 1966,
Foreign Relations of the United States, https://history.state.gov/historicaldocuments/
frus1964-68v27/d184 (accessed December 14, 2021).

27. "Memorandum from the President's Special Assistant (Komer) to President
Johnson," May 28, 1966, *Foreign Relations of the United States,* https://history.state
.gov/historicaldocuments/frus1964-68v27/d182 (accessed December 14, 2021).

304 / Notes to Chapter 4

28. Frank L. Jones, *Buying Time, 1965–1966* (Washington, D.C.: U.S. Army, Center of Military History, 2015), 41.

29. Jones, *Buying Time,* 42–43.

30. John Prados, *The Blood Trail: The Ho Chi Minh Trail and the Vietnam War* (New York: John Wiley & Sons, 1998), 153; Willard J. Webb, *The Joint Chiefs of Staff and the War in Vietnam, 1969–1970* (Washington, DC: Office of Joint History, 2002), 135.

31. "Information Memorandum from the Director of the Office of Southeast Asian Affairs (Trueheart) to the Assistant Secretary of State for East Asian Affairs (Bundy)," April 18, 1966, *Foreign Relations of the United States,* https://history.state.gov/historicaldocuments/frus1964-68v27/d181 (accessed December 14, 2021).

32. "Cambodia and the Vietnamese Communists: A New Phase?," June 13, 1966, *Central Intelligence Agency,* https://www.cia.gov/readingroom/docs/CIA-RDP79T 00826A000800400001-3.pdf (accessed December 14, 2021).

33. "Memorandum from the President's Special Assistant (Rostow) to Secretary of State Rusk," June 21, 1966, *Foreign Relations of the United States,* https://history.state.gov/historicaldocuments/frus1964-68v27/d183 (accessed December 14, 2021).

34. "Memorandum from Acting Secretary of State Ball to President Johnson," June 29, 1966, *Foreign Relations of the United States,* https://history.state.gov/historicaldocuments/frus1964-68v27/d185 (accessed December 14, 2021).

35. Quoted in Clymer, *Troubled Relations,* 65.

36. "Memorandum from the Joint Chiefs of Staff to Secretary of Defense McNamara," September 24, 1966, *Foreign Relations of the United States,* https://history.state.gov/historicaldocuments/frus1964-68v27/d192 (accessed December 14, 2021).

37. "Telegram from the Commander in Chief, Military Assistance Command, Vietnam (Westmoreland) to the Commander in Chief, Pacific (Sharp)," October 2, 1966, *Foreign Relations of the United States,* https://history.state.gov/historicaldocuments/frus1964-68v27/d194 (accessed December 14, 2021).

38. "Memorandum from the Joint Chiefs of Staff to Secretary of Defense McNamara," December 19, 1966, *Foreign Relations of the United States,* https://history.state.gov/historicaldocuments/frus1964-68v27/d198 (accessed December 14, 2021).

39. "Memorandum from the Joint Chiefs of Staff to Secretary of Defense McNamara," December 19, 1966, *Foreign Relations of the United States,* https://history.state.gov/historicaldocuments/frus1964-68v27/d198 (accessed December 14, 2021).

40. "Special National Intelligence Estimate," January 26, 1967, *Foreign Relations of the United States,* https://history.state.gov/historicaldocuments/frus1964-68v27/d199 (accessed December 15, 2021).

Notes to Chapter 4 / 305

41. "Memorandum from the Deputy Director of Intelligence and Research (Denny) to Secretary of State Rusk," undated, *Foreign Relations of the United States,* https://history.state.gov/historicaldocuments/frus1964-68v27/d200 (accessed December 15, 2021).

42. "Action Memorandum from the Chairman of the Cambodian Study Group (Unger) to the Under Secretary of State (Katzenbach)," May 1, 1967, *Foreign Relations of the United States,* https://history.state.gov/historicaldocuments/frus1964-68 v27/d205 (accessed December 15, 2021).

43. "Action Memorandum from the Chairman of the Cambodian Study Group (Unger) to the Under Secretary of State (Katzenbach)," May 1, 1967, *Foreign Relations of the United States,* https://history.state.gov/historicaldocuments/frus1964-68 v27/d205 (accessed December 15, 2021).

44. This statement alone is notable, in that the military operations desired by MACV were not to punish Phnom Penh for failure to stop the use of Cambodian territory by foreign elements; in fact, MACV gave little thought to the Cambodian government.

45. "Memorandum from the Assistant Legal Advisor (Aldrich) to the Assistant Secretary of State for East Asian and Pacific Affairs (Bundy)," September 11, 1967, *Foreign Relations of the United States,* https://history.state.gov/historicaldocuments/ frus1964-68v27/d208 (accessed December 15, 2021).

46. "Memorandum from the Assistant Legal Advisor (Aldrich) to the Assistant Secretary of State for East Asian and Pacific Affairs (Bundy)," September 11, 1967, *Foreign Relations of the United States,* https://history.state.gov/historicaldocuments/ frus1964-68v27/d208 (accessed December 15, 2021).

47. "Memorandum from the Assistant Legal Advisor (Aldrich) to the Assistant Secretary of State for East Asian and Pacific Affairs (Bundy)," September 11, 1967, *Foreign Relations of the United States,* https://history.state.gov/historicaldocuments/ frus1964-68v27/d208 (accessed December 15, 2021).

48. "Action Memorandum from the Deputy Assistant Secretary of State for East Asian Affairs (Habib) to the Under Secretary of State (Katzenbach)," September 14, 1967, *Foreign Relations of the United States,* https://history.state.gov/historicaldoc uments/frus1964-68v27/d209; "Action Memorandum from the Deputy Assistant Secretary of State for East Asian Affairs (Habib) to the Under Secretary of State (Katzenbach)," September 14, 1967, *Foreign Relations of the United States,* https:// history.state.gov/historicaldocuments/frus1964-68v27/d210; "Memorandum from the Assistant Secretary of Defense for International Security Affairs (Warnke) to Secretary of Defense McNamara," October 5, 1967, *Foreign Relations of the United States,* https://history.state.gov/historicaldocuments/frus1964-68v27/d211; "Telegram from the Commander in Chief, Military Assistance Command, Vietnam (Westmoreland) to the Joint Chiefs of Staff," December 5, 1967, *Foreign Relations of the*

306 / Notes to Chapter 4

United States, https://history.state.gov/historicaldocuments/frus1964-68v27/d213 (accessed December 15, 2021).

49. "Telegram from the Commander in Chief, Military Assistance Command, Vietnam (Westmoreland) to the Joint Chiefs of Staff," December 5, 1967, *Foreign Relations of the United States,* https://history.state.gov/historicaldocuments/frus19 64-68v27/d213 (accessed December 15, 2021).

50. "Notes of Meeting," December 5, 1967, *Foreign Relations of the United States,* https://history.state.gov/historicaldocuments/frus1964-68v27/d216 (accessed December 15, 2021).

51. "Notes of Meeting," December 5, 1967, *Foreign Relations of the United States,* https://history.state.gov/historicaldocuments/frus1964-68v27/d216 (accessed December 15, 2021).

52. Quoted in David M. Barrett, *Uncertain Warriors: Lyndon Johnson and His Vietnam Advisors* (Lawrence: University Press of Kansas, 1993), 78.

53. "Notes of Meeting," December 5, 1967, *Foreign Relations of the United States,* https://history.state.gov/historicaldocuments/frus1964-68v27/d216 (accessed December 15, 2021).

54. "Notes of Meeting," December 5, 1967, *Foreign Relations of the United States,* https://history.state.gov/historicaldocuments/frus1964-68v27/d216 (accessed December 15, 2021).

55. "Notes of a Meeting," December 5, 1967, *Foreign Relations of the United States,* https://history.state.gov/historicaldocuments/frus1964-68v27/d214 (accessed December 15, 2021).

56. "Memorandum from the President's Special Assistant (Rostow) to President Johnson," December 5, 1967, *Foreign Relations of the United States,* https://history .state.gov/historicaldocuments/frus1964-68v27/d215; "Telegram from the President's Special Assistant (Rostow) to President Johnson in Texas," December 27, 1967, *Foreign Relations of the United States,* https://history.state.gov/historicaldocuments/ frus1964-68v27/d223; "Telegram from the President's Special Assistant (Rostow) to President Johnson in Texas," December 29, 1967, *Foreign Relations of the United States,* https://history.state.gov/historicaldocuments/frus1964-68v27/d225; and "Telegram from the President's Special Assistant (Rostow) to President Johnson in Texas," January 3, 1968, *Foreign Relations of the United States,* https://history.state.gov/his toricaldocuments/frus1964-68v27/d226 (accessed December 15, 2021).

57. "Telegram from the President's Special Assistant (Rostow) to President Johnson in Texas," January 3, 1968, *Foreign Relations of the United States,* https://history .state.gov/historicaldocuments/frus1964-68v27/d226 (accessed December 15, 2021).

58. Cosmas, *MACV: The Joint Command in the Years of Escalation,* 446–47.

59. "Draft Memorandum from Secretary of Defense McNamara to President Johnson," November 1, 1967, *Foreign Relations of the United States,* https://history .state.gov/historicaldocuments/frus1964-68v05/d375 (accessed December 15, 2021).

Notes to Chapter 4 / 307

60. Cosmas, *MACV: The Joint Command in the Years of Escalation,* 462–63.

61. Cosmas, *MACV: The Joint Command in the Years of Escalation,* 466.

62. Pierre Asselin, *Vietnam's American War: A History* (Cambridge: Cambridge University Press, 2018), 152–54.

63. Adrian G. Traas, *Turning Point, 1967–1968* (Washington, D.C.: Center of Military History, United States Army, 2017), 11.

64. Traas, *Turning Point,* 19–21.

65. Traas, *Turning Point,* 48; see also Graham A. Cosmas, *MACV: The Joint Command in the Years of Withdrawal, 1968–1973* (Washington, D.C.: Center of Military History, U.S. Army, 2006), 29–48.

66. Daddis, *Westmoreland's War,* 141.

67. Cosmas, *MACV: The Joint Command in the Years of Withdrawal,* 88–89.

68. "Telegram from the Commander, Military Assistance Command, Vietnam (Westmoreland) to the Commander in Chief, Pacific Command (Sharp) and the Chairman of the Joint Chiefs of Staff (Wheeler)," February 12, 1968, *Foreign Relations of the United States,* https://history.state.gov/historicaldocuments/frus1964-68 vo6/d68 (accessed December 17, 2021).

69. "Notes of a Meeting," February 12, 1968, *Foreign Relations of the United States,* https://history.state.gov/historicaldocuments/frus1964-68vo6/d70 (accessed December 17, 2021).

70. "Report by the Joint Chiefs of Staff," March 1, 1968, *Foreign Relations of the United States,* https://history.state.gov/historicaldocuments/frus1964-68vo6/d96 (accessed December 17, 2021).

71. Cosmas, *MACV: The Joint Command in the Years of Withdrawal,* 93–97.

72. "Notes of Meeting," March 4, 1968, *Foreign Policy of the United States,* https://history.state.gov/historicaldocuments/frus1964-68vo6/d104 (accessed December 17, 2021).

73. Cosmas, *MACV: The Joint Command in the Years of Withdrawal,* 100.

74. Air operations over North Vietnam—Operation Rolling Thunder—were halted on November 1, 1968. Thereafter, under the Johnson administration, aerial missions over the North were limited to unarmed reconnaissance flights, although MACV had the authority to send fighter escorts into North Vietnamese airspace if the enemy fired on the reconnaissance plans.

75. Traas, *Turning Point,* 73.

76. Cosmas, *MACV: The Joint Command in the Years of Withdrawal,* 129.

77. "Notes of Meeting," March 4, 1968, *Foreign Policy of the United States,* https://history.state.gov/historicaldocuments/frus1964-68vo6/d104 (accessed December 17, 2021).

78. "Memorandum from Secretary of Defense Clifford to President Johnson," July 18, 1968, *Foreign Relations of the United States,* https://history.state.gov/histori caldocuments/frus1964-68vo6/d302 (accessed December 17, 2021).

308 / Notes to Chapter 4

79. Westmoreland notably remained steadfast. Just weeks before his swearing in as Army Chief of Staff, Westmoreland proposed the use of B-52s, tactical air assaults, and artillery strikes against infiltration routes and known sanctuaries in Cambodia. See "Action Memorandum from the Assistant Secretary of State for Far Eastern Affairs (Bundy) to Secretary of State Rusk," May 27, 1968, *Foreign Relations of the United States,* https://history.state.gov/historicaldocuments/frus1964-68v27/d234 (accessed December 17, 2021); and "Memorandum from the President's Special Assistant (Rostow) to President Johnson," May 28, 1968, *Foreign Relations of the United States,* https://history.state.gov/historicaldocuments/frus1964-68v27/d235 (accessed December 17, 2021).

80. See, for example, "Note from President's Special Assistant (Rostow) to President Johnson," March 19, 1968, *Foreign Relations of the United States,* https://history.state.gov/historicaldocuments/frus1964-68v27/d232 (accessed December 17, 2021).

81. Cosmas, *MACV: The Joint Command in the Years of Withdrawal,* 29.

82. "Memorandum from the Deputy Director for Intelligence of the Central Agency (Smith) to the President's Special Assistant (Rostow)," April 22, 1968, *Foreign Relations of the United States,* https://history.state.gov/historicaldocuments/frus1964-68v27/d233 (accessed December 17, 2021).

83. Cosmas, *MACV: The Joint Command in the Years of Withdrawal,* 129.

84. "Information Memorandum from the Deputy Assistant Secretary of State for East Asian and Pacific Affairs (Brown) to Secretary of State Rusk," July 29, 1968, *Foreign Relations of the United States,* https://history.state.gov/historicaldocuments/frus1964-68v27/d241; "Memorandum of Meeting with President Johnson," July 30, 1968, *Foreign Relations of the United States,* https://history.state.gov/historicaldocuments/frus1964-68v27/d242 (accessed December 17, 2021); and "Memorandum from the President's Special Assistant (Rostow) to President Johnson," September 16, 1968, *Foreign Relations of the United States,* https://history.state.gov/historicaldocuments/frus1964-68v27/d248 (accessed December 17, 2021).

5. A Widening War

1. For more on Nixon and Vietnam, see Jeffrey Kimball, *Nixon's Vietnam War* (Lawrence: University Press of Kansas, 1998); Larry Berman, *No Peace, No Honor: Nixon, Kissinger, and Betrayal in Vietnam* (New York: Touchstone, 2002); and David F. Schmitz, *Richard Nixon and the Vietnam War* (Lanham, Md.: Rowman & Littlefield, 2014).

2. "Editorial Note," *Foreign Relations of the United States,* https://history.state.gov/historicaldocuments/frus1969-76v06/d5 (accessed December 18, 2021). For an incisive exploration of Kissinger's geopolitics, see Gerard Toal, "Problematizing Geopolitics: Survey, Statesmanship and Strategy," *Transactions of the Institute of British Geographers* 19, no. 3 (1994): 259–72.

Notes to Chapter 5 / 309

3. "National Security Study Memorandum 1," January 21, 1969, *Foreign Relations of the United States,* https://history.state.gov/historicaldocuments/frus1969-76 v06/d4 (accessed December 18, 2021).

4. "Special National Intelligence Estimate," January 16, 1969, *Foreign Relations of the United States,* https://history.state.gov/historicaldocuments/frus1969-76v06/d1; and "Memorandum Prepared in the Central Intelligence Agency," January 24, 1969, *Foreign Relations of the United States,* https://history.state.gov/historicaldocuments/frus1969-76v06/d6 (accessed December 18, 2021).

5. "Minutes of National Security Council Meeting," January 25, 1969, *Foreign Relations of the United States,* https://history.state.gov/historicaldocuments/frus1969-76v06/d10 (accessed December 18, 2021).

6. "Minutes of National Security Council Meeting," January 25, 1969, *Foreign Relations of the United States,* https://history.state.gov/historicaldocuments/frus1969-76v06/d10 (accessed December 18, 2021).

7. "Minutes of National Security Council Meeting," January 25, 1969, *Foreign Relations of the United States,* https://history.state.gov/historicaldocuments/frus1969-76v06/d10 (accessed December 18, 2021).

8. Graham A. Cosmas, *MACV: The Joint Command in the Years of Withdrawal, 1968–1973* (Washington, D.C.: Center of Military History, United States Army, 2006), 281.

9. See Arnold R. Isaacs, *Without Honor: Defeat in Vietnam and Cambodia* (Baltimore: Johns Hopkins University Press, 1983); Jeffrey Trimball, *Nixon's Vietnam War* (Lawrence: University Press of Kansas, 1998); and William Shawcross, *Sideshow: Kissinger, Nixon, and the Destruction of Cambodia,* rev. ed. (New York: Cooper Square Press, 2002).

10. Johannes Kadura, *The War after the War: The Struggle for Credibility during America's Exit from Vietnam* (Ithaca, N.Y.: Cornell University Press, 2016).

11. Much of the planning for Vietnam was conducted by a select group of advisors known as the Washington Special Actions Group (WSAG).

12. Cosmas, *MACV: The Joint Command in the Years of Withdrawal,* 143.

13. "Memorandum from the President's Assistant for National Security Affairs (Kissinger) to President Nixon," September 18, 1971, *Foreign Relations of the United States,* https://history.state.gov/historicaldocuments/frus1969-76v07/d257 (accessed December 18, 2021).

14. Cosmas, *MACV: The Joint Command in the Years of Withdrawal,* 143. See also Pierre Asselin, *A Bitter Peace: Washington, Hanoi, and the Making of the Paris Agreement* (Chapel Hill: University of North Carolina Press, 2003).

15. Thomas C. Schelling, *Arms and Influence* (New Haven, Conn.: Yale University Press, 2020 [1966]), xviii.

16. Schelling, *Arms and Influence,* 2.

17. Schelling, *Arms and Influence,* 72.

310 / Notes to Chapter 5

18. Scott S. Gartner, "Differing Evaluations of Vietnamization," *Journal of Interdisciplinary History* 24, no. 2 (1998): 243–62; Karlyn K. Campbell, *The Great Silent Majority: Nixon's 1969 Speech on Vietnamization* (College Station: Texas A&M University Press, 2014); David L. Prentice, "Choosing 'the Long Road': Henry Kissinger, Melvin Laird, Vietnamization, and the War over Nixon's Vietnam Strategy," *Diplomatic History* 40, no. 3 (2016): 445–74.

19. Spencer C. Tucker, *Vietnam* (Lexington: University Press of Kentucky, 1999), 157.

20. "Memorandum from Secretary of Defense Laird to President Nixon," March 13, 1969, *Foreign Relations of the United States,* https://history.state.gov/historicaldocuments/frus1969-76v06/d38 (accessed December 18, 2021).

21. "Memorandum from Secretary of Defense Laird to President Nixon," March 13, 1969, *Foreign Relations of the United States,* https://history.state.gov/historicaldocuments/frus1969-76v06/d38 (accessed December 18, 2021).

22. "Minutes of National Security Council Meeting," March 28, 1969, *Foreign Relations of the United States,* https://history.state.gov/historicaldocuments/frus1969-76v06/d49 (accessed December 18, 2021).

23. "Address to the Nation on Vietnam—May 14, 1969," *Nixon Foundation,* https://www.nixonfoundation.org/2017/09/address-nation-vietnam-may-14-1969/ (accessed December 18, 2021).

24. Berman, *No Peace, No Honor,* 50.

25. Jeffrey Kimball, "The Nixon Doctrine: A Sage of Misunderstanding," *Presidential Studies Quarterly* 36, no. 1 (2006): 59–74; at 65.

26. Richard M. Nixon, "Informal Remarks in Guam with Newsmen," July 25, 1969, *The American Presidency Project,* https://www.presidency.ucsb.edu/documents/informal-remarks-guam-with-newsmen (accessed July 8, 2022).

27. Cosmas, *MACV: The Joint Command in the Years of Withdrawal,* 145.

28. Willard J. Webb, *The Joint Chiefs of Staff and the War in Vietnam, 1969–1970* (Washington, D.C.: Office of Joint History, 2002), 131.

29. "Letter from the Deputy Secretary of Defense (Nitze) to the Under Secretary of State (Katzenbach)," October 1, 1968, *Foreign Relations of the United States,* https://history.state.gov/historicaldocuments/frus1964-68v27/d250 (accessed December 17, 2021).

30. "Memorandum from Marshall Wright of the National Security Council Staff to the President's Special Assistant (Rostow)," October 15, 1968, *Foreign Relations of the United States,* https://history.state.gov/historicaldocuments/frus1964-68v27/d252 (accessed December 17, 2021).

31. "Telegram from the Chairman of the Joint Chiefs of Staff (Wheeler) to the Commander in Chief, Pacific (McCain)," November 7, 1968, *Foreign Relations of the United States,* https://history.state.gov/historicaldocuments/frus1964-68v27/d254 (accessed December 17, 2021).

Notes to Chapter 5 / 311

32. "Telegram from the Commander in Chief, Pacific (McCain) to the Chairman of the Joint Chiefs of Staff (Wheeler)," December 18, 1968, *Foreign Relations of the United States,* https://history.state.gov/historicaldocuments/frus1964-68v27/d261 (accessed December 17, 2021).

33. "Telegram from the Commander in Chief, Pacific (McCain) to the Chairman of the Joint Chiefs of Staff (Wheeler)," December 29, 1968, *Foreign Relations of the United States,* https://history.state.gov/historicaldocuments/frus1964-68v27/d263 (accessed December 17, 2021).

34. "Telegram from the Commander in Chief, Pacific (McCain) to the Chairman of the Joint Chiefs of Staff (Wheeler)," December 18, 1968, *Foreign Relations of the United States,* https://history.state.gov/historicaldocuments/frus1964-68v27/d261 (accessed December 17, 2021).

35. "Memorandum of Meeting between the President's Assistant for National Security Affairs (Kissinger), Secretary of Defense Laird, and the Chairman of the Joint Chiefs of Staff (Wheeler)," January 30, 1969, *Foreign Relations of the United States,* https://history.state.gov/historicaldocuments/frus1969-76v06/d12 (accessed December 20, 2021).

36. "Memorandum from Secretary of State Rogers to President Nixon," February 5, 1969, *Foreign Relations of the United States,* https://history.state.gov/historical documents/frus1969-76v06/d18 (accessed December 20, 2021).

37. Arc Light was the code name for aerial bombing campaigns of B-52 Stratofortresses. Between June 18, 1965, and August 18, 1973, U.S. officials approved 126,663 combat sorties for B-52s, of which 126,615 were launched; these missions expended more than 3.5 million tons of conventional ordnance. Approximately 12 percent of Arc Light operations were conducted over Cambodian territory. See Robert D. Launius, "Arc Light Operations," in *Dictionary of the Vietnam War,* edited by James Olson (New York: Peter Bedrick, 1987), 23–24.

38. Cosmas, *MACV: The Joint Command in the Years of Withdrawal,* 284.

39. "Memorandum from the President's Assistant for National Security Affairs (Kissinger) to President Nixon," February 19, 1969, *Foreign Relations of the United States,* https://history.state.gov/historicaldocuments/frus1969-76v06/d22 (accessed December 20, 2021).

40. Cosmas, *MACV: The Joint Command in the Years of Withdrawal,* 285.

41. "Memorandum from the President's Assistant for National Security Affairs (Kissinger) to President Nixon," February 19, 1969, *Foreign Relations of the United States,* https://history.state.gov/historicaldocuments/frus1969-76v06/d22 (accessed December 20, 2021).

42. "Memorandum from the President's Assistant for National Security Affairs (Kissinger) to President Nixon," February 19, 1969, *Foreign Relations of the United States,* https://history.state.gov/historicaldocuments/frus1969-76v06/d22 (accessed

312 / Notes to Chapter 5

December 20, 2021). See also Cosmas, *MACV: The Joint Command in the Years of Withdrawal,* 286.

43. "Memorandum from the President's Assistant for National Security Affairs (Kissinger) to Secretary of Defense Laird," February 22, 1969, *Foreign Relations of the United States,* https://history.state.gov/historicaldocuments/frus1969-76v06/d23 (accessed December 20, 2021).

44. Robert D. Sanders, *Invasion of Laos, 1971: Lam Son 719* (Norman: University of Oklahoma Press, 2014), 55.

45. "Message from Secretary of Defense Laird to President Nixon," February 25, 1969, *Foreign Relations of the United States,* https://history.state.gov/historicaldocuments/frus1969-76v06/d25 (accessed December 20, 2021). Notably, although Laird disagreed with the operation, he informed Nixon that he would carry out his orders as instructed.

46. "Memorandum of Conversation," March 8, 1969, *Foreign Relations of the United States,* https://history.state.gov/historicaldocuments/frus1969-76v06/d32 (accessed December 20, 2021).

47. "Memorandum from the President's Assistant for National Security Affairs (Kissinger) to President Nixon," March 10, 1969, *Foreign Relations of the United States,* https://history.state.gov/historicaldocuments/frus1969-76v06/d35 (accessed December 20, 2021).

48. "Memorandum from the President's Assistant for National Security Affairs (Kissinger) to President Nixon," March 10, 1969, *Foreign Relations of the United States,* https://history.state.gov/historicaldocuments/frus1969-76v06/d35 (accessed December 20, 2021).

49. "Editorial Note," *Foreign Relations of the United States,* https://history.state.gov/historicaldocuments/frus1969-76v06/d33 (accessed December 20, 2021).

50. "Editorial Note," *Foreign Relations of the United States,* https://history.state.gov/historicaldocuments/frus1969-76v06/d33 (accessed December 20, 2021).

51. "Memorandum from Secretary of Defense Laird to President Nixon," March 13, 1969, *Foreign Relations of the United States,* https://history.state.gov/historicaldocuments/frus1969-76v06/d38; "Memorandum for the Record," March 15, 1969, *Foreign Relations of the United States,* https://history.state.gov/historicaldocuments/frus1969-76v06/d39 (accessed December 20, 2021).

52. "Editorial Note," *Foreign Relations of the United States,* https://history.state.gov/historicaldocuments/frus1969-76v06/d41 (accessed December 20, 2021).

53. "Editorial Note," *Foreign Relations of the United States,* https://history.state.gov/historicaldocuments/frus1969-76v06/d41 (accessed December 20, 2021).

54. "Memorandum from the President's Assistant for National Security Affairs (Kissinger) to President Nixon," March 16, 1969, *Foreign Relations of the United States,* https://history.state.gov/historicaldocuments/frus1969-76v06/d40 (accessed December 20, 2021).

Notes to Chapter 5 / 313

55. Cosmas, *MACV: The Joint Command in the Years of Withdrawal*, 287–88; Webb, *Joint Chiefs of Staff*, 136–37.

56. Sanders, *Invasion of Laos*, 57.

57. Webb, *The Joint Chiefs of Staff*, 137.

58. Berman, *No Honor, No Peace*, 51; Schmitz, *Richard Nixon*, 50. For additional details on the bombing, see Ben Kiernan, "The American Bombardment of Kampuchea, 1969–1973," *Vietnam Generation* 1, no. 1 (1989): 4–14; William Shawcross, *Sideshow: Kissinger, Nixon, and the Destruction of Cambodia*, rev. ed. (New York: Cooper Square Press, 2002); Taylor Owen and Ben Kiernan, "Bombs over Cambodia," *Walrus Magazine*, October 2006, 62–69; and Ben Kiernan and Taylor Owen, "Making More Enemies Than We Kill? Calculating U.S. Bomb Tonnages Dropped on Laos and Cambodia, and Weighing Their Implications," *Asia-Pacific Journal* 13, no. 16 (2015): 1–9. In the end, Nixon's bombing campaign would prove mostly ineffectual in achieving the hoped-for objectives. As described in an assessment provided by the CIA, "The B-52 bombing effort has been the least valuable, for several reasons. In general, there is a dearth of suitable targets in Cambodia such as massed forces and concentrated storage areas. . . . Most important, however, we simply do not have enough high-quality targeting information to provide certain or even probable targets for many of the B-52 strikes now run against Cambodian territory." See Central Intelligence Agency, "The Employment of U.S. Air Power over Cambodia Between 1 July and 15 August 1973," https://www.cia.gov/reading room/docs/CIA-RDP80T01719R000400320002-4.pdf (accessed January 9, 2021).

59. Donald M. Seekins, "Historical Setting," in *Cambodia: A Country Study*, edited by R. R. Ross (Washington, D.C.: U.S. Government Printing Office, 1990), 3–71; at 32–34.

60. Hood and Ablin, "Path to Cambodia's Present," xxii.

61. Kent Helmers, "Rice in the Cambodian Economy: Past and Present," in *Rice Production in Cambodia*, ed. H. J. Nesbitt (Manila: International Rice Research Institute, 1997), 1–14; at 4.

62. Donald Kirk, "Cambodia's Economic Crisis," *Asian Survey* 11, no. 3 (1971): 238–55; at 240.

63. Hood and Ablin, "Path to Cambodia's Present," xxii–xxiii.

64. Ben Kiernan, "The Samlaut Rebellion, 1967–1968," in *Peasants and Politics in Kampuchea, 1942–1981*, edited by Ben Kiernan and Chanthou Boua (New York: M. E. Sharpe, 1982), 166–205; at 168.

65. Helmers, "Rice in the Cambodian Economy," 5; Stian Rice, *Famine in the Remaking: Food System Change and Mass Starvation in Hawaii, Madagascar, and Cambodia* (Morgantown: West Virginia University Press, 2020), 153.

66. Chandler, *The Tragedy of Cambodian History*, 163–66; see also Ben Kiernan, "The Samlaut Rebellion, 1967–1968," in *Peasants and Politics in Kampuchea, 1942–1981*, edited by Ben Kiernan and Chanthou Boua (New York: M. E. Sharpe, 1982), 166–205.

314 / Notes to Chapter 5

67. Manning, *Transitional Justice*, 43.

68. Kiernan, "Samlaut Rebellion," 166.

69. Hood and Ablin, "Path to Cambodia's Present," xxiii.

70. Webb, *Joint Chiefs of Staff*, 141.

71. Jeffrey Kimball, *Nixon's Vietnam War* (Lawrence: University Press of Kansas, 1998), 197–98.

72. David P. Chandler, *A History of Cambodia*, 3rd ed. (Boulder, Colo.: Westview Press, 2000), 208.

73. "Memorandum of Conversation," April 4, 1970, *Foreign Relations of the United States*, https://history.state.gov/historicaldocuments/frus1969-76v42/d5 (accessed June 3, 2022).

74. Shawcross, *Sideshow*, 112.

75. "Intelligence Memorandum: Implications for Cambodia of the Move Against Sihanouk," March 19, 1970, *Central Intelligence Agency*, https://www.cia.gov/read ingroom/docs/DOC_0002909551.pdf (accessed June 1, 2022).

76. "Memorandum from the President's Assistant for National Security Affairs (Kissinger) to President Nixon," March 17, 1970, *Foreign Relations of the United States*, https://history.state.gov/historicaldocuments/frus1969-76v06/d202 (accessed December 22, 2021).

77. "Minutes of Washington Special Actions Group Meeting," March 19, 1970, *Foreign Relations of the United States*, https://history.state.gov/historicaldocuments/ frus1969-76v06/d203 (accessed December 22, 2021).

78. "Memorandum from the President's Assistant for National Security Affairs (Kissinger) to President Nixon," March 19, 1970, *Foreign Relations of the United States*, https://history.state.gov/historicaldocuments/frus1969-76v06/d205.

79. "Memorandum from the President's Assistant for National Security Affairs (Kissinger) to President Nixon," March 19, 1970, *Foreign Relations of the United States*, https://history.state.gov/historicaldocuments/frus1969-76v06/d205.

80. "Memorandum from the President's Assistant for National Security Affairs (Kissinger) to President Nixon," March 19, 1970, *Foreign Relations of the United States*, https://history.state.gov/historicaldocuments/frus1969-76v06/d205.

81. "Memorandum from the President's Assistant for National Security Affairs (Kissinger) to President Nixon," March 20, 1970, *Foreign Relations of the United States*, https://history.state.gov/historicaldocuments/frus1969-76v06/d206 (accessed December 22, 2021).

82. Isaacs, *Without Honor*, 201.

83. Isaacs, *Without Honor*, 201.

84. Donald M. Seekins, "Historical Setting," in *Cambodia: A Country Study*, edited by R. R. Ross (Washington, D.C.: U.S. Government Printing Office, 1990), 3–71; at 43–44. Khmer Rouge members of GRUNK claimed that it was not a government-in-exile because Khieu Samphan and other officials remained in Cambodia. Publicly,

Notes to Chapter 5 / 315

neither Pol Pot, Ieng Sary, nor Nuon Chea were identified as top leaders—although political and military authority was firmly in their hands.

85. Norodom Sihanouk, "The Future of Cambodia," *Foreign Affairs* 49, no. 1 (1970): 1–10; at 4–5.

86. Cosmas, *MACV: The Joint Command in the Years of Withdrawal*, 293.

87. "Vietnamese Communist Intentions in Cambodia Prior to April 28, 1970," June 12, 1970, *Central Intelligence Agency*, https://www.cia.gov/readingroom/docs/LOC-HAK-537-2-6-7.pdf (accessed December 22, 2021).

88. "Memorandum from Director of Central Intelligence Helms to the President's Assistant for National Security Affairs (Kissinger)," March 23, 1970, *Foreign Relations of the United States*, https://history.state.gov/historicaldocuments/frus1969-76v06/d208 (accessed December 22, 2021).

89. "Memorandum from Director of Central Intelligence Helms to the President's Assistant for National Security Affairs (Kissinger)," March 23, 1970, *Foreign Relations of the United States*, https://history.state.gov/historicaldocuments/frus1969-76v06/d208 (accessed December 22, 2021).

90. Cosmas, *MACV: The Joint Command in the Years of Withdrawal*, 295. See, for example, U.S. General Accounting Office, *U.S. Assistance to the Khmer Republic (Cambodia)*, October 10, 1973, https://www.gao.gov/assets/210/200096.pdf (accessed January 27, 2021).

91. "Memorandum for the Record," April 10, 1970, *Foreign Relations of the United States*, https://history.state.gov/historicaldocuments/frus1969-76v06/d225 (accessed December 22, 2021). See also "Minutes of Washington Special Actions Group Meeting," April 14, 1970, *Foreign Relations of the United States*, https://history.state.gov/historicaldocuments/frus1969-76v06/d230; "Memorandum from Director of Central Intelligence Helms to the President's Assistant for National Security Affairs (Kissinger)," April 15, 1970, *Foreign Relations of the United States*, https://history.state.gov/historicaldocuments/frus1969-76v06/d232; "Memorandum from the Senior Military Assistant (Haig) to the President's Assistant for National Security Affairs (Kissinger)," April 16, 1970, *Foreign Relations of the United States*, https://history.state.gov/historicaldocuments/frus1969-76v06/d235 (accessed December 22, 2021). The first delivery of munitions—1,500 AK-47s and 100,000 rounds of ammunition—took place on the night of April 21–22 and by April 28 over 4,000 AK-47 rifles had reached Phnom Penh. See Webb, *The Joint Chiefs of Staff*, 151.

92. Cosmas, *MACV: The Joint Command in the Years of Withdrawal*, 295.

93. "Memorandum from the President's Assistant for National Security Affairs (Kissinger) to President Nixon," March 27, 1970, *Foreign Relations of the United States*, https://history.state.gov/historicaldocuments/frus1969-76v06/d215 (accessed December 22, 2021).

94. Cosmas, *MACV: The Joint Command in the Years of Withdrawal*, 296; Webb, *Joint Chiefs of Staff*, 153.

316 / Notes to Chapter 5

95. Cosmas, *MACV: The Joint Command in the Years of Withdrawal*, 296.

96. "Memorandum from the President's Assistant for National Security Affairs (Kissinger) to President Nixon," April 1, 1970, *Foreign Relations of the United States*, https://history.state.gov/historicaldocuments/frus1969-76v06/d216 (accessed December 22, 2021).

97. Webb, *The Joint Chiefs of Staff*, 144–45.

98. "Memorandum from the Senior Military Assistant (Haig) to the President's Assistant for National Security Affairs (Kissinger)," April 3, 1970, *Foreign Relations of the United States*, https://history.state.gov/historicaldocuments/frus1969-76v06/d219 (accessed December 22, 2021).

99. "Memorandum from Secretary of Defense Laird to President Nixon," April 4, 1970, *Foreign Relations of the United States*, https://history.state.gov/historicaldocuments/frus1969-76v06/d221 (accessed December 22, 2021).

100. "Backchannel Message from the Ambassador to Vietnam (Bunker) to the President's Assistant for National Security Affairs (Kissinger)," April 8, 1970, *Foreign Relations of the United States*, https://history.state.gov/historicaldocuments/frus1969-76v06/d224 (accessed December 22, 2021).

101. "Editorial Note," *Foreign Relations of the United States*, https://history.state.gov/historicaldocuments/frus1969-76v06/d239 (accessed December 22, 2021).

102. "Memorandum from the Acting Chairman of the Joint Chiefs of Staff (Westmoreland) to Secretary of Defense Laird," April 21, 1970, *Foreign Relations of the United States*, https://history.state.gov/historicaldocuments/frus1969-76v06/d244 (accessed December 22, 2021).

103. Cosmas, *MACV: The Joint Command in the Years of Withdrawal*, 293.

104. "Vietnamese Communist Intentions in Cambodia Prior to April 28, 1970," June 12, 1970, *Central Intelligence Agency*, https://www.cia.gov/readingroom/docs/LOC-HAK-537-2-6-7.pdf (accessed December 22, 2021).

105. "Memorandum from President Nixon to His Assistant for National Security Affairs (Kissinger)," April 22, 1970, *Foreign Relations of the United States*, https://history.state.gov/historicaldocuments/frus1969-76v06/d245 (accessed December 22, 2021).

106. Cosmas, *MACV: The Joint Command in the Years of Withdrawal*, 296.

107. "Editorial Note," *Foreign Relations of the United States*, https://history.state.gov/historicaldocuments/frus1969-76v06/d248 (accessed December 22, 2021).

108. "National Security Council Decision Memorandum 56," April 22, 1970, *Foreign Relations of the United States*, https://history.state.gov/historicaldocuments/frus1969-76v06/d249 (accessed December 22, 2021).

109. "Memorandum from Roger Morris, Winston Lord, and Anthony Lake of the National Security Council Staff to the President's Assistant for National Security Affairs (Kissinger)," April 22, 1970, *Foreign Relations of the United States*, https://history.state.gov/historicaldocuments/frus1969-76v06/d250 (accessed December 22, 2021).

Notes to Chapter 5 / 317

110. "Editorial Note," *Foreign Relations of the United States,* https://history.state.gov/historicaldocuments/frus1969-76v06/d254 (accessed December 22, 2021).

111. "Memorandum of Conversation," April 24, 1970, *Foreign Relations of the United States,* https://history.state.gov/historicaldocuments/frus1969-76v06/d255 (accessed December 22, 2021).

112. "Memorandum of Conversation," April 24, 1970, *Foreign Relations of the United States,* https://history.state.gov/historicaldocuments/frus1969-76v06/d255 (accessed December 22, 2021).

113. Webb, *Joint Chiefs of Staff,* 156–58.

114. "Transcript of Telephone Conversation between President Nixon, His Assistant for National Security Affairs (Kissinger), and the Chairman of the Senate Armed Services Committee (Stennis)," April 24, 1970, *Foreign Relations of the United States,* https://history.state.gov/historicaldocuments/frus1969-76v06/d256 (accessed December 22, 2021).

115. "Transcript of Telephone Conversation between President Nixon, His Assistant for National Security Affairs (Kissinger), and the Chairman of the Senate Armed Services Committee (Stennis)," April 24, 1970, *Foreign Relations of the United States,* https://history.state.gov/historicaldocuments/frus1969-76v06/d256 (accessed December 22, 2021).

116. "Memorandum of Conversation," April 24, 1970, *Foreign Relations of the United States,* https://history.state.gov/historicaldocuments/frus1969-76v06/d257 (accessed December 22, 2021).

117. "Memorandum from the President's Assistant for National Security Affairs (Kissinger) to President Nixon," April 26, 1970, *Foreign Relations of the United States,* https://history.state.gov/historicaldocuments/frus1969-76v06/d259 (accessed December 22, 2021).

118. Schmitz, *Richard Nixon,* 87.

119. "Notes of a Meeting," April 27, 1970, *Foreign Relations of the United States,* https://history.state.gov/historicaldocuments/frus1969-76v06/d261 (accessed December 22, 2021).

120. "Memorandum from Secretary of Defense Laird to President Nixon," April 27, 1970, *Foreign Relations of the United States,* https://history.state.gov/historicaldocuments/frus1969-76v06/d263 (accessed December 22, 2021).

121. "Background Message from the President's Assistant for National Security Affairs (Kissinger) to the Ambassaor to Vietnam (Bunker)," April 27, 1970, *Foreign Relations of the United States,* https://history.state.gov/historicaldocuments/frus1969-76v06/d265 (accessed December 22, 2021).

122. "Backchannel Message from the Ambassador to Vietnam (Bunker) to President Nixon," April 27, 1970, *Foreign Relations of the United States,* https://history.state.gov/historicaldocuments/frus1969-76v06/d266 (accessed December 22, 2021).

318 / Notes to Chapter 5

123. In anticipation of the invasion, Nixon initiated a massive global campaign of disinformation and propaganda. On the recommendation of Helms, the United States developed a "worldwide clandestine propaganda effort to support the present government and call attention to the flagrant violation of Cambodian territory by the North Vietnamese." In so doing, the United States also worked to "discredit Sihanouk's effort to create a government in exile." By April 14 an international propaganda effort was "well under way" with other clandestine measures being considered. See "Memorandum from Director of Central Intelligence Helms to the President's Assistant for National Security Affairs (Kissinger)," March 23, 1970, *Foreign Relations of the United States,* https://history.state.gov/historicaldocuments/frus1969-76v06/d208; and "Memorandum from the President's Assistant for National Security Affairs (Kissinger) to President Nixon," April 14, 1970, *Foreign Relations of the United States,* https://history.state.gov/historicaldocuments/frus1969-76v06/d229 (accessed December 22, 2021).

124. "Memorandum of Meeting," April 28, 1970, *Foreign Relations of the United States,* https://history.state.gov/historicaldocuments/frus1969-76v06/d267 (accessed December 22, 2021).

125. Schmitz, *Richard Nixon,* 45.

126. Schmitz, *Richard Nixon,* 75.

127. Kimball, *Nixon's Vietnam War,* 210.

128. Quoted in Shawcross, *Sideshow,* 145.

6. The Perfidy of Geopolitics

1. Central Intelligence Agency, *National Intelligence Estimate Number 14.3/53–61,* "Prospects for North and South Vietnam," August 15, 1961, https://www.cia.gov/readingroom/docs/DOC_0000024387.pdf (accessed April 21, 2022).

2. Central Intelligence Agency, *National Intelligence Estimate Number 14.3/53–61,* "Prospects for North and South Vietnam," August 15, 1961, https://www.cia.gov/readingroom/docs/DOC_0000024387.pdf (accessed April 21, 2022).

3. Richard M. Nixon, "Address to the Nation on the Situation in Southeast Asia," April 30, 1970, *Miller Center,* https://millercenter.org/the-presidency/presidential-speeches/april-30-1970-address-nation-situation-southeast-asia (accessed July 12, 2022).

4. David F. Schmitz, *Richard Nixon and the Vietnam War* (Lanham, Md.: Rowman & Littlefield, 2014), 90.

5. James A. Tyner and Mindy Farmer, *Cambodia and Kent State: In the Aftermath of Nixon's Expansion of the Vietnam War* (Kent: Kent State University Press, 2020), 14.

6. Juan de Onis, "Nixon Puts 'Bums' Label on Some College Radicals," *New York Times,* May 2, 1970, https://www.nytimes.com/1970/05/02/archives/nixon-puts

Notes to Chapter 6 / 319

-bums-label-on-some-college-radicals-nixon-denounces-bums.html (accessed July 13, 2022).

7. "Telegram from the Acting Chairman of the Joint Chiefs of Staff (Moorer) to the Commander in Chief, Pacific (McCain), and the Commander, Military Assistance Command, Vietnam (Abrams)," May 1, 1970, *Foreign Relations of the United States,* https://history.state.gov/historicaldocuments/frus1969-76v06/d273 (accessed January 3, 2022). On May 5 MACV proposed six additional operations against enemy bases in Cambodia, with additional proposals submitted throughout May. See "Memorandum from the President's Assistant for National Security Affairs (Kissinger) to President Nixon," May 5, 1970, *Foreign Relations of the United States,* https://history.state.gov/historicaldocuments/frus1969-76v06/d279; "Memorandum of Conversation," May 11, 1970, *Foreign Relations of the United States,* https://history.state.gov/historicaldocuments/frus1969-76v06/d286; "Memorandum for the Record," May 12, 1970, *Foreign Relations of the United States,* https://history.state.gov/historicaldocuments/frus1969-76v06/d288; "Memorandum for the Record," May 14, 1970, *Foreign Relations of the United States,* https://history.state.gov/historicaldocuments/frus1969-76v06/d292 (accessed January 3, 2022).

8. "Minutes of Washington Special Actions Group Meeting," May 4, 1970, *Foreign Relations of the United States,* https://history.state.gov/historicaldocuments/frus1969-76v06/d275 (accessed January 3, 2022).

9. "Editorial Note," *Foreign Relations of the United States,* https://history.state.gov/historicaldocuments/frus1969-76v06/d276 (accessed January 3, 2022).

10. Robert D. Sanders, *Invasion of Laos, 1971: Lam Son 719* (Norman: University of Oklahoma Press, 2014), 74.

11. "Editorial Note," *Foreign Relations of the United States,* https://history.state.gov/historicaldocuments/frus1969-76v06/d276 (accessed January 3, 2022).

12. "Memorandum for the President's File," May 7, 1970, *Foreign Relations of the United States,* https://history.state.gov/historicaldocuments/frus1969-76v01/d66 (accessed January 3, 2022).

13. "Memorandum of Conversation," May 6, 1970, *Foreign Relations of the United States,* https://history.state.gov/historicaldocuments/frus1969-76v01/d65 (accessed January 3, 2022).

14. "Memorandum for the President's File," May 7, 1970, *Foreign Relations of the United States,* https://history.state.gov/historicaldocuments/frus1969-76v01/d66 (accessed January 3, 2022).

15. Sanders, *Invasion of Laos,* 75; Schmitz, *Richard Nixon,* 92–95.

16. Isaacs, *Without Honor,* 204.

17. "Memorandum from President Nixon to the Chairman of the Washington Special Actions Group (Kissinger)," National Archives, Nixon Presidential Materials, NSC Files, Box 510, Country Files, Far East, Cambodia, Vol. VIII, 20 June

320 / Notes to Chapter 6

1970–20 July 1970, https://history.state.gov/historicaldocuments/frus1969-76v06/d339 (accessed January 3, 2021).

18. "Interview with President Nixon," July 1, 1970, *Foreign Relations of the United States,* https://history.state.gov/historicaldocuments/frus1969-76v01/d67 (accessed January 4, 2022).

19. "Memorandum of Conversation," May 6, 1970, *Foreign Relations of the United States,* https://history.state.gov/historicaldocuments/frus1969-76v06/d281 (accessed January 3, 2022).

20. "Memorandum of Conversation," May 7, 1970, *Foreign Relations of the United States,* https://history.state.gov/historicaldocuments/frus1969-76v06/d282 (accessed January 3, 2022).

21. "Transcript of Telephone Conversation between Secretary of State Rogers and the President's Assistant for National Security Affairs (Kissinger)," May 8, 1970, *Foreign Relations of the United States,* https://history.state.gov/historicaldocuments/frus1969-76v06/d283 (accessed January 3, 2022).

22. "Telegram from the Department of State to the Embassy in Cambodia," May 9, 1970, *Foreign Relations of the United States,* https://history.state.gov/historicaldocuments/frus1969-76v06/d285 (accessed January 3, 2022).

23. See for example "Editorial Note," *Foreign Relations of the United States,* https://history.state.gov/historicaldocuments/frus1969-76v06/d300; "Editorial Note," *Foreign Relations of the United States,* https://history.state.gov/historicaldocuments/frus1969-76v06/d303; "Memorandum for the Record," May 25, 1970, *Foreign Relations of the United States,* https://history.state.gov/historicaldocuments/frus1969-76v06/d304; "Editorial Note," *Foreign Relations of the United States,* https://history.state.gov/historicaldocuments/frus1969-76v06/d311; and "Editorial Note," *Foreign Relations of the United States,* https://history.state.gov/historicaldocuments/frus1969-76v06/d314 (accessed January 4, 2022).

24. "Telegram from the Embassy in Cambodia to the Department of State," May 15, 1970, *Foreign Relations of the United States,* https://history.state.gov/historicaldocuments/frus1969-76v06/d293 (accessed January 4, 2022).

25. "Telegram from the Embassy in Cambodia to the Department of State," May 15, 1970, *Foreign Relations of the United States,* https://history.state.gov/historicaldocuments/frus1969-76v06/d293 (accessed January 4, 2022).

26. "Memorandum from the Senior Military Assistant (Haig) to the President's Assistant for National Security Affairs (Kissinger)," undated, *Foreign Relations of the United States,* https://history.state.gov/historicaldocuments/frus1969-76v06/d294 (accessed January 4, 2022).

27. "Memorandum from the President's Assistant for National Security Affairs (Kissinger) to President Nixon," May 26, 1970, *Foreign Relations of the United States,* https://history.state.gov/historicaldocuments/frus1969-76v06/d307 (accessed January 4, 2022). For Haig's conversation with Sirik Matak, see "Memorandum from the

Notes to Chapter 6 / 321

President's Assistant for National Security Affairs (Kissinger) to President Nixon," May 26, 1970, *Foreign Relations of the United States,* https://history.state.gov/histor icaldocuments/frus1969-76v06/d308 (accessed January 4, 2022).

28. "Memorandum from the Senior Military Assistant (Haig) to the President's Assistant for National Security Affairs (Kissinger)," undated, *Foreign Relations of the United States,* https://history.state.gov/historicaldocuments/frus1969-76v06/d294 (accessed January 4, 2022).

29. Nixon apparently believed that Rives was in over his head in Phnom Penh. See "Record of Meeting," July 18, 1970, *Foreign Relations of the United States,* https://his tory.state.gov/historicaldocuments/frus1969-76v06/d344 (accessed January 4, 2022).

30. "Memorandum from President Nixon to His Assistant for National Security Affairs (Kissinger)," April 22, 1970, *Foreign Relations of the United States,* https://his tory.state.gov/historicaldocuments/frus1969-76v06/d247 (accessed January 4, 2022).

31. "Memorandum by Director of Central Intelligence Helms," May 12, 1970, *Foreign Relations of the United States,* https://history.state.gov/historicaldocuments/ frus1969-76v06/d289 (accessed January 3, 2022).

32. "Memorandum by Director of Central Intelligence Helms," May 12, 1970, *Foreign Relations of the United States,* https://history.state.gov/historicaldocuments/ frus1969-76v06/d289 (accessed January 3, 2022).

33. "Memorandum from the President's Assistant for National Security Affairs (Kissinger) to President Nixon," May 19, 1970, *Foreign Relations of the United States,* https://history.state.gov/historicaldocuments/frus1969-76v06/d299 (accessed January 4, 2022).

34. "Memorandum from the President's Assistant for National Security Affairs (Kissinger) to President Nixon," May 25, 1970, *Foreign Relations of the United States,* https://history.state.gov/historicaldocuments/frus1969-76v06/d306 (accessed January 4, 2022).

35. See for example, Central Intelligence Agency, "The Impact of the Fighting in Cambodia on the Economy," June 1, 1970, https://www.cia.gov/readingroom/ document/cia-rdp85t00875r001600030085-5 (accessed January 9, 2021).

36. "Memorandum of Conversation," May 31, 1970, *Foreign Relations of the United States,* https://history.state.gov/historicaldocuments/frus1969-76v06/d313 (accessed January 4, 2022).

37. "Cable to Henry Kissinger from Alexander Haig," May 26, 1970, *Central Intelligence Agency,* https://www.cia.gov/readingroom/docs/LOC-HAK-503-2-13-6 .pdf (accessed January 5, 2022).

38. "Memorandum from the Director of the Program Analysis Staff of the National Security Council (Lynn) to the President's Assistant for National Security Affairs (Kissinger)," June 5, 1970, *Foreign Relations of the United States,* https://his tory.state.gov/historicaldocuments/frus1969-76v06/d318 (accessed January 4, 2022).

39. Richard Nixon, "Report on the Cambodian Operation," June 30, 1970, https://www.presidency.ucsb.edu/documents/report-the-cambodian-operation

322 / Notes to Chapter 6

(accessed January 5, 2022). See also "National Security Study Memorandum 95," June 6, 1970, *Foreign Relations of the United States,* https://history.state.gov/histori caldocuments/frus1969-76v06/d319 and "Memorandum from President Nixon to the Chairman of the Washington Special Actions Group (Kissinger)," July 7, 1970, *Foreign Relations of the United States,* https://history.state.gov/historicaldocuments/ frus1969-76v06/d339 (accessed January 4, 2022).

40. See for example "Minutes of Washington Special Actions Group Meeting," June 19, 1970, *Foreign Relations of the United States,* https://history.state.gov/histor icaldocuments/frus1969-76v06/d331; "Memorandum from the President's Assistant for National Security Affairs (Kissinger) to President Nixon," June 22, 1970, *Foreign Relations of the United States,* https://history.state.gov/historicaldocuments/frus19 69-76v06/d332; and "Memorandum from the President's Assistant for National Security Affairs (Kissinger) to President Nixon," June 23, 1970, *Foreign Relations of the United States,* https://history.state.gov/historicaldocuments/frus1969-76v06/d333 (accessed January 4, 2022).

41. "Memorandum from the President's Assistant for National Security Affairs (Kissinger) to President Nixon," July 14, 1970, *Foreign Relations of the United States,* https://history.state.gov/historicaldocuments/frus1969-76v06/d341 (accessed January 4, 2022). For an optimistic assessment forwarded by Lloyd Rives, see "Memorandum from the President's Assistant for National Security Affairs (Kissinger) to President Nixon," July 14, 1970, *Foreign Relations of the United States,* https://history.state.gov/historicaldocuments/frus1969-76v06/d342 (accessed January 4, 2022).

42. See Schmitz, *Richard Nixon,* 100–103.

43. "Memorandum from the President's Assistant for National Security Affairs (Kissinger) to President Nixon," undated, *Foreign Relations of the United States,* https://history.state.gov/historicaldocuments/frus1969-76v06/d346 (accessed January 4, 2022).

44. Schmitz, *Richard Nixon,* 101.

45. "Memorandum from the President's Assistant for National Security Affairs (Kissinger) to President Nixon," undated, *Foreign Relations of the United States,* https://history.state.gov/historicaldocuments/frus1969-76v06/d346 (accessed January 4, 2022).

46. Chester Pach, "'Our Worst Enemy Seems to Be the Press': TV News, the Nixon Administration, and U.S. Troop Withdrawal from Vietnam, 1969–1973," *Diplomatic History* 34, no. 3 (2010): 555–65; at 556.

47. Pach, "'Our Worst Enemy,'" 557.

48. "Editorial Note," *Foreign Relations of the United States,* https://history.state .gov/historicaldocuments/frus1969-76v01/d36 (accessed January 4, 2022).

49. "Editorial Note," *Foreign Relations of the United States,* https://history.state .gov/historicaldocuments/frus1969-76v01/d38 (accessed January 4, 2022).

Notes to Chapter 6 / 323

50. "Minutes of the National Security Council Meeting," September 12, 1969, *Foreign Relations of the United States*, https://history.state.gov/historicaldocuments/frus1969-76v06/d120 (accessed January 4, 2022).

51. "Memorandum from the President's Assistant for National Security Affairs (Kissinger) to President Nixon," July 20, 1970, *Foreign Relations of the United States*, https://history.state.gov/historicaldocuments/frus1969-76v06/d347 (accessed January 4, 2022).

52. "Memorandum of Conversation," July 21, 1970, *Foreign Relations of the United States*, https://history.state.gov/historicaldocuments/frus1969-76v06/d348 (accessed January 4, 2022).

53. "Memorandum from the President's Assistant for National Security Affairs (Kissinger) to President Nixon," July 29, 1970, *Foreign Relations of the United States*, https://history.state.gov/historicaldocuments/frus1969-76v07/d6 (accessed January 5, 2022).

54. "Special National Intelligence Estimate," August 6, 1970, *Foreign Relations of the United States*, https://history.state.gov/historicaldocuments/frus1969-76v07/d9 (accessed January 5, 2022).

55. See for example "Transcript of a Telephone Conversation between President Nixon and His Assistant for National Security Affairs (Kissinger)," December 9, 1970, *Foreign Relations of the United States*, https://history.state.gov/historicaldocuments/frus1969-76v07/d83 (accessed January 5, 2022).

56. "Summary of Conclusions of a Meeting of the Washington Special Actions Group," August 4, 1970, *Foreign Relations of the United States*, https://history.state.gov/historicaldocuments/frus1969-76v07/d9; "Memorandum from the President's Assistant for National Security Affairs (Kissinger) to President Nixon," August 10, 1970, *Foreign Relations of the United States*, https://history.state.gov/historicaldocuments/frus1969-76v07/d18 (accessed January 5, 2022).

57. "Letter from President Nixon to Cambodian Prime Minister Lon Nol," August 20, 1970, *Foreign Relations of the United States*, https://history.state.gov/historicaldocuments/frus1969-76v07/d26 (accessed January 5, 2022).

58. "Letter from President Nixon to Cambodian Prime Minister Lon Nol," August 20, 1970, *Foreign Relations of the United States*, https://history.state.gov/historicaldocuments/frus1969-76v07/d26 (accessed January 5, 2022).

59. Isaacs, *Without Honor*, 206.

60. Quoted in Iver Peterson, "Cambodian Says Only Aid from U.S. Will Bar Defeat," *New York Times*, August 6, 1970, https://www.nytimes.com/1970/08/06/archives/cambodian-says-only-aid-from-us-will-bar-defeat.html (accessed January 5, 2022).

61. Isaacs, *Without Honor*, 207.

62. "Memorandum from the President's Assistant for National Security Affairs (Kissinger) to President Nixon," September 1, 1970, *Foreign Relations of the United*

324 / Notes to Chapter 6

States, https://history.state.gov/historicaldocuments/frus1969-76v07/d30 (accessed January 5, 2022).

63. "Summary of Conclusions of a Meeting of the Senior Review Group," October 16, 1970, *Foreign Relations of the United States,* https://history.state.gov/historicaldocuments/frus1969-76v07/d51; see also "Memorandum from K. Wayne Smith of the National Security Council Staff to the President's Assistant for National Security Affairs (Kissinger)," September 14, 1970, *Foreign Relations of the United States,* https://history.state.gov/historicaldocuments/frus1969-76v07/d39; and "Summary of Conclusions of a Meeting of the Senior Review Group," September 15, 1970, *Foreign Relations of the United States,* https://history.state.gov/historicaldocuments/frus1969-76v07/d40 (accessed January 5, 2022).

64. "National Security Decision Memorandum 89," October 26, 1970, *Foreign Relations of the United States,* https://history.state.gov/historicaldocuments/frus1969-76v07/d61 (accessed January 5, 2022).

65. "Telegram from the Department of State to the Embassy in Cambodia," November 4, 1970, *Foreign Relations of the United States,* https://history.state.gov/historicaldocuments/frus1969-76v07/d64 (accessed January 5, 2022).

66. Gideon Rose, *How Wars End: Why We Always Fight the Last Battle* (New York: Simon & Schuster, 2010), 162.

67. "Conversation among President Nixon, Vice President Agnew, and the President's Assistant for National Security Affairs (Kissinger)," December 16, 1972, *Foreign Relations of the United States,* https://history.state.gov/historicaldocuments/frus1969-76v09/d181 (accessed January 7, 2022).

68. Frank Snepp, *Decent Interval: An Insider's Account of Saigon's Indecent End Told by the CIA's Chief Strategy Analyst in Vietnam,* Twenty-Fifty Anniversary Edition (Lawrence: University Press of Kansas, 2002), 50–51.

69. Quoted in Thomas Alan Schwartz, "'Henry, . . . Winning an Election Is Terribly Important': Partisan Politics in the History of U.S. Foreign Relations," *Diplomatic History* 33, no. 2 (2009): 173–74; original audio recording, http://tapes.millercenter.virginia.edu/clips/1972_0803_vietnam/ (accessed June 29, 2022).

70. Asselin, *A Bitter Peace,* 183–84. See also Jeffrey Kimball, "The Case of the 'Decent Interval': Do We Now Have a Smoking Gun?" *SHAFR Newsletter* 32, no. 3 (2001): 35–39; Frank Snepp, *Decent Interval: An Insider's Account of Saigon's Indecent End Told by the CIA's Chief Strategy Analyst in Vietnam* (Lawrence: University Press of Kansas, 2002); Jussi Hanhimaki, "Selling the 'Decent Interval': Kissinger, Triangular Diplomacy, and the End of the Vietnam War, 1971–73," *Diplomacy & Statecraft* 14, no. 1 (2003): 159–94; Ken Hughes, "Fatal Politics: Nixon's Political Time Table for Withdrawing from Vietnam," *Diplomatic History* 34, no. 3 (2010): 497–506. For a more critical take on the "decent interval" thesis, see Pierre Asselin, "Kimball's Vietnam War," *Diplomatic History* 30, no. 1 (2006): 163–67.

71. Kadura, *War after the War,* 45.

Notes to Chapter 6 / 325

72. "Memorandum of Conversation," July 9, 1971, *Foreign Relations of the United States,* https://history.state.gov/historicaldocuments/frus1969-76v17/d139 (accessed June 29, 2022).

73. "Memorandum of Conversation," July 10, 1971, *Foreign Relations of the United States,* https://history.state.gov/historicaldocuments/frus1969-76v17/d140 (accessed June 29, 2022).

74. "Memorandum of Conversation," May 27, 1972, *Foreign Relations of the United States,* https://history.state.gov/historicaldocuments/frus1969-76v14/d290 (accessed June 29, 2022).

75. "Memorandum of Conversation," June 21, 1972, *Foreign Relations of the United States,* https://history.state.gov/historicaldocuments/frus1969-76v17/d232 (accessed June 29, 2022).

76. Asselin, *A Bitter Peace,* xi–xii.

77. "Memorandum of Conversation," January 29, 1973, *Foreign Relations of the United States,* https://history.state.gov/historicaldocuments/frus1969-76ve08/d104 (accessed January 7, 2022).

78. "Memorandum from William Stearman of the National Security Council Staff to the President's Assistant for National Security Affairs (Kissinger)," August 6, 1973, *Foreign Relations of the United States,* https://history.state.gov/historicaldocuments/frus1969-76v10/d99; "Memorandum from the Director of Central Intelligence (Colby) to the President's Assistant for National Security Affairs (Kissinger)," September 12, 1973, *Foreign Relations of the United States,* https://history.state.gov/historicaldocuments/frus1969-76v10/d106 (accessed June 2, 2022).

79. Asselin, *A Bitter Peace,* 145.

80. "Message from the Chairman of the Joint Chiefs of Staff (Moorer) to the Commander in Chief, Pacific (Gayler) and the Commander in Chief, Strategic Air Command (Meyer)," December 17, 1972, *Foreign Relations of the United States,* https://history.state.gov/historicaldocuments/frus1969-76v09/d184 (accessed January 7, 2022).

81. Asselin, *A Bitter Peace,* 152.

82. Shawcross, *Sideshow,* 56.

83. "Conversation Between President Nixon and the President's Deputy Assistant for National Security Affairs (Haig)," December 12, 1972, *Foreign Relations of the United States,* https://history.state.gov/historicaldocuments/frus1969-76v09/d161 (accessed July 29, 2022).

84. Stanley Karnow, *Vietnam: A History* (New York: Viking Press, 1983), 654; see also James H. Willbanks, *Abandoning Vietnam: How America Left and South Vietnam Lost Its War* (Lawrence: University Press of Kansas, 2004), 183.

85. "Memorandum of Conversation," November 24, 1972, *Foreign Relations of the United States,* https://history.state.gov/historicaldocuments/frus1969-76v09/d125 (accessed January 6, 2022).

326 / Notes to Chapter 6

86. Asselin, *A Bitter Peace,* 174.

87. Richard Nixon, *The Memoirs of Richard Nixon* (New York: Warner Books, 1978), 724–25, 734–35.

88. "Address to the Nation Announcing an Agreement on Ending the War in Vietnam," January 23, 1973, https://millercenter.org/the-presidency/presidential-speeches/january-23-1973-address-nation-announcing-agreement-ending-war (accessed January 7, 2022).

89. "Backchannel Message from the Ambassador to Vietnam (Bunker) to the President's Assistant for National Security Affairs (Kissinger)," February 1, 1973, *Foreign Relations of the United States,* https://history.state.gov/historicaldocuments/frus1969-76v10/d7 (accessed January 7, 2022).

90. Clymer, *Troubled Relations,* 130.

91. Quoted in Isaacs, *Without Honor,* 212.

92. Kadura, *The War after the War,* 47.

93. Weyand replaced Creighton Abrams as Commander (MACV) in June 1972; Vogt served as the commander of the Seventh Air Force and deputy commander (MACV).

94. "Backchannel Message from the Vice Chief of Staff of the Army (Haig) to the Ambassador to Vietnam (Bunker)," January 21, 1973, *Foreign Relations of the United States,* https://history.state.gov/historicaldocuments/frus1969-76v09/d323 (accessed January 6, 2022).

95. "Transcript of a Telephone Conversation between the Chairman of the Joint Chiefs of Staff (Moorer) and the Vice Chief of Staff of the Army (Haig)," January 23, 1973, *Foreign Relations of the United States,* https://history.state.gov/historicaldocuments/frus1969-76v09/d332 (accessed January 6, 2022).

96. "Transcript of a Telephone Conversation between the Chairman of the Joint Chiefs of Staff (Moorer) and the President's Assistant for National Security Affairs (Kissinger)," January 27, 1973, *Foreign Relations of the United States,* https://history.state.gov/historicaldocuments/frus1969-76v09/d339 (accessed January 6, 2022).

97. "Minutes of a Washington Special Actions Group Meeting," January 24, 1973, *Foreign Relations of the United States,* https://history.state.gov/historicaldocuments/frus1969-76v09/d334 (accessed January 6, 2022).

98. Quoted in Isaacs, *Without Honor,* 213.

99. Isaacs, *Without Honor,* 213.

100. "Telephone Conversation Between President Nixon and the President's Assistant for National Security Affairs (Kissinger)," January 31, 1973, *Foreign Relations of the United States,* https://history.state.gov/historicaldocuments/frus1969-76v10/d5 (accessed January 7, 2022).

101. "Minutes of Washington Special Actions Group Meeting," January 29, 1973, *Foreign Relations of the United States,* https://history.state.gov/historicaldocuments/frus1969-76v10/d2 (accessed January 7, 2022).

Notes to Chapter 6 / 327

102. "Ceasefire Developments (February 9—4:30 P.M. EST)," *Central Intelligence Agency,* https://cia.gov/readingroom/docs/LOC-HAK-30-6-27-2.pdf (accessed January 7, 2022). See also Snepp, *Decent Interval,* 51.

103. Central Intelligence Agency, "Taking Stock in Cambodia," February 18, 1972, https://www.cia.gov/readingroom/docs/CIA-RDP85T00875R002000110043-7.pdf (accessed January 9, 2021).

104. "Minutes of Washington Special Actions Group Meeting," February 6, 1973, *Foreign Relations of the United States,* https://history.state.gov/historicaldocuments/frus1969-76v10/d9 (accessed January 7, 2022).

105. "Minutes of Washington Special Actions Group Meeting," February 23, 1973, *Foreign Relations of the United States,* https://history.state.gov/historicaldocuments/frus1969-76v10/d23 (accessed January 7, 2022).

106. With the resumption of limited air strikes against Cambodia on February 9, the center of U.S. military operations shifted westward, from South Vietnam to Thailand. On March 29, MACV was formally deactivated and the remaining U.S. combat troops departed South Vietnam; the only residual U.S. military presence (aside from 159 U.S. Marines who remained to guard the U.S. Embassy in Saigon) was the newly formed Defense Attaché Office and its 50 officers and approximately 1,200 U.S. civilians. In Thailand, however, the U.S. Special Advisory Group (USSAG) was established at Nakhon Phanom, intended, in part, to coordinate the bombing of Cambodia. See Snepp, *Decent Interval,* 51; Willbanks, *Abandoning Vietnam,* 187.

107. "Memorandum of Conversation," February 15, 1973, *Foreign Relations of the United States,* https://history.state.gov/historicaldocuments/frus1969-76v35/d6 (accessed June 2, 2022).

108. "Memorandum of Conversation," May 18, 1973, *Foreign Relations of the United States,* https://history.state.gov/historicaldocuments/frus1969-76v38p1/d11 (accessed June 2, 2022).

109. "Memorandum of Conversation," February 10, 1973, *Foreign Relations of the United States,* https://history.state.gov/historicaldocuments/frus1969-76ve12/d1 (accessed January 7, 2022).

110. Isaacs, *Without Honor,* 217.

111. Isaacs, *Without Honor,* 225.

112. Shawcross, *Sideshow,* 294–95.

113. Kadura, *War after the War,* 77.

114. "Memorandum of Conversation," May 18, 1973, *Foreign Relations of the United States,* https://history.state.gov/historicaldocuments/frus1969-76v38p1/d11 (accessed June 2, 2022).

115. Kadura, *War after the War,* 75.

116. "Joint Resolution Making Continuing Appropriations for the Fiscal Year 1974, and for Other Purposes," July 1, 1973, https://www.congress.gov/93/statute/STATUTE-87/STATUTE-87-Pg130.pdf (accessed June 2, 2022).

328 / Notes to Chapter 6

117. Kadura, *War after the War,* 80; see also Willbanks, *Abandoning Vietnam,* 195–96.

118. "Transcript of Telephone Conversation Between the President's Assistant for National Security Affairs (Kissinger) and the Director of Central Intelligence (Schlesinger)," June 26, 1973, *Foreign Relations of the United States,* https://history .state.gov/historicaldocuments/frus1969-76v10/d87 (accessed June 2, 2022).

119. "Transcript of Telephone Conversation Between the President's Assistant for National Security Affairs (Kissinger) and Secretary of Defense Schlesinger," July 30, 1973, *Foreign Relations of the United States,* https://history.state.gov/historicaldocu ments/frus1969-76v10/d95 (accessed June 2, 2022).

120. "Minutes of Washington Special Actions Group Meeting," July 10, 1973, *Foreign Relations of the United States,* https://history.state.gov/historcialdocuments/ frus1969-76v10/d92 (accessed January 3, 2021).

121. Central Intelligence Agency, "Political Improvement in Cambodia, Obstacles and Possibilities," July 24, 1973, https://www.cia.gov/readingroom/docs/CIA -RDP80T01719R000400310003-4.pdf (accessed January 9, 2021).

122. "Memorandum of Conversation," June 15, 1973, *Foreign Relations of the United States,* https://history.state.gov/historicaldocuments/frus1969-76v10/d85 (accessed January 3, 2021).

123. "Minutes of the Washington Special Actions Group Meeting," March 28, 1973, *Foreign Relations of the United States,* https://history.stat.gov/historicaldocu ments/frus1969-76v10/d36 (accessed January 3, 2021).

124. "Telephone Conversation Between President Nixon and the White House Chief of Staff (Haig)," March 30, 1973, *Foreign Relations of the United States,* https:// history.state.gov/historicaldocuments/frus1969-76v10/d37 (accessed January 3, 2021).

125. "Minutes of Washington Special Actions Group Meeting," August 7, 1973, *Foreign Relations of the United States,* https://history.state.gov/historicaldocuments/ frus1969-76v10/d100 (accessed June 2, 2022).

126. "Memorandum for the President's File by the President's Assistant for National Security Affairs (Kissinger)," May 30, 1973, *Foreign Relations of the United States,* https://history.state.gov/historicaldocuments/frus1969-76v18/d34 (accessed January 3, 2021).

127. "Memorandum of Conversation," July 6, 1973, *Foreign Relations of the United States,* https://history.state.gov/historicaldocuments/frus1969-76v18/d41 (accessed June 2, 2022).

128. "Minutes of Washington Special Actions Group Meeting," July 10, 1973, *Foreign Relations of the United States,* https://history.state.gov/historicaldocuments/ frus1969-76v10/d92 (accessed June 2, 2022).

129. "Transcript of Telephone Conversation Between President Nixon and the President's Assistant for National Security Affairs (Kissinger)," August 3, 1973, *Foreign*

Notes to Epilogue / 329

Relations of the United States, https://history.state.gov/historicaldocuments/frus19 69-76v10/d97 (accessed June 2, 2022).

130. Sydney H. Schanberg, "Lon Nol Says U.S. Vows Full Support," *New York Times,* January 8, 1973, https://www.nytimes.com/1973/01/08/archives/lon-nol-says -us-vows-full-suppport.html (accessed January 21, 2021).

131. "Minutes of Washington Special Actions Group Meeting," August 7, 1973, *Foreign Relations of the United States,* available at https://history.state.gov/historical documents/frus1969-76v10/d100 (accessed June 2, 2022).

132. "America's Stake in Vietnam" speech, available at https://iowaculture.gov/ sites/default/files/primary-sources/pdfs/history-education-pss-vietnam-stakes -source.pdf (accessed June 29, 2022).

133. Quoted in Thomas Alan Schwartz, "'Henry, . . . Winning an Election Is Terribly Important': Partisan Politics in the History of U.S. Foreign Relations," *Diplomatic History* 33, no. 2 (2009): 173–74; original audio recording available at http://tapes.millercenter.virginia.edu/clips/1972_0803_vietnam/ (accessed June 29, 2022).

134. "Memorandum of Conversation," July 14, 1973, *Foreign Relations of the United States,* https://history.state.gov/historicaldocuments/frus1969-76ve08/d137 (accessed June 2, 2022).

135. "Memorandum of Conversation," July 10, 1973, *Foreign Relations of the United States,* https://history.state.gov/historicaldocuments/frus1969-76v15/d134 (accessed June 2, 2022).

136. "Minutes of Washington Special Actions Group Meeting," August 7, 1973, *Foreign Relations of the United States,* https://history.state.gov/historicaldocuments/ frus1969-76v10/d100 (accessed June 2, 2022).

Epilogue

1. "Memorandum by the Southeast Asia Aid Policy Committee to the Secretary of State and the Secretary of Defense (Marshall)," October 11, 1950, *Foreign Relations of the United States,* https://history.state.gov/historicaldocuments/frus19 50v06/d565 (accessed July 28, 2022).

2. "Memorandum of Conversation," April 21, 1975, *Foreign Relations of the United States,* https://history.state.gov/historicaldocuments/frus1969-76v10/d248 (accessed July 28, 2022).

3. Daniel Yergin, *Shattered Peace: The Origins of the Cold War and the National Security State* (Boston: Houghton Mifflin, 1977); John Lewis Gaddis, *Strategies of Containment: A Critical Appraisal of Postwar American National Security Policy* (New York: Oxford University Press, 1982); Melvyn P. Leffler, *A Preponderance of Power: National Security, the Truman Administration, and the Cold War* (Stanford: Stanford University Press, 1992); Anders Stephanson, *Manifest Destiny: American Expansion and the Empire of Right* (New York: Hill & Wang, 1995); Andrew J. Bacevich,

330 / Notes to Epilogue

American Empire: The Realities and Consequences of U.S. Diplomacy (Cambridge, Mass.: Harvard University Press, 2002); Charles A. Kupchan, *The End of the American Era: U.S. Foreign Policy and the Geopolitics of the Twenty-First Century* (New York: Vintage, 2002); Neil Smith, *The Endgame of Globalization* (New York: Routledge, 2005); Michael Adas, *Dominance by Design: Technological Imperatives and America's Civilizing Mission* (Cambridge, Mass.: Belknap Press of Harvard University Press, 2006).

4. "Memorandum of Conversation," March 24, 1975, *Foreign Relations of the United States,* https://history.state.gov/historicaldocuments/frus1969-76v10/d191 (accessed July 29, 2022).

5. Quoted in Ben Kiernan, *The Pol Pot Regime: Policies, Race and Genocide in Cambodia Under the Khmer Rouge, 1975–1979* (New Haven, Conn.: Yale University Press, 1996), 22.

6. See Gregory Procknow, *Khmer Rouge: Recruitment and Selection & Training and Development* (Phnom Penh: Documentation Center of Cambodia, 2009); Yuichi Kubota, "Territorial Control and Recruitment in the Cambodian Civil War, 1970–75: Case Studies in Battambang Province," *Asian Security* 7, no. 1 (2011): 1–26; and Yuichi Kubota, *Armed Groups in Cambodian Civil War: Territorial Control, Rivalry, and Recruitment* (New York: Palgrave Macmillan, 2013).

7. For more extensive discussions of the Cambodian genocide, see Craig Etcheson, *The Rise and Demise of Democratic Kampuchea* (Boulder, Colo.: Westview, 1984); Michael Vickery, *Cambodia, 1975–1982* (Chiang Mai, Thailand: Silkworm Press, 1984); David Chandler, *The Tragedy of Cambodian History: Politics, War, and Revolution since 1945* (New Haven, Conn.: Yale University Press, 1991); Elizabeth Becker, *When the War Was Over: Cambodia and the Khmer Rouge Revolution* (New York: Public Affairs, 1998); David Chandler, *Voices from S-21: Terror and History in Pol Pot's Secret Prison* (Berkeley: University of California Press, 1999); Steve Heder, *Cambodian Communism and the Vietnamese Model: Imitation and Independence, 1930–1975* (Bangkok: White Lotus Press, 2004); Alexander Hinton, *Why Did They Kill? Cambodia in the Shadow of Genocide* (Berkeley: University of California Press, 2005); Philip Short, *Pol Pot: Anatomy of a Nightmare* (New York: Macmillan, 2005); Kamboly Dy, *A History of Democratic Kampuchea (1975–1979)* (Phnom Penh: Documentation Center of Cambodia, 2007); James A. Tyner, *The Killing of Cambodia: Geography, Genocide and the Unmaking of Space* (Aldershot, UK: Ashgate, 2008); James A. Tyner, *From Rice Fields to Killing Fields: Nature, Life, and Labor under the Khmer Rouge* (Syracuse, N.Y.: Syracuse University Press, 2017); James A. Tyner, *The Nature of Revolution: Art and Politics under the Khmer Rouge* (Athens: University of Georgia Press, 2018); James A. Tyner, *The Politics of Lists: Bureaucracy and Genocide under the Khmer Rouge* (Morgantown: West Virginia University Press, 2018); and James A. Tyner, *Red Harvests: Agrarian Capitalism and Genocide in Democratic Kampuchea* (Morgantown: West Virginia University Press, 2021).

Notes to Epilogue / 331

8. "Minutes of Cabinet Meeting," Ford Library, National Security Adviser, Memoranda of Conversation, Box 11, 4/16/75, available at https://history.state.gov/historicaldocuments/frus1969-76v10/d234 (accessed January 23, 2021).

9. Memorandum of Conversation, "Secretary's Meeting with Foreign Minister Chatchai of Thailand," November 26, 1975, http://nsarchive.gwu/NSAEBB/NS AEBB198 (accessed February 15, 2016). Others in attendance included U.S. Deputy Secretary Robert Ingersoll and Brent Scowcroft, member of the National Security Council.

10. Kissinger is referring to the evacuation of Phnom Penh whereby millions of people were forced at gunpoint to relocate to agricultural collectives throughout the country. This forced removal is part of the prosecution's case on crimes against humanity and genocide at the Khmer Rouge Tribunal.

11. Chatchai's question refers to the dominant narrative of the domino theory, a geopolitical realist position that held if one country fell to communism, so too would the neighboring countries, and so on.

12. Alfred W. McCoy, *In the Shadows of the American Century: The Rise and Decline of US Global Power* (Chicago: Haymarket, 2017); Andrew Bacevich, *The Age of Illusions: How America Squandered Its Cold War Victory* (New York: Metropolitan, 2020); Andrew Bacevich, *After the Apocalypse: America's Role in a World Transformed* (New York: Metropolitan, 2021).

13. Amos A. Jordan, William J. Taylor Jr., and Michael J. Mazarr, *American National Security*, 5th ed. (Baltimore: Johns Hopkins University Press, 1999), 81.

14. "Memorandum from Michael Armacost and Michel Oksenberg of the National Security Council Staff to the President's Assistant for National Security Affairs (Brzezinski) and the President's Deputy Assistant for National Security Affairs (Aaron)," February 18, 1977, *Foreign Relations of the United States,* https://history.state.gov/historicaldocuments/frus1977-80v22/d105 (accessed July 28, 2022).

15. Gareth Porter, "The Decline of U.S. Diplomacy in Southeast Asia," *SAIS Review* 1, no. 1 (1980–81): 149–59; at 149.

16. "Address by President Carter," May 22, 1977, *Foreign Relations of the United States,* https://history.state.gov/historicaldocuments/frus1977-80v01/d40 (accessed July 28, 2022).

17. "Memorandum from the President's Assistant for National Security Affairs (Brzezinski) to President Carter," December 2, 1978, *Foreign Relations of the United States,* https://history.state.gov/historicaldocuments/frus1977-80v01/d100 (accessed July 28, 2022).

18. "Memorandum from the President's Assistant for National Security Affairs (Brzezinski) to President Carter," December 26, 1979, *Foreign Relations of the United States,* https://history.state.gov/historicaldocuments/frus1977-80v12/d97 (accessed July 28, 2022).

332 / Notes to Epilogue

19. "Memorandum from Director of Central Intelligence Turner to President Carter, Vice President Mondale, Secretary of State Vance, Secretary of Defense Brown, and the President's Assistant for National Security Affairs (Brzezinski)," January 15, 1980, *Foreign Relations of the United States*, https://history.state.gov/his toricaldocuments/frus1977-80v12/d168 (accessed July 28, 2022).

20. David S. Painter, "Oil and Geopolitics: The Oil Crisis of the 1970s and the Cold War," *Historical Social Research* 39, no. 4 (2014): 186–208; at 200–201.

21. "State of the Union Address 1980," January 23, 1980, *The Jimmy Carter Presidential Library and Museum*, https://www.jimmycarterlibrary.gov/assets/documents/speeches/su8ojec.phtml (accessed July 28, 2022); see also "Editorial Note," *Foreign Relations of the United States*, https://history.state.gov/historicaldocuments/frus19 77-80v19/d16 (accessed July 28, 2022).

22. Robert E. Osgood, "American Grand Strategy: Patterns, Problems, and Prescriptions," *Naval War College Review* 36, no. 5 (1983): 5–17; at 12.

23. Luis da Vinha, "Dangers on the Edge of the Map: Geographic Mental Maps and the Emergence of the Carter Doctrine," in *Geopolitics and International Relations: Grounding the World Anew*, ed. David Criekemans (Boston: Brill Nijhoff, 2022), 258–86; at 258.

24. "Editorial Note," *Foreign Relations of the United States*, https://history.state.gov/historicaldocuments/frus1981-88v03/d177 (accessed July 28, 2022).

25. Jordan et al., *American National Security*, 84.

26. John W. Dower, *The Violent American Century: War and Terror Since World War II* (Chicago: Haymarket, 2017), 60.

27. "Peace: Restoring the Margin of Safety," August 18, 1980, *Ronald Reagan Presidential Library and Museum*, available at https://www.reaganlibrary.gov/archives/speech/peace-restoring-margin-safety (accessed July 28, 2022).

28. Michael Adas, *Dominance by Design: Technological Imperatives and America's Civilizing Mission* (Cambridge, Mass.: Belknap Press of Harvard University Press, 2006), 353.

29. Bacevich, *After the Apocalypse*, 20.

30. Bacevich, *Age of Illusions*, 66.

31. Phyllis Bennis, *Before & After: US Foreign Policy and the War on Terrorism* (New York: Olive Branch, 2003), 59.

32. Hal Brands, "Saddam Hussein, the United States, and the Invasion of Iran: Was There a Green Light?" *Cold War History* 12, no. 2 (2012): 319–43.

33. Hal Brands and David Palkki, "'Conspiring Bastards': Saddam Hussein's Strategic View of the United States," *Diplomatic History* 36, no. 3 (2012): 625–59; at 625, 641.

34. Lawrence Freedman and Efraim Karsh, *The Gulf Conflict 1990–1991: Diplomacy and War in the New World Order* (Princeton, N.J.: Princeton University Press, 1993), 25.

Notes to Epilogue / 333

35. Freedman and Karsh, *The Gulf Conflict*, 67; Amos A. Jordan, William J. Taylor Jr., and Michael J. Mazarr, *American National Security*, 5th ed. (Baltimore: Johns Hopkins University Press, 1999), 396.

36. Bennis, *Before & After*, 61–62.

37. Jordan et al., *American National Security*, 396.

38. Dower, *The Violent American Century*, 76.

39. Quoted in E. J. Dionne Jr., "Kicking the 'Vietnam Syndrome,'" *Washington Post*, March 4, 1991, available at https://www.washingtonpost.com/archive/politics/1991/03/04/kicking-the-vietnam-syndrome/b6180288-4b9e-4d5f-b303-befa2275524d/ (accessed July 26, 2022).

40. Fraser Cameron, *US Foreign Policy After the Cold War: Global Hegemon or Reluctant Sheriff?* (New York: Routledge, 2002), 15.

41. Cameron, *US Foreign Policy*, 15.

42. *National Military Strategy of the United States*, January 1992, https://nssarchive.us/wp-content/uploads/library/nms/nms1992 (accessed July 26, 2022).

43. Colin L. Powell, "U.S. Forces: Challenges Ahead," *Foreign Affairs* 71, no. 5 (1992): 32–45; at 32.

44. Powell, "U.S. Forces," 35.

45. Powell, "U.S. Forces," 35.

46. Powell, "U.S. Forces," 36.

47. Powell, "U.S. Forces," 36.

48. Dower, *Violent American Century*, 80.

49. *National Military Strategy of the United States*, January 1992, https://nssarchive.us/wp-content/uploads/library/nms/nms1992 (accessed July 26, 2022).

50. Kupchan, *End of the American Era*, 15; Bacevich, *American Empire*, 56–57.

51. Bacevich, *American Empire*, 6.

52. John Tures, "United States Military Operations in the New World Order: An Examination of the Evidence," *American Diplomacy* 8, no. 1 (2003), https://ciaotest.cc.columbia.edu/olj/ad/ad_v8_1/tuj01.html (accessed July 26, 2022).

53. Bacevich, *American Empire*, 61.

54. Bacevich, *American Empire*, 79.

55. Bacevich, *American Empire*, 88.

56. "Remarks of Anthony Lake: From Containment to Enlargement," September 21, 1993, https://www.mtholyoke.edu/acad/intrel/lakedoc.html (accessed July 27, 2022).

57. "Remarks of Anthony Lake: From Containment to Enlargement," September 21, 1993, https://www.mtholyoke.edu/acad/intrel/lakedoc.html (accessed July 27, 2022).

58. Bacevich, *American Empire*, 105.

59. Chalmers Johnson, *The Sorrows of Empire: Militarism, Secrecy, and the End of the Republic* (New York: Metropolitan, 2004), 64, 154.

334 / Notes to Epilogue

60. Patrick Porter, "Why America's Grand Strategy Has Not Changed: Power, Habit, and the U.S. Foreign Policy Establishment," *International Security* 42, no. 4 (2018): 9–46; at 21.

61. Robert S. Litwak, *Rogue States and US Foreign Policy: Containment after the Cold War* (Washington, D.C.: Woodrow Wilson Center Press, 2000); Pinar Bilgin and Adam D. Morton, "Historicising Representations of 'Failed States': Beyond the Cold-War Annexation of the Social Sciences?" *Third World Quarterly* 23, no. 1 (2002): 55–80; Pinar Bilgin and Adam D. Morton, "From 'Rogue' to 'Failed' States? The Fallacy of Short-Termism," *Politics* 24, no. 3 (2004): 169–80.

62. Anthony Lake, "Confronting Backlash States," *Foreign Affairs* 73, no. 2 (1994): 45–55; at 45.

63. Bilgin, and Morton, "Historicising Representations," 66.

64. Bilgin, and Morton, "Historicising Representations," 66.

65. Colin Dueck, "Ideas and Alternatives in American Grand Strategy, 2000–2004," *Review of International Studies* 30, no. 4 (2004): 511–535; at 523.

66. Bilgin and Morton, "From 'Rogue' to 'Failed' States?" 171.

67. Dueck, "Ideas and Alternatives," 526.

68. Dueck, "Ideas and Alternatives," 527.

69. Department of Defense, *Quadrennial Defense Review Report,* September 30, 2001, https://dod.defense.gov/Portals/1/features/defenseReviews/QDR/qdr2001.pdf (accessed July 27, 2022).

70. Office of the Press Secretary, "President Delivers State of the Union Address," January 29, 2002, www.whitehouse.gov/releases/2002/01/20020129-11.html (accessed July 29, 2022).

71. See for example Alex Callinicos, *The New Mandarins of American Power: The Bush Administration's Plans for the World* (Cambridge: Polity, 2003); Ivo H. Daalder and James M. Lindsay, *America Unbound: The Bush Revolution in Foreign Policy* (Washington, D.C.: Brookings Institute Press, 2003); Larry Everest, *Oil, Power, and Empire: Iraq and the U.S. Global Agenda* (Monroe, Me.: Common Courage, 2003); Douglas Keller, *From 9/11 to Terror War: The Dangers of the Bush Legacy* (Lanham, Md.: Rowman & Littlefield, 2003); William Engdahl, *A Century of War: Anglo-American Oil Politics and the New World Order,* rev. ed. (London: Pluto Press, 2004); William R. Clark, *Petrodollar Warfare: Oil, Iraq and the Future of the Dollar* (Gabriola Island, B.C.: New Society, 2005); Andrew J. Bacevich, *America's War for the Greater Middle East: A Military History* (New York: Random House, 2017); and Pinar Bilgin, *Regional Security in the Middle East: A Critical Perspective,* rev. ed. (New York: Routledge, 2019).

72. Bacevich, *America's War,* 361.

73. For broad overviews of both Obama's and Trump's grand strategies, see Colin Dueck, *The Obama Doctrine: American Grand Strategy Today* (Oxford: Oxford University Press, 2015); Jacob Shively, *Hope, Change, Pragmatism: Analyzing Obama's*

Notes to Epilogue / 335

Grand Strategy (New York: Palgrave Macmillan, 2016); Hal Brands, "Barack Obama and the Dilemmas of American Grand Strategy," *Washington Quarterly* 39, no. 4 (2017): 101–25; and Hal Brands, *American Grand Strategy in the Age of Trump* (Washington, D.C.: Brookings Institution Press, 2018).

74. Brands, "Barack Obama," 101.

75. John Lewis Gaddis, *Surprise, Security, and the American Experience* (Cambridge, Mass.: Harvard University Press, 2004), 85.

76. There is, of course, nothing to prevent a revival of this simplistic spatial reasoning.

77. Walt W. Rostow, *The Stages of Economic Growth: A Non-Communist Manifesto* (New York: Cambridge University Press, 1960), 166–67.

78. Rostow, *Stages of Economic Growth*, 107.

79. Peter H. Liotta, "To Die For: National Interests and Strategic Uncertainties," *Parameters* 30, no. 2 (2000): 46–57; at 47.

Index

Abrams, Creighton, 159–61, 165, 169, 175–77, 180, 189–92, 196, 197, 200, 201, 206
Acheson, Dean, 18, 21, 37, 38, 45–47, 49, 50, 132
Adas, Michael, 26, 248
Afghanistan, 247, 257, 258
Agnew, John, 2, 48
Agnew, Spiro, 194, 225, 231, 236
Agroville program, 288n115
Aldrich, George, 152–54
Annam, 20, 33, 39, 108, 270n101
anticommunism, 6, 21, 41, 44, 46, 48, 71, 97, 106, 113, 117, 120, 130, 155, 171, 224, 248
Army of the Republic of Vietnam (ARVN), 73, 87, 138, 167, 190–92, 195, 199–201, 206, 208
Asselin, Pierre, 74, 228
Associated State of Vietnam, 48–50, 62
Auriol, Vincent, 44

Bacevich, Andrew, 37, 249, 252, 257
Ball, George, 93, 99, 138, 139, 143, 148, 292n160

Bao Dai, 39, 44, 45, 53, 54, 62, 72
Bao Dai solution, 39, 40, 43–48, 53, 54, 62, 72
Bidault, George, 30
Biden, Joseph, 258
Bigart, Homer, 73
bipolarity, 250, 251
borders: Cambodian–Vietnamese, 1, 101, 110, 127, 136, 138, 140, 143, 172, 175, 184, 189, 205, 211, 230, 237; cross-border operations, 86, 132, 137, 139–42, 145, 146, 148–53, 156, 176, 177, 180, 181, 184, 190–96, 216, 218; security, 4, 128, 144, 148, 174, 187; surveillance, 82, 86, 128; Vietnamese–Laotian, 64
Bowles, Chester, 89, 90
Brands, Hal, 5, 36, 44, 61, 105, 209, 249, 257
Bruce, David, 44, 45, 47
Brzezinski, Zbigniew, 246, 247
Bundy, McGeorge, 79, 84, 92, 93, 97, 132, 138, 156, 287n107
Bundy, William, 138–41, 145, 173
Bunker, Ellsworth, 163, 175, 176, 189, 191, 192, 200, 221, 232

338 / Index

Bush, George H. W., 250–52
Bush, George W., 255–57

Caffery, Jefferson, 44, 45
Cambodia: betrayal by the United
States, 221–24, 236–40, 242–43;
bombing campaign of 1973, 231–36;
centrality of, 204–21; colonialism,
20, 44, 106; communist movement
in, 123–27; coup, 181–84; domino
theory and, 78, 103; France and,
109–11; incursion, 188–202; independence, 87; neutrality, 147; North
Vietnam and, 124–26; Operation
Menu, 171–81; sanctuaries, 143,
146, 149, 154, 171, 172, 174, 177, 190,
194, 199–201, 204, 205, 211, 213, 218,
223, 233, 308n79; South Vietnam's
border and, 80, 81, 83, 86, 94–96,
101, 105, 141, 148, 158; United States'
covert operations in, 136–46; United
States' military aid toward, 110, 111,
113, 114, 121, 130, 149; United States'
military operations in, 121, 148–57;
United States' strategy toward, 2,
22, 90, 107, 108, 112–15, 117, 120,
122, 127–33, 150, 151, 154, 155, 165,
184–88, 195, 226–31, 245
Carter, Jimmy, 245–47
Carter Doctrine, 248
Carver, George, 203, 234, 235, 237
Catton, Philip, 72
Central Highlands (Vietnam), 86, 146,
149, 157, 158, 172
Central Office for South Vietnam
(COSVN), 83, 158, 175–77, 194, 197,
200, 201
Chandler, David, 120
Chauvel, Jean, 30
Chayes, Abram, 85
Cheney, Richard, 256

China. See People's Republic of China
Choonhaven, Chatchai, 243–45
Church, Frank, 208
Civilian Irregular Defense Group
(CIDG), 86, 131, 132
Clifford, Clark M., 39, 155, 159, 160
Cochinchina, 20, 33, 39, 270n101
Colbert, Evelyn, 31
Collins, J. Lawton, 21
colonialism, 26–29, 31, 34, 46, 48, 65,
68, 124
communist bloc, 80, 115–17, 121, 125,
126, 171
Communist Party of Kampuchea. See
Khmer Rouge
containment, 6, 14, 47, 55, 67, 136, 241,
245–48, 251–53, 255, 258
Cooper, Chester, 92
Cooper, John, 208
Cooper-Church amendment, 208
Cosmas, Graham, 156, 160, 165, 166
counterinsurgency, 79, 80, 82, 88, 94,
143
covert operations, 18, 86, 96, 139, 152,
153, 204, 221, 292n159
credibility, 15, 52, 115, 121, 140, 167, 169,
171, 178, 201, 203, 204, 212, 225, 227,
228, 230, 236, 239, 260
Cronin, Bruce, 15
Cushman, Robert, 196

Daalder, Ivo, 26
Dalby, Simon, 2, 13, 135
Dap Chhuon, 118–120
Davis, Arthur, 109, 110
decent interval, 216, 226, 227, 239
Democratic People's Republic of
Korea, 51, 53, 293n163
Democratic Republic of Vietnam:
Cambodia and, 111, 146, 147, 184;
formation of, 31; independence of,

31, 32; Khmer Rouge and, 123–27, 234, 235; "North-first" policy, 74; recognition of, 48, 146; "Resolution 15," 75; strategy of, 89; United States' bombing of, 155, 159, 171, 178, 229, 230; United States' policy and, 1, 40, 71, 85, 95–100, 144, 157, 168, 184, 204, 209, 210, 215, 225
DeSoto patrols, 97, 292n163
Dien Bien Phu, 64, 65, 68, 70
Dillon, C. Douglas, 109
Dobrynin, Anatoly, 178, 240
domino theory, 67, 169, 209, 245, 258, 331n11
Dubrow, Eldridge, 118
Dueck, Colin, 256
Dulles, Allen, 122
Dulles, John Foster, 25, 65, 66, 69, 70, 107, 115, 116

Earle, Edward Mead, 10
Ebihara, May, 126
Eden, Anthony, 27, 31
Einstein, Lewis, 11
Eisenhower, Dwight D., 62–70, 71, 73, 87, 88, 116–17
Eliot, Theodore, 185
Ely, Paul, 65
Élysée Accords, 44, 47
England. *See* United Kingdom
Eurasia, 11, 15, 18, 19, 21, 37, 69
extra-territoriality, 16

failed state, 137, 255
Feaver, Peter, 5
Felt, Henry, 128
Fergie, Dexter, 10, 12
Ferguson, John, 19
First Indochina War. *See* Franco–Viet Minh War
First World War, 1

Fishhook, 172, 174, 175, 177, 194, 196–201
Forces Armées Nationales Khmères (FANK), 108, 128, 186, 210, 211, 221, 223, 233
Ford, Gerald, 240, 241
Forrestal, Michael, 132
France: American nomos and, 8, 15, 19, 30, 33, 38, 40, 43, 68; Cambodia and, 107–11; colonialism and, 20, 29, 123, 204, 245; Dwight D. Eisenhower and, 62–70, 109; Indochina and, 31–35, 39, 44, 108; Franklin D. Roosevelt and, 28, 29; Harry S. Truman and, 30, 32
Franco–Viet Minh War 62–70, 123
free security, 7, 8
French Indochina, 20, 123, 204, 245. *See also* Indochina

Gaddis, John, 41, 45, 258
Galbraith, Kenneth, 91
Geneva Accords, 70–72, 74, 76, 80, 85, 87, 89, 107, 108, 111, 124, 231, 233, 279n118
geopolitical codes, 6, 19
geopolitics: American, 12, 17, 108, 122, 239, 242; critical, 2, 23; defined, 2, 10, 48, 92; European, 20; Indochina and, 20; military strategy and, 57; practical, 2, 6, 18, 119, 165, 204, 258; Southeast Asia and, 116
Giap, Vo Nguyen, 33, 64, 74
Gottman, Jean, 10
grand strategy: George H. W. Bush, 250–52; George W. Bush, 255–57; William J. Clinton, 252–55; definition of, 4–6, 79, 105, 258; Dwight D. Eisenhower and, 68; "flexible response," 78–79; Indochina and, 21, 136, 143, 169; Lyndon B. Johnson

340 / Index

and, 94, 165; John F. Kennedy and, 79–80; "Massive Retaliation," 78; Middle East, 245; military strategy, 4–5, 57; national security and, 2, 6–12; Richard M. Nixon and, 169, 198, 245; normative function, 5; peripheral importance and, 2, 4, 13, 19, 21, 23, 35, 37, 38, 40, 41, 44, 46, 54, 55, 60, 70, 105, 121, 145, 165, 204, 226, 241, 250, 258–60; post-Vietnam, 245–60; spatial order, 6, 70, 241, 258; Harry S. Truman and, 252
Great Britain. *See* United Kingdom
Great Powers, 15, 19, 33, 256
Gromyko, Andrei, 227
Gulf of Tonkin incident, 97–98
Gulf of Tonkin Resolution, 97, 216
gunboat diplomacy, 7

Habib, Philip, 243
Haig, Alexander, 176, 213–17, 229, 232, 233, 239
Ha Long Bay Accords, 39
Harkins, Paul, 86
Harriman, W. Averell, 90, 132
Hatfield, Mark, 208
Heath, Donald, 107
Helms, Richard, 185, 188, 194, 196, 197, 199, 210, 214, 220, 221, 318n123
Herring, George, 97
Herter, Christian, 119, 120, 122
Hess, Gary, 28, 47
Ho Chi Minh, 29, 31, 32, 35, 39, 40, 44, 45, 48, 62, 73, 74
Ho Chi Minh Trail, 88, 89, 95, 128, 192
Huber, Matt, 3
Hull, Cordell, 9, 27, 29
Hussein, Saddam, 249–50

Ieng Sary, 126, 187, 243, 314n84
Ieng Thirith, 126

Immerman, Richard, 72
imperialism, 7
Indochina: American nomos and, 23, 29, 38, 40, 47, 60–62, 240, 242, 245; Cambodia and, 106, 107, 109, 147, 222, 238; Cold War and, 20, 21; French control of, 30, 32, 33, 43; Second World War and, 28; United States' involvement in, 29, 32, 47, 50, 51, 53, 58, 136; United States' policy and, 20, 21, 27, 30, 31, 34, 35, 37, 40, 41, 44, 46, 48, 49, 57, 69, 70–76, 76–87, 165, 168, 226–28
insurgency, 3, 50, 74–76, 82–84, 100, 101, 103, 127, 128, 130, 137, 143, 144, 157, 168, 184, 185, 187, 221, 231, 234, 238
Iran, 20, 246, 247, 249, 286n94
Iraq, 249–51, 257, 258
Isaacs, Arnold, 186, 223, 234
isolationism, 9, 11

Japan: domino theory and, 78, 97, 209; resources and Southeast Asia, 37, 41–43, 51–52, 59, 67, 69, 116; Second World War and, 11–12, 19, 28, 31, 36, 104, 106, 135
Johnson, Alexis, 185, 196, 210
Johnson, Louis, 49
Johnson, Lyndon B.: Cambodia and, 139, 142, 144, 145, 147, 148, 154, 161, 201; counterinsurgency and, 96, 149, 154; grand strategy and, 94, 165; Gulf of Tonkin incident, 97; Gulf of Tonkin Resolution, 97; Kennedy assassination and, 92; military operations and, 96, 98, 100, 136, 138, 149, 157, 159, 161; policy on Vietnam, 93, 98, 100, 101, 132, 133, 140, 148, 156, 215
Johnson, Robert, 129, 130

Index / 341

Jorden, William, 95
Josselyn, Paul, 34

Kahin, George, 71
Karamessines, Thomas, 185
Karnow, Stanley, 229
Kennan, George F., 15, 19, 21, 22, 37,
39, 40, 41, 45, 46, 54, 171, 269n80,
271n106
Kennedy, John F.: Cambodia and, 129,
132; Laos and, 87–91; Vietnam and,
76–86
Kent State University, 205–7
Kerwin, Walter, 175
Khmer Issarak, 123, 131
Khmer People's Revolutionary Party
(KPRP), 123, 124, 127
Khmer Rouge, 123–27, 183, 187, 221,
231, 232, 234, 235, 238, 242, 243, 245
Khmer Serei, 131, 132, 148, 194
Kimball, Jeffery, 69
Kissinger, Henry: bombing of Cambodia, 176, 177, 179, 180, 184, 198, 239,
240; Cambodia, 174, 185, 186, 191–93,
196, 202, 207, 210, 211, 215, 216, 223,
228, 229, 237–40, 242, 245; Democratic Republic of Vietnam, 184, 190,
219, 220, 227, 229, 244; diplomacy,
166, 167, 178, 179, 230; domino theory, 244, 245; Khmer Rouge, 234,
235, 243–45; military operations
in Cambodia, 165, 179, 191, 194,
196–98, 202, 206, 210, 211, 223, 233,
234, 237; national security, 165, 166,
226; People's Republic of China, 227,
229, 234, 235, 239, 244; Republic of
Vietnam, 225–28, 237–39; strategy,
163, 201, 219, 220, 240, 241, 245
Komer, Robert, 81, 145
Korean War, 51–55, 170, 225, 235, 248,
237

Ladd, Jonathan, 218
Laird, Melvin, 167–69, 174, 176–78,
180, 189, 191, 194, 196, 197, 199–201,
210, 219
Lake, Anthony, 195, 253–55
Lansdale, Edward, 129
Laos: borders and, 1, 81, 83, 94, 129;
civil war, 87–91; combat operations
in, 63, 64, 76, 81, 84, 88, 100, 152,
159, 174, 180, 215, 222, 232, 234;
Democratic Republic of Vietnam
and, 124, 125; domino theory and,
78, 88; Indochina and, 20, 33, 44,
108, 109; supply routes, 63, 80, 86,
89, 94, 96, 98, 105, 114, 131, 143, 144,
161; United States' policy and,
88–91, 122, 129, 131, 173, 190, 193,
199, 208, 238, 242, 245
Lawrence, Mark, 27, 32
Layton, Peter, 5
Le Billion, Philippe, 3
Le Duan, 74
Le Duc Tho, 74, 184, 229, 230
Lee, Steven, 51
Leffler, Melvyn, 14
Liddell Hart, Basil H., 4
Lilienthal, David, 155
Liotta, Peter, 260
Lodge, Henry Cabot, 8, 9, 91–93, 138,
291n147
Lodoen, George, 113, 114
Logevall, Fredrik, 39, 43, 75
Lon Nol, 186, 189, 211–21, 221–24,
238–39, 242
Lord, Winston, 195
Luce, Stephen, 8
Lynn, Lawrence, 217

MacArthur, Douglas, 53
Mackinder, Halford, 11
Mahan, Alfred Thayer, 8, 11

342 / Index

Makins, Roger, 66
manifest destiny, 7, 257
Mansfield, Mike, 72, 98, 292n160
Marshall, George, 34, 35
Marshall Plan, 37, 48, 90
Matthews, H. Freeman, 62
McCain, John, 173, 174, 180, 189, 192, 193, 206, 210
McClintock, Robert, 108–11, 114, 115, 117, 121
McCone, John, 93, 133
McGovern, George, 208
McNamara, Robert: cross-border operations, 95, 105, 136, 138; Gulf of Tonkin incident, 97; pacification, 86; policy recommendations, 84, 97, 99, 100, 105, 144, 156; South Vietnam, assessment of, 94, 95, 103, 104, 144, 155
McNaughton, John, 98
Mekong Delta, 86, 94, 146
Mendenhall, Joseph, 80
Middle East, 36, 69, 77, 121, 240, 245–47, 249, 250, 254, 257
Military Advisory Command, Vietnam (MACV): Cambodia and, 141, 148, 149, 157, 160, 164, 165, 172, 175, 180, 181, 189–91, 193, 197, 206, 210, 221; combat operations and, 143, 157, 158; command structure, 86, 96, 159; establishment of, 86
Military Advisory Command, Vietnam-Special Operations Group (MACV-SOG), 96, 292n158, 292n159
Military Assistance Advisory Group (MAAG), Cambodia, 109–11, 113, 128, 129, 279n118
Military Assistance Advisory Group (MAAG), Indochina, 51, 108

Military Assistance Advisory Group (MAAG), Vietnam, 73, 79, 82, 84, 86, 129
Military Defense Agreement (MDA), 111
military strategy, 4–5, 57
Mitchell, John, 201
modernization, 79, 110, 111, 292n158
Moffat, Abbot Low, 34
Moorer, Thomas, 196, 232, 233
Morris, Roger, 195
Murphy, Daniel, 235

National Liberation Front (NLF), 76, 80, 81, 83, 103, 125, 178, 184, 288n115
national security: George W. Bush and, 256–57; Cambodia and, 2–3, 25, 112–18, 122, 150, 202–4, 224, 240; Jimmy Carter and, 245–47; William J. Clinton and, 253–54; defined, 3–6, 135; Indochina and, 29–48, 60–62; Lyndon B. Johnson and, 94, 132, 147–48, 203; John F. Kennedy and, 76–91, 129, 132; Henry Kissinger and, 161, 163, 166, 179, 194, 197, 202, 226, 245; Richard M. Nixon and, 161, 163, 166, 179, 194, 203–4, 226, 245; Southeast Asia and, 120–22, 240, 242; strategic frontier and, 16–20, 37; United States and, 2, 6–12, 13, 15–21, 25, 29–48, 55, 58–59, 77, 242, 245–60; Vietnam and, 76–87, 122, 226–27, 245
National Security Action Memorandums (NSAMs): NSAM-52, 82, 83; NSAM-273, 94
National Security Council (NSC) reports: NSC-7, 38, 58; NSC-48/5, 52; NSC-68, 18, 19, 49, 50, 54, 278n113; NSC-162/2, 68, 69;

Index / 343

NSC-5404, 69; NSC-5404, 69;
NSC-5612/1, 116, 117, 121, 122
National Security Council Decision
Memorandums (NSCDMs):
NSCDM-56, 194, 195, 197;
NSCDM-57, 199; NSCDM-89,
224
National Security Study Memorandum
1 (NSSM-1), 163
Navarre, Henri, 63, 64
Navarre Plan, 64
Neiberg, Michael, 8
Ngo Dinh Diem: Agroville program,
288n115; assassination of, 20, 91, 93,
105, 145; Cambodia and, 120, 122,
137, 128, 130; Democratic Republic
of Vietnam and, 76; "Denounce the
Communist" campaign, 74; state
building and, 73; United States and,
72–75, 81–83, 86, 92, 129, 229
Ngo Dinh Nhu, 118
Nguyen Van Thieu, 192, 213, 219, 226,
229, 231
Nitze, Paul, 59, 61, 62
Nixon, Richard M.: bombing of Cambodia, 231–36; Cambodian policy,
204–10, 210–21, 222–24; Christmas
bombings, 229; credibility, 225;
deescalation, 168–69, 219; foreign
policy in Indochina, 165–71, 226–28,
236–40; grand strategy, 169, 198,
245; incursion into Cambodia, 1, 23,
83, 124, 165, 188–202, 209, 218; Kent
State University, 206–7; Lon Nol
and, 186, 189, 211–21, 221–24, 238–39,
242; madman theory; Nixon Doctrine, 170–71; Norodom Sihanouk
and, 106, 186–87; Operation Linebacker II, 229; Operation Menu,
171–81, 189, 198; peace talks, 225–31;
presidential election of 1972, 225; as

vice president, 65, 106; Vietnam
policy, 163–65, 169–70; Vietnam-
ization, 165–70, 198, 218, 220;
widening the war, 184–88
Nixon Doctrine, 170, 171, 212, 224
nomos: American, 12, 13, 15, 17, 19, 21,
23, 25, 78, 84, 91, 166, 171, 204, 209,
226, 229, 254, 257, 259, 260;
defined, 5, 6
Non-Aligned Movement, 141
Nong Kimny, 114, 119
North Korea. See Democratic People's
Republic of Korea
North Vietnam. See Democratic
Republic of Vietnam
Nuon Chea, 127, 187, 314n84

Obama, Barack, 257, 258
O'Daniel, John W., 82
Operation Crimp, 146
Operation Daniel Boone, 146, 150, 151,
153, 154
Operation Linebacker II, 229
Operation Marauder, 146
Operation Matador, 146
Operation Menu, 171–81
Operation Plan 34–A (OPLAN-34A),
96, 97, 292n159
Operation Rolling Thunder, 98, 160,
307n74
operations, 5, 57, 61, 79
organic defense, 7

pacification, 86, 101, 103, 136, 143, 156,
157, 160, 163, 164, 213, 288n115,
292n158
Packard, David, 176, 179, 197
Paris Peace Accords, 230, 231
Parrot's Beak, 172, 193, 194, 196, 197,
199–202
Pathet Lao, 87, 89, 129

344 / Index

People's Army of Vietnam (PAVN), 101, 137, 141, 142, 144, 145, 148, 150, 151, 153, 157, 158, 160, 172, 173, 177, 182, 183, 187, 191, 194, 212, 237

People's Liberation Armed Forces (PLAF), 83, 98, 101, 136, 137, 143, 145, 148–51, 153, 157, 158, 160, 172, 173, 177, 182, 183, 187, 191, 194, 212, 237

People's Republic of China, 2, 9, 15, 43–43, 47, 49–50, 53, 55, 60, 62, 66, 70, 85, 90, 98, 104, 111, 115, 122, 124, 130, 139, 170, 182, 186–88, 201, 209, 226, 236, 238, 245, 254, 257

Philippines, 11, 29, 30, 37, 47, 60, 78, 90, 97, 203, 251

Phouma, Souvanna, 87

Phoumi Nosavan, 87

Pol Pot, 126, 127, 187, 314n84

Powell, Colin, 250, 251

Prados, John, 53

Preliminary Convention of 1946, 33

Preston, Andrew, 7, 8

Radford, Arthur, 65, 116

Reagan, Ronald, 248, 249, 251

Reagan Doctrine, 248

Reed, Charles, 59

Republic of Korea, 51, 52, 97, 99, 225, 254, 278n111

Republic of Vietnam: diplomatic recognition, 146, 230; Dwight D. Eisenhower and, 110–11; formation of, 70–76; insurgency in, 136–46, 154, 158–60, 205–6; Lyndon B. Johnson and, 91–101, 103–5, 132; John F. Kennedy and, 76–87, 132; Richard M. Nixon and, 165–71, 179, 198–202, 213–21, 225–31; State of Vietnam, 70–73, 108; and United

States' objectives in, 58, 122, 125, 128, 131, 136, 165, 188, 203, 222, 237; and United States' spatial order, 47, 49, 53, 58, 209, 259

Ridgway, Matthew, 21, 65, 69

Rives, Lloyd, 212–14, 321n29

Robertson, Reuben, 116

Robertson, Walter, 110

Rogers, William, 163, 164, 174–76, 178, 179, 186, 191, 194, 196, 199, 200, 201, 207, 211, 212

Roosevelt, Franklin D., 3, 10–12, 27–29

Roosevelt, Theodore, 7

Rosenberg, Emily, 7, 10

Rostow, Walt, 79, 83–85, 95, 129, 135, 136, 156, 255, 259

Rumsfeld, Donald, 256

Rusk, Dean, 79, 84, 85, 90, 91, 141, 142, 144, 155, 156

Sam Sary, 118, 119

sanctuaries, 143, 146, 149, 154, 171, 172, 174, 177, 190, 194, 199–201, 204, 205, 211, 213, 218, 223, 233, 308n79

Sangkum, 112, 118

Scherrer, Edward, 128

Schlesinger, James, 235

Schmitt, Carl, 5

Scowcroft, Brent, 236

Second World War: Cambodia and, 106, 123; Indochina and, 20, 27, 29, 33, 51; Soviet Union and, 13, 19, 38, 46; United States' national security and, 2, 6–12, 14, 17, 25, 26, 41, 77, 135, 241, 246, 251

Schelling, Thomas C., 19, 167

Sharp, Ulysses, 141, 158

Sihanouk, Norodom: civil unrest, 182–84; communism and, 112–14, 120, 123–27, 128, 130, 137, 147, 187;

coup, 20, 118, 120, 181–84, 222; cross-border operations and, 142, 144, 145, 148, 165, 172, 180, 184, 188; Democratic Republic of Vietnam and, 125, 127, 146, 220; domino theory and, 125; France and, 106, 107; independence, 106, 111, 112, 124; Khmer Rouge, 123–27, 186, 235, 238; military operations, 119, 139; neutrality, 112, 125, 140, 145, 172, 204; People's Republic of China, 139, 146, 186, 188; Republic of Vietnam, 118, 120, 125, 129, 139, 204; socialism and, 113; Soviet bloc, 115, 117; Thailand, 118, 129; United States and, 107, 108, 112, 114, 117, 119, 122, 128–32, 136, 138, 140, 144, 145, 148, 172, 175, 190, 191, 195, 204, 229, 237

Sihanouk Trail, 125, 128
Sirik Matak, Sisowath, 183–85, 213, 243
Souphanouvong, Prince, 87
Southeast Asia: communism and, 44, 47, 53, 66, 67, 70, 71, 73, 84, 97, 108, 110, 114, 120, 173, 187, 209, 242, 245; domino theory and, 60, 69, 77, 78, 121; geopolitics and, 59, 61, 70, 116, 121, 130, 131, 165, 230, 239, 240; resources in, 29, 30, 41–43, 69, 78, 154; United States' policy and, 29, 34, 40, 41, 59, 62, 69, 85, 88–91, 113, 115, 122, 148, 156, 168, 191, 200, 217, 220, 236, 243, 246
South Korea. *See* Republic of Korea
South Vietnam. *See* Republic of Vietnam
sovereignty: Cambodian, 106, 107, 112, 141, 145, 152, 156, 175, 186, 205, 231; concept, 48, 92, 259; French, 28, 30, 34, 43, 44, 50; Republic of Vietnam,

46, 49, 92, 93, 168; United States, 15, 16
Soviet Union, 2, 13–19, 29, 33, 35, 39, 43, 48–55, 69, 70, 90, 115, 124, 126, 130, 164, 182, 188, 201, 209, 236, 241, 247–53, 258
spatial order, 6, 12–23, 25–27, 34, 40, 58, 69, 70, 89, 91, 104, 165, 241, 250–53, 255, 259
Special Operations Group (SOG), 96, 292n158, 292n159
Sprout, Harold, 10, 25
Sprout, Margaret, 10, 25
Spykman, Nicholas, 1, 10
State of Vietnam. *See* Republic of Vietnam
Stennis, John, 198, 199
strategic frontier, 16–20, 37
Strategic Hamlet program, 288n115
Strom, Carl, 117–20
Studies and Observations Group (SOG). *See* Special Operations Group
Stump, Felix, 113
Sullivan, William, 235
Swank, Emory, 214

tactics, 4, 5, 58, 61
Taylor, Maxwell, 83–85, 99, 132
territorial integrity: Cambodia, 107, 112, 145, 154, 156, 175, 185, 186, 195, 222, 231; Republic of Korea, 52; Republic of Vietnam, 50, 71, 78, 82, 88, 93, 94, 136, 215, 216, 230; United States, 8, 14, 117
territorial trap, 48–55
Tet Offensive, 157–59
Thompson, John, 11, 17
Tonkin, 20, 33, 39, 60, 108, 270n101
Tou Samouth, 127
Tracy, Benjamin, 8

346 / Index

Tran Kim Phuong, 238
Trimble, William, 126, 128, 130
Truehart, William, 146, 147
Truman, Harry S.: France and, 30, 32,
48; Indochina and, 32, 44, 48, 53,
165; Korea and, 52; national security
and, 13, 14, 18, 35, 36, 252; Soviet
Union and, 17, 35, 26, 49
Truman Doctrine, 35, 36, 41, 251
Trump, Donald, 257, 258

United Kingdom: American nomos
and, 15, 19; colonialism and, 31, 62;
France and, 29, 30, 62; Indochina
and, 29, 62; Second World War
and, 33
United Nations, 15, 51, 85, 106, 138, 154,
251

Vagts, Alfred, 10, 12
Vandenberg, Hoyt, 21, 60, 61
Vichy France, 28, 29, 106, 123
Vickery, Michael, 112
Viet Minh, 29–33, 35, 38, 39, 50, 51, 63,
64, 74, 82, 107–9, 123, 128

Vietnamization, 163, 166, 167, 169, 171,
191, 196, 198, 201, 210, 211, 213, 215,
216, 218–20, 224
Voorhees, Tracy, 42

War Powers Resolution, 237
Weinberg, Albert, 10
Westmoreland, William: assessment
of Vietnam, 99, 157; bombing
requests, 154, 308n79; Cambodia
and, 142, 143, 148–50, 152, 154,
193, 308n79; military operations,
100, 146, 152; strategy in Vietnam,
101; troop requests, 98, 141, 157,
158
Wheeler, Earl, 173–77, 179, 194, 196,
197, 199
Wheeler, James, 138, 155, 158, 159
Williams, Samuel T., 82, 286n94
Wilson, Charles, 70, 71
Wilson, Woodrow, 253
Woodward, C. Vann, 7, 8

Young, Kenneth, 115
Young, Marilyn, 29, 31, 32, 45, 71, 85

JAMES A. TYNER is professor of geography at Kent State University and a fellow of the American Association of Geographers. He is author of several books, including *War, Violence, and Population: Making the Body Count*; *The Alienated Subject: On the Capacity to Hurt* (Minnesota, 2022); and *Dead Labor: Toward a Political Economy of Premature Death* (Minnesota, 2019).

Printed and bound by CPI Group (UK) Ltd, Croydon, CR0 4YY

21/05/2024

14505110-0002